THE NATURAL HISTORY
OF A COUNTRY SCHOOL

First published in 2005 by

WOODFIELD PUBLISHING
Bognor Regis, West Sussex, England
www.woodfieldpublishing.com

ISBN 1-903953-99-5

Cover illustrations:
Front cover, above titles: West Buckland School in summer [Mrs. Lorraine Millar]
Front cover, below titles: West Buckland in winter [School Archive]
Back cover: West Buckland in winter [Paul Berry]

The Natural History of a Country School

BERWICK COATES

Woodfield

Aerial view of the School. [School Archive]

To think of putting a school here at all was a feat of imagination and optimism.

Contents

Preface

At the end of 2000, after two years as the School Archivist, I published a book entitled simply *West Buckland School*. It was not a straight history – rather a series of sideways looks at features of the School's past. These reflections might be triggered by a teacher's report, an old prospectus, a file of yellowing letters, a seventy-year-old blazer, a faded portrait, anything. I have now taken this process a stage further.

In his famous *Natural History of Selborne*, by writing about scores of local species, Gilbert White composed a very full portrait of a rural community of two hundred-odd years ago, which has struck chords of recognition and sympathy with many people then and since, most of whom have never been near Selborne.

I have tried to do the same with a school. By writing about it through the eyes of a junior pupil, a secretary, a headmaster, a foreign student, a sportsman, a founder, a benefactor, and so on, I hope to make it more intelligible. Add some essays on subjects like school heroes, changing fashions in the curriculum, the history of examinations, and the impact of war. Sprinkle with dozens of little vignettes, anecdotes, coincidences, and generally useless information. With luck, most people should find something here with which they can identify.

Everybody has been to school, so everybody is an expert on education. Everybody also thinks he or she is tolerant, broad-minded, and fair. Well, perhaps by saying in effect, 'Have you thought of looking at it this way?' we can – um – enhance that expertise just a little.

This is not a paean of praise for the Old School Tie. It is simply an effort to show that schools like West Buckland exist, that they are in many ways far more ordinary than many of their critics would have us believe, and that they are filled with ordinary people who believe in them, and whose virtues are enhanced by their loyalty to them.

Over a million parents send their children to independent schools; that is a pretty sizeable slice of the educational life of the nation. That slice is growing, and it is time some of the schools in it were better understood.

A school does not have to be a celebrity in order to be interesting. It does not have to be perfect. It does not have to burst with highest common factors or appeal to lowest common denominators.

It has simply to be human.

Introduction

In an age of increasing urbanisation, increasing standardisation, and increasing brain-washing by mass-communication, the word 'country' can evoke a conditioned response which is often little more than an amalgam of clichés and snap judgments – a distillation of threadbare prejudices, tabloid headlines, and soap-opera sagas. People are unwilling to attribute to other social units, with which they are not familiar, the variety, strength, validity, and subtlety which they see daily in their own.

So 'the country' – to a lot of town people – can conjure up a world which is light years away from the real thing. By the same token, so can 'public school' and 'boarding school' to those who have never attended or even visited one.

Yet the country has been there a lot longer than the cities; public schools go back much further than most state secondary schools; and, until about a hundred years ago, most young people who were sent anywhere for whatever kind of education which obtained at the time were usually expected to live in – going right back to medieval pages and apprentices. The boarding principle, public schools, and the country are still with us – and doing nicely, thank you very much.

Why? Wherein lies their longevity?

The countryside has survived, over the centuries, crises like the destruction of vast stretches of woodland for charcoal-burning and ship-building; civil wars, pestilence, and depopulation; unemployment and misery resulting from enclosure and machinery; the spread of urbanisation and industry; the depredations of tourism; the impact of chemical farming and its inroads into the vigour and variety of wildlife. It will no doubt survive too the attack on blood sports and any other assault on its way of life which a city culture, in its envy, ignorance, high morals, or plain ill disposition, chooses to unleash upon it. For all its alleged shortcomings and outdated ideas, it is still a place very much worth living in – as is testified by the thousands of city-dwellers who save to buy houses there.

Despite the onward march of socialism and equal opportunities for all, there has been, and no doubt still is, a healthy tradition of egalitarian politicians sending their offspring to independent schools, and the revival of such education generally is ample testimony to the fact that the great comprehensive experiment has not delivered anything like as many of the goods as its prophets had expected or claimed. So the Etons and the Harrows, and the scores of second- and third-division private schools up and down the land, cannot still be the festering *foci* of privilege, snobbery, corruption, and anachronism that its critics would have us believe. Over a million parents would not be straining every financial muscle to send their children there if they were.

Finally, the boarding principle. Over the years parents have had scores of very good reasons for deciding to have their children boarded where they are being taught; they cannot all have been heartless, career-obsessed traditionalists blind and deaf to the entreaties of their weeping progeny. Indeed, it is often the parents, who, having decided that the best hope for a good, uninterrupted education is to send their sons and daughters away, are the ones who weep. There is ample evidence that a lot of children *like* boarding schools, even when it would be perfectly practical for them to travel home each day.

This is not the time or the place to enter into the debate about the countryside, the independent schools, or the boarding principle. I simply want to make the point that all three are still with us, and still vigorous, and still making a distinct contribution to the life of the nation. Of course they are not perfect: the countryside has its faults and its prejudices; public schools can still turn out snobs; and some children are made miserable by boarding. But by the same token the opposites are not perfect either: the problems of city life could fill a book twice this size; if state education had fewer faults, there would not be any private education worth having a debate about; and for every child that cries itself to sleep in a boarding school, there is, I venture to suggest, another that cowers before a drunken father or shouts at a feckless mother in a private house.

This book is about a country school which offers a boarding facility to some of its pupils. It is not famous; it is not rich; it is not fashionable. It is not top of the leagues. It wasn't founded by Edward III – or by his mistress. It has not produced a string of prime ministers or captains of industry or foreign ambassadors. But throughout its history (coming up to 150 years) it has consistently done its best for its children according to its lights. And it is more – much more – than a few teachers and a clutch of pupils. I hope with these essays and other fragments to make up a mosaic of a vigorous, many-sided, purposeful, close-knit, valuable, and, on the whole, surprisingly happy place.

Acknowledgments

Once again I am indebted to West Buckland School for the total freedom I have been given to use the resources of its Archive in the preparation of this book. As before, I am also grateful for the interest and support of John Vick, the Headmaster (though I craftily planned for this by subjecting him to interview as a basis for one of the chapters).

In fact I thank all those I interviewed, for their patience, their attentiveness, and their willingness to be subjected to a possibly daunting series of questions.

Books with old pictures demand extra work, and my colleagues Lorraine Millar, Jenni Gale and Stephen Prior have done me many favours, squeezed into a crowded working day, in the process of the computerised alchemy which turns tired and blemished prints into (what I hope are thought to be) attractive and entertaining illustrations. Even the new ones need attention, and Lorraine has been generous again with her time in processing them – besides providing some of the originals herself.

Yvonne Reed willingly took on the chore of proof-reading, and has moreover added to the quality of the book by her many constructive criticisms and suggestions.

As with my previous book on the School, I should like to stress that this is not a West Buckland publication. No authority connected with the School suggested it, persuaded me to start it, tried to insert material into it, or attempted any editorial control whatever. The only changes I have made as a result of outside influence came about because a few of the people I interviewed asked me to correct an error of fact or straighten a slight skew of emphasis – or because Yvonne said it might be a good idea.

So the tone, the flavour, the general tenor, the *raison d'être*, the spirit – what you will – of the book are, for better or worse, mine. If I cause any offence or embarrassment, may I apologise in advance, and say that such was not my intent.

Errors will of course remain, and, if the first book is anything to go by, I shall soon find out about them – from postbag, email box, and ansaphone system. But I can then take comfort from the fact that some people at least have been reading it.

Berwick Coates, 2005

1. The Reverend Regrets

At five minutes past ten on the morning of 24th May, 1912, the Revd. Joseph Thompson, the rector at Warkleigh in North Devon, sent a telegram. It was addressed to 'Taylor, County School, West Buckland, Filleigh.' (Also in North Devon.) It said:

'Afraid unable come Barnstaple please apologise Thompson.'

Thompson was the retired first Headmaster of the School. After he had left the School, he had become the Rector first at Creacombe, then in 1895 at Romansleigh, finally in 1907 at Warkleigh (all parishes in Devon). After thirty years of caring for lively bodies, he married – at 54 (the eldest daughter of the founder, the Revd. J.L. Brereton) – and switched to the care of rural souls. (*He* was 54 – not Miss Brereton.)

But he kept regular contact, and was a familiar sight at Old Boys' Gatherings, as well as a familiar figure, with his black clothes, dog collar, and monocle, in Old Boys' photographs.

Taylor, the man to whom he addressed the telegram, was Adelbert Taylor, long-serving master at the School, and Secretary to the Governors. It was the latter function that was relevant in this case.

The event which Thompson could not attend was the final, ultimate, really, absolutely last meeting to wind up the affairs of the Devon County School. It was to be presided over by the official liquidator, and its sole purpose was, in the words of the statement issued by the liquidator himself, Fred. B. Wyatt, to lay before a General Meeting of the Devon County School Company Ltd. ('in voluntary liquidation'), an account 'showing the manner in which the winding up has been conducted and the property of the Company disposed of', and so and so on.

The process had been begun in 1907, and a new form of government for the School had been set up, with governors instead of directors, a grant from the County Education Committee, and fee-paying parents instead of shareholders. But these processes involve a lot of detail and clearing up, and the business was, apparently, not complete until Fred Wyatt convened his meeting in Bridge Buildings in Barnstaple on Friday, 24th May, 1912.

It was no doubt merely a formality, and was certainly no surprise, but, to Thompson, after so many years, as Headmaster, shareholder, and kind of proud parent, and later, gruff great-uncle, the event must have meant something. He knew the School was on a safer financial basis than it had been on for decades, and it had a new, dynamic, and popular Head. The numbers were beginning to rise. The future looked, or at any rate was beginning to look, bright.

But he had been there first, and he had seen it grow, from only three pupils in the parlour of a farmhouse. What dreams and ambitions he, as a young man of twenty-one, must have had for his pioneer West Buckland Farm and County School. (Within only a few years, it had lost the 'Farm' dimension, and became simply the 'Devon County School', and that was how he built it.) He had talked fondly of this and other feelings at the Old Boys' Dinner just after he had retired in 1888.

He remembered, he said, going round with the Revd. Brereton to decide exactly where the School was going to be built. He had watched the School rise, stone by stone. He also remembered the grounds – at first all bare, and later growing in grace and beauty. Every tree and shrub had been planted under his eye, many to commemorate some particular event. Now they were, as he said, rich and mature, and ornaments to the place.

Above all he cherished the regard of generations of boys, and the family atmosphere over which he had presided for so long. This, he said, was the greatest pleasure of his position. (This may be laying on the sentiment somewhat thickly, but one can easily forgive such softness of heart in a man reminiscing among well-fed, well-disposed listeners after a lifetime of such total service as he had given.)

For thirty years as Headmaster, and for a further twenty-four, he had watched the School through its ups and downs.

Now it wasn't the Devon County School any more; it wasn't the school whose name had gone round England as the pioneer, the forerunner of the middle-class county schools, to be followed and imitated in one county after another. It had another name – West Buckland School. Not much of a change, perhaps, to an outsider, but it must have given him a twinge. It was a bit like a parent, after four or five decades, having to get used to the child he had nurtured and loved changing his name from Sam to Fred. His head must have told him that it was the same underneath, but his heart told him that it wasn't – not quite.

Was that why he sent that telegram to Taylor to say that he couldn't come?

2.   No Stone Unturned

When readers meet a writer whose recently-published book they have just read, it is a temptation very difficult to resist to tell him about some mistakes they have detected in it.

Misprints come high on the list. No matter how many times you read through the proofs, misprints have a truly Pimpernellish knack of avoiding detection. They never become blindingly obvious until they are pointed out by somebody else; then you wonder how on earth you could have missed them. Hence, therefore, I had to writhe in impotence when I realised that it appeared that I did not know how to spell the name of the famous musician-doctor-philosopher Albert Schweitzer. If that last sentence ever sees the light of printed day – and it must have done if you have just read it – be assured that I shall have read through it about twenty times.

Then there are the real gapers, when the writer gets local names wrong. And I don't mean merely spelling. In my previous volume on the School (entitled simply *West Buckland School*), I managed to allocate a lady to the wrong husband! Oh – and I actually did spell the husband's name wrong as well. Luckily the lady's son, who rang me up to tell me about it, was very kind and tolerant. Beyond giving it as his opinion that his late mother, had she known, would have turned in her grave, he took it very well.

Finally, there are the interesting mistakes – indeed mistakes which I had no idea at the time had any potential to *be* mistakes. Mistakes which create mysteries, the solution of which leads to yet more mysteries.

The business of the foundation stone is one that comes under this heading. Indeed, I toyed with the idea of putting as the title 'Who Moved the Stone?', but decided that the possible alignment of it with the mystery of the Resurrection was a mite presumptuous.

However, let us begin, as the King of Hearts suggested, at the beginning.

There are two foundation stones in the School. Well, actually, there must be several – arts blocks and science blocks and gyms and what-have-you. But I am talking about the two stones in the main building – the two 'proper' foundation stones if you like.

The first is the foundation stone-foundation stone – the one laid by the second Earl Fortescue on 4th October, 1860, to mark the beginning of the transition of the newly-born School from its rustic digs in local farmhouses to proper accommodation in permanent buildings just up the road. It is a tribute to the energy of local workmen that the completed edifice was ready for occupation almost exactly a year later. The stone itself, incidentally, is also a tribute to the masonic loyalties of the second Earl, because the inscription makes reference to 'the Great Architect of the Universe'.

So far, so good. No problem there.

The second stone is the one commemorating the beginning of the Memorial Hall, which arose on the site of the buildings destroyed by the famous fire of 1930. The laying took place on 12th October, 1932. This time the workmen did even better; the completed building was ready for official opening within not twelve months, but seven; the Bishop of Crediton did the honours in May, 1933. (I have just found another error for myself, before anyone has been able to tell me. Looking at the relevant page in the book – page 87 – I have just noted that I put in a caption declaring that the building was opened on 12th October, 1932, when in fact it was the foundation stone that was laid on that date. It is satisfying, once in a while, to beat the error-mongers to it.)

Now – to the real point. Another photograph on page 87 of the book depicts the foundation stone itself, with its inscription clear: 'This foundation stone was laid by Hugh, fifth Earl Fortescue K.C.B. on 12th October, 1932.' And other remarks about the presence of the Chairman of Governors, Dudley Bush, and the Headmaster, Ernest Harries.

What is wrong with that? Have we got the dates wrong? No – not so far as I know – not until another error-terror writes to me anyway. Was the Chairman of Governors indeed Mr. Bush? Oh, yes. And the Headmaster Mr. Harries? Of course.

But – and here we come to what P.G. Wodehouse would call the 'nub' – the man who laid the stone was not the fifth Earl Fortescue. It sounds like the punch line in the third act of a Victorian courtroom melodrama, doesn't it? – 'That man is not my husband!'

Does this mean that the man who did the business with the trowel and mallet was an impostor? By no means. He was in fact the fifth Earl's father. We are almost back to the Victorian melodrama again.

This is what I meant when I said that there are some errors which you have no idea have the potential to be errors. If you quote from something which is, quite literally, set in stone, you don't expect to be making a mistake.

None of this would have come to light if I had not received an interesting letter from one of those very eagle-eyed readers I have been knocking (I hope, in a friendly way). Mr. Ian Provis told me a story of something that happened in the nineteen-forties, when he was a boy at the School.

The 4th Earl Fortescue lays the Foundation Stone for the Memorial Hall. [School Archive]

Apparently, a gang of workmen descended one day upon the premises, concentrated round the front of the Memorial Hall, and dug out the foundation stone. It sounds as if it must have been a risky operation, for the stone was large, and set, naturally, in the foot of the wall. However, no doubt some tricks of the trade, which are esoteric mysteries to outsiders, helped to accomplish this feat. Not only that; a second stone was inserted in the place of the first. This stone also bore an inscription; it stated that it had been laid by the *fourth* Earl Fortescue.

I went out to check. Yes, there it was – 'fourth'.

Nobody needs to get out the magnifying glass and deerstalker hat to be able to ask, 'How come?' Why carve a stone with the fifth Earl's name on it when the Hall was going to be opened by the fourth Earl?

If indeed it was. Bells of memory began to jingle a little. I was almost sure that the fourth Earl had died in 1932. I checked. Yes, he had. Well, then, did that solve the puzzle? No, it didn't. If the fourth Earl died before the opening, then the original stone, with the fifth Earl's name on it, was the correct one. If he didn't die before the opening, why didn't they carve 'fourth Earl' on the original stone? And if the old Earl *did* die, and his son *did* perform the honours, which made the original stone correct, why did they change the stone a decade later and put 'fourth' on it?

There was a possible, a barely possible variant on this. Say the fourth Earl was old and ill (he was certainly old in 1932). Say he decided, as the great day approached, that he was not fit to do his aristocratic benefactor's duty. So he asked his son to stand in for him. The organisers were told, and decided that it was a proper compliment to the fourth Earl's heir that he should have his own name carved on the stone. And then – *then* – and this is the clever part, Watson – the fourth Earl recovered for a bit, and said, 'Dammit, I think I'll do it myself.' And did. How about that?

Yes, I know. It still does not explain why they waited to change the stone from 'fifth' to 'fourth' a decade later.

It was time to go to the fountainhead, to family headquarters, to the mouth of the horse. I braced myself and put in a telephone call to Lady Margaret Fortescue. One does not ring up the daughter of a hundred earls every day of the week, and it is never easy to summarise the nature of one's enquiry to anybody in a few words and in a logical fashion. But Lady Margaret is a good listener, and she grabbed it straight off the bat at once.

Had she any memory of the opening ceremony? No. Well, she had been very young. Had she any explanation of the mystery of the two stones? No, she hadn't. Indeed, she wasn't even aware that a mystery existed. Did she know the exact date of the death of her grandfather, the fourth Earl? No. But she could help me there. *Burke's Peerage* was lying at the end of her arm. (It's at times like that that you might be tempted to envy the aristocracy; how many of us have our telephones so conveniently adjacent to such repositories of reference information? The best most of us can manage is the Yellow Pages under the umbrella stand or the plumber's phone number scrawled on the back of an envelope behind the clock.)

However, Lady Margaret joined in the search with great willingness, and duly came up with the information needed, plus a bit more: her grandfather had been born in April, 1854, had married in July, 1886, and had died on 29th October, 1932. 29th October – seventeen days after the laying of the stone. So he could have done it.

How to prove that he did.

There was in the Archive a file containing bits and pieces about the Memorial Hall – a programme, a cutting or two, and so on. Was there anything there? Yes, there was. An account, presumably prepared for the local press. The proceedings began with a 'luncheon'. They are a hungry lot out at West Buckland; practically every public function of any consequence of which records remain, going right back to 1859, seems to have begun with a 'luncheon'. All the usual VIP's were there – mayors, governors, old boys, and of course the Earl (not 'numbered', so we don't know if it was the fourth or the fifth). There was a choir (the boys had been scrubbed and polished, and hoicked into cassocks and surplices), a procession, a service, and the 'customary formalities'.

The stone was mentioned of course, and the full inscription quoted. The *fifth* Earl. So we still hadn't got there.

At the bottom of the file, under all the cuttings, was a photograph. It showed an elderly gentleman with a white moustache doing the honours. It *had* to be the fourth Earl. I sent a copy of the picture to Lady Margaret, and she replied confirming my guess. It was indeed her grandfather, the fourth Earl.

Which at once raised another mystery. Why – if it was the fourth Earl, and they quoted the inscription about the fifth Earl – did nobody see fit to draw attention to this anomaly? Was it because of embarrassment? If so, why quote the inscription at all?

But somebody – indeed quite a lot of people – must have known about the mistake. How many red faces were there among the Governing Body? Or among the Hall Foundation Committee? Did the Chairman of it find a sudden reason for emigrating? Did he at least do the decent thing and resign? Were grovelling letters of apology written to Castle Hill in a vain attempt to shut stable doors after the horse had bolted?

Perhaps it wasn't a governor's fault at all. Perhaps it was the work of a remarkably careless (or evilly-disposed) mason. Or the negligence of a harassed clerk of the works. Did anybody among the working classes find himself suddenly sent to Newgate or Devil's Island?

The mistake must have been known, or it would not have been put right. But why did it take so long to put it right? In order to find out, someone will have to trawl through a decade of Governors' Minutes, and even then he may not find it.

The *Register* of November, 1932, however, weighs in with a nugget of information which deserves to have the last word on this little saga. In his reported speech beside the stone, the fourth Earl made mention of the fact that 'he expected he was the only survivor of those who saw his grandfather lay the first stone of that School over seventy years ago'. Remember? Lady Margaret had said he was born in 1854.

So how's that for a link with the past? Lady Margaret, who is very much alive, knew the man who was present at the foundation of the School over 140 years ago.

3. Shining Examples

In the summer term of 1913, a new boy arrived in the School. He came from Delhi. His name was Farmer. He left to join the Forces in 1917 – it would seem, as soon as his age permitted. In the intervening four years, he notched up a series of sporting successes that it would now be difficult to approach, never mind surpass.

His activities embraced football, cricket, athletics, cross-country, fives, shooting, and swimming – to say nothing of becoming Company Sergeant-Major in the cadet force. The cumulative effect of this achievement would surely have generated a pretty awesome groundswell of hero-worship. Such an emotion one would expect among pupils, but it is interesting to come across evidence of genuine admiration among teachers. The writer of the report on the Athletics Sports of 1917, and presumably a teacher, was moved to say, 'Nothing was more delightful than to see the ease and grace with which he took part in any sport.'

A fine compliment. And testimony to the idea that a true hero should not only achieve great things, but should achieve them without having to strain every muscle in order to do so. He should do it with 'ease and grace'. Or at any rate without conscious striving after the teeth-gritting satisfaction of becoming better than anybody else. A true hero just does his best, because it is the thing to do at the time; if his best turns out to be better than that of anybody else, that is merely a bonus, which he shrugs off with a modest smile.

If any of Farmer's teachers had been crystal-gazers, they might have been able to forecast some sterling achievements for this thirteen-year-old stripling from the other side of the world, sent to compete and survive, alone, six thousand miles away, by a parent in the Indian Army or Civil Service. I have no proof that his father served in either of these organisations, but think about it. A father called Farmer, obviously an Englishman, is working in Delhi, in 1913, at the high-tide of Empire. He has to be a soldier or a civil servant. At the very least an engineer or something. Hardly a missionary; he would not have been able to afford the fees or the fares.

If further evidence of the father's imperial loyalties were needed, you have only to look at young Farmer's Christian names – Cecil Stanley Redvers. The boy had been born in 1900. And who were three of the most heroic, and imperial, names in 1900? Cecil Rhodes, Henry Morton Stanley, and General Sir Redvers Buller.

Buller may be in eclipse these days; indeed his name was in eclipse long before the Boer War was over. (He was the Commander-in-Chief who was sacrificed on the altar of British shame at early defeats by the Boers.) But

Rhodes is still well known, if not much admired, for his concept of a band of British territory stretching from the Cape to Cairo, and Stanley's reputation lives on as the man who picked up the torch of African exploration let fall by the dying Livingstone.

So, with a trio of names like that – Cecil Stanley Redvers – which the bearer himself might have regarded as an affliction (we don't know) – it would not be surprising if his teachers wondered what the boy might achieve.

All of which leads one to speculation on what sort of person a boy of the early twentieth century would be expected to admire, or want to admire? Who inspired young Farmer? Yes, of course, Rhodes and Stanley and Buller. He could hardly help it. But who else?

I came across a clue to this when I found a large framed picture – a full colour reproduction print – under a pile of old and neglected archive material. It showed a young sailor beside a huge gun. He was impeccably dressed, his complexion was clear and fair, and no trace of the ordeal he was undergoing showed on his face except for a frown of determination.

For the caption at the bottom informed me that the boy – for that was what he was – was John Cornwell, and the picture was designed to illustrate an incident from the great battle between the British and German High Seas Fleets off Jutland in May, 1916. The picture was produced to illustrate Cornwell's bravery. The rest of his gun crew were either killed or wounded by a German shell. Cornwell himself was wounded as well, but remained at his post with the gun until he too collapsed. He later died of his wounds. He was sixteen years old. He was awarded a posthumous Victoria Cross.

It was the stuff of legend. Countless pictures, of varying degrees of inaccuracy and romanticism, were published to illustrate the incident. The fact that one reached a remote little boarding school in the fastnesses of rural Devon is a testimony to its popularity.

This might be understandable in time of war, when the British were all right and the Germans were all wrong. By the same token, Buller was a hero in 1899, when the British were all right and the Boers were all wrong. Buller was unlucky in that he did not win a battle, he did not win the war, and he did not die gloriously. He was made the scapegoat for a bad war strategy, and sacked, and it was left to Roberts and Kitchener – two more heroic figures – to grind down the enemy by unspectacular if effective methods.

Young Cornwell's exploit, however, survived, because of its very brevity and unalterability. It proved, beyond argument, that stiff upper-lippery had won the war, and would go on to win the peace in a glorious future of success and empire and Britishness that would help the world to go round –

in the world's best interests, you understand. John Cornwell was considered to be the ideal personality to be held up as an example to the youth of the late-war and post-war generation. His story contained all the elements of perfect heroism – youth, unthinking bravery, unquestioning patriotism, steadfastness, duty, and death.

Small wonder that a large, framed picture of him found its way to an obscure moorland school. How many years, one wonders, did it hang on a classroom wall? How many ponderous morals were drawn from it by hectoring schoolmasters?

Cornwell joined the pantheon of great British heroes (and heroines) like Livingstone, Scott, Florence Nightingale, and Grace Darling (and Rhodes and Stanley – poor Buller soon faded away). Heroes of fact. To say nothing of the heroes of fiction in the novels of Stevenson, Henty, and Rider Haggard, and, later, John Buchan. Intrepid upholders all – of Britishness (well, in the case of RLS, of 'Scotchness' – or 'Scottishness', if you prefer), of Empire, of playing the game, of seeing it through.

It is interesting that young Farmer, in the course of his time at the School, followed a regular tradition by presenting several books to the School Library. They included works by Arthur Conan Doyle, R.M. Ballantyne, and W.H.G. Kingston – all of them jolly-good-lads-doing-your-bit novels of travel and adventure and taking the values of the Empire into every corner of the globe. Predictably, another of the books he gave was by Winston Churchill, and was called *From London to Ladysmith*.

By the time Farmer joined up in 1917, the exploit of John Cornwell a year earlier would have rung round the entire English-speaking world. It seems inconceivable that the boy would not have heard of him. He would also know about Roberts, and Kitchener, and, earlier, Livingstone and Gordon. He would know too about the very earliest (unless you count the semi-fictitious, and endless, early Christian saints) – Grace Darling.

Curiously, she is the one who comes perhaps closest to Cornwell. She performed her great feat, like Cornwell, at sea. Both displayed great courage and presence of mind. Both she and Cornwell were doing their job – or, as the legend-makers would say, their 'duty'. Cornwell, a gunner, stuck to his gun. Grace, a lighthouse-keeper's daughter, rowed out, with her father, to rescue some shipwrecked travellers who were marooned on a large rock among the Farne Islands, just off the coast of Northumberland.

In the noise and confusion, it is unlikely that Cornwell stopped much to think about what he was doing. He did what he had been trained to do. Similarly, Grace was born to the sea and storms and rowing and tough conditions. She genuinely thought nothing of what she did. And, incidentally, one can not imagine her father risking her life on a hare-brained quest with scant chance of success.

Nevertheless, to be fair to both of them, not every sixteen-year-old boy would have stayed at his post, alone and wounded, in the heat of battle; and not every young woman would have leapt at the chance of rowing nearly a mile in an open boat in the North Sea in autumn within hours of a storm which had wrecked a large steamer.

Why then did they become heroes? Why did these two, otherwise unremarkable young people come to be held up as shining examples to their nation?

A combination, perhaps, of two things.

First, for all that the English like to think of themselves as a 'seafaring nation', the truth is that it is only those who go on ships who are really seafaring. The rest of us know very little about it. So, to the public of the First World War, locked in battle against the 'beastly Hun', Cornwell and his fellow-sailors were our 'gallant lads in blue'. (In Nelson's time they were 'jolly jack tars'.) It was all too easy to heap praise on to the dead shoulders of a boy whose exploit seemed to epitomise the values of what the nation thought it was fighting for – British pride, courage, honour, playing the game, beating the wicked enemy, and so on. (For similar reasons, the Australian public in the late nineteen-twenties and -thirties, prostrate from the world slump, fell on the figure of Don Bradman, who seemed to be the only Australian in the whole sub-continent who could knock hell out of the English, indeed out of the whole world.)

Similarly, Grace's feat appealed to a nation which, barely twenty-five years after Nelson, prided itself still more on its affinity with the sea, but which in fact saw it only through a veil of romance. Waves were 'billows'; the sea was 'the foaming main'. In addition to that, Grace offered the perfect combination of virtues that her contemporaries thought they admired. She was young, she was a dutiful daughter, she was brave. She was modest too; she honestly could not see what all the fuss was about. She died unmarried, and before she was thirty. Youth, modesty, obedience, virginity, heroism, and finally early death – the mixture produced an elixir of mass appeal which was totally intoxicating. Finally, her name – Grace Darling. If every novelist, poet, and journalist in the land had sat down together for a month, they could not have come up with anything better.

The second factor which secured the fame of both of them was the press. Once the newspapers got hold of their stories, their exploits swept the nation like a tidal wave (an appropriate simile perhaps for sea heroes and heroines). In Cornwell's case, the legend has not proved quite so enduring; one might stop a dozen people in the street, and find that not one had heard of him. But a fair number of them would have heard of Grace Darling.

Perhaps mercifully, the flood of mementoes, busts, prints, poems, portraits, and songs has abated; you would scour a girls' annual these days – if there are indeed many girls' annuals about – and scour it in vain, for a reference to her. Or to Cornwell in boys' books. You would have to rummage in an old maid's loft to find a kitsch china statue of Grace, and you would have to wade through the dust of neglected school archive, as I did, to come across John Cornwell.

Cecil Farmer's name has not rung down the century either; I had to labour in the furrows of old school magazines to find evidence of his existence, never mind his achievement. But in its small, local way, his school career was the stuff of legend. Perhaps not his academic career, one must admit. I found no evidence of prizes at speech days, and only one instance of his participation in the proceedings of the school debating society. And in a school whose headmaster was crackers about Gilbert and Sullivan, and who promoted a full production of a G. and S. opera every year, Farmer's name is conspicuous by its absence even from the humblest of chorus lines or teams of backstage dogsbodies.

But put this boy out of doors, and there was nobody who could touch him. The OTC (Officers' Training Corps – 'cadets' today) I have already mentioned. That was, to be sure, no great achievement, in an Edwardian-type school in wartime, but he did rise to the top – Company Sergeant-Major. However, it was on the sporting field that he came into his own. In four short years, from 1913 to 1917, he took part in, and usually excelled at, seven different activities.

He won his colours for both cricket and football. He won prestigious awards at shooting. He was runner-up in the School open fives competition when still only sixteen. He was the junior swimming champion, and good enough, at fourteen, to compete in the open races as well.

The School was famous for its cross-country runs. Well, on the edge of Exmoor, it would be, wouldn't it? In 1914, he ran in three races, without much distinction. (He was only fourteen, and competing against boys three and four years older.) The following year, he ran twice, and won twice – getting into his stride, as you might say. Then, in the course of 1916 and 1917, he ran in twenty races and won nineteen of them. In the twentieth, he came second, because of an 'accident' which the magazine did not specify. But it did pause to offer sympathy, so it looks as if he had been the hot favourite.

But it was on the School Sports Day that he must have made jaws drop, for his talent, his versatility, and his stamina. To say nothing of his 'ease and grace'.

There is no record of his participation in the Sports of 1913, which took place on 12th May – quite early. Elsewhere the magazine says he arrived in the summer term. As he had travelled all the way from India, it is quite possible that he arrived after that date.

In 1914, he got under way by winning three events, coming second in two, and becoming Junior Champion. In 1915, still under sixteen, he not only won all the events in his age group; he also won the open mile and half-mile. All these events, remember, took place *on the same day*.

He completely dominated the Sports of 1916, winning six open events and coming second in a seventh. He was now showing not only the remarkable stamina that had become his trade mark, but his versatility; the events were as varied as the mile, the half-mile, the 100 yards, the long jump, the steeplechase, and throwing the cricket ball. His total of points for his house nearly trebled that of his nearest rival.

By the time the Sports of 1917 came round, on Whit Monday, as the *Register* wryly recorded, '. . . the only interest was to see if he could break any records'. He beat one of his own, equalled another, and set up a new one in a third event. He won the mile, the half-mile, the quarter-mile, the 100 yards, the hurdles, the long jump, the steeplechase, and the cricket ball. He had to make do with second in the high jump; otherwise it would have been a clean sweep. He amassed 142 points for his house, while his nearest competitor lagged behind with a mere 85. The boy who came third had only 37. Total domination. And – to repeat – all in one day. A day, moreover, which had begun with storms, and which continued with wind. The conditions were so bad that the decision was not taken to go ahead until one o'clock. So this remarkable athlete not only competed in the most awful conditions; he polished it all off *in one afternoon*.

Before he was eighteen he had left to join an 'Officers' Cadet Battalion'; he served in, and survived, the First World War, or what was left of it.

Would such a record put the holder in line for hero-worship today? Are children still mesmerised by sporting achievement? Or does it depend on the sport? Does, say, a javelin-thrower or a triple jumper attract the same following as a footballer? Or are children harder to impress now? They have access to much more travel, information, money, and entertainment, so who are their heroes now?

Must we go through the ranks of young millionaire soccer or rugger players? Do we search the pop charts or the Hollywood gossip columns? Pore over the prison records of notorious protesters – whether on behalf of civil rights, nuclear disarmament, ethnic self-determination, free access to drugs, or the abolition of all forms of censorship? Sort out the rival champions of the ozone layer, the disabled, the rain forest, the seals, the badgers, the whales, the rhinos, the tigers? Examine the lists of Nobel Prize winners? Look for a sudden rash of new Christian names inflicted by admiring parents, like Winston after 1940, or Dorothy after *The Wizard of Oz* in 1939?

Or am I being too cynical? Is there still, out there somewhere, a small handful of young, devoted, uncomplicated, brave, un-self-conscious, talented, dead people whose very names make the blood race? So that merely to dream of emulating them causes the adrenalin to flow, and the hair to rise on the back of a young neck?

It would be nice to think so.

4. Passing Tribute

West Buckland School is placed roughly equidistantly between the villages of East and West Buckland. Indeed, the parish boundary goes right through the middle of the School, and in the early days scratch football teams in the School could, and did, name themselves after each village with total legality.

The co-founder, the Revd. J.L. Brereton, was Rector of West Buckland, but it was the other church, at East Buckland, which became the regular School church, because it was more closely bound up with the estates of Earl Fortescue, the other co-founder. And it was Fortescue who had the money, the land, the prestige, and the influence.

The Fortescues go back a long way, to Norman times, but the village almost certainly goes back much further. Devon settlements have a deep, deep past. Saxons were not great pen-pushers, and their settlements may be short on documentation, but the Normans left a lot of writing behind. East Buckland is one of scores, possibly hundreds, of Devon villages and/or manors (scholars write whole books about the difference) which are recorded in the Domesday Book, that amazing survey of the land of England, and its inhabitants and appurtenances, which was commissioned by the Conqueror at Christmas, 1085, and was delivered, complete, only eight months later, at Salisbury, in August, 1086.

'Buckland', incidentally, has nothing to do with bucks, or deer. 'Buckland' was originally 'bookland' – that is, land held by special charter or deed or grant from another owner (usually higher up the scale of wealth or society), as opposed to 'folkland', which was land held by immemorial custom or folk-right. This explains why there are so many 'Bucklands' around – 14 in Devon alone. Some of them gained, over time, a second name, partly no doubt to help to distinguish them from the others – like Buckland Filleigh, Buckland Brewer, Egg Buckland (nothing to do with eggs, but to do with an owner called Hecche), Buckland Monachorum (belonging to the monks of Buckland Abbey), and so on.

The two either side of the School became known simply as East and West Buckland. In the eastern part, there were, in Domesday Book, three manors all bearing the Buckland name, and they were all held by Geoffrey de Montbrai, Bishop of Coutances in Normandy, and one of the original companions of the Conqueror. He held dozens of manors all over the South-West, and elsewhere too. He was also, conveniently for him perhaps, one of the Domesday Commissioners who helped to draw up the Great Survey (it wasn't called 'Domesday Book' until a century later, by which time it had built up a fearsome reputation as the authority of last resort, beyond which there was no appeal).

According to the entry for these East Buckland manors (the three bearing the name, and a fourth, since identified as Brayley), the population consisted of '3 farmers, 3 cottagers, 9 labourers, 8 cattle, 46 sheep, and 15 goats'. They did not as a rule count women and children. Its taxable value was £2.00. (I am indebted for much – though not all – of this information to the research of Mr. R.P. Chope, the indefatigable Old Boy, historian, and antiquarian whose myriad activities are recorded elsewhere in this book – see 'Lorna Doone at West Buckland' and 'Chope's Choice'.)

So the total of adult males was 15 – in 1086. The Minutes of the Parochial Church Council, on 11th April, 1928, recorded the total of 'members' on the electoral roll as 21. If this took in the 'new' female voters enfranchised by the recent Act of Parliament, it meant that the numbers of male voters could have been even *lower* than in 1086.

Look at it another way. If you add in a wife for everybody and only three children for each family in that Domesday survey, you arrive at a total population of about 75. In a small pamphlet recording the history of the village, printed in 1969, the population of the village in 1901 was given as 96. Both instances are classic examples of the old idea that nothing much has happened in Devon for the past nine hundred years. Small wonder that Devonians are not exactly noted for their pioneering and adventurous radicalism.

Jumping several hundred years, and leaving Geoffrey de Montbrai far behind, the village (and its church, which appeared in the thirteenth century, and could well have been built on the site of one even earlier – they often were), passed to the Densell family, one of whose daughters married a Fortescue. So here we are.

The Fortescue family provided help, money, and connections for Brereton's brain child – the West Buckland Farm and County School in its first incarnation – but when it came to worship, the second Earl preferred the church at East Buckland to Brereton's on the other, western, side.

One thing you have to hand the Fortescues – they seem always willing to back their convictions with their money. In 1859, for instance, when a large wood-built dormitory was constructed on a farm site to accommodate the growing numbers of pupils (the permanent structure had not yet been built), Earl Fortescue said, at its opening, that he had been initially sceptical of the whole enterprise, but, now that he saw how far the project had come, and how promising it was beginning to look, he was willing not only to make a public recantation, but to pay for the whole building. A fine gesture. (See *West Buckland School* – pp. 13-15.)

So it was now, too, with the church. His Lordship had agreed to support the new school, so he had the church rebuilt to provide room for the pupils – and admittedly for the benefit of the village too – and he endowed the School chaplaincy for good measure. The Fortescues, like many a noble family, may have enjoyed their noble status and their privileges, and took steps too, no doubt, to preserve them; but they took their nobility seriously as well, and appreciated that rank carried with it some inescapable responsibilities. They understood what it meant to be a 'proper' noble. (See 'Who Wants to be a Benefactor?')

The School grew rapidly during the first decades of its history, apparently more rapidly than was expected, and the church must have seemed cramped again. The *Register* (the School magazine) for midsummer, 1870 recorded that 'to meet the increasing requirements of the School' an extension was 'being made at the west end by means of which about sixty new sittings will be provided'. I bet Fortescue paid for that too. With fees at only 25 guineas (£26.25) a year for boarders, and 6 guineas (£6.30) for day boys, it is hard to see how the School could have raised the wherewithal. The combined fee income of the whole school for the entire academic year did not come to £2,000 as late as 1908. Admittedly, the School was bigger in the 1870's than it was in 1908, but the budget surplus at either time would have been pressed to provide a new set of tools for George Balment, the School handyman, never mind a church extension.

This willingness on the part of Earl Fortescue to pay towards the care of the pupils' souls gives added poignancy to the complaint of the Rural Dean which was recorded in 1874, to the effect that boys from the Devon County School were defacing the new seats in the church. He opined that the punishment should fit the crime, and that the School should pay for the damage. If the School ever did, bang went George Balment's new tools.

Schoolboys have always shown irreverence towards dignity and formality, and this has come out too in scurrilous entries in the church's visitors' book, where the easier medium of ink and paper, as opposed to penknife and matured oak, and the greater freedom thereby afforded by the much greater speed available, have given adolescent iconoclasts freer rein to their capacity for cheek. In the 'Remarks' column, which is usually garnished with pious platitudes like 'so peaceful' and 'lovely church', have appeared verdicts of crushing criticism, like 'singers can't sing, ringers can't ring, and preachers can't preach'. Alternatively, other commentators have given rampant expression to their radical politics with complaints about 'bourgeois oppression' or injunctions like 'power to the republic'.

George Balment, extreme right, with School servants, very early 1900s.
At the back stands Mr. Knight, the Headmaster, and, almost certainly, his wife. [School Archive]

These latter morsels of gossip were fed to me by the man who must know East Buckland Church better than any other man alive. Sam Heath has been churchwarden, bellringer, unofficial gardener, archivist, and general nanny to the church for forty years now. He gave me the full tour. (Incidentally, it was his father-in-law who wrote the short history of East Buckland Church to which I referred above.)

Sam Heath – the name fits him like a glove – did not get much of a start in life. He was raised in an orphanage in Croydon till he was about ten, at which time he was lucky enough to acquire a foster-mother. Then, by the terms of one of the many acts of Parliament designed for the benefit of children, he was uprooted and moved back to Devon, where he had been born. One enlightened clause had stated that an orphan had to 'report back' to the place of his birth. Another clause said that his foster-mother was not allowed to adopt him because she was not married. So he finished growing up, along with 56 other kids, in the workhouse in Barnstaple. (Later the Alexandra Hospital, now replaced by a block of flats.)

He was put to work as an agricultural labourer – mostly live-in – at a succession of local farms – in Parracombe, Stoke Rivers, and so on. He generously recalled that one home was a 'good' one, and another was a 'Christian' one.

Then, in the village of Charles, forty-odd years ago, he met May Cotsford and got married. Her father was in charge of the bells at East Buckland Church. His official title was 'Captain of the Tower'. (I am about to perpetrate an awful pun, but it is, in the context, unavoidable.) This title has a splendid ring to it – redolent of ancient warders and Beefeaters and halberds and American tourists and cameras clicking in the sunshine.

Anyway, Sam thus began his long association with East Buckland Church, which has continued to the present day.

His father-in-law introduced him to bell-ringing. By a useful coincidence, the School had begun bell-ringing again in 1958, the year of its centenary. The School Chaplain, the Revd. J.H.B. Andrews, had introduced it in 1936, but of course the War had put a stop to it (bells were to be rung only in the event of imminent invasion or outright victory). Then a Mr. Bailey had presented a set of handbells to the School. An instructor was found, interest was generated, and it was a natural progression for an approach to be made to East Buckland Church for permission to use the bells there for some 'real' ringing.

By the mid-sixties Sam, who had himself become proficient by about 1963, was involved with this School group.

It was by no means his first contact with the School. Two of the many farms he had worked at were Huxtable Farm and Higher Pitt. Some of their fields, where Sam worked, were adjacent to the School grounds (the School owns these fields now). Boys used to enjoy coming over to help with carrying hay and corn, and, later in the year, with lifting potatoes. In the spring, a few assisted with lambing too. It must have offered a welcome change from French irregular verbs and bed-making.

Later on, Sam worked for the Fortescue Estate, in their building department, and learnt new skills and techniques. Round about the same time, he made the acquaintance of the then Headmaster, the Revd. George Ridding, who took the School services at East Buckland. This meeting had a most interesting upshot.

The Revd. Ridding believed in the boys learning as many skills as possible away from their school desks; the School was perpetually short of money; there were a lot of construction jobs that needed doing; and Sam, by virtue of his new employment, had access to all sorts of interesting things like concrete mixers, tractors, trailers, and J.C.B.'s.

Stir into this mixture the Headmaster's initiative and drive, and before long you had teams of boys digging drains, building manholes, shifting mountains of earth, laying acres of concrete, and generally making themselves useful. One suspects that the Headmaster enjoyed himself driving tractors and pulling trailers, and that Sam put in more than his share with his interest, his professional knowledge, his kindness towards the boys and tolerance of their hamfistedness.

The fruits of this partnership included a roof to the swimming pool and a couple of squash courts. All this gave Sam a chance to do what he is happiest doing – sharing his knowledge and transmitting his enthusiasm. It was going to be only a matter of time before he began to share his love of the bells. The association was to continue almost until the present day.

He gave it up only when his eightieth birthday loomed. He had found it too difficult to clamber around, high up, to repair stays, and to keep up with all the hundred and one jobs connected with the maintenance of a working bell tower.

But, for thirty-odd years, he introduced generations of boys to the mysteries of bell-ringing. You might not think that such an activity would appeal to teenage boys in a boarding school. They are not noted, as a rule, for active interest in matters artistic, esoteric, or religious. But look again – especially at that phrase 'boarding school'. Bell-ringing could be performed only, obviously, in the church tower. That meant leaving School. To a boarder (and the vast majority of bell-ringers were boarders) that meant welcome liberation, if only for an hour. No smell of stale dinners from the kitchens, no pong of hundreds of sweaty feet in the changing rooms, no grime and dust from classrooms, no echoing corridors, no prefects, no rules and regulations, no jostle and rush, no forbidding of anything. Just a welcome walk in the fresh air between green hedges to an ancient tower, where Sam, who was no sergeant-major, told them all about bells. If the classes had been in macramé or needle-point with an old maid in a convent, they would still have gone. For the same reason, they had jumped at hay-making and harvesting and lambing.

It must be admitted of course that the delinquent element spotted a Heaven-sent opportunity (in a church! – how much more respectable could it *be*?) for a furtive smoke and a quick swig of communion wine far from prying eyes and retributive canes. For this reason, at least one spoilsport housemaster forbade his charges to be involved at all.

But all those who got there found in Sam rather more than they had bargained for. He is a gentle man, and, as I said, no sergeant-major. But he would brook no half-measures when it came to the bells. He would tolerate nothing but respect for them. He had also to inculcate a sense of awareness; bells are after all extremely heavy objects, and bell-ropes have a life, and a will, of their own.

The learners found out that it is not just a matter of giving a lug on the rope. As with so many other physical activities, until you got the hang of it (another pun – sorry), it could be very tiring. Blisters and burns on hands were frequent, to say nothing of strained stomach muscles. Many boys (and staff – Sam even recruited teachers from time to time) found it extremely difficult to master the intervals and the rhythms and the patterns required; they took a long time to work together. Some never managed it; there was a fair drop-out rate.

But those who stayed grew to appreciate a set of surroundings completely different from those in School. They had the chance to engage in an activity which had nothing to do with lessons or exams or Culture or deadlines or punishments. They learned to concentrate on a task, and to work as a team; they soon realised that, if they didn't, the whole exercise would be useless – possibly even dangerous. Most of them, as one ex-ringer confessed to me, were no angels (indeed, had they been more successful and more law-abiding at School, they would not have thought of escaping to East Buckland in the first place), but they grew to like Sam, and to trust him. He was so different from a schoolmaster or a matron or a secretary. As the ex-ringer said, 'He had shown us that little bit of compassion and kindness detached from the School and given us the chance to be ourselves.'

There grew up a strong loyalty to Sam himself, never mind to the ringing team. Our ex-ringer (let us call him John) said that, even when Sam could not get to the church for a teaching session, they still practised by themselves. Sam had also induced them to assist him in keeping down the grass in the churchyard. John claimed, possibly through spectacles that were ever so slightly rosy, that 'we maintained the graveyard like it was Lord's cricket square'. It must have been something of a minor miracle – to get a bunch of oddly-assorted, not very well-disciplined boys to feel a sense of commitment to such an unusual activity, and 'more importantly not to let Sam down'.

Curiously, the bells made a strong appeal to foreign boys, particularly Asian. (Latterly, some girls too.) No matter how hard the School tries to make these pupils from the other side of the world feel at home, the fact remains that the culture shock must be powerful. It is not every eleven-year-old from Canton or Bangkok who can quickly adapt to sausages and mash, endless wind and rain, and leg-spinners and scrums and *Grange Hill* on the telly. Bell-ringing was completely different, and some of them became more adept than a lot of the natives. The other side of Asia being a long way away, they often could not go back home for the shorter holidays, and so had to remain at School. Bell-ringing was something to do, so they simply did more of it than the others. There was one year when Sam had a whole team of boys from Hong-Kong, including one who called the changes. (What you might call a real Hong-Kong Sing-Song Ding-Dong.)

Once they got the knack, there was the added satisfaction and pride that they could do something that ninety-eight per cent of the others couldn't, and that helped them to keep their heads high in a foreign environment. Sam, with his sympathy and understanding, used to encourage them by awarding them certificates.

The highlight of the bell-ringers' year was the summer outing. These were instituted by David Taylor, the son of 'Judy' Taylor, a long-serving teacher at the School (1895-1929). Judy had worked for years as choirmaster and organist, and his son David maintained the church connection. When he moved away, other willing staff chipped in with the use of their various motor cars. So did parents. Later, much later, the School minibus became available. (Sam apparently was not aware of the limitations of minibuses, and went roaring off down narrow lanes that were familiar to him, but not necessarily to the worried driver behind him, who had to watch Sam, look out for wandering sheep, and keep to the speed limit all at the same time.)

Sam organised peals in church towers all over the county. If it was possible, he would try and stretch his ringers' experience, and test their mettle, by getting them to ring bells that were heavier than those at East Buckland. Sam owns a reference book in which are recorded the weights of every church bell in England, so he would know. (The weight of the tenor bell at East Buckland – the heaviest – is, for anyone who is interested, half a ton.) When they got back to their own bells, they found them that much easier.

Each leg of the journey (during which Sam would frequently pull a bag of humbugs from his capacious pocket) was punctuated by a stop at the house or farm of someone connected with the School (and Sam knew a lot of people too). After each peal, the ringers would be regaled with buns and cakes and cream teas and other 'gastronomic delights', as one teacher recalled. At one farm they once had a huge buffet which included a big joint of home-slaughtered beef. If their travels took them to Exeter, they were given an hour 'off' in the city; at Paignton, they could snatch an ice cream and a quick paddle on the beach. Not much perhaps when put against the more modern and sophisticated delights of a fortnight's ski-ing in Switzerland or abseiling in the Cairngorms. But for boarders in those days, an hour off anywhere was 'a huge perk'.

The list of places they visited reads like a gazeteer of a Devon from some rustic, romantic, bygone age: Bickleigh, Kentisbury, Lapford, Copplestone, Mariansleigh, Exmouth, Iddesleigh, King's Nympton, Broadhembury, Watermouth Castle, Romansleigh, Molland, Morchard Bishop, Monk Okehampton, Broadwood Widger, Widecombe-in-the-Moor, and so on.

All of which makes it such a shame that it is all fading away. The numbers of pupils presenting themselves for tuition have shrunk. Sam is now eighty years old, and unable to keep the tower bell machinery in good repair. His wife is no longer in good health. Money is a growing problem. The School does not insist nowadays on regular Church attendance every Sunday for the boarders – just two or three times a term.

Several times during the tour of the Church and graveyard that Sam gave me he would drop sad little remarks which showed the way things were going. 'People phone me up and say can they ring here.' Well, now they can't; the ropes aren't good enough. 'Now they're all rotting off.' Other bell ropes were ready to go up, but there was nobody left to repair the stays, which prevented the bells from swinging right over and whisking the ropes up and out of sight. The church roof had been repaired 'about ten yure ago', but, if the body of the tower and its machinery were not maintained, it would soon, in Sam's opinion, be in danger of collapse.

Outside it was the same – untreated moss and untended grass. 'Look at all this green stuff. I'd love to get enough money to get this done. I used to keep this so neat.'

But there was a lot of positive talk too; Sam was too fond of it all to confine himself to complaint. Inside, he could hardly move a couple of yards without coming across something worthy of comment. 'See that piece fitted into the door after the fire? Came from a three-hundredweight block at Castle Hill [the home of the Fortescues]. Cut with an ordinary crosscut saw.'

'The safe? Yes – came from Castle Hill.' 'Look at these heaters – about a dozen of them – cost £4,000.' [I bet they came from Castle Hill too.]

So it was no surprise when Sam drew my attention to a plaque behind the altar: 'In memory of Hugh, second Earl Fortescue, K.G., Lord-Lieut. of the County of Devon, who endowed the chaplaincy of the Devon County School and rebuilt and enlarged this church for the joint benefit of the school and of this parish, but died 14th Sept. 1861, just before the completion of his pious work.' [He just missed the opening of the new School building in October, 1861 as well.]

We stopped beside the organ. The fuse for the bellows used to be kept in, said Sam. Not any more; the boys used to get in and play jazz. 'It sounded good too.' For once it was the School rather than the Fortescues who chipped in with some money for the restoration of this venerable instrument. The School's own Chapel Fund had folded, and the money was given to East Buckland instead. [So *that's* where it went. A few years ago, I wrote a piece on the School Chapel that never was, and was always puzzled about a large payment to a firm called 'Eustace and Alldridge'. Presumably, therefore, they were organ-restorers. See *West Buckland School* – 'The Safe Under the Lavatory Basin'.]

The font cover was made by a member of staff. Sam's own wife May had made all the kneelers for the communion rail. *Graffiti* on pews by courtesy of the pupils. Inside the tower, Sam showed me two panels in the door which had been smashed and restored with oak from a cowpen. Apparently, two boys had been up in the tower when the door was locked after a practice; Sam had thought everybody was out. Much later, when the boys descended (quite probably having guiltily satisfied their craving for nicotine), they found themselves locked in. And nobody to come back possibly for days. So they broke the panels and scrambled out. 'They could have rung the bell, but they never thought of it.'

On a wall of the tower was a rough, almost home-made-looking, plaque, on which were painted the names of a team of ringers from the School: 'Ho, Wong, Ashley, Omabgemi, Lau, Brookbank.' Were two of these the phantom panel-smashers of East Buckland, one wonders?

I was shown the bell-ropes. 'Do you want a go?' said Sam. I will spare the reader an account of my puny efforts.

Outside it was a lovely, if bracing, spring day – a stiffish breeze shuffled little ramparts of cloud across a blue sky behind the squat tower. The grass may have been uncut, but it provided a perfect deep-pile, violet-studded carpet for a luxurious amble between the gravestones, which stood awry like lines of tired soldiers wilting in the sun of a long summer parade.

The names on the stones are the ones you would expect for a Devon churchyard:- Ridd, Stanbury, Prideaux, Symons, Witheridge, Clatworthy, Brayley, Tozer, lots of Holloways.

But there are others – of men and women, and children, who were associated in one way or another with the School. The David Taylor I spoke of, the man who began the bell-ringers' outings, was buried here in 1989 – 'man of music and mirth', it said. His father, 'Judy' Taylor, lies here too, along with his (Judy's) wife, whose original home was mentioned – Langholme. The house they lived in was called 'Langholme', and, when the first Preparatory School was set up and housed in the same building, it was given the same name – 'Langholme'.

Round the other side is the grave of Dudley Swinney – ex-pupil, benefactor, governor, President of the Old Boys' Association, and Chairman of the Friends of the School – who died in 1993. His brother, his son, and his grandsons attended the School, and his daughter became the School Matron.

In 1921, they buried here George Balment, who was the very first gardener and handyman the School ever had. Only the infirmity of age forced him to retire in 1916, after 58 years of continuous service. The *Register* ended its tribute with the words 'one of Nature's gentlemen'.

There must be a very tiny grave there somewhere, but I couldn't find it. In the *Register* of Christmas, 1901, there appeared two items about Arthur John Knight, the firstborn son of the Headmaster, Mr. William Arthur Knight. The first announced his birth, on 14th November. The second told of his death two days later, and of his burial in East Buckland two days later again. *Both items were printed on the same page.*

Even sadder is the story of Hugh Douglas Darvill. He was a teacher at the School for six years, and gave sterling service during the harrowing period of the First World War. He had been a tower of strength during what that the *Register* called 'the famous scarlet fever epidemic' (though there had been another memorable one in 1864). He gave loyal support to the OTC. He was best man at the Headmaster's wedding.

He had apparently not been a gregarious soul, which makes his virtues all the more praiseworthy in that they still came through despite his solitariness. A fine testimony to the truth that the transmission of real sympathy does not depend upon show or words. But he had suffered from poor health for a year. When he died suddenly, aged only 32, in November, 1920, it was a shock but not entirely a surprise. The surprise came when the School tried to inform his family. Despite all efforts, it proved impossible to trace them. Not a single member of it came for his funeral. So there was no option but to bury him at East Buckland.

Hugh Darvill, third from right, front row, next to the Headmaster, Harries. The lady on the extreme right is Eleanor Bendall, who married Harries. On the other side of Harries is 'Judy' Taylor, who was on the staff for thirty-four years (1895-1929). He was only forty-five when this picture was taken in 1918, a stark indication of the strain brought on by the Great War. This photo also contains Miss Tamlyn, the first female full-time member of the academic staff, appointed in 1914. She caused quite a stir among this monastic institution. [School Archive]

It can be a lonely life as a bachelor. It can be a lonely life as a boarding school teacher, especially in a tiny school in the remote, rolling fields of North Devon, and long before regular motorised travel. If that man does not communicate easily with his fellows, and moreover can not, because of poor health, join in activities, it can be lonelier still. But most men in such a position have at least the solace of a family to return to during the holidays.

But to have none. . . . or at any rate not to be in contact with it. Had this life just happened to him, or had he chosen it?

Sadder still is the grave of an ex-pupil, Ernest Elias Bland, who died on 11th August, 1892. He had only recently won a place at St. John's College, Cambridge, with which the School built quite a long-standing connection. Its most brilliant pupil of that time, William Stradling, went there at the very end of the century. The entry in the *Register* states that Ernest died 'in his 21st year, at West Buckland, after a short illness'. Well, maybe so. But the grave is oddly placed. All the other graves are orientated east-west. Ernest Bland's grave is at the very edge of the churchyard, right up against the boundary wire, and it is orientated north-south. The suggestion is therefore that he took his own life. Suicides could not be buried in consecrated ground. It is possible that, though the stone is in the churchyard – just – the actual body was buried outside. If this young man did in fact do away with himself, it could be an early instance of a student who could not cope with the stresses of university life, away from the comforts and consolations of home.

Not far from Bland's nevertheless impressive gravestone lies the grave of another Ernest – the School's greatest headmaster, the Revd. Ernest Charles Harries. His mother, Ellen Priscilla Harries, was buried here first – in 1921, having lived to be 87. (It is a rare headmaster's mother who gets herself in the annual photographs of the Staff, and on the frontispiece of the School magazine.) Then, after twenty-seven years as Headmaster, and another twenty years of retirement, Harries joined her. As another headmaster recorded with fond brevity, 'one pleasant noon in May, his ashes were buried by the side of his mother'. He was 86. The members of the Harries family were a long-lived lot. In 1985, Harries' widow Ellie was buried beside them, only five months short of her hundredth birthday. I don't know whether the quotation is a commonly-used one, but I liked the inscription on Harries' stone – which, it seems probable, he chose himself. 'Sis mihi, Christe, comes.' 'Christ, be a companion to me.'

I have no doubt that instances like this of a village churchyard cherishing the bones of many souls associated with a nearby school can be repeated up and down the British countryside. But their ubiquity neither diminishes their dignity nor cheapens their worth. Thomas Gray understood this very well:

> 'Far from the madding crowd's ignoble strife
> Their sober wishes never learned to stray;
> Along the cool sequestered way of life
> They kept the noiseless tenor of their way.
>
> Yet even these bones from insult to protect
> Some frail memorial still erected high,
> With uncouth rhymes and shapeless sculpture decked,
> Implores the passing tribute of a sigh.'

5. Lorna Doone in West Buckland

Most schools with any kind of a history have a Chope tucked away in it somewhere. This Chope would have had a worthy career at the School as a boy; he had a worthy career in business or public service; he became a force in the Old Boys' association. He attended nearly every School and Old Boys' function; he placed his talents and energies, unremittingly, at the disposal of the School; he funded a prize in his name to be given away each year at Speech Day; he was an inveterate layer of foundation stones; and he had a school building named after him.

West Buckland's Chope was born Richard Pearse Chope, at Hartland, in 1862. His family was of yeoman stock, and, predictably therefore, his father sent him to the new school for the sons of tradesmen and farmers in North Devon – the Devon County School at West Buckland. He did well. In the Cambridge Local Examinations of 1877 (the GCSE equivalent of the day for schools of this type, though this is a very loose comparison – see 'Tried and Tested') he was First Junior out of 2,885 in the whole of England. It was this distinction which got him into the foundation-stone-laying business before he had even left school. In 1880, he and another First Junior were accorded the honour of laying the foundation stone of the new Fives Courts. The stone is still there, though the court has gone.

He later won Honours in both the Oxford and Cambridge Locals Senior Section. He took part in the first Shakespearian production at the School of which records survive – *The Merchant of Venice* in 1881. A photograph of this was printed in the first *West Buckland School* book (p.152). Of course, Chope played Shylock.

He played both cricket and football, and was in the cricket XI for two seasons. However, in a *Register* article he modestly admits that he made the innings' highest score only once, when he made 4 out of a team total of 16, on a recently re-turfed assault course at Eggesford. His reminiscences of the time he served beforehand as scorer could almost fill another chapter on their own.

Needless to say, he was chosen to be Head Prefect, and he won the Fortescue Medal, before proceeding on a major scholarship to Trinity College, Cambridge. (The Fortescue Medal, as the name suggests, was instituted by the third Earl, to be awarded to the boy – or, much later, girl – who achieves high academic and athletic distinction. It is by no means awarded every year.) He read Maths, got a First (of course), and decided to enter the Civil Service. He spent most of his working life in the Patent Office, nearly twenty years of which he spent as Principal of the Abridgments and Printing Branch.

If that sounds a mite dull, it was certainly not a cushy number. During the course of his service, he was responsible for a yearly issue of about 14,000 specifications – full descriptions – of the new inventions patented, most fully illustrated. In case readers found the full versions too indigestible, he published over 100 *volumes* of illustrated shortened versions. (Well, it was the Abridgments Department.) He also found time to publish a weekly illustrated journal.

Away from the Patent Office – if he ever got away much – he pursued a staggering variety of interests and hobbies. He was a keen historian and archaeologist; he was a more-than-dilettante student of philology; he contributed a stream of articles to local and scholarly publications; he lectured on local history; he began and built a healthy amateur theatrical company in his home town of Hartland; he was a generous restorer of the local church and Lady chapel; and he had the energy and financial acumen to build his family estates around Hartland to about 1,000 acres. Naturally, he was a local magistrate and churchwarden.

A sample selection of things he wrote gives an idea of his range. One may think that a little local history book about Hartland would not exactly fly to the top of best-seller lists, but we are told in his obituary that a large edition of it sold out in a few weeks. He assisted the Professor of Comparative Philology at Oxford in the compiling of *The English Dialect Dictionary* – which must have been a prodigious undertaking. He contributed papers to the proceedings of the Devonshire Association. He compiled over 200 'Notes of the Past' for the *Hartland Chronicle*. In conjunction with others, he did a complete transcript of the *Pipe Roll of the Bishopric of Winchester, 1208-09*. The average reader is in no position to assess the size or significance of this and many others of his projects, but, taken together, and taken in conjunction with his professional work, they constitute a huge monument to a lifetime of continuous effort and industry.

This is all the more impressive when one considers the amount of travel involved. Obviously, for his work in the Patent Office, he had to live in London. Equally obviously, in order to pursue his multifarious interests in Devon, he had to be in the County a lot of the time. The hours he must have spent on trains. And on carriages and carts, even saddles; not even the late nineteenth-century Devon railway system (which had more lines than a Riviera dowager's face) could take him anywhere near Hartland.

His was a constant presence at Old Boys' dinners in London and Exeter, where he contributed to the entertainment of the evenings by giving recitations in the Devon dialect. These gatherings were not merely annual affairs; for several years, other, more informal 'social' gatherings were held each month during the winter, sometimes in London, sometimes in Exeter.

Chope was a regular attender (he had been on the committee set up to arrange these extra evenings). Indeed, he had been a pioneer in setting up the Old Boys' Association in the first place, and served both as its Treasurer and as its President. During his two years of presidency, he raised the membership from 100 to 320. Not content with that, he served for years as the Association's representative on the Governing Body of the School.

These meetings of Governors (or Directors, as they were called in the early days, when the School was a private company, complete with shareholders) therefore brought Chope to West Buckland a lot – a village which is not noted – even now – for the comprehensiveness or modernity of its communications. If he had not been a Director, he would still have come, if only for the annual Whitsun Gathering of Old Boys, which could last for three or four days. Guess who would read the lesson in East Buckland Church on Sunday.

Once at West Buckland, he could focus his fearsome attention on every aspect of School welfare. Through decades of benefactions, he loaded the School with gifts, books, pictures, magazine articles, photo slides, prizes, quizzes, and 'useful' ideas.

For example, he donated a stereoscope to the School, and, later, scores of photographic plates that were clearly the fruit of his work in the Patent Office – beautifully detailed reproductions of gadgets and inventions from the Industrial Revolution onwards. There were portraits too, of historical worthies, and a lot of local views. These still remain, in their original boxes, in the Archive.

Chope also gave pictures. There were cartoons from *Vanity Fair* – cartoons of celebrities associated with the School – the third Earl Fortescue, Harold Hilton, the golf champion, Archbishop Longley, who had presented the prizes in 1863. It would be interesting to know what happened to these.

He gave photographs – groups of staff and prefects and sports teams from the 1880's. He could not resist adding the picture of the production of *The Merchant of Venice*, in which he had played the starring role. We have these pictures still.

He gave books, endlessly – anything and everything from *Crystallography* ('with a set of 40 models of crystals') and *Stag Hunting on Exmoor* to *Tom Brown's Schooldays*, *Moby Dick*, *The Last of the Mohicans*, and *The Story of King Alfred*. As with the photographs, he could not resist adding his own *The Story of Hartland* ('2nd revised edition').

Inevitably, he wrote articles for the *Register* (the School magazine, begun in 1863 – we have edition 'Number I', and every other one till its demise under that title in 1998). By way of example, in only seven years, between 1906 and 1913, he regaled his readers with details of the careers of Old Boys in the Navy, in the Army, in the Lower Civil Service, in the medical profession, in holy orders. This output was augmented with treatises on local geology (eight pages), the 'march of inventions' (eight pages), East and West Buckland in Domesday Book (six pages), Old Boys as athletes, cricket in the past, football in the past, and lists of Head Monitors, Prefects, Champion Athletes, and Honours in the Local Examinations. He even unearthed a legend that the Lorna Doone stories had first seen the light of day in a West Buckland school dormitory. The midwife of these stories was a garrulous member of that dormitory, who span his late-night yarns years before Blackmore published his book.

The Editors found it all pretty heavy going. In the editorial of October, 1906, they are saying that they are 'as usual, indebted to Mr. R.P. Chope for help in the compiling of the *Register*'. They had already, in the summer of that year, referred to Mr. Chope's 'unflagging industry', but he did not take the hint. In October, 1907, Mr. Chope is continuing his 'laborious researches'. In February, 1908, their thanks were due to their 'indefatigable contributor'.

There was clearly something unstoppable about Chope. One tough set of editors did manage to put a temporary brake on his efforts; they bravely decided to hold over one article until the following edition of the *Register*. It was no use. Further articles came thick and fast, and when that following edition of the *Register* came out, the editors lamely admitted that they were 'in the happy position of having to choose from an embarrassment of riches in making up the present number'. They decided, even more bravely than their predecessors, that 'some articles. . . . had to suffer severe condensation'. One wonders what Mr. Chope would have thought of that. Perhaps he decided that he was far enough ahead in the game not to worry. The index for the years 1905-08 listed five other contributors of articles besides Chope; they produced eight pieces between them, and three of those were only obituaries. In the same period, Chope swamped the editors with sixteen, and that was only the ones they published. One wonders how many were quietly 'held over' indefinitely.

But he got his own back. He attacked on another front. He designed a new cover for the *Register*, and the editors responded inscrutably by saying that 'our readers cannot fail to be struck with the change'. The new cover first appeared in February, 1906, and was used continually until December, 1965. Nearly 60 years, and 164 numbers of the *Register*. But Chope wasn't finished. He followed this up, within a term, by designing a bookplate to be used inside all the School's library books. The editors responded, rather more gallantly this time, by remarking that the bookplate 'adds much to the dignity of the books'.

It is a wonder that he did not turn his awesome attention to the Headmaster's notepaper, or the football team's strip, or the School uniform. Perhaps he did, and somebody diplomatically headed him off. It must have been a bit like having a combination of Charles Dickens, Leonardo da Vinci, and Napoleon at large on the campus; you never knew where this awesome loose cannon was going to rumble to next.

It was round about this time – the Edwardian era – that Chope came to a decision: the boys of the Devon County School were pretty ignorant when it came to general knowledge. (He would find plenty to agree with him today – including the pupils themselves.) So he devised a General Knowledge Exam paper, had it set, had it printed, and funded a prize for it which was to be awarded at Speech Day. This General Knowledge Prize was awarded continually right up to the Second World War – with Chope's name attached to it, naturally. It reappeared, mysteriously, as the 'Carter General Knowledge Prize' in 1947, and continued until 1965. By 1966 it was gone.

And still Mr. Chope would not let the editors off the hook; he persuaded them to print some of the most entertaining wrong answers in a later edition. (See 'Chope's Choice', p.105.) So at least he had some kind of a sense of humour, if only a slightly heavy and pedantic one.

In 1935, two years before he died, he received the immortality that you feel he had been seeking, if only subconsciously, all the time. The new workshops were named after him. The plaque is over the door now. He deserved it.

Richard Pearse Chope, and his design for the front cover of the *Register* in 1906.
'Read and Reap' was the School motto – deliberately chosen to avoid the usual
Latin quotation. This cover lasted for sixty years. Look at the design for the new one
in 1966. . . . Yes, exactly. [School Archive]

6.   Nuts and Bolts

Explosive Situations

The Editor of the *Register* for June, 1916, recorded, *a propos* of nothing:

> 'Owing to the dearth of teachers in Science the Head Master has temporarily taken that branch of School work, and after one very narrow escape has survived his practical experiments up to the present.'

A splendid example of economy – a great deal is left to the reader's imagination. A fine testimony to caution – note the 'up to the present'. And a tribute to the Head Master's honesty – the overwhelming probability is that he himself was the Editor; it was wartime, and he did practically everything else.

In the same number of the *Register,* it was noted:

> 'The miniature range has been entirely rebuilt, and it will now be possible to fire at sky targets on it.' [One hopes that the Royal Flying Corps gave it a wide berth.]

Fun and Flames

At the end of 1958, the School got what looks like its first television set. An agreement document survives, which states that the School would rent ('with full maintenance'), from Strandways Ltd., of 19, Cross Street, Barnstaple, a PAM Model 550 I.T.V. [sic] Television Set with J-Mast Aerial. The deposit was to be £8.12p., and a further £3.00 for the aerial. The monthly rental was to be £2.3½ p., plus another 47½ p. for the aerial.

In the same folder as the TV rental agreement there lay an annual licence costing £1.00, issued under the terms of the Small Lotteries and Gaming Act of 1956. Now what on earth were the pupils – or the staff – up to at the end of the 1950's?

At the same time as the School was apparently setting itself up as a rural casino, it was still running as a demolition depot; letters survive from the same time, in which the School was reminded about renewing its licence to store petroleum spirit (25p. per year), and also renewing its Explosives licence (5p.). Explosives!

Working Round the Clock

William Cockram was one of those faithful servants who believed not only in loyalty to one's employers, but in loyalty to one's tools. He served the School from before the First World War until well after the Second. During that time, he became, among many other things, the official driver of the official School motor car – a venerable Austin which had already done substantial service with Mr. Taylor, one of the masters.

It was to do even more with William, and was still on duty when he retired in 1952. He heard some time afterwards that the authorities had decided to replace it, that it was to go, at last, to that Great Big Garage up in the sky. His disgust was deep and genuine; the decision, he thought, was both unwise and unfair. He reckoned that it still had a lot more miles left in it. After all, it had only done just over 800,000.

Keeping the Menials in their Place

The new Headmaster, Mr. C.C.S. Bland, brought one or two family problems with him when he took up his appointment in succession to the first HM, the Revd. J.H. Thompson. This was how the Governors resolved them:

> 'Jan. 11. 1889. Some discussion then took place as to the amount to be charged for the Board [sic] of Mr. Bland's child and her nurse and it was resolved that for the child the charge should be 5/- [25p.] per week up to the age of 10 years. That the nurse should board with the servants of the School and be charged at the rate calculated for them, a rate equal to that charged for the boys, 8/- [40p.] per week.'

> 'Sept. 7. 1889. It was agreed that the charge for Head Master's visitors should be fixed at 2/- per day.'

[From the Minutes of the Governors' (or Directors as they were then) Meetings.]

Service with a Smile

In the pre-War days when there were waiters to serve dinner in the School hall, the chef ruled proceedings with a rod, or rather a ladle, of iron. An ex-pupil remembers one of the young waiters being cheeky to him. There was no argument; the chef simply leaned through the hatch and clouted him with his ladle.

Family Connections

One of the first things any new arrival learns about West Buckland is that nearly everyone he meets has some kind of connection with somebody else – whether by family, by marriage, by friendship, by common employment, by shared experience, by geography, or whatever.

Failure to become acquainted with the intricacies of this network can lead to anything from mild amusement to grave, if unwitting, offence. It is for the reader to decide, depending upon his inclinations and viewpoint, whereabouts on the scale the following anecdote comes. My own feeling is that it tends to grow extra dimensions the more you think about it.

A boy called Cockram was becoming bored with a lesson, and was gazing out of the window – as boys do – at the distant groundsman, bent over his mower on the playing fields.

The master called the boy to order, and tried to make a moral out of the situation by suggesting that if he didn't pay proper attention to his lessons, he might end up like that poor fellow out there on the playing field.

The 'poor fellow' was in fact Bill Cockram, the boy's father.

[I know I called him 'William' Cockram on p.36, but you know him better by now.]

7.   Holding the Fort I – William Watson

What is the source material for a biography of a caretaker headmaster in an obscure rural boarding school in the middle of the nineteenth century? Frankly, not much. There are a few references to him in the official history of the School, and a few more in the pages of the *Register*. He pops up *en passant* in the history of a similar county school founded by the tireless Brereton in the North Country. As he was a clergyman, I was able to pick the brains of a very helpful gentleman on the editorial staff of *Crockford's*. There remains in the Archive the printed text of his farewell sermon preached to the School in 1870. There is also an engaging memoir of him written by his grandson over forty years ago, in the pages of a local newspaper of 1958. Finally, there is some suggestive negative evidence, of which more later.

William Watson was born in Nottingham round about 1843 or 1844. We have no information concerning his family background or education. The first fact to emerge is that he left home in January, 1864 to take up a post as 'third master' (he soon became 'second master') at the Devon County School. His pay was to be £35 – a year! Board, lodging, 'and washing' were thrown in. (I should think so.) Incidentally, there were about a hundred applicants for the job.

In that paragraph lies the first surprise. Not that his pay was so low. It probably wasn't, not by the standards of the time. Get hold of any copy of *The Times* for the eighteen-sixties, run your eyes down the columns of adverts on the front page, and look at the wages on offer for thousands of live-in jobs.

Nor is it therefore a surprise that there were so many applicants. The fact that such paltry wages could be in such demand appears to indicate that the economic balance in the 1860's was very much in favour of the employer. Population was galloping up.

No – the surprise is that he got the job, and without any degree or special experience, when he was barely into his twenties, if that. In that hundred or so unsuccessful candidates there must have been some men with degrees, dog collars, glittering testimonials, and relevant experience. Why then did Watson get it?

Of course we can never know for sure. It is possible that there were *no* men with degrees, dog collars, glittering testimonials, and relevant experience, that all hundred were impecunious, callow young men desperate for work – any work – and that Watson was the best of a bad bunch (a very large bunch). But it still seems, on balance, unlikely.

There is too the unquestioned fact that the man who must have appointed him – Mr. J.H. Thompson, Headmaster of the Devon County School – had himself been appointed at the age of twenty-one, without either degree or dog-collar. Headmasters in those days were of course appointed by the Governors, but the appointment of other staff was usually left to the discretion of the new Headmaster. Indeed, the earliest document we have about the 'Terms as to the Appointment of Head Master' specifically states that 'the Head Master will have the appointment of Assistant Masters, subject to the general control of the Governors as to the number to be appointed, and the sum to be allowed for the salary of each'. It takes its origin from a Deed of Trust of 1860, and remained the authority all the time that the School was a private company – which it was until the early 1900's.

Thompson owed his own appointment to the very fact that he had neither degree nor dog-collar. This was almost certainly the founder, J.L. Brereton's, way of announcing to the world that his new foundation was not going to be like any other previous private school. He had no intention of setting up yet another rural academy for forcing down the unwilling throats of the sons of gentlemen the turgid diet of Latin, Greek, and more Latin and Greek – with a bit of Bible thrown in for the good of their souls.

He wanted the education in his school to be modern, practical, relevant, and healthy. Plenty of Bible, naturally, but not sectarian Bible. Brereton was what was known as a 'broad' churchman. Basic Christianity was a solid enough rock on which to build boys' characters; it didn't have to be High Anglican or Evangelical, much less Methodist or Baptist. The timetable was going to include Maths, Science, Land Management, and so on (remember its first name was 'the West Buckland Farm and County School'). And, with all that open space and fresh air, there was to be no lack of exercise and sport – even if it was only cricket and 'foot-ball'.

It seems wholly consistent, then, with this philosophy and background, that the young candidate from Nottingham should be in with a very good chance. Thompson could well have looked at him and seen himself a few years before. He too had come from the north of England, with little but his youth, energy, and eagerness to serve. No doubt the all-pervasive Brereton put in his two-penn'orth as well.

Whether or not the interview was a harrowing experience, Watson's arrival to take up his duties most certainly was. He reached Barnstaple after dark – in January, remember – with only sixpence in his pocket, and discovered that the only way to reach the School was by hiring the post carriage at the Fortescue Hotel. So his first act was one of supreme optimism – the hope that the School which was going to pay him only £35 a year was to cough up for the carriage when he arrived well into the night.

His troubles were not over when he arrived (think of bouncing over Leary Hill late on a cold January night, with only a grumpy driver for company). The School was locked up – naturally. After much banging on doors, he roused the Matron. His luck turned. The Matron must have been a jewel of her profession – kindly, resourceful, not to say liberated. She found, and cooked, some pork chops for him, and allowed him to smoke a pipe in her sitting room while she found him a bed. (A pipe – at twenty!)

It is a curious thing, but if you speak to many long-serving members of staff today (even, sometimes, pupils), they will all have their own stories of their journey, or their arrival, or their first glimpse of the school, or of the odd characters they met when they came for interview, or whatever. And what good 'dining-out' stories they are too.

They will also, as often as not, go on to say what a hefty work-load they soon had heaped upon their young shoulders. It seems to be a tradition of West Buckland that the 'authorities' get their pound of flesh when it comes to the burden of responsibilities, and this goes right back to the earliest days. Watson was no exception.

He came to a School which was growing fast. As is well known (well, round here anyway) it had started in 1858 with only three pupils; a prospectus of 1867 speaks of 'nearly 100'. In 1864 when Watson arrived, the *Register* recorded about 60 boarders, plus a scattering of day boys. By 1866 it had leapt to 96.

As for staff, that prospectus of 1867, which lists all the trustees, refers to only two teachers – Thompson and Watson – and to the Chaplain and the Secretary. However, we know from other evidence that a Mr. Thomas arrived in the summer of 1864, six months after Watson. He was to be 'Third Master'. He was nineteen. And an Old Boy's reminiscences referred to the Revd. Lillington, and to 'a quaint old gentleman, Mr. Palfreman, who taught something or other'. Lillington left in June, 1864, but another teacher arrived from Marlborough – Arthur Martin – who was to become a great friend of Watson. No doubt there were part-timers as well, and probably a teacher of 'Drill' (he is mentioned in connection with an event of 1859).

Between them, Thompson, Watson, and the others would have had to provide instruction in English, Geography, History, Mathematics ('including Arithmetic, Algebra, Euclid, and Higher Mathematics'). Book-keeping and Land Surveying were taught 'to those who desire them', and French was offered 'without extra charge'. 'Vocal Music' was also available. No doubt it was here that the part-timers played their part, and the Chaplain of course took charge of 'the Scriptures'. If you wanted your son to be taught Latin and Greek, it would cost you a further five guineas a year. Drawing lessons set you back only three guineas.

That was indoors. Outside, there were the games to be organised, super-vised, and often participated in – cricket, football, and the cross-country runs. Fives began in 1864. The swimming 'pond' didn't come until 1870.

Such a regime was 'such as to fit pupils for Agricultural or Mercantile pursuits, for the Civil Service Examinations, for the Oxford and Cambridge Local Examinations, and, in general, to prepare them for honourable and independent positions in life'.

And the School was doing well. Watson came to a thriving institution. No less a personage than the Archbishop of Canterbury, who had come to present the prizes in 1863, had complimented the School on its progress, and freely admitted that it had 'assumed dimensions beyond what I expected when I first heard of it'. Its progress, he said, entitled it to 'rank among the first educational establishments of the country'.

Of course, you would expect guests to say things like that when they are thanking their hosts – singing for their supper, if you like. But it is worth noting that His Grace was sufficiently impressed to be willing to go and lay the foundation stone for another such school – the Surrey County School (later known as Cranleigh) – and, in the course of his speech there, to refer to the Devon County School in the most effusive terms.

Watson therefore had to pull his weight, and make a full contribution to the life of this moorland academy which had such a healthy pioneering reputation that even an archbishop sang its praises far afield. A variety of subjects in the classroom, a vigorous effort on and around the games field, and of course the never-ending responsibilities of a resident teacher in a boarding school. There was a Matron (she of the pork chops), but she couldn't do everything. When he became Second Master, he would also have been expected to share the burden of administration and public relations. And – to repeat – he was only twenty.

He was not a particularly robust young man either. Nor, apparently, very athletic; his name does not appear in the interminable and exhaustive cricket scoresheets of the time – except one unique mention of the occasion when he was called in to make up the numbers of a 'Twenty-Two' against the First XI. This was in 1864 – his first summer. He was never asked again. The same raconteur who recalled the quaint Mr. Palfreman mentioned that Mr. Watson, while he was 'an excellent teacher', was 'troubled with ill-health and a liver, which affected his temper'. The smaller boys christened him 'Vinegar'. To be fair, the writer did say at the end, 'Peace be with him; he did good work.'

He had his good moods too. When so disposed, he could entertain the boys with stories of the famous Notts cricketer, Dick Daft. Remember, Nottinghamshire was his home county.

The picture that begins to emerge is of a young man, not especially strong or gifted, who was keen to do well in his chosen profession, who found himself sucked into numerous duties and responsibilities that possibly threatened to engulf him from time to time. As a bachelor in a lonely Exmoor boarding school, he would have found it difficult to maintain much private space for himself – either physically or psychologically. As a very young man, he would have had few yardsticks to give him points of reference as to what was moderate and what was extreme. His two closest associates were also young men who were committed to the same demanding regime. Thomas was strong, and no doubt better at surviving. But even Thompson, for all his vigour and commitment, was to break down under the strain later on. The extraordinary fact was that, in the mid-1860's, the ruling triumvirate of this pioneering School consisted of three young bachelors whose average age was about twenty-four. Was this normal? Then again, such schools were still in single numbers, founded in imitation of West Buckland, and only a few years old, so what constituted 'normality'?

It seems quite likely that Watson, whose only guiding lights were conscience, respectability, and Victorian sense of duty – plus the harsh economic fact that if he argued with the regime, there were plenty more where he came from – kept his head down and did his best. Whether this effort induced his ill health, or whether his ill health made the effort harder, we do not know. But, either way, it might explain his lapses of temper.

His task was not made easier by those extra, unclassifiable chores which cropped up, if only occasionally, and which were added to a young master's load as a matter of course. Take the business of providing for the accommodation of boys who could not get home for the Easter holidays. Watson had not only to find such accommodation, but to share it. Thompson expected him to walk the ten miles to Hunter's Inn to book the rooms – which he did – in company with his boys, presumably. They then spent the Easter holidays there, some of them sleeping in blankets on the floor, and existing, so he recalled, on a diet that consisted largely of bread, butter, and eggs.

It says a great deal for his professionalism that he found time and energy, in this all-consuming life, to try and improve himself. He matriculated at London University in 1866, and took his degree two years later. The studies must have been a little rudimentary, because, as he said himself, he had 'to cram himself while cramming others'; he had learned his Chemistry by heart 'without much understanding it'; and he gained his qualification in this subject 'without having seen a single experiment performed'.

But he wasn't satisfied, not by a long chalk. He then embarked on studies for the Church, became a deacon in 1869, and was ordained priest in 1870. He was appointed curate at East Buckland Church and Chaplain of the School – as if he didn't have enough to do already. That boosted his income – £50 a year as curate, and £40 a year as Chaplain – which may well have been an additional incentive to his studies in the first place.

One wonders what the Revd. Brereton would have thought of all this enterprise and self-improvement. One of Brereton's ideas was that the way to make his new school different was *not* to have either a graduate or a priest as headmaster. He did not wish to emulate the fashionable public schools. Yet here was his deputy head aiming for both – degree *and* dog-collar. Was it a case of pure self-improvement? A means of strengthening the CV, with a view to seeking improvement elsewhere? Or was it a case of the young school, flushed with early success and flexing its muscles, and feeling that it could, if it put its mind to it, join the super league of the top establishments? Maybe even Brereton was beginning to change his mind. We don't know.

Nor do we know whether Watson's decision to get married round about this time was the result purely of youthful passion, or partly the realisation that it might do him a bit of good if he took a wife. Perhaps the Victorian world did not look too charitably on bachelor curates who appeared set on a firm course towards a solitary middle age. Though, on the other hand, neither Thompson nor a later head, Harries, felt the matrimonial urge till each was turned fifty; but then they weren't on the circuit applying for headships.

Be that as it may, the fateful meeting happened when he, as a young ordinand, took his testimonials for signature to the rectory at the nearby village of Charles, where the incumbent was the Revd. Richard Blackmore. (It was his nephew who was the novelist.) His niece (who was also therefore a cousin of the author of *Lorna Doone*) was staying there. This was early in 1869. They became engaged in the summer of 1870, and cut a half-crown in two to mark the occasion. (So there *was* some romance.)

Meantime, Earl Fortescue, who worshipped frequently at East Buckland Church, and who had, out of his own pocket, refurbished it for the use of the School, had made his acquaintance. He was invited to take services at Filleigh Church, and afterwards to come to lunch at Castle Hill, Fortescue's stately lair. It was Fortescue's influence that helped him to be appointed to the nearby living of Yarnscombe later in 1870.

The stipend was a healthy £139 a year 'with 40 acres of poor glebe', but he still hesitated to get married on it. However, something happened towards the end of 1870 that may have pushed him into a couple of cavalier decisions. He borrowed £100 from a relative, and another £150 from his future father-in-law, admitting that he was appalled as he contemplated his own rashness. A few days after Christmas, 1870, he and his bride walked up the path to Molland Church between huge banks of piled snow.

The happy couple reached London the same evening (try that on our train system today – Molland to Paddington in an afternoon), and took a room at the Great Western Hotel. They had enough money left over from the wedding expenses (and father-in-law's loan) to go out the next morning 'to secure lodgings, a sitting-room, bedroom, and dressing-room in Oxford Street'.

They spent one day at Teddington, visiting Mrs. Watson's cousin by marriage, the author of *Lorna Doone*, and another applying for a new job.

And here we come back to what made Watson change his mind about marrying sooner rather than later. Had he decided to improve himself and go for a headship, and thus made it imperative that he snap up this eligible spinster from Charles and take her with him? Or had his impending marriage, or his bride-to-be, brought in upon him the thought that a move to a headship was more in keeping with his new status? Again, we don't know. (Of course, there is always the possibility that has no doubt already occurred to nine readers out of ten – that the future Mrs. Watson was in an interesting condition. But, since the courtship must have been carried on in either the parlour of Charles rectory, or the pupil-frequented room of the overworked young master at the Devon County School – which doesn't seem to be a situation exactly bursting with opportunity; and since not the slightest breath of scandal must attach itself to the budding career of a young ordinand eager to prise a profitable living out of the local aristocrat, the possibility of such careless – nay, reckless – lovemaking seems remote. No records of the date of birth of Watson's children have come down to us, so we must remain in ignorance. And perhaps rightly so. Even the subject of a modest little biography is entitled to a modicum of privacy.)

Perhaps it was his recent experience at the Devon County School that turned his mind in the direction of self-improvement. For Thompson too had taken it upon himself to go for a degree and a dog-collar. He applied for, and gained from the Directors, leave of absence from 1867 to 1871, to read Mathematics at Jesus College, Cambridge, and to prepare himself for the priesthood. He took a B.A. degree with honours, and was ordained deacon. He was appointed curate at East Buckland Church, and also Chaplain to the School. It must be something of a record for a Headmaster to succeed his own Deputy Head both as School Chaplain and as curate at the local church. The coincidence is so close that one wonders whether it was Watson's initiative in going for degree and ordination that prompted Thompson to do the same. Or was it the other way round? Their two respective courses of study overlapped so closely that, at this distance of time, it is impossible to tell.

At any rate, Thompson was going to be absent for three or four years, and someone had to mind the shop while he was away. His Second Master was the natural choice, but it must say a lot for Watson's work, sense of duty, and integrity that (despite his youth – still only about twenty-three) the Directors agreed to entrust him with the responsibility.

He seems to have risen to the occasion with commendable zeal. The timetable was administered with the same attention to detail, and large numbers of boys were regularly entered for the Oxford and Cambridge Local Examinations. These 'Locals' were the public exams which had been instituted by the two universities to extend their teaching and influence beyond their own members, and to provide a nationwide yardstick for schools such as West Buckland. The chief pioneers in this movement were Dr. Temple (later Archbishop of Canterbury, who used to visit the School), Sir Thomas Dyke Acland (a governor of Devon County School), the second Earl Fortescue, and the ubiquitous Revd. Brereton. Brereton must have been particularly pleased with himself in 1858; the School and the Locals were set up in the same year. (See 'Tried and Tested'.)

The School did well in these exams, and the *Register* proudly printed every detail of their success – seniors, juniors, honours, distinctions, first class, second class, nothing was overlooked. And why not? They had plenty to be proud of. In 1867, they obtained more Cambridge certificates than any other school in the country – for the third year in succession. In 1868, one boy, J.T. Woolcock, came first in English in the whole country. In 1869, J.M. Odger was the best senior in England, and T.H. Aplin the best junior. M.B. Snell did it again in 1870. Moreover, by 1869, the School had notched up a total of 338 certificates from Oxford and Cambridge combined – the best in England, 50 ahead of their nearest rivals, and, incidentally, 109 ahead of Manchester Grammar School. So Watson was doing more than keeping the ship afloat – much more.

And not just in the classroom. Because of the School's commitment to a good Christian education, cohorts of boys were regularly presented for confirmation, and the record was good here too – 25 in 1868, 24 in 1869, 20 in 1870. It compared very favourably with what had gone before. Watson must have had something to do with this, both as director and as participator, because from 1869 he was School Chaplain and Curate of East Buckland Church. So he was fulfilling his duties here too.

Under his direction, the School continued to grow – 96 pupils in 1866, 99 in 1867, 112 in 1868, 115 in 1869. It necessitated fresh building; a third side was added to the Quadrangle. Shortly afterwards work was begun on a fourth – the north side. In 1870, the Directors 'resolved upon' even bigger extensions – a whole new west wing, no less. In the same year, East Buckland Church was enlarged; an extension was added at the west end to accommodate seating for about sixty, specifically 'to meet the increasing requirements of the School'.

Meanwhile, it looked as if it was going to be made easier for boys to travel to School, and from further away. During Watson's caretakership, schemes were mooted, money raised, plans drawn up, labour hired, and track laid for a new railway line between Taunton and Barnstaple, with a station at Filleigh, barely a stone's throw, by Devon standards, from the School. It seems inconceivable that the two 'growths' did not interact upon each other.

Brereton's ideas of a healthy outdoor life were not neglected either. Cricket and 'foot ball' (two words, though a hyphen soon came to be inserted) thrived. Asphalt had been laid upon the surface of the covered playground, and fives soon began. A new bathing pond was added in the spring of 1870, and one of the recently-confirmed pupils, one William Cade, proved his muscular Christianity by being the first bather – in a chill Exmoor April. The annual Exmoor hare-and-hounds race was, of course, run every year without fail. (See 'A Shot of the Good Side'.)

Watson was not himself a great sportsman, judging by what the *Register* does not say. No appearance in a cricket XI or a foot-ball XI or XV is recorded. Nor did he take part in the laying of a trail in the *Exmoor*. It seems unlikely, therefore, that he would have felt tempted to join Master William Cade in the School pond. Interestingly, though, he took part in the very first game of bowls 'played on the new Bowling Green in front of the School'. More sedate, and perhaps more in his line. Yet he was still only in his early twenties.

In addition to all this, of course, there were the hundred and one duties and chores of a headmaster and housemaster. Watson lived in, and so was involved in the non-stop cares and worries of looking after upwards of ninety boarders. He stayed on the premises during the holidays, especially the short ones – Easter and Michaelmas – when several boys could not get home. He organised end-of-term suppers, with all the toasts and responses. He continued the tradition of the Fire and Fireworks on 5th November. He laid on excursions, sometimes for the whole School – to places like Lynton, Westward Ho!, and 'Combmartin'. He made contributions to School plays and other entertainments. (Look at the *Register* for almost any year in the last four decades of the 19th century; you will find the names of masters in the cast lists of a host of 'dramatic presentations'.) He organised tributes to friends of the School, like the Revd. Scriven, who had shown such kindness and hospitality to boys of the School during holidays, and during the tense outbreak of scarlet fever, when the whole School had had to be evacuated. Money was raised for Scriven's Church Restoration Fund at Martinhoe. He helped Thompson to raise a substantial tribute to the Revd. Brereton, on the occasion of his leaving West Buckland to take up a living at Little Massingham in Norfolk in succession to his late father. (More of Norfolk later.)

He entertained the visiting examiners from Oxford and Cambridge. One would think that the occasion might have been somewhat stilted, and hardly conducive to conviviality. On the contrary. Dinners and parties were held in the evening after the exams were over. Songs were sung by both School and examiner. Each called for three cheers for the other. It was all very jolly. The examiner from Oxford, the Revd. F.H. Curgenven, Fellow of Corpus Christi, came nine times in succession, and clearly enjoyed it. He must have been met like an old friend. (See *'Toujours la Politesse'*.)

Watson also met VIP's of much more illustrious rank. The *Register* recorded with evident pride that two headmasters of distinguished public schools, Marlborough and Winchester, had visited the School – presumably to see how these new county schools were coming along. Clearly the word had got around.

Increasing numbers had necessitated new staff. Mr. Roberts arrived in 1867, Mr. Llewellin in 1868, Mr. Pugh in 1870. Now we come to one of the puzzles. Were these appointments the work of Watson, or were they made by Thompson, who naturally came back to Devon from time to time during his studies at Cambridge? Was Watson, as acting Headmaster, given a headmaster's authority, or did Thompson keep some of the reins in his own hands? After all, he could argue that Watson would have to leave the hot seat when he, Thompson, came back, and it would be Thompson who would have to live with the new men.

The answer, on the available evidence, would appear to be that Watson had very little to do with it. For a start, nobody ever called him 'Headmaster', for all that he was doing the job – and, on the evidence above, doing it pretty well. He is constantly referred as the 'Second Master' – 'Mr. Watson, the Second Master, will be in Exeter on the Monday until the train leaves St. David's Station at 4.2 for Barnstaple.' (This from the *Register* of January, 1868, detailing arrangements for boys returning after the holidays.) Elsewhere he is plain 'Mr. Watson'. Except for the year 1870, when he was ordained. Then the authorities did bend to correctness so far as to call him 'the Rev. W. Watson', but never 'Headmaster'.

When Earl Fortescue wrote (from the French Riviera) to congratulate the School on its recent successes in the Locals, he wrote to Thompson – two full paragraphs of fulsome praise – 'I do indeed most sincerely rejoice and exult in this success', and so on. He was, however, enough of a gentleman to say in the same letter (in a P.S.) that he had also written to 'Mr. Watson', offering 'special congratulation on the efficient manner in which he…..carried on the system you had so successfully set on foot….' Fortescue felt 'it due to him'. But the tone of the letter seems just a little double-edged.

In December, 1868, there was the usual celebratory supper in the Dining Hall in honour of the visiting examiner from Cambridge. Thompson was the one who made the speech of thanks. When Mr. Willis, the examiner, concluded his speech of reply, he called for three cheers 'for the Head Master'. Three pages later in the *Register*, it was 'Mr. Watson, the Second Master', who would 'be in Exeter on Tuesday until the train leaves St. David's Station at 4.10 p.m. for Barnstaple'.

Thompson continued to play cricket for the 'D.C.S. Cricket Club'; Lilly-white's *Cricketers' Companion* for 1869 describes him as a 'fast under-hand bowler'. Watson does not seem to have played at all. Thompson was President of the Club; Watson was only the Treasurer.

There must have been times when Watson wondered whether he was ever going to get Thompson out of his hair, and whether his ever-present principal was keeping enough terms at Cambridge to get his degree. Thompson popped up to give out prizes for the Locals. He took the Harvest Festival service. He was for ever dropping in to stiffen the bowling attack of the 'D.C.S. Cricket Club' with his 'fast under-hand' bowling.

And as for Prize Day! In the list of those dignitaries attending in 1868, Watson comes twenty-eighth. In the list for 1869 he is twenty-seventh. In 1870, he was twenty-ninth. When Thompson is mentioned, way up the list, he has '(Head Master)' after his name. Brereton did mention Watson in one of his speeches, but only to place him clearly second after Thompson ('the head master') in his awarding of thanks for their 'highly creditable' work. All Thompson said in 1868 was that he felt he had to 'express the great obligation the School is under to the other masters, particularly Mr. Watson, who has been here for five years. . . . ' 'Who has been here for five years'! Was that all he could bring himself to say?

It seems that the audience thought otherwise. When Thompson had finished and the cheers had died down, Watson was 'loudly called upon'. He 'briefly returned thanks'.

The following year, Thompson contented himself with the sentiment of simple appreciation for 'the assistance he had received from the other masters'. He thanked the School Secretary, and presented a silver salver and cricket bat to the retiring School Chaplain, the Revd. J.L. Francis, but mentioned no teacher's name. And nobody asked Watson to say anything at all. (It makes one wonder how Watson came to be appointed the new School Chaplain. Perhaps he had won Fortescue to his side. Fortescue had invited him to lunch at Castle Hill, and had possibly helped him to secure the living at Yarnscombe. Was Thompson jealous of his subordinate's success with the nobility?)

What was going on? Was this normal treatment for a caretaker headmaster? Or was there some kind of a feud between Thompson and his understudy? Did Thompson come back a mite too often because he didn't trust Watson, or was he just being broody about his baby? Did Watson resent this constant 'presence' breathing down his neck, or was he a man of saintly patience? (It does not square with a notorious short temper, a dodgy liver, and a nickname like 'Vinegar'.)

In 1870, however, the Directors tried to make up for this apparent neglect by giving him a good send-off. Watson had resigned – in dudgeon and frustration? Or merely to take up his new living at Yarnscombe? Or had he begged Lord Fortescue to get him a living so that he could get away from Thompson's interference? We don't know. We do know that the Governors, in their Report of 1870, said that 'while regretting the loss of so valuable and efficient a master as Rev. W. Watson has shown himself to be for so many years, [they congratulated] him on the recognition of his services to Middle Class Education in his presentation to the Rectory of Yarnscombe by the Lord Chancellor'. (Had Lord Fortescue been pulling some strings? Or was the living of Yarnscombe – only about ten miles away – in his gift?)

We know too that, at the prize-giving of December, 1870, when, one would have thought, the Headmaster would have been present to say a few kind words about Watson's hard work, both as Second Master and as caretaker, Thompson was not there. Not there at all. The *Register* takes the trouble to mention 52 people by name, but not Thompson. And Thompson, as a rule, never missed anything. Why?

You would have thought that a headmaster, one who seems to have let slip no opportunity to 'drop into' the School to keep contact (to put it at its most charitable) during his four years of 'dropping out', and who presumably was intensely concerned with the welfare of the School while he was away, would have made the time to come along and say a few words of thanks to the man who, for better or worse (and, by the record, for better), had borne the burden for the best part of four years. It was left to the Head Boy, M.B. Snell, to make the speech and the presentation.

The 'masters and boys' were generous; Watson received 'a handsome silver tea and coffee service'. (One is constantly surprised at the apparent generosity of the donors of these going-away presents – silver salvers, silver coffee sets, silver inkstands, silver cream jugs, gold pencil cases, gold watches. We are not among wealthy, aristocratic parents or clusters of towering town houses, yet prices of such valuables seem to be within the reach of quite ordinary groups of people.)

Watson was clearly affected by the moment. He said what most people do say on these occasions: he was gratified by the compliments the School had received; he too had, while helping others to learn, learnt a great deal himself. He paid tribute to the monitors, especially the Head Monitors, who had served during his time as acting Head – or as he put it – 'during Mr. Thompson's absence'. He thanked them for backing him up when unpleasant decisions had to be taken. He expressed his gratitude to 'the assistant masters for the readiness they had shown in working with him for the good of the school'.

He singled out one man for special mention – Mr. Arthur Martin, the School Secretary – for his help, his kindness, and his advice. He paid tribute to Earl Fortescue for 'the encouragement and countenance he had ever received from him', and wound up by assuring all those listening that he would treasure his present, which would always remind him of his time at the Devon County School.

Not once did he mention Thompson, except to refer to his long absence.

All this was on Thursday, 8th December. There was another affecting scene three days later, when Watson preached his farewell sermon to the School in East Buckland Church.

He took as his text two verses from Genesis xlviii (15,16): 'The God which fed me all my life long unto this day, the Angel which redeemed me from all evil, bless the lads.'

It is not a surprise that he chose something to do with boys; it *is* a surprise to come across the word 'lads', with its modern, almost colloquial ring, in the midst of Jacobean prose. But there it is; I looked it up to make sure. '*Bless the lads.*' It shows not only a knack for the apt choice of text, but also the depth of Watson's Bible knowledge. How many readers of this paragraph would have known of its existence?

It was about the ageing, dying Jacob meeting his son Joseph and his grandsons Ephraim and Manasseh for what was going to be a farewell. Its relevance was obvious, and Watson made no bones about it. He naturally offered advice, both to those who were, like himself, leaving that Christmas, and to those whose time had not yet come. Much of it was predictable, but inlaid amongst the moralising about sin and angels and redeemers, like precious ormolu, were thoughts and sentiments which ring uncannily true today, and which are all the more remarkable for having come from the parting thoughts of a man still only in his mid-twenties.

For instance, people tend to think of each other as they were, not as they are. Talk to anyone who has been to a reunion, and they will say, 'It's amazing; they haven't changed.' Watson knew this: 'The reputation you have at School will stick to you as long as you live……. When you grow up to be men, you will think of and remember each other, not as you will be then, but as you are now….'

He was alive to the value of example. Ideally of course Christian example. But he didn't want them to be milk-and-water goody-goodies. 'Do not think for a single moment that I would make you effeminate; no, not for an instant. What Christianity wants now is *men* [his italics, not mine]; men who by their manliness will extort admiration from the world.' What a splendid choice of word – 'extort'. And so rare to see it used in a good sense.

He was aware of the mixture of feelings which comes to all school-leavers who harbour any kind of soft sentiment towards their school. 'To young people healthy in body and mind, there must be a pleasurable excitement in the thought that boy-life proper is ended, and active life is about to begin. It would be unnatural if it were not so. It would be unnatural if the change were not hailed with ardour. And yet, I am sure, that there is not one of you who does not, at this moment, feel that this ardour is tinged with sorrow.'

He understood the unwelcome truth which always comes as a shock to the ego – namely – that, no matter how great is our influence in a place, no matter how popular or successful we have been there, the minute we leave it the waters close over our heads. 'You may stay here no longer. You are wanted elsewhere. *Very soon your place shall know you no more.*' [My italics this time.]

I cannot but repeat that this is remarkable maturity for a man in his mid-twenties.

He had one more formal occasion at which to officiate – the supper held for the visiting examiner on Friday, 16th December, 1870. But Thompson was not there this time to receive the compliments from the examiner on how well the School was being run. He did not present any prizes. He did not say a few words by way of farewell to 'the Rev. Watson, Second Master'. It was the School Secretary, Mr. Martin, who made the final tribute: '…the boys would long remember the master, whom they were losing; they would remember him not only for his able management of the school in Mr. Thompson's absence, but for his unfailing kindness, his fairness in dealing with them, and the genuine interest he had taken in them all.' He called for three cheers, and 'the boys warmly responded'.

Now of course, boys always do 'respond'. But words like 'kindness' and 'fairness' do not always figure in leaving tributes, so, when they do, one is disposed to believe them. Watson had singled out Martin in his own speech of thanks, and Martin was now returning the compliment. Both seem genuine.

As a tailpiece to this occasion – and as a piece of perfect dramatic neatness and symmetry – a gold watch and chain were presented to the Matron, Miss Wells. She of the pork chops? Oh, yes – please let it be so.

[So Watson left, and Thompson returned to take over the reins of leadership. He presided in full, unrivalled pomp at the Prizegiving of 1871. The *Register* mentioned 32 people by name, including 11 other local clergymen besides Thompson and Brereton, but not Watson. He had not been invited, and he was only up the road at Yarnscombe – ten miles away as the crow flies. They had expected the Earl of Devon to make the trip from beyond Exeter.

But, despite what he had said in his farewell sermon, the waters did not close over his head – not completely, or rather not at once. After two years as Rector at Yarnscombe, he was mentioned once more, in the *Register* of Midsummer, 1872: 'The Rev. W. Watson, late second master of the Devon County School, has been appointed to the head-mastership of the Norfolk County School, established under the patronage of the Prince of Wales.'

Brereton's work, almost without a shadow of a doubt. Attentive readers, of whom no doubt you are one, will recall that the Revd. Brereton, when he left West Buckland in 1867, went back to take up the rectorship in his home village of Little Massingham, where his father had been the incumbent for fifty years, and *his* father before *him*.

He had clearly flung himself into the life of the county with the same abandon he had shown in Devon, and one of the fruits of this energy was the creation of another County School. It needed a headmaster. Better the Devil you know than the Devil you don't know. However, it is more than likely that Watson, during his tenure of office in DCS, had shown that he was capable of running a school in his own right. Fortescue clearly liked him – even if Thompson didn't. And Brereton, whose finger was on the pulse of the School as much as anybody's, must have seen what he could do.

He remained Headmaster at the Norfolk County School for the next fifteen years or so. But it did not do well. Watson's health broke down – it had never been robust. Perhaps he tried too hard. Once again, we don't know. He was forced to step down, and he was replaced by Brereton with one of his own sons, Francis Lloyd Brereton, who had recently been made Headmaster at the North-Eastern County School, yet another result of Brereton's passion for middle-class education. Earl Fortescue laid the foundation stone in 1883. Brereton senior practically forced his son to make the change, just when he was getting his North-Eastern County School off the ground. But the rescue attempt was not successful. The Norfolk County School closed in 1891. (See 'Founding Father'.)

By that time Watson had died – in 1889. He left a widow and eleven children. He was still a few years short of fifty. The *Register* of 1889 devoted a whole page – out of a total of only twelve – to an obituary of Watson's friend, Arthur Martin, who had also died that year. There was no mention of Watson at all.]

8. A Bitter Pill

The Masters' and Boys' football team of 1895-96 had to put up with the frustration of seeing their unbeaten record broken, and not through any particular fault of their own. During that season, they won eleven games out of the twelve they played, and scored 101 goals against only 12. Their undoing came in the second match against Somerset County School at Wellington.

This was the more unwelcome as the first meeting had resulted in a victory so popular that 'the excitement at the School on receiving the news and, later, on the return of the Team, baffles description'.

But in the second encounter, the team had not only the opposition to contend with – the Somerset County School Masters' XI – but the weather. There was a spot of bad feeling even before the kick-off, because the opposition, 'after postponing the Match on account of weather chose about the worst day possible to imagine'. Almost as if they were in league with the god of storms. The suspicion grew when the match began. . . .

> 'We do not grudge our friends their victory for one single instant, but we *do* [their italics] think that had the game been played in anything like favourable weather we should have won. For the first half we played with the terrific gale that was blowing and simply pressed our opponents from start until the whistle blew half time, being prevented from scoring more than once owing to the skilful manner in which our opponents packed their goal.'

But the combination of capricious gods and suspected sharp practice was to become even stronger. . . .

> 'In the second half to add to our discomfort heavy sleet began to pour down into our faces and with the wind increasing in force we were at a double disadvantage. They scored three times, two of the goals being kicked by our backs who instead of seeing the ball proceed up the field towards our opponents' goal as they might naturally expect, had the mortification of watching it ascend in the air and come sailing back over their heads and through the goal which was some 30 yards behind them. *And then, too, most of us thought that second half much longer than the first.*' [My italics this time.]

Delirious reactions to success at home, goal-packing by the other side (rotters!), and jolly bad luck – it could be a tabloid account of World Cup ups and downs.

If this wild celebration of a football success, which 'baffles description', is true – and there is no reason to think it isn't – it highlights two things. First, that in a remote boarding school like this one, there wasn't a great deal going on that could *be* celebrated, so of course the team was feted on its return. And it wasn't a very big school either – well under 100 in 1896. Boys simply didn't get out much, so the ones who did generated intense interest. As late as the 1960's, boarders were allowed into town only twice a term.

And second, however much we may today, with our much-travelled sophistication and our worldly access to the wonders of technology, turn a scornful smile at the intensely parochial 'play-up-and-play-the-game' ethos adopted by the writers of schoolboy stories of Victorian and Edwardian England, it is just possible that those writers were only echoing what was actually going on at the time they wrote. It was not pious moralising; it was a reflection of total truth; it was what everybody – then – understood and accepted.

9. Other People's Letters

One of the most permanent lessons I ever learnt about 'Life' came when I was ten years old. I was in my first term at grammar school (I was a bit young for my year). I had been charged with the delivery of the 'Absence Book' to the secretary's office. It was about ten o'clock in the morning. The thinking ran that you should wait for about an hour or so after the start of the school day. Boys who came in during that time could be labelled 'Late' and, after the Deputy Headmaster had heard their breathless recital of extenuating circumstances, receive their usual punishment. Anyone who was still not present after that time could be safely regarded as more than officially 'Late'; they were truanting, dead, or propped up on the pillows at home – at any rate, a fit study for investigation by somebody much more important than the Late Monitor; you were in the realm of Absence Notes and Doctors' Certificates and, in the most severe cases, Letters from the Headmaster.

Our School Secretary was a lady of indeterminate age (when you are ten, nearly every adult is of indeterminate age) called Mrs. Jelley.

You showed her the relevant page of the book, signed by the teacher in your class at that moment, and she copied the names inscribed there into a master record book on her desk. I stood at her right elbow, waiting patiently while she finished a phone call. As this was my first experience of premises as important as secretaries' offices, I took the opportunity to look about me.

Her desk was huge – much bigger than our dining table at home. Papers were strewn across its vast acreage like autumn leaves in a park. Huge memoranda in foolscap, enigmatic notes on very small sheets like secret agents' messages, great sheaves of records held together with brass split pins, letters both closed and open. One of the latter was tipped towards me. It had a most impressive printed heading.

Nobody had ever sent me a letter with printed headings at the top of the first sheet. I wondered what illustrious personage had thought fit to communicate with Mrs. Jelley. I craned my neck slightly to get a better look, just as Mrs. Jelley put down the receiver.

I cannot remember a word of what she actually said, but I carried away from her office that morning the very clear understanding that One Did Not Read Other People's Letters. The lesson has remained with me ever since. I may have picked up many other faults on the rugged road through life, but I can go before my Maker safe in the knowledge that at least I have not Read Other People's Letters. (I tell a lie; I did, only about a couple of weeks ago. The circumstances were almost identical: I was standing at a counter waiting for another secretary to give me her attention, and I found myself glancing at the address on an envelope that I knew perfectly well had nothing to do with me. It was only a venial sin, compared with the mortal crime of actually reading an open letter, but at once I was catapulted in the mind back over fifty years to Mrs. Jelley's office. I even had to confess the sin to the lady behind the counter.)

What Mrs. Jelley had done – and done so permanently – was to engrave upon my memory one of the hundreds of good manners which a well-brought-up boy was expected to learn. In so doing she had exhibited one of the hundreds of functions which a school secretary was expected to have in her professional machinery – namely, that of Dragon.

That does not mean that every school secretary was a dragon all the time – far from it. Neither was Mrs. Jelley. On the contrary, as I got to know her, I discovered that she was a charming lady, with a great sense of humour. Totally professional. Those were the days when a headmaster and a secretary, between them, could run an entire grammar school of nearly four hundred and fifty boys. She also had the most sharply clear handwriting; she could hold the phone in one hand, steady a wayward sheet of paper with her elbow, and scribble down at great speed, with half a pencil, what the speaker was saying, in writing as near copperplate as made no difference.

I have seen similar standards of calligraphy in the work of a secretary of West Buckland from a hundred years ago, though of course I cannot suggest that I was around to see Mr. Taylor's technique with the telephone and wayward sheets of paper. But I have many examples of his writing, both in ink and pencil, and it is a joy just to gaze at it.

He was a fine example of several common features of the early administration of the School. For a start, he was male; lady secretaries did not appear until after the First World War. Well, they didn't at West Buckland. A meanly-disposed critic may sneer that this is one more example of how behind the times the School was – in its secluded, remote, moorland eyrie. More likely, the appearance of ladies – in school offices and common rooms – was a sign of the beginnings of female liberation set in train by the War, and of the necessity of finding people to fill the gaps left in male ranks by the appalling casualties.

Secondly, Mr. Taylor was involved in the financial management of the School too. There remain in the Archive balance sheets drawn up and signed by him. So he combined the role of Secretary and Bursar.

Thirdly, he applied for, and was given, the post of Secretary to the Governors. If you look at the salaries that people like Taylor received, you can not be surprised. Just after the turn of the nineteenth to the twentieth centuries, the annual salary *for the Headmaster* was only £200.

Finally, Mr. Taylor ('Judy' Taylor to the boys because he had a voice, it was said, like that of Mr. Punch) was a full-time teacher. His range encompassed Drawing, Shorthand, Geography, Music, Book-keeping, and 'Manual Instruction'. He ran the School Choir and he was the village organist at East Buckland. He was also the Secretary of the Old Boys' Association. He was a family man too.

So school secretaries then could be, and usually were, male; and they could carry so many duties that one is left wondering how they found time to eat and go to sleep.

School secretaries now do not do what Mr. Taylor did; no school secretary of my acquaintance teaches in the classroom even part-time (though I have worked for a headmaster in a tiny church school in a northern city who was his own secretary; every Wednesday afternoon, he shut himself away in a garret above the classrooms and caught up with his paper-work).

Mrs. Helen Clark, who has just left her post of School Secretary, did not have to confine her activities to Wednesday afternoons in a garret; she had a roomy office with all the latest gadgetry. Nor did she teach; she had far too much else to do.

Which brings us back to the point that secretaries today, just like Mr. Taylor, have to turn their hand to a lot of things. Helen may not have been the Bursar, or the Choir-mistress, or the Secretary to the Governors, but she has filled millions of unforgiving minutes with sixty seconds' worth of distance run. And, like Mrs. Jelley, she knows that firmness is a prime quality which all secretaries need to call upon at will.

Dragon? No . . . . Anyone who has known Helen for the briefest of time soon realises that she, like Mrs. Jelley, is a very charming lady. And a very kind and gentle one; the very word 'Dragon' would never come naturally to the mind when thinking of her. But I have no doubt that she has had, many times, to exercise firmness.

And not just with children. With staff, parents, and visitors too – with everybody. Visitors have to be eased out of offices when it is quite clear that they have long since finished conducting the business for which they came. Parents have to be steered towards the door when they have been assured, for the twentieth time, that Lucy will have delivered to her the games kit that she forgot when she went out of the house in the morning. Staff who have met each other in the office have to be told that their joint reminiscences would be better expressed in the more relaxed atmosphere of the Common Room.

It is here that we touch on one of the commonest misconceptions about what a secretary does. So many people – and we all have to go to the Secretary's Office at some time or other – assume that a secretary is there simply to see to us. This misconception comes about, paradoxically, because of the secretary herself (I say 'her' because they are all ladies now); Helen, and her opposite numbers in other schools, are so good at 'seeing to us' that we come to expect immediate attention. From there it is a short step to assuming that that is all they do. Their very courtesy, professionalism, and generosity with their time draw us into this mistake.

Helen went further when I asked her about this. Of course, if you pressed people, they would say that a school secretary works for the Headmaster, and they understand that. But, she said, they conclude that a secretary simply carries out orders. 'They think that there is little initiative involved.'

In my work as Archivist, I have an office in the headquarters block of the School, and I see secretaries at work more than a teacher does. Believe me, initiative is going on all the time. On a mundane level, you would be surprised at the creativity shown when dealing with importunate parents on the telephone, or with prospective parents who cannot bring themselves to end an exploratory conversation about the School, or with a host of other unclassifiable callers obsessive about something or other.

I asked Helen for a bigger example from her daily round. 'There are many occasions when you pick up the pieces.' She did not mean that she is the US cavalry coming to the rescue; she meant that there are many occasions when, at a given moment in a tricky negotiation or the making of a hard choice, she may be able to offer extra information, or arrange material in a particular pattern, which may be of great assistance to the Headmaster in coming to his decision. He cannot possibly be aware of everything, and a good secretary offers the right detail, or the right combination of detail, at the right moment. It can often call for fine judgment and fine timing. And nobody outside the Headmaster's office will ever know.

How a secretary gathers these skills – which, for all their unobtrusiveness, are nevertheless vital – is a matter of mystery. There are no exams in judgment and timing; there are no certificates for parent-handling or for keeping callers away from the Headmaster. Helen has her paper qualifications in short-hand and typing, naturally. She picked up computer skills as she went along. She can chat up a VIP, clear up a misunderstanding, call up reinforcements, and rustle up a mean cup of coffee. That is all, you may say, common sense. True. But it goes further than that.

It is what she is; it is the dedication which she has brought to her work; it is her willingness to learn anything that needs learning; it is her unfailing kindness and sheer interest in her fellow-beings; it is her sense of humour which helps her, and her colleagues, to bear the burdens of the day; it is her sense of mischief which enables her, and her colleagues, to *laugh* at the burdens of the day – it is all that, and a lot more, which has given her the other skills I have been talking about.

When I asked her what she considered the most congenial part of her work, she answered without hesitation, 'Dealing with people. I enjoy that. I don't have to count up to ten very often – put it that way.'

And you never know what you are going to find when you walk in first thing in the morning. Helen said, that, by contrast, the most difficult part of her work was sorting out which things had to be done first, and which could be left for a bit. To use modern jargon – 'prioritising'.

She had not sailed straight into secretaryship, as a military cadet at Sandhurst sails into a commission. After a convent education, her working life began in a bank. Then she got married – to a young teacher who had been appointed Head of Chemistry at West Buckland. She met him backstage in a local amateur dramatic company. (How David Clark found time for courting and amateur dramatics, in between teaching Chemistry, running the department, coaching numerous sports, living on the campus, and dealing with the problems of young boarders, is another minor mystery.)

The course of true love was not without its hitches. West Buckland was going through a bad time during their courtship – so bad in fact that the most unkind rumours floating round North Devon had it that the School was only a couple of jumps ahead of the sheriff's posse. The manager of Helen's bank, mindful of the welfare of his employees, particularly his young and vulnerable ones, took it upon himself to offer some pastoral advice. Did Miss McKiernan really understand the true nature of the instability of West Buckland's finances? Did she really want to trust her future to a young man who might have a broken career in front of him?

Yes, indeed, Miss McKiernan really did. They were married in 1971. She was fond of her manager, and grateful to him, but between his sturdy common sense and David's obvious charm there was no contest. 'Did he but realise it,' she said, 'I was so besotted that I'd have married David if he had had no prospects at all.'

She stopped work to have her two sons, and started again in 1983 – at West Buckland. Only part-time at first, 'so I was always at home to meet them'. She only went full time when her younger son went to university.

Her first job was in the Reprographics Department. The word 'Department' is used very loosely; what she actually had was 'a filthy duplicator' in a lobby outside the Bursar's office. If the machine went too fast, it threw out ink everywhere.

She did get cleaner machines later, but the accommodation was no bigger. Her room was later modified into a pair of toilets – and very small toilets at that.

From there she moved 'up' to reception secretary, and later assistant to the incumbent Secretary, a Mrs. Thornhill, who was to hold the office for twenty-five years. When she retired, Helen stepped naturally into her shoes – though, after a twenty-five-year tenure, it must have seemed a hard act to follow.

All this time, her husband David had been developing his own career. He became a housemaster, Senior Master, and finally Second Master (Deputy Head), in between doing a hundred and one other things on the way – Cadets, Duke of Edinburgh Award, games coaching, and running foreign trips (which Helen accompanied and helped with).

So, when John Vick, the new Headmaster, arrived in 1997, he found the unusual situation of having a husband-and-wife team either side of him, as it were, one member of whom was his deputy, and the other his chief secretary. It could have been awkward, and there were those who said so. It speaks a great deal for all three that they made it work as well as it did – the Headmaster for his tolerance, broadmindedness, and willingness to judge things on their merits; and Helen and David for their massive integrity and total discretion.

One of the first things Helen said to the new HM was this: 'Please do not assume, because David knows something, that I do too – and vice versa.' Each was totally professional; each was able to separate work from home life. Here was another mild surprise. Every observer I have spoken to has emphasised the total dedication of both Helen and David, yet this evidence shows that they have been able to make a clear distinction between professional and private life. Helen observed, 'My *home* is my domain. When I left my office, it took me five minutes to take away my bits and pieces – my shorthand dictionary, a stationery basket which was a present from Martin [her younger son], and a couple of pens.'

After twenty years, had she noticed many changes, say, in the pupils? Yes, she said, a few. 'There is more money now than there was then. They can get into town more.' Very true – affluence and mobility. Or, if you prefer, mobility and affluence. So many nowadays have their own cars; many who do not can get lifts. Once in town, they can spend more than they did. 'They have many more casual clothes – and more stylish ones.'

And yet, either in spite of or because of this, Helen observed, 'I'm sure they find it more difficult to entertain themselves. They expect more material items.'

But her natural bonhomie soon asserted itself; her final verdict was much more positive. 'I think the children here now are great – absolutely great.'

What about the staff? Had they changed much? 'I don't think so. They moan a bit, but they moaned then.' After more thought (Helen thought a lot over her answers), she said, 'They're a bit better off. Staff then would have had one holiday per year, and didn't go very far. Now they have two or more, and go to more distant places like the USA.'

She then offered the opinion that they were 'less eccentric'. This could well be, as she freely admitted, because we remember the unusual characteristics of our past colleagues, and the humdrum details slide into limbo. Whereas we see today's colleagues in the round, warts and all, but the warts don't stand out so much because we can set them against everything else.

What about the School itself? The main modern trend she deplored was the growing need to put things in writing. This was one of the main reasons for going on to computers. It was all time-consuming and therefore tedious. But necessary – in a world where litigation was one of the ever-spreading plagues; one had to protect one's back. An example? Well, for example, 'we had never a school rule book before'.

She thought that size was a factor which had to be watched. A school could get too big. A secretary's job could get too big. 'The *amount* of work causes pressures. Small is beautiful – once it grows and you start delegating, you begin to lose touch.' And there was a danger of this because of the growth in legislation (and litigation), and because of the increased expectations of both parents and governors.

What was she looking forward to? 'Time for myself – probably top of the list'. Or again – 'sitting down and not feeling guilty'. 'I really do have time to think now. I've had an organised day for a long time.' Certainly she is not short of ideas – I have heard horse-riding mentioned, and a return to study of the piano. I know she and David are shortly off to visit the Czech Republic. (He has just retired too.) So travel will play its part.

Such plans and energy are typical of a lady who, in between being a dedicated secretary and a wonderful listener (she even listens to us when we talk about nothing in particular – and we all do our fair share of that), managed to help with make-up for the School plays, stood in as a sort of second mother to the boys in David's house, went shopping for the boarders, and so on.

Whatever comments or verdicts Helen offered, a few common threads were detectable, and the strongest of these was her conviction that her job was not just 'Secretary' but 'Headmaster's Secretary'. 'You act as a buffer for the Headmaster.' First loyalty is to the Headmaster. That did not stop her being the most sociable of colleagues. Few were more genuinely pleased to see you in the morning, at a social gathering, bumping into you in the street.

Nobody, absolutely nobody, had a greater fund of local information, family lore, and school history. Not to say good, old-fashioned gossip. If you asked Helen a question, you would not only get the answer to it; you would get the answer to the next fifteen questions which you didn't know you were going to ask.

But it was always in her own office and on her own terms. She was – is – known and liked universally, but she was not seen all that often in the Common Room. 'I probably knew less of what was happening than some staff; I was too busy.'

More likely, she was being discreet. If she was not in the Common Room, she could not be quizzed about the Headmaster or about his decisions. It always came back to discretion.

Helen may have been a bottomless fund of information, but she never told you anything you were not supposed to know. She was doing, all the time, what she regarded as the most important part of her job – protecting the Headmaster. She never let any cat out of the bag. Nor – like some people who enjoy the thrill of it – did she drop hints that she had a cat *in* the bag. With Helen, you wouldn't even know that there was a *bag*, never mind a cat. The only piece of advice that she thought worth offering was 'discretion is all'.

Would she do it again? 'Certainly. I enjoyed it.'

10. The North-South Divide

In the Archive is a cutting from the *North Devon Journal* about the opening of the Memorial Hall in May, 1933. Out of curiosity, I turned it over to see what was on the other side. It was a long article about a protest meeting of the League of National Life, called to object to the idea of setting up a birth control clinic in Barnstaple.

The speakers included the vicar of Barnstaple, the Bishop of Exeter, and the wife of a former headmaster of Blundell's School. Among the points made, by these and other speakers, were:

'Did they really mean that weak women were to be mechanised and poisoned in order to be protected from their husbands?'

'Was there no alternative to a medical officer sending a woman to Exeter because she could not control her lusts and the husband could not control his?'

'The back-bone of the arguments against birth prevention was the essential wrongness of the practice.'

'Anything. . . . that tended towards birth control tended towards immorality.' A time was approaching when 'all that . . . .children would ask would be "tell me where is the nearest reliable chemist's shop".' [Oddly prescient.]

'It was argued that from the point of view of social reform birth control was needed. . . . That was starting at the wrong end. Instead of limiting families they [the Government] should . . . . see that there were enough houses for the people to live in. . . . sooner or later they would have to evolve something in the nature of a system of family allowances. . . . to make it possible for people to live decently and in decent surroundings, and . . . . they would not do it by limiting the number of children that were born.' [Years ahead of the Welfare State.]

It would be uncharitable to laugh too readily at some of the above sentiments, and others expressed in the piece, because tucked away inside and behind them are some still-worthy feelings about duty, and family, and discipline, and priorities, and religion, and Right and Wrong, and sticking to principles, plus a little prophetic common sense.

But perhaps we can allow ourselves a little wry smile at the expense of the Mayor of Barnstaple, who was clearly a most reluctant chairman of this meeting. He and the Town Council, he said, were not going to express an opinion 'on such a controversial and far-reaching matter', and he fell back on a time-honoured North Devonian tactic: 'There were ample facilities at Exeter, [which] seemed to show that they were probably not needed at Barnstaple.'

11. Something in the Air

There have been fifteen headmasters at West Buckland since the School's foundation in 1858 – including the present incumbent. The School's history throws up all sorts of coincidences as one thumbs through old magazines and governors' minutes, usually on totally unrelated quests. One such coincidence concerns children.

Well, what a surprise! Study the history of a school, and you come across children. But I do not mean pupils; I mean children of the headmaster himself. It is a curious fact that there was a run of headmasters, from 1888 to 1940, who all fathered children while they were in office – or came very close to it.

I am not suggesting that two of them came close to considering the actual act of procreation; I mean that the births in question fell just outside their terms of office. The first was Mr. Bland, who arrived in 1888 with a ready-made infant, as you might say, but the Governors (or the Directors, as they were then) were concerned as early as January, 1889 with provision for the baby's care. (See p.37.) So it was a sort of near-miss. He went on to father two more children in 1890 and 1891, and twins in 1894. They were all baptised in East Buckland Church.

The second was Mr. Badger, who left in July, 1940 to join the Armed Forces. The *Register* of March, 1942 congratulates 'Major and Mrs. Badger' on the birth of a daughter. So the child was conceived within a year of its father's departure. So that just about counts too.

No argument about the rest.

When Mr. and Mrs. Challen arrived in the Headmaster's house in 1895, Mrs. Challen was already *enceinte*. John Bonamy Rhys Challen was baptised on 10th October. His father's middle name was also Bonamy. Three and a half years later, the happy couple were congratulated by the *Register* of June, 1899 on the birth of a daughter, Esther Vardon. (Unusual name – especially for a girl.) She was moreover christened, like her brother, at East Buckland Church, on Thursday, 9th March, 1899, and by 'the Revd. J.L. Challen' – presumably either the Headmaster's brother or his father.

In December, 1900, the *Register* recorded the engagement announcement of the new Headmaster, Mr. Knight. As it related, very correctly but benignly, 'At the conclusion of the concerts, the opportunity was taken to present to the Headmaster a combined standard lamp and table, and, at the same time, to offer him the hearty congratulations of the whole School on the occasion of his approaching marriage with Miss Ferguson Davie, whom they were all very pleased to see present that evening.'

So there was good reason to expect a happy event in the not too distant future. Nor were they disappointed – well, not at first.

There was a unique entry in the *Register* for December, 1901. On one and the same page, they announced that Mrs. W.A. Knight had been safely delivered of a baby son, Arthur John, 'at the Devon County School', on 14th November; and immediately below, in a black square, they sadly recorded that the 'three-day-old son' of Mr. and Mrs. Knight had died. He was buried in East Buckland churchyard. (See 'Passing Tribute'.)

Mr. Knight, whose teaching timetable, as recorded by the visiting inspectors, ran to twenty-seven hours a week, whose slender staff did not run to substitutes, and whose School budget did not run to supply teachers, had to smother his grief, and go back into the classroom and teach dozens of lively children. Poor man!

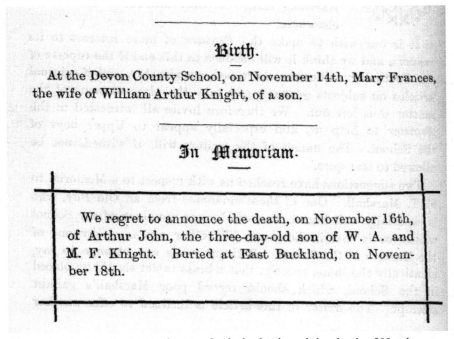

Birth.

At the Devon County School, on November 14th, Mary Frances, the wife of William Arthur Knight, of a son.

In Memoriam.

We regret to announce the death, on November 16th, of Arthur John, the three-day-old son of W. A. and M. F. Knight. Buried at East Buckland, on November 18th.

From the *Register* for 1901, showing both the birth and the death of Headmaster Knight's firstborn son. [School Archive]

However, the editors of the *Register* had another joyful event to impart to their readers in the issue of January, 1903 – namely, that another son had been born to Mrs. Knight – again at Devon County School.

Because both children were born at the School, one is tempted to wonder whether this was by choice or by necessity, and whether the absence of hospital facilities and all-round care had helped to precipitate the trouble which had caused the death of the first child. Indeed, I scanned the later pages fearfully, in case there was to be another sad announcement about the second son, but thankfully found none. On the contrary, I found an entry for October, 1906, which recorded that on the previous 19th September, Mr. and Mrs. Knight had had a third son.

The chances are that these men – Bland, Challen, and Knight – were only in their thirties (if that), but one does not associate the status of headmaster with comparative youth. Much less with 'new' paternity. This applies particularly to Victorian and Edwardian heads. Heads were lofty, fearsome creatures who did not simply come into a room; they manifested themselves there. One does not readily associate simple, ordinary emotions and situations with these supermen. Just look at the photographs of them – all those gowns and mortar boards and watch-chains and formal poses, and above all those moustaches. We are misled by the whiskers. True, Challen did not in fact wear a moustache, but he still looked pretty forbidding. Knight did though, and very impressive it was. Bland's was truly portentous – almost of Wyatt Earp proportions. So – I repeat – headship and paternity do not readily go together in the minds of students of Victorian England. To put it another way, you can not easily see such towering figures being involved in anything so mortal as having kids.

Another surprise came nearly twenty years later, when the Revd. Harries, who had, one would imagine, long since established the impression of unregenerate bachelorhood, embarked on matrimony at fifty. Making up for lost time, he sired three sons in as many years, including twins. He was the second head in forty years to father twins. (And incidentally, the Revd. Thompson, who retired in 1888 and married three years later at fifty-four, also produced a son, who also became a clergyman.)

Harries' successor, Lt.-Commander Westall, kept up what had by now become almost a tradition, and duly produced a daughter while in office. He already had three children, sired during his previous service at Blundell's. Not content with that, when he moved to take over the Headship at Kelly College, he fathered another child there too. As his daughter put it to me in a 'phone conversation about her parents, 'They had children everywhere.'

There followed the Badger episode, as I have related above. Then, the thread snapped. The War of course, which upset everything. Badger left to join the Forces. His successor, Mr. Smith, was a bachelor summoned from retirement to be wartime caretaker (see 'Holding the Fort – II'); and when he retired – again – his caretaker successor was another bachelor – Mr. Howells, who died in office in 1952. (See 'Sam and Jimmy'.)

There has been no child born in the Headmaster's house since. Odd – thirty years at the outset, from 1858 to 1888, and sixty-odd years since, from 1941 to the present day. None. But in the middle fifty years or so – just 36% of the full time – combined tally 16.

Other heads have arrived since 1941 with families already established, but their combined tally comes nowhere near 16. Now – what was it that produced that run of magisterial fertility while in office?

12. The Sporting Life

Swimming Notes

[This piece appeared in the *Register* of autumn, 1956, and is a splendid example of three things all at once: bland, deadpan reportage typical of a school magazine; barefaced euphemism; and unconscious expression of a school's values and priorities.]

'Owing to the very low rainfall since January [almost unique in West Buckland's history, I should think], the swimming bath contained no more more than a few inches of water and all hopes of its filling were unfulfilled. [It remained an open-air pool until the 1970's.]

'The opportunity was taken to repair the bath and the surrounds, and when the rains came in August [the summer monsoon, regular on Exmoor – set your watch by it], the bath quickly filled with crystal clear water. [An Old Boy said that one of his sharpest memories of the School was the scum on the surface.]

'Swimming commenced on September 24th and is still in full swing at the end of November.'

[Note the 'is' in the last paragraph – and 'full swing'! Open-air swimming, beside Exmoor, in November! And how much longer did it go on? No wonder ex-pupils coped easily with Army barracks life and prisoner-of-war camps in the Second World War.]

Quick Learners

The School switched from playing football to playing rugby in the winter term of 1925. Only three years later, in the season of 1928-29, the First XV, the Second XV, and the Colts XV all won all their school matches. Who was coaching these adaptable prodigies? Could a modern Six-Nations manager study his methods with profit?

Where Have All the Run-Makers Gone?

1913, apparently, provided a very dry summer, even in North Devon. Wickets must have broken bowlers' hearts. Well, they did in the senior house matches. Scores were prodigious, and games 'took several days to finish'. (Enough to make a cricket master's eyes fill with green water today.) In only five matches – admittedly double-innings – the total of runs scored came to over 2,400. There were two nail-biters. In a match where 615 runs were scored, the Brereton beat the Fortescue by three runs. In another the total was 770, and the Courtenay won by only two. How many writers of schoolboy stories would have dared to pen such cliffhangers?

However, the Junior batsmen seem to have made very heavy weather of the heartless wickets. In a Junior House cricket match during that same season of 1913, eleven boys from the Courtenay House made a little bit of history. On 26th May, playing against the Brereton, they managed, in their second innings, to get themselves dismissed for 0 – nought – zero – nothing. That is, all of them, together, added up, *in toto*. They rated a mention in the general cricket report for that year: 'In the Junior Matches a record was made by the Courtenay team, who were dismissed by the Brereton before they could score a single run.' And 'Extras' didn't score either.

(In fairness to the Courtenay, let it be mentioned that the following year, 1914, the Junior team achieved another record: they scored 218, a record innings total for a junior house match. If they had a coach, the poor man must have wondered what they were going to do next.)

Eye on the Ball

A Nigerian boy who joined the School was picked out straight away as a potential rugby player by virtue of his great size and strength. The only snag was that he did not know the first thing about the game. But he was a willing lad, keen to learn, and anxious to have a go.

So the games teacher took him on one side and said, 'There are only two things you need to know. If you see someone running with the ball, tackle him. If you get hold of the ball yourself, run like mad for the line at the end of the field, and don't let anybody stop you.'

After about ten minutes, the teacher had to halt the game to tell the boy, 'You only tackle the person with the ball if he is wearing a different shirt from you.' The game resumed, with our Nigerian recruit just as keen.

So keen, in fact, that in the second half he scored a try. But the teacher had to take him on one side again – to explain that, as the teams had changed ends, it was the *other* touchline that he had to run for.

13. Abroad Spectrum

Considering that the idea of the founder, the Revd. Brereton, was to set up a school which would provide a sound, cheap education for the local middle classes, West Buckland has come a long way.

This is particularly true with regard to the word 'local'. True, the old lists of pupils are full of Balments and Beers and Blackmores and Chuggs and Corks, Dallyns and Geens, Huxtables and Kingdons, Millers and Smales, Stanburys and Withecombes. These and other local dynasties are still well represented in this, the twenty-first century.

But the number of foreign names has grown steadily, and by 'foreign' I don't just mean 'grockle'; I mean really 'foreign' foreign names. Luckily for the School authorities, the 'foreigners' referred to have to learn English, and Devonian English at that. We do not have to learn their bewildering variety of tongues. Just as well – it is becoming an awesome feat just to be able to read the register.

But what an exotic spice and lavish variety they have, between them, brought to this moorland academy in the backwoods of the West. Try your hand at some of these names, and you will see what I mean:-

Lacava	Adeniji	Bogiatjis	Chong	Yip
Dansubutra	Du	Gharavi	Hamoudi	Cheung
Hoontrakul	Lam	Li	Gergely	Kwok
Chewprecha	Kudaras	Olszewski	Makarova	Bauch
Abb	Tang	Leung	Hermijanto	Mallannah
Lau	Mohamedbhai	Mogghadam	Pialek	Ng
Obi	Okumura	Amagai	Ojomoh	Namboka
Ongsaranakom	Phuchanakit	Pourmogadham	Quaishi	Siu
Sayidzadeh	Szoke	Ubogu	Watanabe	Zaouk
Yim	Zareh	Wijesekeva	Poisson	Ngui
Wing-Yiu	Djajasaputra	El Nabulsi	Fodio	Hemmatat
Tantisuvanichkul		Karnasuta [I wonder what his nickname was?]		

14. Founding Father

What should a founder be like? Pretty jolly eminent, don't you think? Well, ideally, that is. Degrees, decorations, distinctions and whatnot. Famous if possible – so that future generations of pupils, or members, or patients, or whatever they are, can boast that they were once the recipients of the favour and the attention of the celebrity in question. We all like to make the leap of unreason which allows us to think that, if we can establish a connection with somebody eminent, however tenuous, a tiny smudge of that eminence somehow rubs off on us.

Rich too. After all, let us be practical: there is not much point in a celebrity, however eminent or famous, trying to set up something unless he can provide the launch-pad of money to set it off into orbit.

It would also help if the founder could be around for a while afterwards, so that he, or she, can keep an eye on things, give his (or her) ewe lamb the attention it may need, help it over early stiles, see that it is not too easily shorn by wicked predators on its perilous path to the golden sunrise – be, in effect, a mixture of resourceful midwife, attentive godfather, and proud uncle. And of course a generous one.

By these standards, the Revd. Joseph Lloyd Brereton, begetter of the West Buckland Farm and County School in 1858, hardly fits the bill. He had a degree, it is true, and he was in holy orders. But he had no claims to eminence beyond that, unless you think that a Prebendary Stall in Exeter Cathedral qualifies its holder for such a distinction.

He was not famous, or anything approaching it; when he set up West Buckland School, he was the rector of a tiny, remote village in Darkest Devonshire. He was certainly not rich, and never became so. Indeed, most of his life was spent struggling, and usually failing, to make ends meet. His debts were to become a burden to his surviving family members for nearly half a century after he died.

Finally, he remained in West Buckland for only nine years after the foundation of his school; in 1867, he moved to Norfolk, to the village of Little Massingham, to take over the living left vacant by the death of his father. And there he stayed till he died in 1901.

What sort of a founder is that?

A very unusual one, and for more reasons than have appeared so far. There were many dimensions to Joseph Lloyd Brereton: depending on which circle he was moving in, or which idea he was pursuing at the time, or which colour his bank balance was currently appearing in, he could be visionary, authoritarian, charming, entertaining, contentious, devoted, child-like, infuriating, selfish, imaginative, prophetic, devious, untrustworthy, and downright impossible.

One of the first surprises you get when you make his acquaintance is his appearance. He was dashed good-looking. A high, noble forehead. A long, classical nose. What the novelists used to call well-chiselled features. A good head of fine hair – which, from its curls at the sides, looks as if it was well cared for – a symptom, perhaps, of the vanity and self-centredness that was part of his character.

He was certainly handsome enough to win the hand of a seventeen-year-old clergyman's daughter. Probably the heart too, because apparently both families were 'dismayed' at the match, so the couple would have had to be pretty determined. Such determination does not normally spring from mere formality. Frances was only a daughter of the cloth; Brereton certainly did not marry her for her money. Young Joseph (he was twenty-nine at the time) had poor health and few prospects, but he did have charm, and his head was buzzing with ideas. Perhaps his courtship is an early example of this powerful combination of energy, mental fertility, and impulsiveness. It is just possible that he swept young Frances off her feet, in spite of what her family may have thought.

However, the marriage proved very successful, especially if you judge by its fruitfulness (Brereton's fertility was not merely mental); Frances bore him sixteen children, of whom eleven reached maturity. (Another authority says seventeen.) In all the vicissitudes of a long life – and there were a lot – this huge family group was unswerving in its loyalty to him.

Frances was an attractive girl, and could, one would have thought, have had a pretty wide choice of suitor. So it says something for what we might call the Valentino factor in Brereton's make-up. The portrait of Frances which hangs in the hall at the School (donated by one of Brereton's grandsons), shows a true blooming English rose. It was painted by George Richmond, R.A., who enjoyed a long career, and a high reputation, as a portrait artist in Victorian England. Another of Brereton's grandsons, Henry Lloyd Brereton, said he had heard it described as the most beautiful portrait Richmond ever painted. Certainly it was one of the most expensive. In the autumn of 2001, there was an exhibition in London of Richmond's work. At the back of the catalogue was a list of all Richmond's known output, plus the prices at which they originally sold. Generally, he seems to have charged, for his portraits, between £30 and £50. The picture of Frances, together with one of her husband, was listed – that is, the pair – at £175.

There is an interesting comment in this list: 'Balance by Lord Fortescue for the two Brereton pictures – £25.'

DEVON COUNTY SCHOOL, WEST BUCKLAND, RECENTLY OPENED BY EARL FORTESCUE.

THE DEVON COUNTY SCHOOL, WEST BUCKLAND.

In the year 1856 the Rev. J. L. Brereton, rector of West Buckland and honorary canon of Exeter, addressed a letter to the late Earl Fortescue, Lord Lieutenant of Devon, suggesting a scheme of "county middle-class education," and which scheme it was carried on, and every successive quarter brought with it an increase in its number. The too small to accommodate the candidates for admission, and three large wooden rooms (a dormitory for twenty boys, a dining-room, and a schoolroom) were added to it. These rooms became crowded, and another farmhouse at the distance of a mile was engaged, to which Mr. Thompson, the Head Master, promoted with the older boys...

Brereton's new school, as reported by the *Illustrated London News* in November, 1861. [School Archive]

It is time to introduce the other half of the partnership which was responsible for the birth of West Buckland Farm and County School – Viscount Ebrington, or Earl Fortescue, as he became on the death of the second Earl, his father, in 1861.

Was Fortescue paying off the last of a series of instalments? Was he the owner therefore of the two paintings? Or did he intend them to be a present to Brereton as a mark of his esteem (they were to enjoy a very long, if turbulent, friendship lasting nearly half a century)? Since they came into the inheritance of one of Brereton's grandsons (also called Joseph), it might be reasonable to deduce that the elder Brereton was the original owner. More likely then – knowing what we know of Brereton's finances – Fortescue was doing what he was to do many times during their association – coming to Brereton's rescue when he was 'temporarily embarrassed', as the saying goes.

The relationship they enjoyed – or endured – bore some similarities to another, more famous, Victorian partnership – that of Gilbert and Sullivan. To say they had their ups and downs would be putting it mildly. Just as Gilbert railed at Sullivan's penchant for the high life when he should have been at his desk composing to meet rehearsal deadlines, so Fortescue constantly complained about Brereton's infuriating lack of perspective and common sense when it came to money. While Sullivan felt continually frustrated at what he considered the frittering away of his talent on trivial comic opera, so Brereton found it difficult to understand why Fortescue – and the rest of the world – did not jump at once to put into practice his brilliant theories and novel ideas.

Interestingly, Brereton possessed within himself characteristics of both theatrical partners; he shared Gilbert's prickliness and passion for quarrels, and he had Sullivan's combination of charm and fecklessness. No wonder Fortescue found him difficult.

But the friendship was always patched up in the end. Brereton had only to write a letter of deep, and no doubt genuine, contrition for Fortescue to respond with equally genuine relief and chivalrous generosity. Brereton seems to have possessed something of the charm of Toad; he could drive his friends to distraction, but Ratty and Mole and Badger could never stay furious with him for very long. Neither could Fortescue with Brereton. It was difficult to remain at odds with a man who could write, with obvious sincerity, that he valued their decades of friendship as 'the salt of my soul'.

There is another parallel with Gilbert and Sullivan. It was chance that brought that famous pair together; they moved in different circles and had not sought each other out. Chance in the shape of Richard d'Oyly Carte, an enterprising theatre manager, who saw the possibilities of a collaboration between England's leading dramatist and her most feted composer, and who arranged the first meeting.

It was chance that brought Brereton and Fortescue together, though the chance came not through the gumption of a theatre manager but through plain ill health.

Brereton was born in 1822, the third son of a Norfolk rector, one of eleven children in all. (Eleven might be said to run in the School family; eleven of Brereton's own children were to survive. The second Headmaster at West Buckland, the Revd. William Watson, died leaving eleven children.) He was not a strong boy, and was educated at home in his early years, by his parents. Perhaps because of this, he was to fall more than was usual under their influence. His mother was an emotional woman, and his father was of a stern and dominant disposition – perhaps in reaction against the mercurial nature of his wife. (It could of course have been the other way round; she was nervy and prone to swift changes of mood in order to cope, so she hoped, with his hectoring and disapproval.) The Revd. C.D. Brereton, when he was not disciplining his large brood, spent a lot of his time churning out polemical pamphlets on the Poor Law and the social functions of the clergy.

Whatever the Freudian interpretation of all this, Brereton took on something of his mother's emotionalism on the one hand, and his father's energy and contentiousness on the other. For example, there was a long period when he was involved, largely through his own fault, in Byzantine litigation with brothers and sisters. It is also interesting that he too developed the knack of moulding a very large family to total acquiescence in his chosen line of activity. Only two of his many daughters, for instance, managed to get married.

But he did not inherit his father's health. After what appears to be an unsuccessful, and not very happy, spell at a day school in Islington, he arrived at Rugby School at the age of fifteen, still a bit soft, and not easily able to cope with the 'coarseness and tyranny' that was reckoned an inescapable part of all public schools, including Thomas Arnold's Rugby (more of Arnold later). It is likely that he suffered from what was called in those days 'consumption' (diseased lungs); two of his sisters died of it.

His energy and determination got him through, but only just. Ill health prevented him from attaining scholastic distinction at Oxford. After ordination, he held curacies in Norwich and London, but was forced to find more bracing air in Paignton in 1851, where he kept the ship afloat by giving private lessons. It was bracing air which brought him to West Buckland in 1852 (armed now with Frances), a living which he may well have secured through knowing the right people (the Brereton charm again). He began to get better, but as late as 1857 still found it helpful to winter in Egypt.

Fortescue on the other hand, four years older than Brereton, was born and bred in Devon. As the eldest son of an aristocrat, he was destined for a career in politics. After a spell as private secretary to his father (Lord Lieutenant of Ireland) at Dublin Castle, he served as M.P. for Plymouth, and later for Marylebone, and was also Secretary to the Poor Law Board. Then, while inspecting a military hospital, he caught a very bad infection of the eye, and in the end lost the sight of it. He withdrew from London politics, and settled at the family seat at Castle Hill, barely three miles from Brereton. Ill health had brought them both to West Buckland for the foreseeable future

Fortescue – or Lord Ebrington, as he was until he inherited his father's title in 1861 – was, like Brereton, an admirer of Arnold, though it is unlikely that he ever espoused Arnold's philosophy with quite the devoted and single-minded passion that Brereton did.

Here we return to Brereton the sickly boy. He was fifteen when he first came under Arnold's sway. This influence was deepened and enriched when he moved into the Sixth Form and into Arnold's house. He was not an outdoor type; he had none, it seems, of the beery, back-slap, ruggernaut approach to life of the typical public schoolboy. Sensitive, unathletic, scholarly, impressionable, probably unhappy (he had once asked his father to take him away), he would have naturally given his attention, and, later, his loyalty and admiration, to such a man as Arnold, with his fearsome righteousness and his passionate certainties. (I can think of one or two of my own schoolmasters in this context; I did not necessarily agree with their philosophy, but I envied their certainty.)

This influence continued when he went up to University College, Oxford; his tutor there was Arthur Stanley, who had also been one of the great man's sixth-formers, and who carried his intense admiration into and through the pages of his biography. It seems inconceivable that Brereton would not have read it.

Years later, he observed, 'To have been one of his [Arnold's] pupils I esteem to have been in some sense the chief privilege not only of my boyhood but of my whole life.' Arnold marked him – permanently – and he knew it: 'Who are we – what can we do – what can we become if we would not be utterly unworthy of our school and our schoolmaster?' Thanks to his powerful father, and his even more powerful headmaster, Brereton seems to have been a driven man. He was sincere and creative, to be sure – there was the engine. But it was Arnold, and his father, who provided the fuel; he strained all his life somehow to be worthy of them. They gave him his reason for striving, for never forgetting what he saw as his ideals.

What were these ideals? What did he want?

One hardly knows where to begin. . . . Let it be with Arnold, the main-spring of Brereton's effort, if not of his creativity. Arnold found a system which was, as Lytton Strachey said in his essay on Arnold in *Eminent Victorians*, 'anarchy tempered by despotism'. He maintained the despotism, but went some way to lessening the anarchy with his famous prefect system. His three main priorities were religious and moral principle, gentlemanly conduct, and intellectual ability – in that order. After Arnold, 'the worship of good form' became universal. After Arnold, 'no public school could venture to ignore the virtues of respectability'. (Strachey again.) Arnold, like his predecessors, still beat boys (though not *en masse*); he still domineered, he still preached and moralised and hectored; but he did, by comparison with what had gone before, civilise his charges. He also provided those pupils who admired him with an indestructible pair of rose-tinted glasses. Thomas Hughes, the author of *Tom Brown's Schooldays*, was invited to be a guest at the Devon County School's prizegiving in 1868, and for years afterwards his book figured in the list of prizes presented to scores of small boys.

Brereton would not have disagreed with any of that. Indeed, he was probably the one who suggested Hughes as the guest. But he took it further, much further. Arnold, for instance, gave very short shrift to Science. Brere-ton was all for a modern curriculum – especially where science was involved with agriculture (his school was first called the West Buckland Farm and County School). Latin would be available only on demand, and by special arrangement. The School's first headmaster was not going to be a Classical scholar, but a teacher trained in one of the new training colleges.

He was not going to be a clergyman either. Brereton took issue with Arnold here too. He believed in a broad-based Christianity. Religion, of course, was inseparable from education, but it was not to be over-prescrip-tive. As the first Headmaster, Thompson, was fond of saying, it was Christian 'feeling' that he taught and encouraged, not Christian dogma, much less sectarian dogma. If you like, it was the Christianity of the Samari-tan, not of the Pharisee. Brereton's idea was to attract as broad a spectrum of potential parents as possible; ideally even secularists might be attracted by the modernity and efficiency of the curriculum, and would be prepared to overlook any partisan holiness which might seep into their son's subcon-scious in the process. This tolerant view of religious instruction, set against the strength, and the variety, and often the narrowness, of the shades of Christian opinion in nineteenth-century England, puts Brereton's philoso-phy way ahead of its time. More ink was spilt on the nature of the religious education to be inflicted on schoolchildren than on all the other subjects in the curriculum put together. Brereton, if he had had his way, could have bypassed a lot of that.

Another of the reasons why the new Headmaster was not going to be a classical cleric was that Brereton had no intention of setting up just another specially-patented public school. Here again he departed from Arnold. It is interesting, and perhaps ironic, to note the extent to which Brereton diverged in practice from the philosophy and approach of the man he so much admired.

Arnold started from the top; how was he going to lick into shape the youth of England's rulers? Brereton was altogether more ambitious; his glance took in the whole of society before he decided on his strategy. At the top, he said, were about a million 'free men', who had 'more than enough to live on without working at all'. At the bottom were another million or so, of 'paupers', a 'half-slavish class', who couldn't pay for anything, and who depended largely on charity. Brereton wasn't interested in charity; he believed it degraded the recipient without improving his situation. He remembered the many attacks his father had made on the allowances paid out under the old Poor Law in the early decades of the century, which gave the honest labourer no incentive for hard work and thrift. (He might also have noted that the other half of this pernicious equation was the derisory wages that were being offered by farmers, who were themselves being impoverished by having to pay the ever-rising poor rate. But crusaders often ignore, or choose to ignore, the full picture in their search for just causes and neat slogans.)

By the same token, Brereton had no time for the charity-based primary education that was on offer from Government grants, for all that it was being administered (and being haggled over) by religious societies and organisations. It was almsgiving gone mad, and it was, moreover, Government interference. This was another of the whole apiary of bees that whizzed around inside his bonnet. (Had he stopped to consider, he might have seen that these annual grants were not a sign of the Government interfering, but a sign of the Government trying to wash its hands of the business by doling out some cash to religious do-gooders and thereby shutting up the noisy reformers.)

However – to pursue Brereton's analysis, errors and all. In between these two extreme millions lay, obviously, the rest, everybody else, the ones in the middle, the 'Middle Class' – perhaps 'twenty millions', he estimated, 'who with more or less reserve of capital are earning their living by services rendered to others'. Here was where he could, perhaps, do what Jeremy Bentham, the famous utilitarian philosopher, called 'the greatest good' for 'the greatest number'.

This group, by its very size and position, was, by blinding obviousness, the core, the hub, the bastion, the bedrock of the nation. The education that this group could procure for itself would therefore be the true yardstick of the quality of the whole nation's education. It followed in turn that the greatest possible leap forward that could be made would be in developing the educational level of this group. And it was to this end that Brereton was to devote much of his enormous energy for the rest of his life.

At the very centre of this central group, by Brereton's theory, was the yeoman farmer – his 'midmost man' – occupying between 200 and 300 acres. 'The education which that man has received, or can procure for his sons, would seem to me the true measure of general English Education.'

Having argued himself into this position of apparently impregnable logic, Brereton set about trying to bring his system into practice, without stopping sufficiently to consider whether the various human (or financial) factors in his equation would fit. But it was a praiseworthy concept. The coat of arms which was devised for his new school at West Buckland summed up his aspirations – a wheatsheaf over an open book, with the motto 'Read and Reap'. No rampant heraldic animals and fancy Latin mottoes for his rustic students of Land Surveying and Arithmetic, Algebra and Euclid, History and Geography, Grammar and Analysis, with the mud still clinging to their hobnailed boots from where they had been out on the School farm learning their trade and helping to keep the School solvent with the profits of their labour.

The full name of the School was the 'West Buckland Farm and County School'. The 'Farm' element in the title was obvious. But why 'County'? Here we come to another of Brereton's passions – self-help.

If ever there was a century when people believed in the virtues of hard work, putting your shoulder to the wheel and your nose to the grindstone, knuckling down to it, getting on with the job, it was the nineteenth. In the early heady days of the Industrial Revolution, it seemed as if anyone could make a fortune if he was prepared to work. It followed therefore that those who did not were somehow not working hard enough; and those who had no money at all, and who had sunk to the bottom of the pile, had lost out and sunk because they were idle, feckless, and probably stupid as well. So it served them right. The opportunities were there for everybody; why didn't these people take them? Why was it that the only thing they took was charity? Charity only staved off immediate crisis; it did nothing to produce long-term improvement. That would come only with a change of attitude on the part of the recipients of the charity.

Brereton's father had been writing about these topics for as long as young Joseph could remember, and he swallowed the philosophy of self-help whole. In that sense his idea was a throw-back. In another, it is prophetic; one of the great modifications of the world effort to help under-developed peoples in the twentieth century was the idea of creating schemes of improvement that the recipients could run for themselves – to make them willing partners instead of piccaninny bowl-sippers.

This principle Brereton applied to education. There was no national education system. Very well; Brereton would construct one. But not a Government one. If there was one thing he loathed, it was Government 'interference'. This opposition by English gentlemen to interference in their lives also goes back a long way, and was to have a very long innings in the nineteenth century. There was a long rearguard action afterwards too, arguably up to the present day, still detectable in complaints about the nanny state. It explained why the first income tax was opposed as 'intrusive'; why police forces were regarded as potential vehicles of military dictatorship; why municipal piped water was an insult – 'we prefer to take our chance with the cholera' – and so on.

Far better, said Brereton, and many others, to rely on the time-honoured systems of self-regulation and self-help that existed at local levels. The old Saxon traditions of self-government at the level of village, hundred, and shire took on a fresh lease of life in his eyes. (When he was a young curate, Brereton had published a periodical called *The Anglo-Saxon*, the expenses and premature demise of which were an early indication of his feeble business instincts.) So the new school for his middle class was to be rooted in the life of, and nurtured by, the county – hence County School.

Brereton being Brereton, it was not enough to have a county school in Devon, where he was living at the time; there must be county schools all over England. And – thanks to his drive, persistence, and unflagging energy – there soon were. Before he died, there had appeared county schools in Somerset, Dorset, Bedford, East Devon, Hampshire, Suffolk, Surrey, Oxfordshire, Norfolk, Shropshire, Gloucestershire, and Durham. Some barely blinked at the light of day, and others folded later; but some survived, albeit under other guises. His own firstborn – the Devon County School – re-emerged as plain West Buckland School; Surrey County School became Cranleigh; Suffolk metamorphosed into Framlingham; the North-Eastern County School was translated into Barnard Castle. Brereton did not play an active part in all of them; but he was aware of them, he took an interest in them, and he must have felt pride in the movement he had created.

Brereton again being Brereton, it was not enough either to let boys collect a certificate or two and go off into the wide world at the age of fifteen or sixteen. Provision would have to be made for their further education, to fit them for the many civic professions that an increasingly industrialised society was demanding. So county schools were to be succeeded by county colleges, which would award county degrees.

One thing you have to say for Brereton, incidentally, at this stage. Unlike a lot of doctrinaire left-wing politicians, who, while trumpeting the virtues of comprehensive schools, quietly sent their own offspring to Harrow and Oundle and Charterhouse, Brereton was quite prepared to submit his own sons, and daughters, to his new creations. His eldest, William, went to the Devon County School; two more, Francis and Henry, went to the one in Norfolk. Brereton even turned down an offer for Francis to go to Marlborough, explaining with touching honesty to the would-be benefactor that he could hardly champion the virtues of the county schools if he chose to exclude his own son from one of them. He also sent Francis and Henry to his new county college foundation at Cambridge.

This was a typical Brereton Quixotic effort. He conceived a nationwide system of county colleges, affiliated to and watched over by the traditional universities. These colleges would award degrees below that of honours degrees, but of sufficient standing to allow their holders to proceed to a wide variety of employment, especially teaching. For Brereton was well aware that all these new schools would only be as good as the teachers they could recruit to work in them. This is a good example of how sharp, and at the same time how obtuse, Brereton could be. County schools were a good idea; so, arguably, were county colleges. He was also practical enough to see the need for trained teachers of modern subjects rather than languid Oxbridge classicists or pallid clerics, but he went about it all the wrong way.

He became so convinced of the logic and the rectitude of his schemes, and the crying need for them, that he steered himself into the conviction that they were all financially viable. The sincerity of the desire was its own justification. His papers are strewn with jottings about comparative costs – of tuition, boarding, salaries, buildings, and so on, punctuated with impractical estimates of the amounts that could be raised by the sale of shares in a limited liability company. In his published writings, he went into infinitesimal detail about examination fees and secretarial costs, about estimates for coal, meat, vegetables, beer (beer!), laundries, housemaids, and a host of related topics – estimates which 'proved' that such and such a function could be made self-supporting or viable. He 'demonstrated' that the headmaster of one of his county schools could expect a salary of £900 a year; in fact, over thirty years later, the actual headmaster of West Buckland was in receipt of less than one-third of that sum.

When friends or associates ventured to question his figures or his policies, he saw these comments not as kindly criticism but as mischievous obstacle-strewing. Hence some of his frequent spats with Fortescue.

The limited liability company was yet another of that apiary of bees in his bonnet.

Capital would be raised by the sale of shares; part of the profits (profits!) would be set aside for endowing scholarships (another splendid idea in principle – giving a leg up to the bright boy from a poor home); the rest of the profits would be distributed as dividends; and interested benefactors – or delighted shareholders – would chip in with further private endowments.

It sounded wonderful. It fitted too with his gospel of self-help. Farmers would pay modest fees for their sons' schooling, and not have their characters warped by excessive charity; they would also derive satisfaction from the boys' modern education, to say nothing of the profits from the shares. He even expected labourers to be able, and willing, to afford fees for the elementary schools at least, because 'the average money wages of the agricultural labourers in England have notoriously been on the rise for many years, and are stated to be, at the present time, twelve shillings [60p] a week'. (*County Education*, 1861, p.7.) In many cases, of course, they were not. The whole edifice was based on a time-honoured unit of local life – the county. It kept out Government interference. It was perfect.

It is Toad all over again. Remember when he showed Mole and Rat his new gypsy caravan? It was new, it was exciting, it would solve all the problems of existence. It was 'the real thing'. It was 'change, interest, excitement'. And 'look at all the arrangements'. Toad had planned them all himself – sleeping bunks, folding table, cooking stove, lockers, bookshelves, a birdcage with a bird in it, and so on. Toad had thought of everything – 'biscuits, potted lobster, sardines. . . . soda water here – baccy there – letter paper, bacon, jam, cards and dominoes'. It was his boast that 'nothing whatever' had been forgotten, 'when we make our start this afternoon'.

Brereton, like Toad, had thought of everything, and couldn't wait to get stuck in. Just as Toad's enthusiasm swept his friends along with him, so Brereton's childlike keenness and energy conjured money out of scores, probably hundreds, of people over the years, for schemes which in their more sober moments they might have consigned to the waste paper basket. Putting together all his schools and colleges and associations for a moment, one can draw up a list of contributors which included, at one time or another, Lord Northbrook (Viceroy of India), the Earl of Leicester, the Earl of Devon, Fosters the Cambridge bankers, W.H. Smith the stationer, the Duke of Devonshire (Chancellor of Cambridge University), Sir Stafford Northcote (Cabinet Minister), Viscount Clifden (whom he persuaded to become a director of West Buckland), the Duke of Marlborough, the Duke of Bedford, and the Prince of Wales. Sundry bishops and archbishops were beguiled into giving their vocal support, into visiting, presenting prizes, and so on. Surrey County School managed to recruit as benefactors the Duke of Cambridge and the King of the Belgians. Of course, not all these men were directly recruited personally by Brereton, but since he was more closely associated with the 'county' movement than anybody else, and since he gave more of his life to it than anybody, he deserves the lion's share of the credit for pulling these big names on to prospectuses and shareholders' lists.

Brereton still wasn't finished – not by a long chalk. With his massive logic and all-embracing thinking, it was only a matter of time before he turned his attention to girls' education. Or rather only a matter of his many daughters growing up, which, by its very inexorability, brought the topic to the forefront of his mind; just as he wanted his sons to be teachers and, later, headmasters, so he envisaged his daughters ending up as headmistresses. For all its wild optimism, it was also practical in a blinkered, crusading sort of way. In the nineteenth century, there was not much future for well-brought-up young ladies; you became a governess, a companion, or you got married. On the other hand, the principal of a girls' school or a college had rank, status, a permanent position, and a good income, by the standards of the time – and would be free from the necessity of getting married and handing over all her property to her husband.

In 1884, the Graduated County Schools Association Limited was formed, with plans to set up girls' schools (many of them 'county' schools of course) in Barnard Castle, Darlington, King's Lynn, Taunton, and Uffculme (in Devon). These were for the younger girls. Older girls were to be provided for in Worcester Park (in Surrey), Bayswater, Blackheath, and Darlington again. The county college idea was transferred to this scheme as well; there were to be hostels in university towns for degree students. (Only one actually materialised – in Cambridge – in Norwich House, which had previously been occupied by Brereton's male county students, before Cavendish College was built.)

The demise of this grandiose plan is a good template for the failure of so many of Brereton's schemes. Fortescue had his doubts about it from the outset. Brereton tried to pay off some of his ancient debt to his long-suffering friend by giving him some shares in the G.C.S.A. – for what they were worth. Because there were a lot of absences from the directors' meetings, Brereton as chairman had a much freer hand than he should have done. The result was disastrous. He spent a lot of money travelling all over the place on association business. Letters went unanswered. Proper accounts, one suspects, were not regularly kept. He 'borrowed' association money for private purposes. The numbers of pupils fell far short of expectations. Despite an original authorised capital of £20,000, by the end of 1886 £5,000 was owed to Fosters' Bank and £800 to teachers, to say nothing of £10,000 to tradesmen.

In 1887, the bank forced it into liquidation. Brereton complained bitterly of disloyal colleagues, of 'neglect of my instructions, opposition to my deliberate advice, and scandalous combinations to tie my hands and blind my eyes'. In other words, it wasn't his fault. The world, once more, was against him. While the association was dying, in the spring and summer of 1887, and, one would have thought, all energy and concentration should have been devoted to preserving it, Brereton was throwing himself into setting up yet another county school in Gloucester.

There was no end to his energies and enthusiasms. He was interested in teacher training. He was both prophet and partisan of the new Oxford and Cambridge Local Examinations (see 'Tried and Tested'), and he took great pride in the successes enjoyed in these exams by his Farm and County School at West Buckland. (At one time they were top of the national league, well ahead of, for instance, Manchester Grammar School.) He was advocate and champion of the boarding principle. 'The true corner-stone of a national system of Education,' he intoned, 'ought to be laid in a model middle-class boarding-school.' (*County Education*, 1874, p. 10.)

This was partly because of the legacy of Arnold, which had so markedly shaped him. He also thought that the rural middle classes – his 'midmost men' – led a 'dispersed' life; boarding would bring more boys together more of the time, would socialise them and, by the example of the teaching, civilise them and make them cultured gentlemen. He wanted the county colleges to be so integrated with the universities that the 'culture' would not evaporate when the young county graduates went back to their farms and villages. (Fifty years later, in the run-up to the First World War, the Headmaster at West Buckland was still taking advantage of a tame prizegiving audience to extol the advantages of boarding over day schooling.)

The population may have been 'dispersed' in the countryside, but it was concentrating in ever-increasing numbers in the burgeoning cities. Brereton lived most of his working life in two tiny villages – West Buckland in Devon and Little Massingham in Norfolk – in two pretty large, empty counties by English standards. He seems not to have fully understood that this teeming urban physical proximity brought with it a huge range of new problems, which would necessitate a range of new solutions. These problems – for instance, of local government, of hygiene, water supply, medicine, factory regulation, law enforcement, and a host of related ones – became so enormous as a result of the galloping population, that the Government, whether it liked it or not, would have to legislate on a national scale simply in order to make life bearable, never mind to improve it. State intervention, which Brereton deplored, was unavoidable.

The same applied to education. The days of private enterprise – especially nationally-organised private enterprise in the shape of Brereton's county associations – were past. The best-run and the best-endowed national associations would never have the resources to provide for the needs of a population which tripled in a hundred years. And Brereton's associations were anything but well run – or well endowed.

Greater density of population would also generate, in time, greater social mobility. Brereton believed in a hierarchical structure for society. His county schoolboys should improve themselves, of course, but they should not improve themselves too much. Remember his rosy view of Anglo-Saxon society – that distant, idealised Arcadia of time-honoured virtues and rustic simplicity, self-help and co-operation, when everybody knew his place – and, by and large, kept to it.

Hence, his plans are shot through with divisions and layers and levels. There should be three levels of education – elementary in the village, secondary at the county school, and 'further' at the county college. Labourers' sons were to be educated at the elementary, because after that they would normally expect to leave. Farmers' and tradesmen's sons would go on to the county schools. If they were bright and worked hard, they could pass the Junior Local Examinations (set up by Oxford and Cambridge University), and, with parental backing (because Father would pay the extra fees), they could proceed to the county colleges, where they could take the Senior Local Examinations. If the county school was a good one – a Second Grade school – it might induce its pupils to stay on till the age of eighteen, and take the Senior Local Examination while still at school. So the county schools themselves were to be divided into three types, or grades – First, Second, and Third. It depended on a combination of criteria – fees, size, leaving age, curriculum, and status of parent who provided the pupil. Brereton, it seemed, was all for social mobility, but not too much of it. It was for him a sort of sociological castor oil: administer small doses to ensure that no painful constriction prevented society operating; but administer too much, and the result would be social dissolution.

It is interesting that so many of the people who have championed the virtues of a hierarchical, almost static form of society have enjoyed a privileged position in it. Brereton was born the son of a country rector, who, traditionally, was one of the triumvirate of authority in the locality – the squire, the parson, and – if the village was lucky – the doctor. He took it in through the pores of his skin, and his father, as we have seen, exerted a huge influence on him. Arnold had wielded absolute power – benevolent, maybe, in the longest of long runs (though the benevolence element may have seemed somewhat elusive to his charges, particularly just after punishment) – but absolute nevertheless.

When he finally settled at West Buckland, he found a situation that exactly fitted his aspirations, his background, and his instincts. His health was braced, at last, by the keen Exmoor air. Local society – with its clearly-visible strata of resident aristocrat, small farmers, and agricultural labourers, and maybe a scattering of local craftsmen – suited him down to the ground. Here he could take his 'natural' place as pastor, adviser, reformer, bringer of light into lives darkened by poverty and ignorance, and general organiser of everything.

He had a loving – or at least a remarkably complaisant – wife, an ever-growing family of obedient children, and a local viscount who was inter-ested in the same things he was. As his family relentlessly expanded, he could add the role of patriarch to his growing repertoire of parts on the village stage which he came to dominate. He wrote poetry too – guess who composed the words for the School Song at West Buckland (and, for all I know, at Elmham and Barnard Castle too).

Incredibly, he found time to add yet further to his many interests. He farmed the church glebe – about thirty acres. The village farmers must have wondered what hit them. He queried the old system of four-course rotation. He doubted the value of the local reliance on cereals. (Such a doubt, in the damp, windy climate and hilly terrain of North Devon, makes sense even to the ignoramus general reader.) He experimented with new types of cattle feed. He used sea sand instead of straw for bedding. He became a sheep-breeder of repute – and lost money doing so, his own and Fortescue's.

He enlarged the village elementary school. He began, with Fortescue, a local agricultural show. He was involved in building a road, and he helped to bring the new railways near; a station was opened at Filleigh, a few miles from his precious school. He laboured to bring in steam traction engines. There is even a reference to his doing conjuring tricks to entertain his parishioners.

It seems, too, that Brereton was not just a tiresome meddler. There are records of his being given a silver cream jug by the parish clothing society. The elementary school gave him a gold pencil case. The United Parishes' Farming Society presented him with a silver inkstand. The very value of these gifts indicates some genuine gratitude; his flock was far from affluent; they could so easily have rustled up some housewives' embroidery or a basket of local produce.

He edited, and wrote much of, two volumes of a West Buckland Year Book, for 1857 and 1860. For what they are, they are sumptuous. There were articles on subjects as wide-ranging as cricket, managing poultry, Shakespeare, Geology, Pig-Hunting in New Zealand, Agricultural Theory, Fishing, Lundy Island ('Embosomed in the centre of the Bristol Channel. . . . '), Devonshire Cream, The 'Steam Horse', and travelling in Egypt (he had wintered there at least once). He could not resist re-printing a batch of his own sermons and sprinkling the text with his own poems.

During all this time, he was launching his county school up the road, corresponding with bigwigs to try and raise money for it, cooking up plans for county schools elsewhere, having endless discussions with Fortescue about middle-class education in general, and writing pamphlets about it, getting involved in the new Oxford and Cambridge Local Examinations, dreaming of his new county colleges, and raising an enormous family. For a man who up to now had suffered very indifferent health, it was a prodigious effort. Heaven knows what he might have done if he had been in *robust* health.

Everything took second place to the 'work', throughout his life. Even his family. There exists in the record his curt dismissal of Joseph Thompson, his school's first Headmaster, when the latter asked for the hand of Anna, his eldest daughter: 'I am sorry, Mr. Thompson, but I need her for the work.' Anna was married in the end – to Thompson – but she had to wait until she was thirty-six (and her groom was over fifty by that time). Only two of Brereton's daughters made it to the altar, the oldest and the youngest. In 1881, he had one of them working as a teacher in the girls' school at Worcester Park. Another was listed in the census of that year as a 'visitor'. Four more were pupils. Everything was to be submitted to the great experiment of 'middle-class education'.

The census of 1901, just before Brereton died, listed no fewer than five of his daughters, all still living at home – Henrietta, Margaret, Jane, Eleanor, and Cicely, aged 42, 38, 33, 32, and 27 respectively. So presumably they were still helping with 'the work' – running a little boarding school for teenage girls and small boys, because the nearby school at Elmham had been closed (see below). It seems most unlikely that their father had made any provision for them; he left little but ample debts.

William, the eldest son, was put into his new school at West Buckland, Francis and Henry into his brain child at Elmham, the Norfolk County School. William escaped into the Army, though, when he died prematurely, *his* son Munster (Brereton's grandson) was put into Barnard Castle; the other two meanwhile were submitted to his new Cavendish College at Cambridge. Henry, like his father, went on to take holy orders, and eventually became, again like his father, rector at Little Massingham – the third member of the family to hold the post. Francis finished up there too, after his retirement from a headship.

Brereton had a hand in that as well. In 1872, he was looking for a head for his new county school at Elmham, in Norfolk. His eye had fallen on the Revd. William Watson, who worked at West Buckland School. Watson, the Second Master, had served as caretaker headmaster while Thompson was reading for a Maths degree at Cambridge. (See 'Holding the Fort – I'.) He must have made a pretty good job of it, because Brereton was happy to offer him the new post at Elmham. (Fortescue clearly liked him too, because he had arranged for Watson to take the living at Yarnscombe when Thompson returned in 1871.) It is quite likely that Watson taught young Francis and Henry while they were pupils at Elmham.

Francis grew up, graduated, and became a schoolmaster. By that time Brereton had helped to found Barnard Castle School in Durham (Fortescue laid the foundation stone in 1883.) The governors were looking for a headmaster. Francis got the job at an extremely young age, much to the chagrin, apparently, of his much more experienced chief rival. They shared a train compartment on the return journey south. The poor man could not resist asking the young appointee, 'Would you mind telling me, Mr. Brereton, how many years of experience you have had as a schoolmaster?' Even allowing for the fact that Francis was an extremely fit, well-set-up young man, it seems inconceivable that his father had nothing to do with it. Especially as brother Henry was appointed as a housemaster as well.

He certainly had everything to do with Francis' resignation in 1887. The County School at Elmham was in danger of closure. Brereton's choice of Headmaster, the Revd. Watson, had apparently had some kind of collapse (he had had liver trouble when he was at West Buckland), and there was a danger that the Elmham school would fail. With Cavendish College struggling, the crisis, like most crises, could not have come at a worse time. Brereton could not afford a failure; it would cast a national doubt on the whole county school movement – his movement. He cast about for the best man to save the situation. His son Francis was going from strength to strength at Barnard Castle. The movement was much more important than any one human component of it. Very well – Francis would have to resign at Barnard Castle and go to Elmham.

Francis understandably did not want to go. But Brereton was implacable. Francis' sister Henrietta ('Etta' in the family) recalled the scene years later as she sat in the Headmaster's house with Francis' son: 'I can remember your father. . . . sitting in front of this grate and brooding as he dug the poker again and again into the fire.'

It is a telling scene, and touchingly illustrates the hold that Brereton had over his family, and the sacrifices that he demanded, and got, from them. Their universal loyalty, in the face of episodes like this, is truly amazing. At this time, too, Brereton was putting son Henry in as Headmaster of the fledgling county school at Gloucester, and it seems almost certain that he wrenched him away from his housemastership at Barnard Castle. The Gloucester school failed as well.

The same grandson, H.L. Brereton, recalls the awesome atmosphere in the rectory at Little Massingham in his grandfather's old age, surrounded by all his spinster daughters. The old man was revered, he said, 'only less than God, and even there the priority seemed to be in question'. It was not till the third generation that the grip began to slide; one of the grandsons remembered saying to his brothers, 'You know the aunts have no doubt that Christ will be seated on the right hand of God in heaven. They are not so certain who will be on the left hand but think it likely to be their Father.' (It is possible of course that these stories are two versions of the same family joke.)

Even so, he also observed, 'From his haunting spirit none could escape .... For good or ill one had to come to terms with him.'

There is, as it happens, part of a happy ending to come out of all this, due to a chance intervention by Fate. The man who succeeded Francis at Barnard Castle died young, and very suddenly. For Francis it was a Divine deliverance. After he had obeyed the paternal will and gone to Elmham, he found that the school was beyond hope. It closed in 1891. So there he was – stuck without a school, without a job, and forced (with brother Henry, another ex-head of a failed school) to give private lessons. And then, at the end of 1893, the extraordinary news arrived from Barnard Castle. He seized the chance, applied for his old job, got it, and remained, a very successful headmaster, till 1924. (And then became rector of – where else? – Little Massingham – successor to brother Henry [1901-17] and brother Philip [1918-24] – till his death in 1942.)

The grandson who supplied much of the above information became a schoolmaster himself, and eventually became a headmaster too – of Gordonstoun. As he said, the old man's influence reached out, well beyond the grave.

Brereton lived to be seventy-eight. But it was clear, before he reached seventy, that much of his work was already in ruins. Some of the county schools barely made it to childhood, never mind maturity. His own foundation, at Elmham, struggled on only to 1891, despite the efforts of his son Francis to give it the kiss of life. (It remains today only as a sign on an Ordnance Survey map – the County School Station. See 'The Game is

Afoot.') The G.C.S.A. – his elaborate scheme for middle-class education for girls – had died in the 1880's. Perhaps his greatest disappointment was the closure of his county college, Cavendish, at Cambridge, in 1892. (It had been given the family name of the Duke of Devonshire, who was Chancellor of the University at the time. Brereton had wanted to name it after Arnold.)

Some of the reasons for these failures have already been indicated. The collapse of Cavendish in particular throws up several more. By now it should go without saying that the finances were unsound. Typically Brereton's dream of 300 students was never fulfilled, so there was not enough fee income, and what there should have been was in arrears. One of the offenders was Brereton himself, who, short of cash as usual, was behind with the payments for his own sons. For the first six years of the college's existence, there were annual deficits. By 1887 the only asset, apart from the buildings (and there was a mortgage on them) was £1,000 in arrears of fees.

There was not enough capital investment either, and shareholders who had trusted him were to find that they often received charming letters of sympathy instead of dividends. One promise that was met, however, was the cheapness of the fees, but the terms were longer than at the University proper, so subsistence allowances had to go further. Fortescue, as an old friend, tried gently to draw Brereton's attention to his shortcomings: 'I have for some time felt a diminishing confidence, not in the soundness of your general views with regard to Middle Class Education, but in your reasonableness in trying to carry them out. You seem to me for some time, especially since your accident, to have resolutely ignored actualities.'

This refers to a train crash in which Brereton was involved in 1882. It is possible that his injuries left a psychological mark, the effect of which was to make worse existing faults in his capacity for judgment – which had not been exactly sober at the best of times.

Brereton reacted predictably. He complained of his friend's 'desertion', and of being 'left to the mercy of traitors and plunderers'. A meeting of dons and directors in 1887 completely re-organised the financial structure of Cavendish; the Duke of Devonshire and Fosters' Bank put in another £5,000 each – a remarkable sign of forbearance and generosity in the face of Brereton's infuriating way of doing business. But there were to be no more dividends; the commercial principle was to be dropped. Brereton, hurt, dismayed, and disgusted, washed his hands of the whole business. They had not invited him to the rescue meeting anyway, quite probably deciding that his absence was the best hope the college had of surviving. Brereton wrote, in one of his many letters on the subject, 'From the bottom of my heart, I protest that I am not the swindler but the swindled.'

For four years more the college struggled on under the control of a new association. New facilities were added to the spartan buildings. But there were still annual deficits, and in 1892 Cavendish College closed. In 1894 it was sold to Homerton College, which for years was to be a teacher training centre for young women. Homerton is now the resting place of thousands of Brereton's letters and papers relating to education. This collection was donated by Canon Philip Lloyd Brereton, yet another of his sons. Here is further witness to his pervasive, and, it seems, permanent, influence on his family. Philip, like his father, had become a clergyman; and he had painstakingly transcribed thousands of letters received by his father over a period of nearly forty years. It is an eloquent testimony to filial devotion.

The weakness and decline of Cavendish can not be explained in terms of finance alone, which might appear to mitigate the case against Brereton, though Heaven knows his poor judgment, lack of planning, and confused methods have a lot to answer for. But he was so intimately bound up with every other aspect of the scheme that, whatever other factor is pinpointed as contributing to failure, some share of the blame falls upon him – despite his oft-repeated recriminations about secrecy and betrayal and deceit. Even in his poetry one finds sentiments like 'such has life been to me, a countering tide of silent opposition'. He almost took refuge behind the wall of obstacles, as he saw it, which so often presented itself.

Take his views on a broad Church. It was praiseworthy, and it was ahead of its time, but it did not attract enough support. Church of England parents thought he was too low, and sectarian parents thought he was too high. These were the days of the Oxford Movement – the resurgence of an Anglo-Catholic church, which struck deep chords of anti-papalism in the psyche of good Anglicans. Anything 'Churchy' was suspect. On the other hand, anything too general and vague would not have the spine to withstand creeping Romishness. There was no room for a middle way of moderation, tolerance, and reason. Brereton could never see that, just because an idea was virtuous, it would not necessarily succeed, no matter how deserving or modern it was.

By the same token, his concept of farmers' sons moving on to his county college simply did not materialise. In 1881, out of the first 142 students, only five were the sons of farmers. The vast majority were from professional backgrounds, attracted possibly by the low fees. The same tendency appeared among Cavendish graduates: over 70% went into the professions – the Church, medicine, education, the law, the Army. The destiny of nearly 30% is unknown. Very few are known to have become businessmen or farmers.

There was, admittedly, a slighter greater admixture of business families in the later years, but the overwhelming impression is that the make-up of the Cavendish student body was, apart from its more tender age, not markedly different from that of the colleges proper. So the very class of people which Brereton hoped most to attract – his 'midmost men' – remained largely unresponsive to his call. Again, the idea, however good or well organised *on paper* – in his endless pamphlets – simply did not work out in practice.

This applied to his schools as well; the farmers, whose offspring he was after, responded to agricultural depression and hard times by making cuts in the one area that they thought they would least miss – the education of their sons. The Great Depression of the 1870's and 1880's cut swathes through the pupil population of the county schools.

So did the rise of other schools whose appearance Brereton so deplored, because it was Government-inspired, because it was a national initiative which went against his precious principle of local self-help. Forster's great Education Act of 1870 offered an attractive alternative for less money – the three R's, Bible and Catechism – and no boarding fees.

Boarding at Cavendish was cheap, certainly, but it was anything but comfortable. Its rooms were so small that special narrow beds had to be made. There was no proper hall, no chapel or library, no proper kitchen or cellars – not in Brereton's time anyway. Perhaps the average student, being younger than the average undergraduate in the other colleges, had less experience of life, and was therefore more long-suffering.

But life as a Cavendish student was by no means all discomfort and penny-pinching. Its position and surroundings were pleasantly rural; there were playing fields. Students could become members of the Union. The college boat was successful on the Cam. As a newcomer, it had to start at the 'bottom of the river'. Races were in fact chases; the boat behind had to catch – to 'bump' – the boat in front. There were two sets of bump races – the 'Lents' and the 'Mays', with four days of racing at each. If a crew caught four of its opponents – made four 'bumps' – each member of the crew was allowed to keep his oar. Most such crewmen had the blade painted with the year, the names of the bumps, and the names of the crew, and kept it for years as a treasured trophy. Francis Brereton won no fewer than four oars. So Cavendish got at least one thing right.

But they were a long way out of town. With such a close-knit society as a university, Cavendish may have been 'in' the river, but they were out of the swim. Many potential students chose to go to the newer city universities, where distances were shorter, and laboratories and lecture rooms were more accessible. There was a body of opinion in Cambridge which regarded the whole Cavendish experiment as pretentious and cheap; put at its worst, it was adolescent bumpkins working for pseudo-degrees and trying to become pseudo-gentlemen. One waspish article described it as a 'butter-substitute turned out cheaply and in a hurry'. . . . 'though its customers may like their margarine in that form, the patrons of the higher butter can scarcely be expected to subsidise its manufacture'. It described the new Cavendish establishment, over a mile out of town down the Hills Road, as an 'isolated brick building which stands like a fever hospital apart from the desolate outskirts of new Cambridge'. . . . 'intended all along to cut off its inmates from the culture of various social contact'.

It was unkind, unfair, and largely untrue, but it was symptomatic of some of the opposition. And it hurt. Brereton retreated to Little Massingham to lick the wounds inflicted on his pride, his integrity, and his bank balance.

All he had left was his Devon County School. The Surrey County (Cranleigh), the Suffolk County (Framlingham), and the North East County (Barnard Castle) – with son Francis at the helm – had all gone their own way by that time.

The scheme for girls' education, the county college plans, Cavendish itself, foundations in Oxford, Gloucester, Dorset, Shropshire, and the rest – they had all gone. Farmers were reeling from a run of shocking harvests and a collapse of agricultural prices largely caused by the massive influx of cheap corn from the vast American prairies and refrigerated meat from New Zealand. His loyalty to the proprietary principle – share capital, self-govern-ment, and dividends – had proved to be misapplied. Self-help was being eroded by increasing Government legislation. Growing millions of people, city life, the extension of the franchise, the march of science, the growth of the press, the spread of the railways, and a host of other features of Victorian life – all were undermining the rural hierarchy and set habits of the life he had grown up in and was trying to perpetuate.

All he could do was to bemoan it. He hated Government 'interference'; he deplored the 'traitors' who met behind his back and changed the organisation of his foundations; if only he had been given more time and more loyalty. . . . He was, quite possibly, jealous of the successes of the educational foundations of his great rival in middle-class education, the Revd. Nathaniel Woodard. He railed at Forster's new elementary schools which were shaping to take away so many of the potential pupils from his county schools. It was all so unfair.

In fact, if West Buckland had not had more than its share of luck – in the shape of Fortescue's generosity – it is more than likely that it too would have gone the way of the rest.

Its very birth was a classic instance of Brereton's methods. On his own admission, it was begun 'without any definite estimate of cost'. (*County*

Education, 1874, p. 11.) If you look at an aerial view of the neighbourhood – over 600 hundred feet up on Exmoor, midway between two remote, tiny villages miles from the main road – you wonder why anyone would want to put a school here of all places. It was typical of Brereton's wild idealism that he saw fit to go ahead with the establishment of 'West Buckland Farm and County School' when he had recruited only three pupils. A young headmaster had been appointed – Joseph Thompson, a graduate of a Yorkshire training college, only twenty-one years old. No fashionable degree, no dog collar. That may have been deliberate, because of Brereton's stated philosophy, but unkind critics insinuated that he was all that Brereton could afford. It is certainly true that Brereton saw West Buckland originally as a third-grade school, with the cheapest fees, and an 'industrial' element to boost income – the 'farm' dimension.

No definite estimate of costs, a headmaster barely out of his teens, an untried business ingredient, and three pupils. It was only then that it seems to have occurred to anybody that they had no school – well, no school buildings. They had to make do with a local farmhouse. After only three weeks of lessons in the parlour, they moved to the sitting room of a house attached to the village elementary school. They moved twice after that – to more farms. Fortescue's father, the second Earl, paid for a barn dormitory. Not till Fortescue, as third Earl, opened the present building in 1861 did they have a permanent home. Within a very short time, it was clear that the idea of the School partially supporting itself with the profits of the farm that the boys were to run as a segment of their education – another of Brereton's bees – was not going to work. The name was quietly shortened to the Devon County School. One way and another, not a very good start.

However, Brereton discovered, perhaps to his surprise, that the fees were coming in so well so that the farm element could be safely dispensed with. The School, amazingly, prospered, and numbers rose swiftly – to about 100 in the first decade, to 150 in the mid-1870's. New buildings were added, and the future looked bright. The results in the new Oxford and Cambridge Local Examinations were among the best in the country – in some years the very best. Headmasters of fashionable public schools visited West Buckland. Thompson hosted a conference of county school headmasters.

The Archbishop of Canterbury (who, as I said, came once to present the prizes) trumpeted its virtues on his other public engagements. The Bishop of Exeter happily went on record to say: 'There is no school in the country which conciliates to itself a larger amount of favourable opinion, and at once disarms hostility more entirely, than this school at West Buckland. I believe that the course here pursued has, at any rate, succeeded in this respect, that it is confessed on all hands that the religious instruction given is really religious, and, on the other hand, I never yet heard of any one who could complain that there was any interference with the rights of conscience whatever.'

Brereton would have been well pleased. He proudly quoted the Bishop's comments in his book *County Education*, published in 1874.

But it did not last. The Great Agricultural Depression referred to above cut into Devon farmers' pockets as much as it did elsewhere. The new primary schools were siphoning away potential pupils. Other schools – Somerset County School (later Wellington) and the Woodard schools (a rival string of new foundations with a distinctly more prescriptive religious tinge to it) – also offered competition. Thompson lost his pension fund in an investment crash; his health broke down, and he had to go abroad for a while. There was a dispute between one of Thompson's successors and the governors in 1899, which resulted in that gentleman's resignation. He took two-thirds of the boys with him when he went off to set up another school in Barnstaple. So, in the year before he died, Brereton had the mortification of seeing his most successful experiment shrinking to 31 pupils, in buildings designed to accommodate over 150. Within half a dozen years, the School came within an inch of closing – twice. It only turned the corner after 1907, with the appointment of a gifted, energetic, and long-staying headmaster, the Revd. Harries.

Survival meant change. Brereton's shade would have had to sit aside and watch a headmaster in holy orders, with a degree, encouraging the teaching of Latin, presiding over a complete change in the School's status (the proprietary nature of it was abolished, and there was a new ingredient in the governing body in the shape of the Devon County Council) – every single one of which he had spent his life denouncing as anathema. The School survived by becoming, to a large extent, what Brereton had set out to avoid.

It is easy to dismiss Brereton, then, as a self-centred visionary, a bully (to his family at any rate), a bumbler (figures on balance sheets were simply chess pieces to be moved around in order to keep the game going), a silver-tongued charlatan who never delivered on his promises, and a serial failure. But this is because the historian has that most perceptive of allies beside his pen – hindsight. With hindsight Brereton's career can be made to look a dreary, unedifying chronicle of broken dreams.

But West Buckland is still there – with about 700 pupils, a campus of 100 acres, clusters of new buildings, a healthy balance sheet, snugly placed in the league tables, and doing quite nicely. For all Brereton's infuriating deficiencies of character, his debts, and his errors, is it fair to deny him any credit at all?

Nobody is perfect, and we all make mistakes. Errors are not the same thing as wrong or misconceived ideas. Brereton's head teemed with ideas, a lot of which would not find many dissidents today – toleration in religion, education for all, a modern curriculum to meet the needs of a modern society, the vital importance of teacher training, provision of facilities equally to north and south.

Again, take his blueprint for a good headmaster. He should have 'a quick and accurate discernment of character'. He should possess 'a true insight into the latent capabilities and subtle peculiarities of his pupils, and of his assistant-masters'. He should have 'moral perception and moral transparency', and 'intellectual penetration, that he should see clearly from surface to principle'. He should have 'readiness of communication', 'physical vigour, or, at least animal spirits'. 'If denseness and cloudiness are a boy's aversion, flatness and dulness [sic] are his abomination.' 'In short, the keen eye, the open countenance, the vigorous presence, to know, to be known, to be felt – these are the qualities of character and intellect which seem to me most requisite in one who is to reign supreme in a boy's world.' (*County Education*, 1874, pp. 91-92.) Granted that such paragons may be rare, that should not deter boards of governors from looking for them today, or at least for the closest possible approximation to them.

Brereton was on to all this. Where he ran into trouble was in persuading people to pay for these highly desirable schemes, and, when the money came in, making them work.

Fund-raisers do not necessarily make the best fund-managers; that is why we have two separate professions for the work today. Anyone who has ever asked a single person for financial support for a cause – even when the money has been promised – knows what a thankless task it is. Yet Brereton worked tirelessly at this most difficult of chores all his life. And there is no denying his charm and his force. As one reads his endless pages of passionate advocacy and detailed plans and bursting enthusiasm and remorseless arithmetic and (apparently) unarguable logic, one is conscious of a faint but definite tug on the cheque book. It all sounds so wonderful; one can understand why well-intentioned peers and princes were persuaded. Here was something practical they could do to improve the lot of their inferiors. Before we smile at their gullibility, we might recall how many times we today have been taken in by mortgage endowment schemes which promised the earth, or insurance policies which appeared to guarantee a lot more medical care than we actually received.

Even now, when we are armed with the knowledge of his failures and his faults of character, we can feel his influence; it reaches out across the yellowing pages and the chasm of the years.

Of course, he had so many worthy causes that anybody could have told him that he had not a hope of realising even a tithe of them. But that did not stop him; his resilience and the obvious thickness of his skin – to say nothing of his charm – seem little short of legendary. Here we come back to the 'Toad' factor again. As early as the second chapter of *The Wind in the Willows*, we have an instance of Toad inveigling his friends into an adventure that the sober Rat could see would probably lead to trouble, or at least to snags and frustration. And, as the Rat had said, it was not as if this was the first time; there had been sailing, punting, house-boating; now it was gypsy caravanning. The final craze, for motor cars, led to all the trouble the Rat had feared – and more. Brereton had the same infectious enthusiasm. Where he differed from Toad was that, whereas Toad gave up his previous passions when he fell upon a new one, Brereton maintained every one of his throughout his life, till old age and massive obstacles forced him into retirement and recrimination in his rectory. Brereton and Toad caused no end of trouble by their impulsiveness, but could always win their friends round with the most charming, and genuine, contrition. It is worth repeating that the people to whom he was the greatest trial – his family – stayed loyal to a man (and to a woman; think of the lives he arguably blighted). It is a tremendous achievement, for all of them.

If you think of *The Wind in the Willows*, it is not Mole, or Rat, or Badger who comes first to mind; it is Toad you think of, first and last. He is the one who drives the plot. Without Toad there would be no plot. Without Brereton there would have been no West Buckland.

Like Toad, Brereton was a beginner, not a finisher. But finishers can do nothing unless someone has started something. What about Fortescue? Was he not interested in education? Was he not in on the ideas at the outset? Did he not provide the land for the School? Did he not come to the rescue time and time again, of both Brereton and the School? Yes, yes, yes, and yes once more.

But, after reading what I have read about these men and their work (and I must admit that I have read more about Brereton than I have about Fortescue), and while trying to give credit where credit is due, I am constrained to suggest that, if Brereton had not been there, Fortescue would not have started it by himself.

It is given to few men to have the spark. Fortescue, for all his tolerance and hard work and sincerity, did not have it; Brereton did. Because Brereton, in the end, failed, history can come up with scores of reasons why he failed, thanks to the great god Hindsight. But supposing he had succeeded. Suppose there hadn't been an Agricultural Depression; suppose there hadn't been an Oxford Movement, which made so many Anglicans, anxious to defend themselves against Romishness, wary of a weak 'broad' Church. Suppose the bike had been invented twenty years earlier, and students had been able to get about Cambridge more easily, and to get in to town from Cavendish in no time at all. Suppose Watson hadn't died at Elmham. Suppose Brereton hadn't been injured in that train crash. Suppose Forster had not brought in his Education Act for another fifteen years, so giving more time for the county schools to become more established.

The books might then have been full of reasons why Brereton had succeeded. But he would have been the same man.

Suppose Jesus had failed. After all, Nazareth was just as much in the back of beyond as West Buckland. If he had failed, the only books about him would have dismissed him as an egotistical, impractical, iconoclastic, unbusinesslike dreamer. (Quite possibly some contemporary writers, deprived of clairvoyance – whose work is now lost to us – did.)

If Brereton's spirit will tolerate this comparison with the Almighty (his daughters would certainly have seen nothing incongruous in it), he shares with Jesus a sort of impossible saintliness that is nothing to do with normal goodness. His daughters, remember, would have put him up there with Jesus on either side of God, so perhaps the comparison is not quite so outrageous as one might think – so long as God has a sense of humour.

Saints and idealists are very difficult people to live with, but the world would be a poorer place without them – though the world, while admiring them, would not fall over itself to have them back. Perhaps this is why the world is so often content to stand by and let its saints become martyrs.

The more one pursues this analogy, the closer it appears to become; one could perhaps make a case that Brereton, having seen the Light about middle-class education, tried to convince endless would-be investors of the Truth of it, and spent his life trying to show the Way. And his Gospel of middle-class education, a broadly practical curriculum, a tolerant creed, and equality for girls would have few dissidents today, any more than Loving Thy Neighbour.

Perhaps we should abandon this line of argument, lest God's sense of humour gives out. Our Lord is, after all, beyond judgment.

But Brereton is not. Even so, let us try – as Jesus would have urged us – to fashion our final verdict out of charity. For all his failures, it is difficult to sneer at a man who devoted his whole life to his dreams. For all his vanity, impracticality, and deviousness, most of which sprang from the urgency of his ideas, it must have been hard for Fortescue to stay furious for long with a man who could write, and mean, that their friendship was 'the salt of my soul'; who could captivate his parishioners with conjuring tricks; who could lay on a free Christmas dinner for 'a large number' of the navvies who were building the new railway line through Filleigh. (These rough men were so grateful that they passed round the hat, collected two guineas – £2.10 – and gave it all for the purchase of a prize to the best footballer in the School each year. This, in 1865, was a considerable sum of money – over twice a labourer's weekly wage. Remember too that navvies were a frightening breed of men; nine people out of ten would have wanted nothing to do with them.)

Let us therefore leave Brereton as Thompson, the first Head, once remembered him. When Thompson retired in 1888, he gave a speech at an Old Boys' Dinner, in which, naturally, he reminisced. One scene he recalled with particular fondness was a visit he made with Brereton to the parcel of land that Fortescue had offered to them for the new School. He remembered the two of them – himself a young man barely into his twenties, Brereton only in his mid-thirties – scrambling over the tussocks of grass, deciding where they were going to put their new buildings.

They were going to design and build a whole new school, of a wholly new type, with a completely new aim and ethos. And there was the open land, up on the windswept hill. The very air must have been intoxicating. Can you not imagine them, like two small boys with a building set?

'We'll have the hall here. . . . The foundation stone? Oh, there, I think, beside the main entrance. . . . How many stables, would you say? . . . . Kitchens near a well, of course. . . . Separate housing for all the oil lamps – stone built, against fire. . . . '

Just like Toad with his gypsy caravan. . . . 'Soda water here – baccy there – letter paper, bacon, jam, cards and dominoes. . . . . Nothing whatever has been forgotten. . . . '[1]

---

[1] I am indebted for much of the material in this piece to Professor John Honey's book – *Tom Brown's Universe* [Millington Books Ltd., 1977], and to Mr. Peter Searby's two articles on Brereton – *Joseph Lloyd Brereton and the Education of the Victorian Middle Class* – Journal of Educational Administration and History, XI, 1979; and *A Failure at Cambridge: Cavendish College, 1877-1892* – Proceedings of the Cambridge Antiquarian Society, LXXII, 1982-3. Plus of course Brereton's own essays, in particular *County Education*, published in 1874. The School still has in its possession Brereton's two Year Books, of 1857 and 1860. Two centenary books from West Buckland School and Barnard Castle School have provided other facts and anecdotes; so have the School Archive, John Edmunds' *History of West Buckland School*, and other general reading, including census information from the Internet.

Despite Brereton's tireless work and long life, his teeming ideas (often ahead of his time), his surviving educational monuments, the many sides to his character, the innumerable pies he had his finger in, and not least the enormous collection of his papers held at Homerton College and in the Norwich Record Office, it is an odd fact that he still awaits a biographer.

15. Heads and Tails

Going Before a Fall?

Examiners produce reports on the examination they have just finished conducting. The Syndicate of the University of Cambridge duly did their duty with regard to the 'Local' examinations of 1868. The *Register* predictably pounced on any individual mention of West Buckland, and proudly printed it, even at the expense of other schools. A splendid self-righteous sideswipe came in the reference to the examination of the Church Catechism:

> 'At very few centres did it appear that good explanations of the Catechism or of Christian doctrine had been given to candidates by their masters. At Cambridge, Norwich, and West Buckland the work was well done; from Bristol, Dorchester, and York, the papers were very feeble.'

[Hang your heads in shame, teachers and candidates of Bristol, Dorchester, and York.]

Deep Waters

Here is a project topic for an 'A' Level candidate in Psychology.

The present and the previous School Bursar both served, during their naval years, in submarines. Not much in that, you may say.

But when one adds that a previous Headmaster, Lt.-Comd. Westall, also served in submarines, during the First World War, the coincidence begins to get a little stretched. (As a matter of interest, too, Westall was present at Gallipolli – where he was torpedoed – and at the Battle of Jutland – *Register* No. 215, Nov., 1934, p. 206.)

Before I proceed to the point, here is another coincidence. Westall, who was born in 1900, was educated, as one would expect young naval cadets to be educated, at Osborne and Dartmouth. And who was a teacher at both Osborne and Dartmouth during the first decades of the century? William Stradling, possibly the most brilliant pupil and sportsman the School produced during its first fifty years.

Was that how Westall first heard about West Buckland? Did Stradling first suggest it to him? If he did, that makes him not only the best all-rounder the School produced in its first half-century, but the best salesman.

Or – and here is my point at last – is there some subconscious vibration among governors that makes them respond to submarines? What do Adler, Freud, and Jung have to say about hidden depths and still waters? Does being cooped up close to your fellow-humans in a submarine mysteriously fit you well for coping with being cooped up with several hundred young people and a batch of staff in a remote school miles from anywhere?

All sorts of theories and philosophical superstructures could be conjured out of research like this. Such a project, if it is well done, could well raise the candidate's overall grade by a full class. Think about it.

A really resourceful candidate could build a whole post-graduate career on it, so long as he had the gift of the gab and appeared on the right chat shows and was seen at the right conferences. Books filled with phrases like 'bathymetric depression medians', 'ratios of human relativity', and 'proximity coefficients' could baffle the average reviewer, bewitch the average education minister, and drive to despair any teacher with a grain of common sense or three months of experience. Such a researcher would become a professor of education at thirty, and could retire to a profitable life on quangos (or is it 'quangoes'?) and visiting lectureships before he was forty. At fifty he could return to the real world as an inspector, and find out the full extent of the damage he had been causing in the previous twenty years.

Doubling Up

On 6th January, 1918, the Revd. F.G. Harries got married at St. John's Church, Clifton, to Ann, youngest daughter of Mr. and Mrs. C.M. Bendall, of Redland Park, Bristol. His brother, the Revd. E.C. Harries, Headmaster and Chaplain of West Buckland School, officiated.

On 21st August, 1918, the Revd. E.C. Harries got married at St. John's Church, Clifton, to Eleanor, second daughter of Mr. and Mrs. C.M. Bendall, of Redland Park, Bristol. His brother, the Revd. F.G. Harries, Rector of West Buckland, officiated.

Among the Old Boys present were two brothers of the bride. One of them, Sidney Bendall, had been Head Boy in 1907. The Headmaster indeed admitted at the reception that he had made the acquaintance of Sidney Bendall's family on the School cricket field nearly twenty years before.

Harries had a trick of notching up unusual achievements. Firstly, not all that many headmasters committed matrimony at the age of fifty, or were lucky enough to secure the affections of a young woman eighteen years their junior. Secondly, even fewer indulged the habit of including their mother in School Staff photographs, or of placing her picture as the frontispiece of the School magazine. Thirdly, it must be a rare venture into paternity to produce twin sons, as Harries did, in his early to mid-fifties.

And finally, the list cannot be very long of headmasters who have married the sister of a previous head boy. How far back in those near-twenty years had the first of Cupid's arrows begun to fly? Or had Miss Bendall's arrival on the Staff only three months before thrown her charms suddenly into greater relief? Or – indeed – had her arrival on the staff been engineered by the Headmaster so as to facilitate his wooing?

Fundamental Insulation

Whenever they plan to change, modify, or abolish – or even when they only criticise – features of venerable institutions which are outworn, outmoded, inefficient, or just plain old, you can always find a champion of them, no matter how outworn, outmoded, inefficient, or old those features are.

At a recent gathering of Old Members, someone was remarking that perhaps it was time that the stone stairs in the main building were due for pensioning off – dusty, worn down in the middle, unsightly, and a deathtrap to the unwary.

One veteran of numerous canings from pre-War days leapt to their defence. He claimed that they were a perfect resource for those who knew they were due for correction. One sat on them, with the trousers (or pyjamas – boys in Harries' day had to present themselves for caning in pyjamas, to prevent books being secreted in the correct spot) drawn tightly across the buttocks, and allowed the cold of the stone to penetrate right into the – um – fundament. When a suitable degree of numbness had been achieved, the owner of the buttocks rushed to present himself for punishment.

Magisterial Marksmanship

Caning was not just a matter of swinging a wand of whippy wood. Seasoned survivors became connoisseurs of a master's skill in such matters. A poor practitioner could leave marks across a boy's body from his middle thighs right up to the small of his back. But the Revd. Harries, it seems, was a virtuoso – a man of rare skill in the business of administering punishment as he was in so many other departments of inter-war schoolmastering. As one veteran of the Bend-Over Brigade recalled, 'That man could give you six of the best, and leave only one weal. One weal.' (But just think what it was like *while it was happening*.)

16. Chope's Choice

Richard Pearse Chope must have been a great force in the School during his life. He entered in 1874, won prizes and distinctions galore, became Head Boy, and left in a cloud of glory to go up to read Maths at Trinity College, Cambridge. His achievements and impact on the School and on Devon life are recorded elsewhere in this book (see 'Lorna Doone at West Buckland'). He is mentioned again here because of his devotion to the cause of General Knowledge; as already explained, he compiled an annual General Knowledge Test Paper, to be taken by candidates from the School who wished to be considered for his General Knowledge Prize presented each year at Speech Day. Such was his influence with the authorities that this question paper was regularly printed in the *Register* for years (whether for entertainment or enlightenment is not made clear). The editors finally wriggled out of it in about 1920.

The questions, when cast today into the searching light of modern thought and idiom, may well strike the reader as a trifle dusty, but knowledge goes in fashions like anything else, and what one generation sees as vital information another will ignore as irrelevant trivia.

Whatever the criteria, the test paper that follows is a terrifying testimony to the standard of general knowledge that Chope considered, if not indispensable, at least desirable in the well-educated boy. It demonstrates too that highly intelligent polymaths are often up in a mental stratosphere of their own; they do not realise the extent to which processes and accomplishments that they consider routine present enormous difficulties to lesser mortals. Moreover, we do not know what Chope's marking methods were, and we do not know how many per cent the winner of the prize actually scored (if indeed the omniscient Mr. Chope ever told anybody).

Present readers might care to try these questions for themselves. They all come from the paper he set for the Chope Prize of 1916. (Remember, it was half way through the First World War.)

I offer it complete with Chope's precise, even finicky punctuation – but at least you know what he meant.

General Knowledge (Paper Set For The Chope Prize, 1916.)

1.- Sketch the ground plan of a house suitable for your Head Master.

2.- Why are the Germans commonly called Huns? What is the difference between Hun and Boche?

3.- Explain the following phrases: (a) The thin red line; (b) The green-eyed monster; (c) The sere and yellow leaf; (d) Born in the purple; (e) A bolt from the blue.

4.- What do you know of any *five* of the following persons: General Serrail, General Smuts, Sir William Robertson, Sir Douglas Haig, McKenna, Von Mackensen, Henry James, Thomas Hardy, Edith Cavell, Clara Butt?

5.- Give the names of (a) ten wild fruits, *or* (b) ten wild birds, *or* (c) ten freshwater fish – used for food.

6.- (a) In what language was each of the following written, and who was its author: Don Quixote, Utopia, Vathek, Il Penseroso, Sartor Resartus?

Or (b) What authors used the following pseudonyms: George Eliot, Lewis Carroll, Peter Pindar, Mark Twain, Carmen Sylva? Name one work of each.

7.- The late Lord Avebury used to tell how he walked from the House with a well-known M.P. across St. James's Park one beautiful moonlight night. "I wonder," speculated his companion, "if we shall ever know how it is that the moon so constantly changes its shape. I suppose that is one of the things we can never hope to know." Can *you* explain?

8.- Name the sources of any *five* of the following quotations, and correct the wording in the selected examples:

(a) To-morrow to fresh fields and pastures new.

(b) Falleth as the gentle dew from heaven.

(c) There's many a gem that's born to blush unseen,

And waste its fragrance on the desert air.

(d) Just cause and impediment.

(e) Small by degrees, and beautifully less.

(f) A man convinced against his will,

Is of the same opinion still.

(g) Wheresoever the body is, there will the eagles be gathered together.

(h) A beggarly array of empty bottles.

(i) When Greek meets Greek, then comes the tug of war.

(j) All that glitters is not gold.

9.- Comment on the following: (a) "Germanism, originally a necessary reaction after Germany's defeats in the Napoleonic Wars, became a chauvinistic obsession, bringing with it a false racial policy based on Germanistic megalomania."

Or *(b)* "If you invest in Exchequer Bonds, your money, capital and interest, is secured on the Consolidated Fund of the United Kingdom, the premier security of the world."

10.- What striking events have taken place during the past year at Anzac, Verdun, Kut-el-Amara, Erzerum, Salonika?

11.- *(a)* A tuck-woman came to the School with apples, of which she sold 50 at two a penny and 60 at three a penny. As the former took longer to sell than the latter, the next week she sold the same number of apples at the average price of five for twopence, but she found she got less money for them. How do you account for this?

Or *(b)* Having a square piece of red cloth, how would you cut it to form the badge of the Red Cross Society, without waste and with the least amount of seaming?

12.- Punctuate the following:-

a)   Every lady in the land
      Hath twenty nails upon each hand
      Five and twenty on hands and feet
      This is true without deceit.

b)   It was and I said not that.

c)   That that is is that that is not is not that is it is it not.

13.- Samuel Johnson observed: "That man is little to be envied whose patriotism would not gain force upon the plain of Marathon, or whose piety would not grow warmer among the ruins of Iona." Explain the full significance of this observation.

14.- Explain *five* of the following terms: Irredentism, Individualism, Contraband of War, Censorship of the Press, Kultur, Guerrilla Warfare, Duma, Reichstag, Trade Mark, Preferential Tariff.

15.- What is the difference between an Act of Parliament and an Order in Council?

16.- What countries are the chief producers of coffee, cocoa, rubber, tin and copper?

17.- Explain the allusions in the following quotations:-

(a) Our Jason has sowed the Field of Ares with dragons' teeth to some purpose, and his crop of armed men is thicker than even the most enthusiastic of our friends ever imagined we could raise. – *The Globe.*

(b) The iron of human destiny is hot in the Vulcan's stithy of the war.- *The Observer.*

[I suspect even Mr. Chope has slipped up here – doesn't he mean 'smithy'?]

> *(c)* A caravan leader needs the arms of a Briareus, and the sleepless vigilance of an Argus. – *Life of Bishop Hannington.*

Any boy who came top in this exercise richly deserved his Chope Prize.

Lest it be thought by his readers that he was nothing but a stuff-shirt, Mr. Chope also caused to be printed the more random, and therefore more entertaining, answers that his questions had provoked. One wonders, though, whether his sense of humour was more the lofty smile of the superior pedant rather than the hearty guffaw of the fair-minded sympathiser. Or it may be that such inaccuracies gave him some pain, because he observed more than once, with a twinge of distress, that such-and-such a piece of knowledge should have been part of the mental armoury of most educated boys (though, to be fair, he did see the funny side now and then).

Nevertheless, a few examples will show that the schoolboy's genius for getting something so very nearly right or unbelievably wrong has shone brightly down the ages:

> 'The Germans are called Huns because the word Hun in the German language means "a pig", which they are supposed to be like.' [Well, it was during the First World War.]

> ' "Born in the purple." The phrase seems to me to have a tincture of slang in it [tincture!], perhaps an abominable Americanism or modernism of some type.' [Clearly the writer was going to have a full future writing complaining letters to the *Times.*]

> 'Cologne is famous for the odour made there.'

> 'Kultur is an ironic name for German brutality.' [The War again.]

> 'Florence Nightingale is one of the greatest singers of the day.'

> 'Blanc-mange is a powder used for making a desert.' [Gobi the instructions on the tin?]

> 'The armadillo lives chiefly in trees, travelling upside down.' [Australian, naturally.]

> 'Cheese is a hard, non-greasy substance, and can be eaten alone, if possible.' [By consenting adults?]

> 'Australia exports wine to England, made from a bird called the emu.' [Well, it makes a change from sweaty saddles and gooseberry stalks.]

> 'A suffragette is a person who wants women. . . . to have a hand in everything and anything.' [Chope himself was constrained to remark that the writer had shown 'unusual political insight'.]

'Belladonna is the same as prima donna, but it is generally applied to old ladies.' [This, as Chope observed, 'hints at a knowledge of artificial aids to beauty that one would hardly expect in a schoolboy'.]

'Kismet is the Mahomedan Bible.'

'A blue-book is a book with a green cover.' [Which shows that the schoolboy's contempt for logic was, and still is, as healthy as ever.]

'A stockbroker is a man who deals with cattle.' [A good old Devon opinion.]

'A refugee is a man who keeps order at a football match.' [Still, alas, true.]

Chope's General Knowledge Prize survived until the Second World War, and reappeared afterwards (well, 1947) in the guise of the Carter General Knowledge Prize. It continued until 1965, when, apparently, it died. There is no mention of it in 1966 or thereafter. But we know the very last winner – R.M. Clarke, in 1965. It must have done him some good – all that encyclopaedic revision; in the entry about him in the *Register* when he left, it says he won an Open Scholarship to Hertford College, Oxford.

The late Mr. Chope would have felt well pleased – and vindicated.

But he didn't have the last word. In 1917, the *Register* printed a parody of the notorious General Knowledge Paper, which showed that not everybody took Chope totally seriously. This parody is attributed to a Mr. Inniss, a member of staff. He came from Trinidad, and in 1915 went back to teach there. This piece did not surface till two years later, but I bet it had already done the rounds of the Common Room, maybe even the Board of Governors and the Old Boys.

MAJOR-GENERAL KNOWLEDGE

1.- On a piece of paper, 6 by 5 inches square, describe an imaginary line, using no instruments. Find its area, and make one 27/8 times as large.

2.- Which would you rather, or go fishing?
(Marks will be given in accordance with the votes.)

3.- What is the exact difference between: a bobolink and a bob a day; antipon and antimacassar; a lac of rupees and a lack of cash; a fisherman and a lyre-bird; a fagocite and the sight of a fag.

4.- Point out any cases of anachronism, hydrophobia, or electrolysis in the following poem of Shakespeare:-

" 'Tis sweet to watch the rosy dawn
Echo across the deep;
When the crystal song of the roses bright
Hushes the rocks to sleep.

"When the blood-red moon, in the blaze of noon,

Is bathed in a crumbling dew,
And the wolf rings out, with a glittering shout,
To-wit, to-wit, to-woo.' "

5.- Either *(a)* Give the life-story of a tiddlywink;
Or *(b)* Describe the growth of a grain of common sense.

6.- Why is a mouse when it spins?
(Plain "Yes" or "No" will not be accepted as an answer.)

7.- Calculate the amount of water displaced in the School bath at 0 degrees and 760mm., when a fat boy, aged 16 years 216¼ days enters, reckoning 1760 yards = 1 mile, £1 = 25 francs, and the atomic weight of a flea = 3.24½ .

8.- Either *(a)* Translate the Japanese irrational motto, "O! Watta Nasa? Yâm!" and compare its weight with that of the London Scottish proverb, "Scots wa' hae!"

Or *(b)* Give a history (with translation) of the famous dictum of the Russian poet, Sneeztwysoffski: "Sanitas, sanitorium, omnibus sanatogen."

9.- Explain the following terms: caterpillary attraction; the twelve signs of the Cognac: parallelogram of velocipedes; the force of gravy; acrobatic scales and archipelagoes (in music); total eclipse of a moving point.

10.- Explain and criticise the following proverbs:-

1) A hair in the head is worth two in the brush.

2) One swallow does not make a drink.

3) All is not banana that fritters.

Let us hope that Mr. Chope had the good grace to crack a smile at all this.

17. Drawing a Veil

In the Governors' Minutes for January, 1936, the Bursar 'called attention to customs and privileges that had grown up and were not in the best interests of the school'. He suggested that the Governors might consider their 'discontinuance'. It was arranged that the Headmaster should report on them at the next meeting.

The Headmaster duly did so, in February. He said he had investigated the matter, and had found that 'the privileges referred to' had come about 'in quite a legitimate manner but had now ceased'.

What on earth were they talking about? A protection racket run by the prefects? A private racing syndicate in the Common Room? A distillery in the Chemistry lab? The Headmaster's *droit de seigneur* over the new serving girls in the kitchen?

Perhaps not, since the Headmaster did say that the 'customs and privileges' had arisen in a 'legitimate manner'. Legitimate. So that would appear to cut out the above options. But think: if the Minutes had said not 'legitimate' but 'natural', then that might have made any of those options a by no means illogical answer. As Holmes often said, 'When you have eliminated the impossible, whatever remains, however illogical, could be the truth.' An entertaining line of speculation for an after-dinner circulation of the port.

Of course, life is not as spicy as that, and the real answer is going to be pretty mundane. But, if the genesis of these 'customs and privileges' *was* so legitimate and beyond reproach, why this delicacy and reticence about providing any solid detail?

18. Bolt from the Blue

Well, from the 'black', actually. All this began at night. It must have been a stinker too – dark as a bag (as they say round here), blowing hard, raining cats and dogs, and a terrific thunderstorm. Sheep were killed. Lightning struck the Bursar's house. A tree or two came down.

This happened towards the end of 1936. At least that is the recollection of a lady who was a little girl of about nine or ten at the time. If not the exact date, the drama of the event is fixed in her memory because of what happened the next morning. The groundsman gave her a little metallic ball, nearly three centimetres in diameter. He had found it in the middle of the games field, at the end of a large seam of burnt grass. It was, he told her, a thunderbolt. He showed her where it had come down. She was, understandably, tremendously impressed.

The 'thunderbolt' became one of her most treasured possessions, cherished and guarded through the years. It was not until she read the first of these books about the history of West Buckland that she decided to relinquish it. Now that the School had an Archive, she felt that the School was the proper repository for such a 'rare relic'.

The little girl in the story was – is – Vyvyan Westall (now Lindsay), who was one of the daughters of the then Headmaster, Lt.-Comd. R.V.H. Westall. (She and her sister, incidentally, were the first girl pupils at the School; their father made special arrangements with the Governors for them to be educated with the boys.)

Young Vyvyan took her thunderbolt to the Natural History Museum. It was examined by the 'top man' in the relevant department. He told her that it was not a meteorite, but a piece of haematite. Haematite, apparently, is a natural North Devon mineral.

That might have disposed of the 'alien body' theory, for the time being at any rate, but it did not explain why a lump of haematite came to be lying in the middle of the rugby field of a West Country school after a thunderstorm. Had some rare disturbance of the earth, caused maybe by a lightning strike, thrown up this object from below the ground? If so, what was it? It was remarkably spherical. Was it a relic of some firearm from the Civil War? It looked too small for a cannon and too large for a musket. And in any case the chances of seventeenth-century soldiers drilling – much less fighting – on the outskirts of a lonely Exmoor village seemed pretty remote.

Was it a slingshot? Again, unlikely. Slingshot was medieval, if not Roman, and would have been buried much deeper than Civil War detritus. Could some enterprising young amateur archaeologist have dug it up? Some bespectacled little swot who was being bullied by a boorish ruggernaut from the First XV? And had our archaeologist challenged him to a midnight duel on the field of his opponent's greatest triumphs, so that he could the better savour his coming victory? Had that Goliath of the second row received his comeuppance from the slingshot of the David of the Second Form, while the Heavens laid on a suitable backdrop of thunder and lightning? No, perhaps not. But what a scenario!

Vyvyan was left with no explanation, but she did still have her storm story and her thunderbolt. Both were precious to her, and it was with this in mind that I embarked on further enquiry.

The first step was the School magazine. I found no reference to the storm, much less to a thunderbolt.

The next step was the Common Room. As I have said elsewhere, one of the great strengths of a common room in a secondary school is that, whatever the subject you bring up, there is somebody there who will know something about it, or who can put you on the right track to the answer you are looking for. A physics colleague took it away for a look, came back, and told me that at least it was not magnetic. Haematite is magnetic. So – the mystery deepened. Was it haematite or not?

Which opened up a further possible problem: if the Natural History Museum was wrong in saying that it was haematite, could it also have been wrong in saying that it was *not* a meteorite?

So the story began to sprout as many bristles as the chin of a stormbound gold prospector. Was there any reason why it could not be a meteorite? Do meteorites fall during thunderstorms? Can meteorites *cause* thunderstorms? For that matter, can thunderstorms cause meteorites, by sort of loosening up the heavens and allowing them to fall? What shape is your average meteorite? Could this one have been somehow sucked up by the storm somewhere else and dropped on the rugby pitch? What was the incidence of meteorites in North Devon? Was it possible that the storm and the 'meteorite' were quite separate happenings, and their joint arrival a gigantic coincidence? And what another coincidence that the groundsman should come across such a small object in such a wide expanse.

Now there was somebody else I could ask, but the trouble was that his answers might be too truthful. And you know the old saying: never ask a question if you are not prepared to face the answer. I had been entrusted with this 'rare relic', which had once been the treasured possession of a little girl, who, now a grown lady, still naturally had a great fondness for it. How would she react if the 'truth' were to be told that it was a valueless, nondescript chunk of metal that just happened to be lying around? And should I take the risk of letting it out of the care of the Archive, just after it had been entrusted to me by its fond, long-time owner?

Luckily, Alan Rogers, Systems Manager in the IT Department, is interested in this sort of thing; he is immensely knowledgeable; and, because of his passion for all things meteorological, I knew he would understand and take great care of it. However, his first two answers delivered a knock to the romantic superstructure of the story. Firstly, he said, there is no such thing as a thunderbolt; it is merely the popular generic term applied to a lightning strike which causes damage. Secondly, there is no way that a bolt of lightning can bring down a meteorite.

On the other hand – by way of shoring up that superstructure again – a meteorite *could*, by its passage through a storm cloud, provide a line of least resistance for a bolt of lightning to travel.

Alan did some straightforward measurements. It was pretty regularly spherical, it weighed about 48 grams, it bore some grooving of about 1 mm. depth, and its approximate density was 4.35gm/cc. It was dark brown to black to look at, and it had a dull gloss finish. The groove, when gently scratched, revealed a surface of a lighter, slightly rusty colour. It was a non-conductor and early tests showed it to be non-magnetic.

Alan then showed it to some 'experts', who suggested alarmingly that the best way to find out what it was to break it in half! Mindful of his responsibility for guarding it with great care, he declined the offer. The same experts, however, did not think it was a meteorite, largely because meteorites 'don't look like that'. Which does not sound very scientific.

Well, if it wasn't a meteorite, what was it? They didn't know. Theories ranged from 'a lump of ore – haematite' to 'a fossilised sea urchin' and 'medieval munitions'.

Alan knew that it was twice the density of ordinary rock – which seemed to dispose of the sea urchins – but it was of less density than metals – which removed the 'munitions' idea. Its density pretty well matched that of haematite, so we were back to the haematite again. Unfortunately, haematite is weakly magnetic, and so far Alan had found no magnetic qualities present.

He resorted to the Internet. There he discovered various kinds of haematite, one of which is Black Botryoidal Haematite (also known as Kidney Ore). He came up with a picture of a piece, which, though much bigger, showed an amalgam of nodules protruding from a central mass, each one of which looked remarkably similar to 'our thunderbolt'. But – and the problem arose again – haematite is magnetic, and, if 'our thunderbolt' was haematite, why wasn't it magnetic?

Back to the bench. Alan refined his tests, which involved rolling small cylindrical magnets across sheets of glass with and without the 'thunderbolt'. Presto – it was indeed magnetic! Fine – it was haematite and it was magnetic. But what connection did it have with the storm? Then Alan remembered an article he had seen in the *Journal of Meteorology* in 1997. There, in discussing the damage caused by a lightning strike to a water main and surrounding electrical equipment, it was stated that lightning travelling through the ground can create tunnels and throw quite large stones considerable distances. Moreover, as 'our thunderbolt' is magnetic, it could have interacted further with the intense electromagnetic field produced by the lightning and been thrown a very long way indeed. Which in turn could explain why it landed in the middle of a games field, and why, as it was so hot, it caused burn marks when it landed.

So how much is left of 'our thunderbolt'? Well, it is no meteorite, it would appear. And it didn't come down on the sharp end of a bolt of lightning. Nor did it cause the bolt of lightning. It is haematite, and it is magnetic. And it could have come from almost anywhere.

Now, if you go back to the original story that young Vyvyan picked up, you will see that that is pretty much what she was told by the Natural History Museum – no meteorite, and haematite. So she might well conclude that, after all that fuss and theorising, we are back to square one. Maybe.

But it has been an interesting quest, and Mrs. Lindsay (as she now is) is still left with most of her memories. There was definitely one hell of a storm. The sheep are still dead. The Bursar's house still copped it. The 'thing' was still there, the groundsman still found it, and there were still the burn marks. A little girl still opened her eyes in wonder, she still took away her 'thunderbolt', and she still treasured it all those years until now.

And, if Alan Rogers' theory is correct, the real explanation of how it got there is every bit as remarkable as the thunderbolt and meteorite theories. It is unlikely that violent thunderstorms cause hundreds of chunks of rock to go whizzing about all over the place, but that is not the point. It is the very rarity of such an occurrence which gives it the drama.

We still have a tremendous storm; we still have a piece of haematite thrown a possibly huge distance by the violent action of a strike of lightning. That little ball of ore could have dropped to earth like a bolt from a heavenly sling just as the clouds rolled and the thunder crashed.

We still have 'our thunderbolt', and we intend to keep it.[2]

---

[2] [I am indebted to Mrs. Vyvyan Lindsay for her reminiscences, and for her thunderbolt, and to Mr. Alan Rogers for permission to quote from his article in the *Journal of Meteorology* for September, 2001.]

19. Penny Packets

Charles Royle Penny came to the School in 1920 and left in 1927. Seventy years later he had printed a small collection of reminiscences of his life, and there was a section in it about West Buckland. I include here a little fistful of gems from the treasury of his long memory.

Any Complaints?

A permanent component of breakfast in Harries' time (1907-1934) – and, I suspect, long before and after – was porridge. It was 'very often lumpy, with scant milk or sugar'. One morning, a boy objected so strongly to this pile of damp concrete on his plate that he took it up with him to complain to the Headmaster, who was himself breakfasting at the masters' table on the dais.

Whatever he was expecting, it was certainly not what he got: without uttering a word, Harries 'took his plate and in exchange gave him his own'.

Dripping with Cholesterol

A regular accompaniment to the inexorable porridge at breakfast between the wars was 'toast and dripping piled up on plates in the centre of the table'. Since each boy was entitled to two slices, there was a lot of spreading to be done in the kitchen. 'This was neatly if roughly accomplished' first by dipping the toast into a huge galvanised bowl of melted dripping, and then by scraping the toast on the edge of the bowl. (Enough to give a modern health expert heart failure, to say nothing of generations of boys. And yet they thrived. No doubt the layers of dripping provided welcome insulation against the rigours of the unheated dormitories and washrooms.)

The Show Must Go On

In the annual performances of Gilbert and Sullivan operas, which Harries championed for so many years, there were never any understudies. (Yet another testimony to the rude health of the inmates.) 'Harries' insurance against coughs and colds was a nightly administered dose of cod liver oil and malt by Mrs. Harries (Nellie) in the Headmaster's kitchen on our way to bed.'

Deus ex Machina

For the School's annual Gilbert and Sullivan productions, the skills of the woodwork teacher, Mr. Adelbert Taylor ('Judy' Taylor, because he had a voice like Mr. Punch) were much in demand. . . .

'In *The Gondoliers*, the Duke of Plazatoro (C.M. Bere – physics and chemistry), the Duchess (Ma Walmsley [one of the first lady teachers]) and their daughter Casilda (myself), plus a gondolier complete with oar (I forget who) make their first act entrance in a gondola. . . . Judy Taylor . . . . had made a beautiful silhouette of a gondola cut out of thick plywood. This was screwed to the side of a 9" x 3" plank on which we had to stand. The plank, in turn, was supported on two small rubber-tyred piano trolleys, one fore and one aft, and a rope was fixed to the fore end of the plank. The whole mechanism was invisible to the audience, being obscured by a low parapet wall which was part of the scenery. From the other side of the stage in the wings, it was then Cockram's job [William Cockram – 'Bill' if you prefer – a long-serving member of the maintenance staff – see pp. 36 & 38.] to pull on this rope and thus sail us into full view of the audience.

Unfortunately, due to inevitable inertia and the not inconsiderable weight of four people, he could not get the thing started, without giving it an almighty jerk. This he did to some purpose and, to the great delight of the whole audience, toppled us all into the Grand Canal.'

Luckily, it was only a dress rehearsal, and Judy Taylor had time to salvage the situation by a system of pulleys, 'which enabled Cockram to make us a very smooth entrance to the applause of the audience'.

Bringing Colour into Music

'Sunday morning service at East Buckland was enlivened by the occasional festival like Confirmation. Also I remember Judy Taylor [the organist] displaying his purple socks when he reached with his foot a pedal placed high up on the organ.'

Not Quite Drake's Drum

'In classroom 3b (below the woodwork room) hanging on the wall at the opposite end to the teacher's desk and dais was a large framed print of an engraving of Francis Drake on his flagship, prior to some battle or other. Drake had his back to the viewer and was bending over to talk to members of his crew, who were sitting on the deck around him.

'One of the boys. . . . had acquired from somewhere an old broken billiard cue, and he was larking about with this, prodding other boys and simulating use of it as a javelin. Suddenly. . . . he caught sight of Francis Drake.

' "How's this for Drake's bum?" he shouted. . . . launching his missile at the target, which he hit fair and square.'

[The glass shattered, and his punishment was 'severe'.]

20. Tried and Tested

As many Devon villages in the nineteenth century enjoyed the facilities of more than one public house, it is doubtful whether the phrase 'the local' would have been much in use in that context; one would not have known which was being referred to. Conversely, around West Buckland School, at any rate after about 1860, the phrase 'the Locals' was very much in use, but it meant something completely different.

The School, remember, was founded in 1858. As it began to grow, it must have exercised the minds of the Headmaster, the founders, and the directors, how they could best enhance the School's reputation and standing in relation to other schools in the South-West, indeed in the whole country. One way was to enter its pupils for a new type of examination, which, coincidentally, had also been set up in 1858. If their pupils could perform well in competition with candidates from these other schools, it could provide welcome ammunition for the Headmaster's report to his directors, and welcome copy for insertion in the next edition of the School Prospectus.

In these days of Key Stage examinations, 16-plus examinations (GCSE), 17-plus examinations ('A-S' Level), and 18-plus examinations (the 'normal' 'A' Level), league tables and comparative performances, such a strategy would seem quite normal. We all turn to examination performance as a ready barometer of a school's worth. No matter how much headmasters may deplore the publicity given to league tables, the fact remains that they offer the immediate attraction to the media, and in turn to the public, of apparent accuracy, and, therefore, reliability. Useless to point out that they do not reflect the percentage of the pupils entered, or the rate of improvement of the average pupil, or the selectivity of the school's entrance policy, and a host of other relevant factors (whole books have been written about this controversy); the fact remains that a school is 279th in the table, or whatever. And it was 218th last year. Therefore it is slipping – Q.E.D. Perception is all, or nearly all.

This universal regard of placing in the league table did not apply in the mid-nineteenth century. This was not because people then did not mind so much about a school's position in the exam league table; it was because the whole principle of examinations themselves was only just beginning to win any kind of acceptance at all.

Indeed, the more you look at it, the more surprising it becomes that so many institutions and ideas relating to education have embedded themselves so deeply in the nation's subconscious, and so quickly; it takes an effort of the imagination to realise that they have a relatively short history.

Even the principle of education itself – for the whole nation – goes back barely further than the history of West Buckland School – that is, about a hundred and fifty years. A national system of primary education goes back only to the 1870's, a system of secondary education only to 1902, a fraction over a century. The rest of the familiar structure – a minister of education, a national inspectorate, a nationwide network of teacher training colleges, county education committees – all these are about the same age too, give or take a decade or so.

What about the universities – what about Oxford and Cambridge? What about the venerable public schools? The ancient town grammar schools? Do they not go back centuries? Yes, of course they do. And that is the trick. Because they *are* so old, and because they *look* so old, and so permanent, we tourists who walk round them, or we proud parents who send our offspring to study in them, make the leap of unreason to assume that everybody who had the money, or the enterprise, or the brains, or the luck, could send their children to schools wherever they may have happened to live, going right back to the Middle Ages.

Well, some of them might have done, but they were in a distinct minority. One must remember too that in past centuries, the population – of all social classes put together – was a very small percentage of what it is today, and the number of schools and universities then was a still smaller one. While the nineteenth century saw the population leaping up decade by decade (it trebled between 1800 and 1900), it did not see a comparable spread of schools, or, therefore, of universities; and the existing universities, and the public and grammar schools, were not especially interested in educating the swarming inhabitants of the industrial city ghettoes. Nor, incidentally, were the parents in these ghettoes very interested in sending their children to any kind of school; they needed them to earn money climbing down mine shafts to work ventilation shutters or crawling under moving machines to clean them. When the Newcastle Commission made its report in 1861, most children were leaving school at eleven (if they had ever attended in the first place), and among the poorer classes only one in twenty received any kind of schooling after the age of thirteen. Many of those who did attend could not expect much in the way of education beyond the alphabet and the Authorised Version.

So, if experience of education itself in the country at large was so scanty and unevenly spread, it follows that awareness of examinations was even more vague and ill-informed. Indeed, in the first half of the century, the whole topic of examinations was little more than the intellectual hobby-horse of an energetic pressure group of pioneers and crusaders. It is almost justifiable to say that the nineteenth century saw the invention of the competitive examination.

It is always a surprise to find that what seem unshakable and eternal features of our lives once needed to be invented – like the castle, or the village, or the hedgerow. So too with examinations. What on earth did they do then – beforehand, that is?

They 'fixed' things, that's what they did. They intrigued, they bribed, they wrote grovelling letters, they sucked up to anybody who would listen to them. Anything to get a job or a place or a commission or a promotion for their son or their nephew. (You didn't have to do it for daughters and nieces; you traded in the marriage market for them. Besides, a husband, generally speaking, was a safer investment, and girls needed protection. What else would a loving father do?) There were no certificates or paper qualifications which anxious parents could brandish, because such things did not exist.

Nobody who mattered spent much time concerning himself with the 'lower classes'. They had always been 'hands' or 'menials', fit only for the work that their parents and grandparents had done, and somebody had to do the fetching and carrying in a pre-industrial and pre-technological society. It was not prejudice; it was common sense, based on the evidence of one's own eyes, and on the habits and traditions of centuries. In any case, had not the Almighty decreed that every human being had his or her place in society, so that to attempt to break out of it was therefore unwise, un-Christian, ungrateful, and unlikely to succeed, much less to bring happiness? This concept of a person's 'place' in society was to persist right through the nineteenth century – and, some would argue, the twentieth as well – and was to bedevil many educational reforms. (As late as the 1950's, my own mother was asked, quite seriously, by one of her sisters, whether it was really a good idea, since none of the family had ever been to university, to encourage me in my quest for Cambridge.)

It followed therefore, from this universal, if random, reliance on greasy palms and the old oil, that there was no great chance of a successful applicant for a job having the natural abilities to enable him to perform it with any particular distinction. Except insofar as his position in society would have given him the background, instincts, and connections without which any job performance would get off to a bad start. Nevertheless, that is what the situation was, and it was tolerated by the great majority of society, from top to bottom. If it had not, it would have been changed much earlier than it was. There is a remark attributed to the King himself, George III, who is supposed to have said that 'anyone was fit to occupy any place he could manage to get'. The saying 'faint heart never won fair lady' would appear to suggest that the philosophy still has some currency at least in the world of courtship.

So where did the change come from? What signalled the assault on the great citadel of Patronage? It came from a variety of sources. I am not qualified to put them in any kind of order of impact, but the mere recital of them, in whatever kind of order, will, I hope, serve to make the point that 'things' do not just 'happen' in history, they do not happen because of only one reason, and they do not happen overnight.

Let us start with the French Revolution. It is easy for an imaginative historian to trace almost everything in the nineteenth century back to the French Revolution, but in this case one can make a case for a pretty strong line of cause and effect. The Declaration of the Rights of Man, and the abolition of all social privilege, both of which stemmed from the early heady days of August, 1789, had let a lot of powerful genies out of bottles. True, they also led to the Reign of Terror, and to guttersnipes in high places, but no reasonable statesman since has seen fit to question the validity of the great 'freedoms' stated by the Revolution – freedom from religious persecution, from arbitrary arrest, from torture, from imprisonment without trial, from capricious dictatorship, from political censorship, and so on.

In the wars which followed in the 1790's and 1800's, France survived invasion, and went on to conquer most of Western Europe, by producing enormous armies which were officered by men who had been selected on the simple basis that they were good at their job. The 'career open to the talents' needed no further justification; the proof of the pudding was in the beating – of nearly everyone else.

True, the Napoleonic Empire failed in the end, and it was defeated by an army led by the Duke of Wellington, who believed that the purchase of army commissions was sound practice. Nevertheless, as with the Rights of Man and the abolition of the blue blood tradition, the career open to the talents, which had produced field-marshals in their thirties, left the idea in men's minds that talent deserved to be rewarded, that it might be more important than breeding.

Second, the Industrial Revolution. This would have been impossible without the emergence of a generation of *entrepreneurs* whose main driving force was the profit motive, who knew that money talked all languages, who understood that victory went to those who made the rules rather than to those who kept them. They proved that anybody with the brains, the gumption, the energy, and the thick skin could make a fortune. The aristocracy, the 'gentlemen' who rested on laurels grown out of ancient lineage and inherited wealth, found it impossible to resist them, and, in the end, were forced to admit them to the ranks of power in the terms of the Great Reform

Act of 1832. New interests entered Parliament. They did not control it; the aristocracy were not as effete as that, and were to show remarkable resources of resilience and flexibility, not to say cynicism and ruthlessness. But the 'new men' were in, and they had got in because of what they did, not because of whom they knew.

Business is competitive, and the Industrial Revolution made competitiveness commonplace. It was so successful that, well before the middle of the nineteenth century, England was selling much more than it was buying. Protective tariffs slowly declined, as more and more men realised that trade did not need such cossetting. Free trade meant lower prices, and lower prices meant more profits, and world trade was an open arena, in which the weakest went to the wall. (This was fine, until, towards the end of the century, other countries, very unsportingly, decided to have industrial revolutions of their own, and began to outsell England. By a strange coincidence, Englishmen began again to see the value of protective tariffs. But that is another story.)

Thirdly, biology. It can hardly be a total coincidence that, round about the middle of the century, when the free trade gospel was achieving almost universal acceptance, Charles Darwin published a book called *The Origin of Species*, in which the principle of the survival of the fittest was first aired. In fact, the first of the competitive examinations I shall discuss, the Oxford Locals, and Darwin's bombshell appeared within twelve months of each other.

Competition was entering the realm of sport too. Games like cricket and football were of course very old, but they developed an enormous fresh impetus during the nineteenth century, and this was, partly at any rate, because they were increasingly encouraged in schools – the public schools of course. This in turn was because some public school headmasters tumbled to the idea that boys would become better behaved if their surplus energy was siphoned off on the games field. Too much free time was merely free time in which to cause damage. The chief 'sin' which stalked caged communities of lusty boys, according to the interminable magisterial sermons of the age, was not sex; it was violence. Mutinies in schools were not exactly regular, but they were by no means unfamiliar. Flashman was not a drug addict or a sex fiend; he was a bully.

By the last third of the nineteenth century, rugby had been 'invented', to make up the great trinity of sports which claimed its millions of devotees – of all classes, incidentally. The great virtue of a gentleman became not gentility, nor breeding, and certainly not a taste for aesthetics; it was 'playing the game', having regard for the rules which bound everybody. One now had to be chivalrous to one's defeated opponent, but *one had still worked to defeat him.*

The Olympic Games, which reappeared in 1896, may have stressed to its participants that the important thing was merely taking part, but the fact remained that a world institution had been re-created based totally on the competitive principle.

Far and away the greatest celebrity and most popular figure of late nineteenth-century England was W.G. Grace, the Gloucestershire cricketer. It was not only because of his towering talent and prodigious performances. It was not only because he played a game which had rules (though he himself was not noted for his regular regard for them). It was not only because he played a game which everyone enjoyed. It was, above all, because *he played to win*, regardless of the state of the game or the status of the opposition. Grace, if such a figure is conceivable, was the High Priest of the Gospel of competition.

The ideals of the French Revolution; the career open to the talents; the free-for-all of the Industrial Revolution; the elevation of competition to the level not merely of virtue, but of necessity – the power and universal applicability of these principles simply had to have effects in all corners of existence. We must now add into the mixture the admiration which many observers had for the new French and Prussian systems of education, which were in the vanguard of European thinking. Englishmen may have been convinced that their Navy and their Empire and their Industry may have been the best in the world, but it would have a taken an Englishman of truly opaque political vision to claim that the English education system was the best anywhere. Indeed, England did not even *have* a system.

In this context it becomes unavoidable to return once again to the phenomenon of population. Time and again, one sees that it was the sheer weight of population increase which made old methods and philosophies unworkable and irrelevant – be it in parliamentary representation, local government, public health, medical reform, poor relief, or, as here, education.

Just as, in politics, the ruling classes found a way of creaming off the top of the industrial energy represented by the successful industrialists – giving them seats in Parliament, so, in education, it would become vital to find a way of creaming off the best potential talent which, by the law of averages, would find its way to the top of the seething ranks of the working population. Keep the old system of patronage, and the danger was that that talent, prevented from entering the higher ranks of society by poverty, privilege and the Old Boy Net, would turn its energies to criticism and, in the end, to sedition. If there was one devil which haunted the nightmares of anybody with property in the nineteenth century, it was 'revolution'. So we come full circle back to the Storming of the Bastille.

Finally, as the country became more mechanised, more mobile, and more sophisticated – and more crowded – so more and more manpower would be required to fill the new professions which would serve this new society – doctors, bankers, surveyors, builders, engineers, and so on. A priest or a politician in the eighteenth century might be able to get by with Latin and Greek and the Bible, but this was clearly totally insufficient for a man who was going to plan a railway station or build a suspension bridge. His knowledge and skill would have to be tested, or lives – and, more important – money would be lost.

So then, it was agreed, among liberal-minded and far-seeing men, that a new method of selection would have to be evolved. What follows is an over-simplification and telescoping of facts, but this is only an essay, not an exhaustive analysis. (For such an analysis, one should turn to a book like *Public Examinations in England, 1850-1900*, by John Roach, to which I am much indebted in the composition of this piece.)

One should bear in mind too that, once accepted as a possibility, the principle of competitive examination did not proceed serenely along a broad and open high road towards universal coverage, total efficiency, and ubiquitous acquiescence. There were ambushes, blockages, and accidents all along the way.

For instance, there were those – and they included J.L. Brereton, the School's founder – who were opposed, for reasons of instinct, temperament, training, and experience, to any kind of State initiative. These men were convinced that such initiative would be the kiss of death to creativity and local energy; the heavy hand of the State was soulless – in both the psychological and the religious sense. In other words, State control would be the trigger for national secularisation. Put even more bluntly, State schools would be godless schools.

In fairness, there were also those who felt a similar fear of too much Church initiative. It was for this reason that the Revd. Brereton, in his promotion of his new nationwide scheme for middle-class education, planned to tack it on to the counties, not on to the dioceses.

This may seem a slight diversion from the main theme of competitive examination, but the two themes were becoming intertwined. The reformers were agreed that competitive examinations might be worth trying. They were also agreed that schools – indeed education in general – needed reforming. It followed – to many of them, though not to all – that the best agency for achieving these desirable objects was the Government; at the very least, it had the money and it had the authority.

The Government did not wholly concur. A nationwide programme of school-building would be expensive, too expensive. Teacher training was becoming increasingly costly. School inspection was soon going to become another drain on the coffers. But then Chancellors thought again. They realised that examinations might be a way to get round all these dragons in the path. Exams would, of course, encourage talent everywhere. They would put schools, and teachers, on their toes. They would raise teaching standards. The competition would force schools to smarten up their act. New subjects offered for examination would broaden the curriculum. And nobody need build anything. It would be nationwide, democratic, fair, modern, attractive, and cheap. It was too good to be true.

An interesting sidelight to this concerns the status of teachers. One of the reasons for the opposition to all this reform was, amazingly, the threatened rise in the number of teachers. Many of the middle and upper classes did not see this as an automatic blessing. Ever since the Government had taken on the responsibility for teacher training, teachers had become another object of the national phobia about State interference. The more these new teachers spread into the elementary (primary) schools, the more they were seen as a threat. They were not 'gentlemen'; they were State-reared nobodies hauled up from God knew where, poseurs who, because of a little book learning, thought they were thereby qualified to enter any rank of society. Heaven knew what socialistic nonsense they were putting into the heads of their pupils.

This prejudice followed them when they began filtering into the newly-created middle-class schools. It may explain why the first Headmaster of West Buckland, J.H. Thompson, was not popular in some quarters; apparently too his rough manners and bluff approach did not go down well with an aristocrat like Earl Fortescue, or with some of the local businessmen. At this distance of time it is impossible to know exactly why Thompson was not liked. Was it the national suspicion of teachers? Was it really because he didn't know which knife and fork to pick up? Was it Devonian wariness of a Yorkshireman? Was it that he represented some kind of vague social levelling-down threat that could not be put into words? Was it that he was indeed, in the opinion of some, of poor calibre? Had Brereton appointed him because he, Brereton, was short of money, and he, Thompson, came cheap? (In fairness, this does not square with the high regard in which Thompson seems to have been held by generations of his old pupils.)

Or did all this suspicion and disregard of teachers go deeper still, back to the days when they were the household slaves of Roman senators? Right on into the eighteenth and early nineteenth centuries, they were, for the most part, little better than household servants, glorified nannies hired to knock the Classics and the New Testament into the heads of listless young aristo-crats who yearned and fidgeted to be upstairs, out of doors, anywhere but where they were. Something of this disrespectful attitude of society seems to have lingered on into this century, when, though we are told that 'nobody ever forgets a good teacher', an established, fully-trained doctor can earn nearly three times what an established, fully-trained teacher gets, and an able lawyer much more. And who helped all those doctors and lawyers to qualify?

If teacher status needs a boost now, it needed an even bigger boost then, and examinations, so the thinking ran, might provide it. Success in getting one's pupils through could do nothing but good for a teacher's reputation, and, by extension, a school's reputation as well.

The result was – for all the reasons cited above, and no doubt for others as well – that the years following the middle of the nineteenth century saw an outbreak of examinations almost of epidemic proportions. The College of Preceptors set up exams for teachers, and, soon after, for grammar and private schools. In 1854 the Society of Arts published its examination schemes for adults studying in Mechanics' Institutes. In 1859 the Science and Art Department set up exams in scientific subjects.

1862 saw the appearance of the Revised Code for awarding grants to ele-mentary schools based upon their pupils' performance in reading, writing, and arithmetic tests. As its architect, Robert Lowe, famously claimed, 'If it is not cheap, it will be efficient, and if it is not efficient, it will be cheap.' Here is not the place to enter into the controversy about what became a notorious system – 'Payment by Results' – which dominated primary teaching for a generation, and which, some said, ground down teaching into mindless swotting (a theme which has been a constant motif in any discussion of examinations ever since). Suffice it to say that the Lowe system fitted into the pattern of events which was unfolding.

The exam bug spread outside schools. In 1853, the India Act opened appointments in the Indian Civil Service to competitive examination. In 1855, a limited form of this practice was introduced into the Home Civil Service, and became universal by decree of Gladstone's Government in 1870.

In 1867, the Second Reform Act very nearly doubled the electorate, thereby prompting the aforementioned Robert Lowe to observe, 'We must now educate our masters.' In 1870, Gladstone's Government again went into action, with Forster's Education Act, which attempted to plug the gaps in the existing elementary education coverage in the country.

But before that, a group of energetic men had already set in motion a scheme for a nationwide system of examinations, not for the elementary sector, but for the secondary sector. They were all connected, one way or another, with West Buckland School. One was the Revd. J.L. Brereton, the School's co-founder. The second was Earl Fortescue (or Viscount Ebrington, as he was then, before he acceded to the title), the other co-founder. The third was Sir Thomas Dyke Acland, a leading Devon landowner, and a shareholder in the original Farm and County School which Brereton and Fortescue set up in 1858. (Acland, incidentally, was also responsible, with the School's head, Thompson, for laying out the course of the *Exmoor*, the cross-country race which became the School's deepest-set tradition. See 'A Shot of the Good Side'.) The last was Frederick Temple, Headmaster of Rugby at this time (1857-69), thereafter Bishop of Exeter, then London, and finally Archbishop of Canterbury. More to the point, he was a friend of Brereton, and a great admirer of West Buckland, visiting once in 1873 to present the annual prizes.

It seems quite remarkable that the four main driving characters of a pioneering, nationwide system of secondary examinations, which was to last for over half a century, should all have been closely associated with a tiny, obscure, remote establishment in the depths of the Devon countryside.

Indeed Brereton had mooted such a scheme when he had first begun to advocate his plans for middle-class schools; it seemed to him a logical necessity to set up, alongside the new schools, the means for maintaining their standards. He had been writing and talking about it, to anybody who would listen, ever since he had arrived at West Buckland as Rector.

Fortescue needed no conversion to the principle of middle-class education, and Fortescue knew everybody. Acland was instrumental, with Fortescue, in setting up a trial examination – what would nowadays be called a 'pilot scheme' – in Exeter in 1857. Just over a hundred candidates turned up, including two boys who had walked twenty miles to attend. Rooms were hired at the Clarence Hotel opposite the cathedral.

Meantime Temple was at work. He had seen the value of Brereton's ideas, but thought that they needed modification in one important area – that of control. Brereton, with his pathological horror of State interference, had based his system on the counties. Temple felt that such a ubiquitous institution would need resources beyond those of the counties. So he came up with a compromise: let there be central control, but let it be, not by the Government, but by the universities – Oxford and Cambridge. Money might come from the Exchequer, but control and administration would be by the two senior academic institutions in the land – which seemed eminently suitable.

He and Acland were both Oxford men. They were both well aware that the universities were not in close touch with the rest of the educational world outside their own venerable walls, and were not noted for a particularly liberal attitude to education, or indeed to anything else – except in one important sphere. They had embraced the idea of competitive examinations as early as the late eighteenth century. By the mid-nineteenth century, a growing number of men in public life owed their entry, and much of their later success, to their strong performance in these examinations. Peel, for example, gained an excellent degree. So did Gladstone. Acland was an exact contemporary of Gladstone, and a close friend all his life (they were born, and died, in the same years).

So Acland and Temple sold the idea of examinations to Oxford. Shortly afterwards, they persuaded Cambridge to buy it too. Both ivory towers accepted the necessity of showing the nation that they were interested in 'the education of all England', as Temple put it. In turn, such a reform could not but make 'all England' interested in, even proud of, Oxford and Cambridge. In 1858, the Oxford and Cambridge Local Examinations were born. A system came into being which would offer an outside, professional, and impartial means of assessing a pupil's performance – by the senior academic institutions in the land – without raising the middle classes' fears of privilege, of 'Churchiness', of secularism, or of State interference. It was not exactly what Brereton had had in mind, but it was the best he was going to get.

Success was due to the efforts, connections, and vision of Acland, Fortescue, and Temple – and others too – but as John Roach observed in his book about public examinations, 'It is fair to say that . . . . the whole movement should, in a sense, be traced back to [Brereton]'. (*op. cit.* p. 67.)

The first Oxford exam was held in June, 1858, and the first Cambridge one in December. There was to be a Preliminary Examination for both Juniors and Seniors. Inevitably there were variations between the Oxford and Cambridge schemes; for instance the cut-off date between Junior and Senior was younger at Oxford, and their religious knowledge exams diverged. There were many other differences, but the general pattern of the two was similar. Unfortunately the two universities, except for a flush of pioneering goodwill in the early days, did not show great willingness thereafter to be co-operative with each other.

Nevertheless, to extend a metaphor, the project, after its pilot scheme in Exeter the year before, soon 'took off'. In the first year, Oxford gathered 750 Junior candidates and 401 Seniors. Cambridge, somewhat slower to start, collected 297 Juniors and only 73 Seniors. But by 1878, Cambridge had overhauled its rival, and amassed 6,435 candidates to Oxford's 2,330. In the twenty years following 1878, Cambridge numbers went up from that 6,435 to 15,941. Oxford rose from 2,330 to 9,136 – which was faster, relatively speaking.

The attractions of this new set of exams crossed the oceans. In 1862, an application was received for a centre to be set up in Trinidad. By the end of the century, there were 36 colonial centres and 1,220 candidates. (These 'Empire' exams were not without their peculiar troubles. In 1898, the exam papers from the Gold Coast did not reach home to be marked by the prescribed time; it was discovered upon enquiry that the acting director of exams had died, and his replacement, the acting chaplain, had also died – they didn't call it 'The White Man's Grave' for nothing.)

Nevertheless, from whichever direction you view it, it seems that the 'Locals' soon settled into the woodwork of secondary school life. They became as much a part of everyday school conversation as 'O Levels' did in the forty years following the Second World War, or 'School Cert.' in the years between the Wars. If the West Buckland School magazine, the *Register*, is anything to go by, schools trumpeted their successes in these termly reports. Well, they would, wouldn't they? Especially since the universities published not only passes and grades, but an order of merit as well. So a boy, or girl, could be not only the most successful candidate in their school in a certain subject, but 'first in England' in that subject too. So league tables are nothing new.

The early numbers of the *Register* are chock-full of every candidate, every subject, every grade, every national success. Indeed several numbers contain little else, beyond the bald information inside the back page that 'Mr. Thomas will meet pupils at Exeter Station on the day before the new term starts'.

But they had something to shout about. Not only did their boys gain first place in their various subjects; some of them were pronounced 'First Junior' or 'First Senior' overall, in the country. One boy, T.R. Potbury, was 'First Junior' in both the Oxford and Cambridge Examinations, in the same year, 1881. Another, William Stradling, the son of a milk roundsman, was 'First Senior' twice. In the Cambridge Examinations of 1864, 1865, and 1866 West Buckland passed the highest number of candidates of any school in England. Top of the league, no less.

Other laurels were won too, though of not quite such a spectacular kind. In December, 1862, Cambridge allowed its examination to be held in the School – the very first to be allowed an exclusive examination centre of its own. It prompted a letter to *The Times*. Apparently it had become regular practice for the newspapers to announce the coming exams, and to print a list of exam centres. In December, 1862, therefore, there appeared a list like this: 'Bath, Birmingham, Cheltenham, Exeter, Leeds, Liverpool, London,

Manchester, Oxford, Southampton, and West Buckland.' R.P. Chope, a regular contributor to the pages of the *Register*, recorded that the mystified letter-writer enquired of *The Times* Editor, 'Where is West Buckland?' Mr. Chope's dry comment was that it was 'a query which would even now be somewhat difficult to answer with any great degree of accuracy'.

J.H. Thompson, the Headmaster, took the brave step of entering whole classes for these exams, instead of just his high flyers. He, and Brereton, felt that it was a good way of raising the overall standards of school work, which would more than make up for the fact that the high flyers, deprived of exclusive coaching, might not achieve the very highest grades. The policy seems to have worked. Cambridge, in its official report, commented on the School's enterprise in this respect. No less a celebrity than Temple himself went further. When he visited the School in 1873, this time as Bishop of Exeter, he pointed out that 'half the whole school' had entered the 1872 Cambridge exam. Seventy per cent of the candidates had passed, twenty-five per cent with honours:

> 'This is the clearest proof that any school can give of the substantial sound-
> ness of the education it bestows. I do not know whether it is absolutely the
> only school in the Kingdom that sends in boys in this way, but certainly, it is
> the only school in the country that sends in anything like that proportion of
> boys, and, I may add, it is the only school in the country that passes that
> proportion of its scholars.'

So – bully for West Buckland. And bully for all those other schools who could, and no doubt did, boast similar successes. However, the Locals did not surge smoothly forward without their teething troubles or their critics.

The first concerned the very early candidates: they did not perform particularly well. This was due, predictably, to inexperience, on the part of both pupils and teachers. Examiners too; the papers had been set by university academics, who had no idea what went on in a classroom or in a schoolboy's mind. Adequate supervision was a problem, as was adequate provision of rooms and other facilities. One English exam was bedevilled by the room having been used for a ball the previous night. One French literature set book proved to be unobtainable from the Paris publishers owing to the siege of Paris in the Franco-Prussian War. One smiles at such stories, but only because one would be bored by the mountain of humdrum evidence to the effect that, generally speaking, things went pretty well.

Criticism was a different matter.

One need not take shelter from the frivolous sniping and the puritanical puffing, which sprang largely from the feminine side of the equation. What would be the main subjects for girls – cooking and flirting, ho-ho? Bringing girls into the examination room would have an unfavourable effect on their characters. It was not a good idea to pit boys and girls against each other; girls might be stimulated towards an unworthy mood of emulation. Girls should not be submitted to public tests of any kind; it would be too much of a strain. You never knew what kinds of undesirable persons you might meet in an examination room. And so on and so on.

More adverse or outrageous remarks came from unsuccessful candidates. One of the Cambridge Examination Syndicate chief administrators, J.N. Keynes, kept a collection of them. A private student who had four failures to his credit referred darkly to 'some hideous undercurrent' which was frustrating his richly-deserved success. One girl candidate wrote to ask if she could buy a certificate: 'Mother would gladly pay double the money to get it rather than me to sit and fail.' A fond father was certain that some mistake had been made, and suggested that, if the mistake could be rectified, he would be glad to send the secretary – and his wife – for a trip to Paris. One respectful, but ill-informed correspondent addressed him as 'The Provost of Keynes'. Such sentiments are worthy only of the basket or the anthology.

Other comments displayed more genuine, and deeper thought – not to say validity. The first, and most obvious, was that exams led to teachers concentrating on their more able pupils, which in turn could lead to overstrain on these boys and girls, and neglect of the less able – a criticism which has had a long pedigree, and is still with us. Also still with us is the one about mindless cramming. A teacher of mine enjoyed telling us that he had failed the Entrance Examination at a Cambridge college because he had translated two more lines of Latin verse than there were on the paper.

Complaints by tired examiners referred to candidates who 'do not take pains to understand the drift of the questions', and who 'waste time in writing answers of which they are wholly ignorant'. They could have come from an examiner's report from last year. *Plus ça change, plus c'est la même chose.* I am not so sure, though, whether an examiner today would get away with this: 'It was curious to observe how in many cases a girl in answer to a question about which she evidently knew nothing, could nevertheless cover a sheet of paper with very fairly expressed English conveying no information whatever either right or wrong!'

The old chestnut about irrelevance and lack of critical faculty was already a chestnut by the 1870's. To say nothing of ignorance – during the resurgence of the notorious 'Eastern Question' in the same decade, the majority of candidates thought that the Suez Canal was a 'scientific discovery'.

So much for the actual mechanics of the exams. Perhaps more searching were the criticisms of their very *raison d'être*. Once again one is struck by what sounds like the modernity of the remarks. Exams, it was claimed, did nothing but test knowledge; they did not test mental powers, potential, creativity, or judgment. Put another way, they tested memory; they did not test imagination or reasoning power. In fact, if we stop to think, we should not be patronising the thinkers of 130 years ago for their modernity; we ourselves should be searching for something rather less derivative to say.

The same too applies to the argument *for* exams as a concept put forward at the outset. This said that the effort, application, persistence, courage, and self-discipline required for the work of the exam course, and the stress of the actual exam, were in themselves excellent training, would enhance the character, and would bestow benefits long afterwards – whether the exam was passed or not. Some of us are still saying the same today.

It did not stop a powerful last-ditch action in 1888 mounted by a celebrity-ridden group of worthies, including novelists and several distinguished historians. They went through the, by now, old arguments about overstrain, mindless memory work which would stifle the love of learning, over-emphasis on prizes and scholarships, and general soulless conformity.

It was too late. The fact was that exams had come to stay, for the simple reason that nobody could think of anything better. The alternative was a return to the old corrupt system of patronage and oily letters. Society, now hugely more numerous, more aware, and more ambitious, simply would not wear it. (Though the 'Who-you-know-not-what-you-know' philosophy still sustains an impressive rearguard campaign.)

The only debate now was how to make the exam system, which even its strongest advocates admitted had plenty of faults, work more efficiently. Substantially, that is what has been happening ever since, at any rate in the worlds of education and public service – which are what it was designed to serve in the first place. What goes on in the world of business recruitment is another matter. Who knows? Maybe the world of education will have something to learn from it.

The Locals came to an end, as is the nature of most institutions. By the second decade of the twentieth century they were being replaced by School Certificate and Higher School Certificate. They in turn were superseded in 1950 by 'O' Levels and 'A' Levels, complemented in the 1960's by CSE's. Now, since 1988, we have had the General Certificate of Secondary Education (GCSE), and, since the turn of the century, A/S Levels and A2 Exams. But, if you compare the dates, the Locals had a good run – better in fact than their successors, unless you include the Eleven-Plus, which is nearly a hundred years old, though admittedly an endangered species.

But – to return to the examples I gave of those things which seemed eternal (the castle, the village, the hedgerow) but which needed to be invented – we must bear in mind that the castle now is a footworn tourist ruin, the village in danger of becoming a holiday-home-cum-dormitory ghetto, the hedgerow the prey of the JCB. Exams, which settled into the national subconscious so quickly, also needed to be invented. Will they too, one day, go? And, if so, what then? Will somebody, somewhere, come up with something?

Just as all the great religions, and great invasions, came out of the East, will another great idea – like middle-class education – come out of the West, out of the fertile imagination of another restless cleric in Devon?

Is there, somewhere in deepest Exmoor, another Brereton pouring his plans into the ears of another Fortescue? Is there another bustling Acland lobbying with another tireless Temple to achieve the next breakthrough? Will West Buckland one day speak to the world again? Let us, as Mr. Asquith said, wait and see.

A certificate from the Cambridge Local Examinations, 1867. [School Archive]

21. A Unity of Nations

I don't know what should be the proper collective noun for nations, but this, by virtue of its optimism, will do as well as any other. It seems appropriate as a reference to the multitudinous colours, races, creeds, and nationalities that have, at some time or other, made their way to West Buckland in the shape of new pupils.

The composition of the following list prompted much brow-furrowing and head-rubbing among those staff with long memories, as well as much thumbing through previous School magazines. It drew out not only names, but delightfully random comments, like:-

'The Iraqis were always fighting the Iranians.'

'Must be about thirty years ago – whenever the boat people were coming out.'

'He became Commander-in-Chief of his country's Armed Forces.'

'Oh, she was the one who would never wear a bra in Geography lessons.'

Nigeria	France	South Africa	Lebanon	Hungary
Brazil	Spain	Hong Kong	Russia	Moldova
Palestine	Thailand	Latvia	S. Rhodesia (as it was then)	
Switzerland	Estonia	Ghana	Iran	China
India	Lithuania	Turkey	Uganda	Germany
Iraq	Sri Lanka	Brunei	Sweden	U.S.A.
Cambodia	Canada	Pakistan	Cyprus	Denmark
Japan	Finland	Austria	Botswana	Trinidad
Bolivia	Jordan	Tunisia	Singapore	Sudan
Holland	Malaysia	Australia	Vietnam	Ireland
United Arab Emirates	Croatia	The West Indies (as they then were)		

Among the most heartfelt memories of these foreign students was one from a boy who hailed from Nigeria. He claimed that when he first arrived at West Buckland his suitcase weighed practically nothing, because he was wearing nearly all his clothes.

22. The Eye of the Beholder

A man grows many faces during his life. Each of these faces, when frozen in a snapshot of a person's reminiscence of him, often seems so much in conflict with the others that one could almost forget that they each reflect a facet of the same man.

The first time I came across Francis Brereton, the second son of the Revd. Joseph (the School's founder), he was a dutiful pupil of the new Norfolk County School. In due course, he went on, as dutiful student, to his father's most cherished creation, Cavendish College, Cambridge.

Here emerges the second snapshot: Francis was a keen sportsman. He rowed for his college so successfully that he won four oars in the Bumps races – no mean feat even today.

The archivist next comes across him as a young, but clearly successful headmaster of yet another of his father's projects – the North-East County School, or Barnard Castle, as it soon became, and remained. He was the first head, and he steered the School to its first successes.

Then the dutiful son reappears. The Norfolk County School – his old school – fell on hard times, and father Joseph decreed that Francis should give up his successful headship at Barnard Castle and go and rescue the struggling academy at Elmham. Amazingly, he went. And failed.

So the next picture is of a bitter, frustrated, unemployed headmaster imprisoned in Norfolk, trying to make ends meet with private lessons. Then Fate – or Providence, or the Almighty, or what you will – took a hand. The Headmaster at Barnard Castle suddenly died, Francis re-applied for his old job, got it, and went on to be a very successful headmaster for another thirty years.

During that time he fathered a family, and one of his sons, in a published reminiscence, remembered him as 'a really vulnerable, sensitive, and very kindly man'. At the same time, he acknowledged that his father had to create a figure of authority, and had to be able to turn on the magisterial wrath to order when the situation demanded. During one of these storms, one charlady who happened to be present was so frightened that she took refuge behind the door till it was over, observing to the son afterwards, 'Oh, I am sorry for your poor mother!'

Francis, like most good schoolmasters, had a nickname. It was 'Kip'. The son thought it had begun as 'Skipper', was later corrupted to 'Kipper', and finally shortened to 'Kip'. Neat little nicknames do not usually stick to nobodies, and they are not usually applied to unpopular figures.

The last two images come from the period when Francis, retired from teaching, went to serve as Rector at Little Massingham, the fifth member of his family so to do. He continued to serve right up to the Second World War. A lady I recently met in that village – a formidable senior personage in rural tweeds and body-warmer, with a sparky little dog beside her on the front seat of the Land Rover – boomed with laughter when I mentioned Francis' name.

'Do I remember him? I should say so. Dull old bugger!'

She then went on to tell me the story of how she and her friends or family – I forget which – had gone up to London for the day, and had spent time, and money, in the famous toy store at Hamley's in Regent Street. They came back with a Whoopee cushion, determined to use it deflate the dignity of somebody who represented, to them, old age, authority, and pomposity. Who better than the aged Rector? They duly inserted this cushion under the Rector's seat in the church, with, apparently, most gratifying results. It was a story she relished telling, and had no doubt relished telling many times.

The final picture of Francis shows him at the age of eighty-four, and still Rector. He was hurrying up a steep hill in the course of a visit to a nearby village, in order to hear the latest news of the War on the 'wireless'. He collapsed and died in the road.

An archivist can come across several of these snapshots in the course of his work. He can file them dutifully under the man's name, but he can not hope to produce a definitive portrait, because the snapshots are so far apart, either in space or in time. He will probably never be able to fill in the gaps; he is a recorder, not a biographer. He can occasionally marvel at the variety of the images, but he is unlikely to be able to make a consistent pattern – not without a liberal admixture of imagination.

However, he can still be left with an impression of a very human individual, who still retains on the yellowing pages a personality of enough dimensions to whet the appetite.

23. *Toujours la Politesse*

You would think that week-long examinations conducted by visiting examiners from Oxford and Cambridge would be sombre occasions. Not necessarily so.

Certainly a lot of serious work must have been done – witness the School's good record in these exams in the first half-century of its existence. At one time it was top of the league in the whole of England. It was also the first school in England to win the privilege of becoming its own examination centre, in 1862. (See 'Tried and Tested'.)

A certain *camaraderie* must have been built up, in a week, between candidates and examiner, the result of shared concentration and effort. It became traditional, after the last day's work, to have a formal tea. This soon developed into far more than a staid, sit-up-straight-and-speak-when-you're-spoken-to, hands-in-the-lap, polite communal silence to impress the visitor with the School's manners.

Speeches were made. Votes of thanks were offered. The 'Head Master' said that the School was 'fortunate in having so kind and courteous an Examiner sent them by the University'. This was the Revd. F.H. Curgenven, M.A., Scholar of Corpus Christi College, Oxford. Mr. Thompson called for three cheers for Mr. Curgenven.

Mr. Curgenven admitted his surprise at this hearty reception. He admitted too that during the week he had been very nosy, in order to 'form a candid opinion of the School'. (He merely administered the exams; he didn't actually ask the questions.) He 'could say very honestly and impartially that he had formed a very high opinion of the School', and he thought the general manner of the boys 'natural and unaffected'.

It got better. Thompson said that he hoped that this 'would not be the only time they would see Mr. Curgenven again'. He was right; the Revd. Curgenven enjoyed himself so much that he came nine years in succession. Each time he was given a royal welcome. The 'tea' became a 'supper'. After the speeches, there were, over the years, 'races and sports', 'music', 'songs and glees', and carrying on generally. The distinguished Examiner was so captivated by the general *bonhomie* that he joined in, on at least two occasions 'presiding at the piano-forte'.

Now *that's* the sort of examiner to have. They don't make them like that any more.

In 1872, the Revd. Curgenven was presented by Corpus Christi College, of which he was by now a Fellow, to the Rectory of Byfield, Northamptonshire – at a stipend of £1,000 *per annum*. Which was pretty generous.

No wonder he stopped being a mere visiting examiner. Did he ever pause, as he visited grumpy parishioners in the rain, to remember the warmth and glow of those teas and suppers, and races and sports and songs and glees, and himself 'presiding at the piano-forte'?

24. Market Forces

A Pretty Dry Day

In the early 1900's, the School was in a bad way financially, and the Governors were constantly looking for ways to economise and cut corners. In the Minutes for 12th June, 1906, 'it was unanimously decided' that at the forthcoming Prize Day 'luncheon be provided as usual, but on as economical lines as possible – drinks to be confined to beer and aerated waters. Proposed by Mr. Sanders, and seconded by Mr. Hiern.'

Aerated waters! But note how they would not give up their 'luncheon', not entirely. Almost every public function at WB simply has to have a luncheon. The tradition seems set in stone. It went right back to the celebrations of the Queen's Birthday and the opening of a new dormitory in 1859, barely seven months after the School was founded. (See 'High Hopes', *West Buckland School*, pp. 13-15.)

Collectors' Items

As I gathered together, from various corners and cupboards, all the bits and pieces that related to the School's past, I was intrigued by the number of prizes that turned up. Books, that is. The name of the prizewinner was on a label stuck inside the front cover, together with the subject of his award, the date, and the signature of the current headmaster.

Why was it that so many had found their way back into the School? One can understand the occasional very Old Boy deciding to make a late presentation out of affection, or a younger relation coming across great-uncle's prize book in the loft, and deciding that his old school was the best place for it. But so many!

Another odd thing was that the subject matter of the prize book often bore little or no relation to the subject for which the pupil had won the prize. I put this point to one Old Boy from the late 'thirties and early 'forties. He confirmed the rumour I had picked up elsewhere, and offered an explanation. It was expected, apparently, that all prizewinners should immediately donate their prize books to the School Library. This practice had stemmed, or so he had been told, from the famous fire in 1930, which had caused so much damage in the old library. So the School authorities had devised this ingenious – or devious, depending on your point of view – scheme, whereby they gained credit for public largesse in giving worthy prizes, and at the same time they could, at no extra charge, re-stock the library shelves with skilfully-chosen volumes donated by a well-drilled phalanx of generous prizewinners. Under these circumstances, then, it did not matter what book they were given.

The Old Boy I had questioned about this had received, for his Maths and Science Prize, a biography of Cardinal Richelieu. . . . Quite right; he didn't.

Cheap at the Price

On Prize Day, Tuesday, 6th December, 1864, 24 prize books were presented, in a school of barely more than 60 pupils – forty per cent. If the surviving prize books are anything to go by, they were sumptuous by today's standards – leather binding, inlaid gold lettering, gold edges, marbled end pages, School crest on the cover. They cost a total of 'about £20'. That was about four-fifths of a single pupil's total fees for a year.

At Speech Day in 2003, there were about 160 prizes presented to a school of roughly 500 pupils. Thirty-two per cent – not all that far away from the forty above. But when it comes to a percentage of fees. . . . They cost, today, an average of just under £14,000 a year for a boarder. I bet the School doesn't give away £11,200 in prizes. It certainly doesn't give books any more. And even if it did, they certainly wouldn't be leather-bound, with inlaid gold lettering, gold edges, marbled end pages, and the School crest on the cover. Imagine!

But *if* it did, and *if* leather-bound books, with inlaid gold lettering, gold edges, marbled end pages, and the School crest each cost today about £70, and *if* they were presented to 160 pupils, that would account for £11,200. What would you think such a book *would* cost today? Exactly. . . .

Them as Don't Ask

An Asian pupil was once awarded a senior School prize – in his day (roughly mid-twentieth century) a book on some topic relevant to his special studies. He wrote, with totally disarming frankness, to the School Secretary, to ask if the book could be replaced by a pewter tankard. He was well aware that a tankard could cost a lot more than the book, and gallantly assured the Secretary that he would be happy to pay the difference. He gave as his reason the facts that he wanted to remember the School all his life, and that he intended to live for a very long time, and a tankard would last much longer than a book. He even detailed the inscription that he wanted engraved on the tankard.

He got it. (But I had better hasten to warn present pupils against trying the same.)

25. Sam and Jimmy

Just over fifty years ago, give or take a twelvemonth or two (especially when one allows for the time taken to produce a book), Sam and Jimmy died. 'Sam' Howells was the Headmaster of West Buckland School from 1941 to 1952; 'Jimmy' James was the Headmaster of Kingston Grammar School (my school) from 1940 to 1949. Jimmy died within a year or two of retiring; Sam died in office.

I was reminded of Jimmy when I came to write something about Sam. I wanted to put up on the wall of the main staircase leading to the Memorial Hall a portrait photograph of Sam as part of a rogues' gallery of headmasters I am preparing, and I intend to place underneath each one, in a small glazed plaque, a short summary of their achievement. It isn't much, but it might give the tiniest idea of what Sam, and other headmasters, accomplished during their term of office.

The problem, naturally, is – how do you put it all into such a short space? Whatever you write, it won't mean much to anybody who didn't know him, and it won't satisfy anyone who did. You don't want to write a hagiography, nor do you want to put in warts just for the sake of it. You need to tell something of his public service, but you need also to say something personal. You have to sit back and you have to go up close. All in about sixty-odd words. Not easy. (Why not write more? Because it would make a bigger plaque, and you don't want to have such a daunting notice on the wall that nobody bothers to read it at all.)

In the end, I came up with something like this:

'Mr. S.E. Howells, Headmaster, 1941-52.

He joined the staff in 1918, and became Headmaster early in the Second World War. He guided the School through the years of wartime hardship and post-war austerity. A bachelor, totally devoted to the School, and a legendary English teacher, he was noted for his discipline and sharp tongue, for his many small acts of kindness, his hospitality, and his gift for friendship.'

It was as I was putting this together that Jimmy came to mind. As I thought about it, the parallels became more and more numerous.

Both Sam and Jimmy had arrived in their respective schools just after the First World War, Sam in 1918 and Jimmy in 1919. Both became Second Master (Deputy Head) in the 1930's. Both were invited by a worried board of governors to take over the School in a wartime crisis – in each case there had been a sudden departure of the previous head. At West Buckland, Mr. Smith left for reasons of physical health; at Kingston Grammar School Mr.

Howse had a nervous breakdown. Both Sam and Jimmy were installed 'for the duration' – on probation, as it were. Both were later 'confirmed' as official heads.

There was more. Both were Biology teachers. (Sam's first love, it is true, was English, but he was also a passionate devotee of Biology, and indeed pioneered its teaching in the School.) Both wore small clipped moustaches. Both were pretty comprehensive smokers: Sam was a slave to Gold Flake; Jimmy was in thrall, I believe, to St. Bruno. Both had their crosses in life, and carried on without making any fuss: Sam had health problems which, I understand, prevented his playing games and, more seriously, doing military service in the First War (and it is difficult for us now to understand the overpowering sense of inadequacy that that thrust upon any young man as he watched the millions go off to the war to end wars); Jimmy lost his only son in the Second War, and had to go back to work with hundreds of vigorous, unfeeling boys who were ready to play him up if he weakened.

And still more. Both Sam and Jimmy had to keep a school ticking over during what was probably the worst decade of the whole century. There were the obvious burdens to bear like rationing – not only of food, but of clothing and petrol. If a commodity was not rationed, it was 'in short supply' – which meant that you had to beg, plead, beseech, wheedle, cajole, intrigue, wheel and deal, and pay Black Market prices in order to get some of it. So many services which had been normal in peacetime were either in tatters or completely defunct between 1939 and 1945, and surprised complaints were usually met with the regular catchphrase: 'Don't you know there's a war on?' Beleaguered heads had to sit by and watch the fabric of their schools begin to crumble because the means of remedying the situation were denied them – supplies, money, and skilled labour.

Most of the young staff had gone off to enlist, and heads had to turn to whatever else was available on the labour market – part-timers, pensioners, barely-qualified bumblers. They had to ask experienced, middle-aged teachers of, say, Modern Languages, to take on some fourth-form Maths and English. All sorts of unlikely non-benders found themselves on the sports field and a whistle shoved into their hand, in the hope that they could control a mob of hoop-shirted banshees determined to work off some energy.

Peace in 1945 did not mean the end of their troubles. Food rationing continued. If anything, it got worse; bread, for instance, which had been off ration throughout the War, went on ration for a while in 1947. Consumer goods were just as hard to buy, because a desperate government was exporting everything that came off an assembly line in order to begin to reduce the nought-laden war debt. Many of those young teachers who had gone off to war did not come back, and staff shortages were just as worrying. Austerity for most people today is just a word in a dictionary; it meant volumes between 1945 and 1950.

Sam and Jimmy rose magnificently to the occasion. Very sensibly, they did not waste time bemoaning what they did not have; they made the very best of what they did. Uppermost was experience, vast experience. They knew boys through and through. They could handle them and they could anticipate them. In the course of a quarter of a century in the profession they had learned right to the very bottom the great lesson that what really pervades a classroom is a constant state of friendly, undeclared war, in which the victory goes to the one who plans, who leads, who inspires, who *knows*, and who exhibits the greatest depths of low cunning.

Time and again, in the tributes to him, writers about Sam mentioned his fearsome discipline – if a weak teacher left the room at the end of a lesson of chaos and the next lesson was Sam's, the room would fall quiet long before his footfall was heard outside. He could reduce a boy to mere inches by a few words. Ex-pupils who saw him in action many years later were often surprised to see how tolerant he was; that was not how they remembered him. But when they stopped to think, they admitted that the tolerance had probably been there all the time, but they had simply not noticed it; boys' eyes are sharp, but they are selective. Even Sam's famous sarcasm – a fearsome weapon in any teacher's armoury, and rarely liked if always respected – was not constant. As someone remarked, 'He never over-used it.'

Napoleon was a great practitioner of the art of surprise. So was Sam. Boys never knew what to expect. Like all good schoolmasters, Sam maintained around himself a last ditch of inscrutability. One of the most fearsome monsters to haunt the classroom is boredom. From the stories, there seems to have been little scope for it in Sam's lessons. He understood completely the value of keeping the little blighters on the hop.

One must stress here that though a boy may not have known what to expect in the way of content, he did know what to expect in the way of character. One of the things a pupil finds most difficult to tolerate is a teacher who is as nice as pie one day and like a bear with a sore head the next. Sam did not change. He was always Sam. If that meant being hard, intolerant of sloppy work, sarcastic, and smelling of tobacco, well, so be it. It did not mean that Sam was not healthily disliked by some. But you did know where you were – in the wrong, and the lowest form of animal life. Curiously, it was comforting.

Ex-pupils who reminisce about a much-respected old teacher are fond of trotting out the familiar stories, and no doubt these stories have been polished and burnished over the years. But, as R.F. Delderfield observed,

they were only polished and burnished because they were prized possessions. They may dazzle, but it is hoped that they do not distort. And even
the dazzle is the result of affection, so it is just as genuine.

Sam was quoted as saying, for instance, that it was a waste of time trying
to make boys perfect. You should recognise a boy's limitations and concentrate on his good points. There must have been thousands of members of his
classes – imperfect schoolboys – who would have appreciated that. I have
noticed over the years that great schoolmasters attract a lot of praise from
boys who were neither very clever nor very hard-working, but they were
grateful for the fact that Old Misery-Guts had noticed something worthwhile about them, and they had responded to it. For example, say the name
'Joe Ellis' to any one of legions of my ex-contemporaries and they will at
once boom, 'Joe Ellis? The only man who ever taught me any Maths.'

And that's another thing. Another hallmark of the great teacher is that,
when he was finished with teaching you, you stayed taught. More than one
Old Boy has gone on record to say that he can still rattle off, word for word,
poems that he was introduced to by Sam. I am no great mathematician, but
I still tackle certain maths problems using the methods I was taught by Joe.
('Joe' was not his real name, incidentally. He got it from Jimmy. Apparently,
where Jimmy came from, everyone who had the surname Ellis was nick-
named 'Joe' – like 'Dusty' with Miller and 'Spud' with Murphy – and the
name stuck with the boys as well as the staff.)

Then there were the harder lessons of Life, which seemed possibly harsh
at the time, but they stayed in the memory. Sam never shrank from showing
a boy an unwelcome truth. If the process was painful, that was just too bad;
he would benefit from the learning of it in later life. The gratitude would
come later too. Along with the understanding that lessons offered in sugar
and cotton wool get forgotten; lessons suffered in pain, surprise, even
outrage, survive.

This sort of confidence also comes only with age and experience. Sam
and Jimmy knew exactly what they were doing. They believed in what they
were doing, and they believed that it was worthwhile. Teachers should lead,
and to do that successfully, you need confidence, and it must show – even
when, at times (because we are all human), it may not always be totally felt.
You could never imagine a man like Sam engaged in navel-contemplation
or breast-beating; he had a job to do, a very difficult one at a difficult time,
and he considered it his supreme responsibility to get on with it, day by day,
as best he could.

Sam Howells – in 1919 – in 1929 – in 1939 – in 1951. [School Archive]

All the stories and remarks I have retailed about Sam I could have repeated, in their respective context, about Jimmy. That prompted me to wonder, since there were hundreds and thousands of schools like ours up and down the country, how many Sam's and Jimmy's there were who did what they did in the 1940's. Men in their middle years, who had beavered at the blackboard and the laboratory bench for two decades or more, who suddenly found themselves behind the headmaster's desk, given a bucket of mud and some wisps of straw, and told to go and make bricks for the duration.

It was all very well, and necessary, that young teachers should dash off to war and do their bit for their country, but those who found it their duty to stay behind and soldier on, in their own equally necessary way, are equally praiseworthy. It was also all very well for those young men, the lucky ones, to come back as seasoned veterans with chestfuls of medal ribbons and rich funds of racy anecdote with which to entertain hero-worshipping boys, and bright ideas on how to revolutionise the profession. What a relief from those crusty old so-and-so's, who now stooped and shuffled and gathered tattered gowns round their stained, baggy suits and spent their time telling everybody what they couldn't do. They were the dedicated few who had kept the ship afloat, and had little to show for their efforts but a battered set of buildings, some declining exam standards, and a lot more grey hairs.

But these men are the true 'old masters', whatever sense of the phrase you care to employ. They are among the unsung heroes of the profession. Their wit and humanity and sense of perspective and unobtrusive hard work kept schools going, and did a lot of good to a lot of children, in a very bad time. If a child ran into a Sam or a Jimmy during formative years, he (or she) could count himself (or herself) that much richer.

26. The Game is Afoot

One of the hazards of an archivist's work is interest. Whenever a freshly-discovered picture or aged school magazine or yellowing report comes into the hand, the danger is that one may become so engrossed with reading it, and relating it to other documents, that the normal business of an archive office can become suspended. By the same token, if an archivist goes off into the outside world in pursuit of particular knowledge, he is in danger of meeting so many informative people, of being shown so much absorbing material beyond his original quest, and of being presented with so many hitherto unsuspected avenues of exploration, that he is in peril of, at the very least, being sidetracked. Or rather 'overtracked' – in that he finds a host of other stories waiting to be recorded.

Take the Brereton-Watson Quest. I have written elsewhere in this book about the School's founder, the Revd. J.L. Brereton (see 'Founding Father'), and about the second, and acting, headmaster, the Revd. W. Watson (see 'Holding the Fort – I'). Brereton, when his father, the rector of Little Massingham in Norfolk, died in 1867, left West Buckland to go and succeed him. He was to stay as rector there till he died in 1901.

Watson, after a spell, as I said, as Acting Headmaster at West Buckland, had so impressed Brereton that when he, Brereton, opened his new county school at North Elmham in Norfolk (only a few miles from Little Massingham), he invited Watson to come and be its first headmaster. Which he did. And stayed till *he* died in 1889.

For family reasons my wife and I wanted to visit that part of Norfolk, so I decided to combine the two errands – mingle with the younger generation, and dig out facts about an older generation during the course of the same weekend. I took time off from daughters-in-law and grandchildren, and spent most of Saturday on Brereton and Watson.

The weather was glorious, if somewhat 'bracing', as the holiday brochures would have it – crystal skies, bright sun, and a wind to keep the bloom on the cheeks. I met several interesting people. Most willing people too; as soon as they became convinced of my *bona fides*, they opened their memories, their scrapbooks, their libraries, and their photograph albums. I was presented with a huge packet of fresh intelligence – though ironically the majority of it was not directly related to either Brereton or Watson. This is my point. Well, two points actually: you never know what you are going to come across, and, whatever you *do* come across – whether it is relevant to your original enquiry or not – it is usually thoroughly engrossing.

I found Brereton all right – in Little Massingham church. In fact I found a lot of Breretons. Members of the family held the rectorship from 1820 till

1942 – five of them. For all I know, there may have been Breretons in the living before that. A most knowledgeable custodian (verger, churchwarden, sacristan, what you will – probably all four, as he told us that there were barely fifty people in the whole village now) told us that Breretons possibly went back to Norman times, since the 'Brere' part of the name signified 'bear' in old French. I can as yet find no confirmation of this, but then I am not the sort of bibliophile who has dictionaries of mediaeval French on his shelves.

My informant also told me that there was a very old connection between the Breretons and Wales or the Welsh Marches, since the family name 'Lloyd' appeared in the names of so many of them. Well, that figures. There was certainly a branch in Cheshire, and a pretty affluent branch by all accounts; an article from the *Daily Telegraph* of 27th July, 2002, which found its way into the School Archive, informed its readers that Sir William Brereton built a pile called Brereton Hall in the late 16th century, and that Sir William was later promoted by Queen Bess to the peerage. The Hall's modern owner recently hosted a gathering of 120 Breretons from all over the world. During my family weekend I also visited an old school friend in the village of Brampton, about twenty miles away, and he told me had a neighbour called Brereton. So I hope I have satisfied the court that there is no shortage of current Breretons.

Not much of a shortage of older Breretons either; above the choir stalls there is a huge plaque recording the names and dates of nineteen of them. Their graves lie just outside the east wall. All five of the rectors – Charles, son Joseph, and grandsons Henry, Philip, and Francis. Two Frances' – both Charles and Joseph married a Frances. Four of Brereton's five spinster daughters. Brereton's eldest son – William, who escaped from the usual Brereton fate of becoming either a clergyman or a schoolmaster, and became a Lieutenant-Colonel in the Royal Munster Fusiliers. William's son was called Munster. How many sons have been inflicted with their father's regiment for a Christian name?

Behind the altar was a splendidly-carved reredos to the memory of Frances, daughter of the Revd. William Martin. She was the seventeen-year-old English rose who had married the young Joseph Lloyd Brereton back in 1851, and who had borne him sixteen children. Small wonder she predeceased him. If ever a woman deserved her memorial, she did.

The customary little printed brochure of the church's history added more family members. It tells the story of a rather rash Brereton who was a cavalry officer in the Civil War. Any student of military history will tell you that a crucial factor in most successes on the battlefield is timing. Well, this young Brereton, no doubt eager to add further glory to the 'bear' of the family name, went and spoilt things by charging at the head of his troop before the signal had been given. King Charles, who was not noted for his military acumen, nevertheless knew enough to understand the significance of the error. He was not known either for the sternness of his military discipline; he is said to have observed mildly, 'Let the bear be muzzled.' Cromwell, one suspects, would have had him tried at a drumhead court-martial.

Be that as it may, the emblem of the family thereafter featured the head of a bear with a muzzle on it. Carved 'busts' of muzzled bears still stand at the ends of the choir stalls in Little Massingham Church.

The old rectory – Brereton's rectory – is gone. Pity. A modern, squarish red-brick house stands in its place. So it is hard to picture the old parlour where the elderly Joseph sat at the head of the family table and lorded it over his five dutiful spinster daughters, who, as the end of the century approached, were slipping into permanent maidenly school-marmery, making ends meet by running a little boarding school for teenage girls and young boys, stitching holy patterns on hassocks, and making cucumber chutney for the summer fete.

This picture of rural obscurity and straitened circumstances does not sit easily with the record of Brereton's long public life of hobnobbing with titled names, floating numerous companies, managing the shares of these companies, travelling all over England in pursuit of the bees escaping from his bonnet, losing several fortunes (which often belonged to other people), and generating debts which his long-suffering family would spend more than a generation paying off. As the best-informed student of his life has remarked, 'In a life shot through with contradictions, perhaps the greatest was [his] compulsion to spend money recklessly while enjoining frugality on others.' (See the list of sources at the end of the chapter on 'Founding Father.')

As for Watson, the man Brereton translated from a rural living in North Devon (he had gone there after leaving West Buckland) to a headship in Norfolk, I found pretty slender pickings. Like Brereton's rectory, his school had long gone. Unlike Brereton's rectory, there had been nothing put in its place.

But *before* it went – ah, that is another story. I already knew that Watson had been forced out of office by ill health, a complaint which also afflicted his Norfolk County School. Brereton's own son, Francis, inserted by his father as Headmaster – against his will – to perform a rescue mission, failed. Before the century was out, the school had closed.

I also knew that the building had subsequently been taken over by the Dr. Barnardo organisation, and that a new school had been opened, a naval training college for orphan boys who intended to proceed to service in the

Merchant or the Royal Navy. But from here onwards, I entered into mostly uncharted waters.

Plenty of material survived about this naval establishment, but very little about the old County School. Well, it was over a hundred years ago. Curiously, the old name of the School still stuck to the local railway station. Brereton, with his customary energy and charm, had prevailed upon the railway company in question to insert a station on their new line through rural Norfolk to serve his County School. (He had done the same with Filleigh Station to serve his new County School at West Buckland.) The line was closed in 1963 – a casualty of the late, unlamented Dr. Beeching – he of the notorious 'cuts'.

Well, the station is still there. In defiance of history, and with that cussed attachment which rural folk have to familiar names, it is still called 'the County School Station', even though it went on to serve the needs, for over fifty years, of the Watts Sea School. Its name is still up above the door and on the platform, and, what's more, is also enshrined in the relevant Ordnance Survey map. A lady who works there at weekends, to provide cups of tea to walkers and railway enthusiasts, showed me, in the waiting room, a print of the laying of the foundation stone of the County School – by the Prince of Wales, no less (he was only just up the road at Sandringham) – on 14th April, 1873.

Another informant showed me an entry in a book entitled *Norfolk Annals*, which described the event in considerable detail. Absolutely everybody was there, of course – the Prince and Princess of Wales, the Bishop of Norwich, Lord and Lady Suffield, Viscount Newry, the Earl of Leicester, Lord and Lady Sondes (a prominent local landowner over whose park the School looked from its hilltop site – West Buckland School was also on rising ground overlooking Lord Fortescue's many acres). The 'large and distinguished company . . . . partook of luncheon in a marquee'. Another parallel here – no event at West Buckland worthy of the name was complete without the 'company' indulging in a 'luncheon'. His Royal Highness still had some room left too; he and the Princess of Wales also took tea with Lord and Lady Sondes before returning to Sandringham 'by special train'.

Guess who read an address to their Royal Highnesses. Right first time – Prebendary Brereton, 'chairman of the Board of Directors'. That man got in everywhere.

But you see what is happening, don't you? I am getting further and further away from the Revd. William Watson. The very essay I am writing about the danger of being sidetracked is itself in danger of being sidetracked by all this talk of opening ceremonies and special trains and the Prince of

Wales' appetite. And the man I was looking for, the Revd. Watson, the Headmaster of this brand-new school, who must have been there, does not get a mention.

He is faceless. Literally. Nobody I spoke to had a picture of him, which is what I really wanted. Nobody knew where one could be found. Nobody knew whether there were any descendants of Watsons still in the area (he had *eleven* children, so the chances are high). The School – West Buckland – has had fifteen headmasters, and I have a photograph of all of them, except one – Watson.

All I knew before I went to Norfolk was that he became Headmaster of the County School at North Elmham, fathered eleven children, fell ill, was forced into early retirement, and died before he was fifty. By the time I came away, I still didn't know any more. I came close once. I went into the village church. The Visitors' Book, as luck would have it, showed, only three weeks before, the record of a visit by an old boy of the Naval School. But nothing, of course, relating to Watson; an old boy of *his* school would have had to be about a hundred and twenty.

However, it did occur to me that Watson could well be buried in the churchyard. Unfortunately, it was our last morning, time was getting on, and we had over three hundred miles to drive. Maybe, when I get back to my desk, a letter or two to the local incumbent or the Norfolk Records Office, or the relevant organ of the local press might push the enquiry further. Moreover, I have since met a great-grandson of Brereton who is embarking on research on Brereton papers in that very Records Office; perhaps he will come up with something.

So I came away. It had been a marvellous weekend: spectacular weather, for April; delightful countryside – Dutch skies, hares scampering along the roadside, phalanxes of ivy-bound oaks, miles of flint walls; a profitable family meeting, in which a few tentative bonds may have been forged between grandfather and grandson; a splendid lunch with an old friend; a fine hostelry which served monumental breakfasts; and – *and* – a series of visits and conversations which, while not adding in great measure to the extent of my existing knowledge of my two quarries, Brereton and Watson, nevertheless provided a tantalising array of beckoning sidetracks which alas! are unlikely to be explored.

So I shall not find out much more about the Chapel which was added to the Norfolk County School in 1883. After the Sea School closed in 1953, the property was sold to a demolition agent. The school buildings were razed to the ground; the outbuildings became a broiler farm and the chapel became a piggery. That, I thought, was that. But it wasn't. I found the chapel in fine condition; it had been bought in 1984, and renovated, by a couple from Sheffield. So life remains – though the couple did not know much about the chapel's history.

The School site, they told me, is about to have some private houses built on it. So life will return there too. But why, one wonders, was such a huge building sold for demolition in the first place? Commentators on its architecture had mentioned its vastness and solidity; comparisons were made between the School and a French chateau, or a battleship! Room for enquiry.

Life will not return to the tiny cemetery on the other side of the road. It contains the graves of about twenty pupils of the Sea School. Two died within twenty-four hours of each other. The lady at the station told me that they had gone off on a foraging expedition in the local woods, deciding apparently that they would live off the land. They devoured some attractive black berries, and fell ill when they returned to their dormitory. Schoolboy – and cadet – honour decreed that one did not snitch on one's mates. By the time the authorities found out that what the boys had actually eaten was deadly nightshade, it was too late. Quite a story there as well.

Did you know that the actor Sir John Mills was born at the Watts Sea School? No – I bet you didn't. Nor that his father was the Headmaster there. Nor that his real name was Lewis Ernest *Watts* Mills.

And I am sure you don't know that an ex-cadet of the Watts Sea School, Frederick Humby, left the School in 1910, and two years later secured for himself a much-envied post as steward on the very latest, and most modern, liner – the *Titanic*. His family and friends contributed to a chapel window in his memory. When the chapel became a piggery, the window was moved to another Barnardo's chapel in Stepney. When *that* closed, in 1968, it was, apparently, put into store – and has not been seen since. It would be interesting to follow that one up too.

And so on and so on. You see? You get interested.

One must know when to stop.

27. Double Rations

West Buckland and its denizens never lose an opportunity for a good meal – usually lunch. Or – as it was in the old days – 'luncheon'. Prize-giving, openings of buildings, visits by distinguished celebrities, or even by undistinguished celebrities – anything is made the occasion of a good tuck-in.

This goes right back to the huge spread laid on by an indefatigable farmer's wife to celebrate the opening of the first custom-built dormitory for the School, way back in 1859. (See 'High Hopes' in the first West Buckland miscellany, *West Buckland School*.)

I have no doubt that another banquet was laid on when Earl Fortescue laid the foundation stone of the main school on 4th October, 1860.

But when the building was finally complete – only a twelvemonth later! – and the Earl's son came to open it (the old Earl had longed to live to do it himself, but, alas, died shortly before the date fixed), the Governors, or Directors, really pushed the boat out.

As the *Illustrated London News* reported on 9th November, 1861, 'His Lordship gave a luncheon to about two hundred of the directors, parents, and friends.'

But that was not the end of it.

In the evening, the local M.P., one Mr. Buller, presided over a dinner in the schoolroom, 'at which a very large number of the gentry, farmers, and tradesmen of the district were present'.

Where did they put it all?

Unless, of course, class distinction was rearing its fastidious head, as it was wont to do in those days. So the 'directors, parents, and friends' – the nibs – got the posh 'luncheon', and in the evening the local M.P., anxious to make sure of his seat, laid on a second (or second-class?) spread for the 'gentry, farmers, and tradesmen' in the evening. Perhaps they had to make do with the left-overs.

Incidentally, it was on this occasion that his Lordship presented to the School the marble bust of the Revd. Brereton, which still sits in lofty, slightly quizzical solitude half way up the staircase to the Memorial Hall.

28. Foreign Legion

A short while ago I gave a talk to a top class in a local primary school, about being evacuated in the Second World War. As an introduction, and in order to focus the problem, I asked them what they thought helps to make us happy when we are children. We put together a list on the blackboard: Mum and Dad, brothers and sisters, home, neighbours, favourite toys and games, friends, household pets, familiar sights and sounds, and so on. We then went through the list, striking out what an evacuee did not have. By the time we had finished, there was hardly anything left.

It made the point. It makes the point too when we consider the position of a foreign pupil walking through the front door to West Buckland for the first time. All right – there are differences. Evacuees were generally younger; pupils from distant countries do not normally come to West Buckland until they are of secondary age. Evacuees were not asked whether they wanted to be evacuated; Hitler was the deciding factor. Foreign pupils come to this school in North Devon because they or their parents wish it, and good money is paid for it. On the other hand, evacuees had some slight advantages over foreign pupils today. They did fit the culture of the places they were sent to, and they did at least speak the language.

Nevertheless, the parallel runs close enough to make it worth using the comparison; it does help, as I said, to focus the problem. These young people from all over the world face a truly daunting prospect when they arrive. By virtue of their circumstances, many of the supports which would normally help them to keep going are stricken from their hands; they have to dig deep into their own personal resources. Most of them manage to survive, one way or another. In such a diffuse mixture, and over such a long period, there will have been the predictable variety of successes and failures, winners and losers, jolly souls and sad sacks. No doubt too their fate will have been the result of both the School's influence and their own personality and efforts.

Down the years, West Buckland has been host to children from over fifty foreign countries (look at the list on page 135). This mere feat of receptivity is in itself a record to take pride in, and the School would not be human if it did not do so. So it will announce in the pages of the School magazine that a Japanese boy played cricket for the First XI, that a Lithuanian was one of two senior pupils to design the School's internet website, that the School Debating Society elected a Hungarian to be its Secretary, that a boy from Uganda became Head Prefect in 1988 and another from Thailand did the same in 2003. Foreign ex-pupils don't do too badly either. One of three Indian brothers became the Commander-in-Chief of his country's Army;

two from Nigeria played rugby for England. Long-standing connections have been built; a successful family of hotelier brothers (nearly all ex-pupils) in Thailand now regularly send their children to the School. Recently we had the first instance (well, the first known to me) of a marriage between a foreign and a British ex-pupil – and the romance began at school. There may well be another in the offing.

These, of course, are the success stories. Are there no failures? No doubt. But it is unlikely that news will reach the School that a former prefect from Bangladesh is now a beach bum in Melanesia, or that a former Brazilian import has set up a drugs cartel in Colombia. If it did, it is not certain that the School magazine would record it. Any more than it would rush to report that one of its *English* ex-pupils had been up to no good with his company's books. Every organisation, be it familial, educational, or commercial, generally prefers to keep its skeletons safely under lock and key in the cupboard.

The commonsense view of this is surely that the majority of foreign students, like the majority of any human group, bowl along and, on the whole, by and large, when all is said and done, taking things all round, do reasonably well. As Damon Runyon said of his guys and dolls on Broadway, they 'do the best they can'.

How do the majority fare, then, during their time at West Buckland?

Perhaps, before we address that, we should offer some reasons why they come here in the first place. Arguably, all the reasons can be boiled down to one word – English. That is, the English language. For better or worse, it has become the most powerful medium of human contact in the world. Therefore, concerned parents in countries where it is not commonly spoken will make efforts to connect their children with this linguistic mainstream. If the best way to achieve this is to commit them to a full-blown English education, so be it.

It is, I suppose, a handsome compliment to the English educational ethos. One might even argue that it is a back-handed compliment to the many wicked English imperialists of the nineteenth century, who, in between enslaving the world and exploiting it, also introduced millions of people to impartial justice, incorruptible administration, efficiency, mechanisation, and the three R's. Anyway – bully for Tom Brown and Billy Bunter.

Because – and this will come as no surprise – it is to the independent schools that these parents send their offspring. Again, I have no figures, but it would seem to be common sense that, if parents can afford to send their children half way round the world, they are not going to commit their sons and daughters to a deprived, inner-city, run-down state comprehensive. Or even to an airy, modern, rural, lively, successful comprehensive. Such schools do not normally have the staff or machinery to receive foreign pupils; they do not have the resources to go out and recruit them; they do not have the facilities to make special provision for them. Finally, there are very few state schools which have the boarding capability to cater for children who need to be accommodated for months at a time (some manage to get home only once a year).

So it is the independents which put out the feelers, which produce CD-Roms about themselves, which send their headmasters to faraway places on recruiting drives. State comprehensives do not normally, I should have thought, advertise on the internet; they have more than enough to cope with dealing with the products of the roads and avenues and estates within a mile of the secretary's office. At the other end of the equation, foreign parents think in terms of a 'traditional English education', and they associate this with the schools which send them material about it. Whether they are right to do so is another matter, but they can only base their decisions on what they are told and what they think they know. So many courses of action are adopted among the human race not because of what *is* happening, but because of what people *think* is happening.

These foreign parents, then, send their children to England for a sound 'English' education, and are encouraged by many independent schools to do so. Even if they commit their sons and daughters to only a year or two instead of the full five or seven, they still expect a dividend. Either way, the School builds contacts all over the world, and its English inmates derive benefit from the admixture of cultures. If it helps young people to understand each other better, it cannot but be a good thing. In short, a fine meeting of interests.

Now, if this process is as successful as the above might lead a reader to believe, why is the School not bursting at the seams with foreign students? Because, if it were, it would no longer be what it is. It could no longer offer a 'traditional English education'. The foreign tail would not be wagging the English dog; it would have *become* the English dog. So the intake has to be rationed.

It is worth noting here that not all the approaches – that is, not all the approaches to West Buckland, but, I would guess, to other independents too – come from parents. We have instances of the initiative coming from the children. One Maltese boy, for example, was turned loose on the internet by his parents, and came up with West Buckland as his first choice. Mum and Dad stood by it. Another, from Thailand, got no help from his parents at all at first; his father spoke no English. But, on his own, he found schools in North Devon. Indeed, his efforts were so successful that he was offered a scholarship in a nearby girls' school. Presumably they had no idea from his Christian name whether he was boy or girl. To be fair to Dad, once the boy had located West Buckland and opened negotiations, he realised his son must be serious, and lent his weight, and his cheque book, to the quest. He later sent his second child too.

Not all families pay the entire bill; a few come on special exchange arrangements between schools, but this is usually for a limited period – a term, or at most a year. (West Buckland has a regular connection, for instance, with a school in South Africa.) Many more come on grants and funds and scholarships. Without them, they could not come at all. Rather like the old eleven-plus and grammar-school system.

So – here they are – forty or fifty of them – from all over the place. What do they think of it?

Probably not much to begin with. Here I shall rely quite heavily on the reminiscences of a Hungarian boy who spent two years in the Sixth Form on a special scholarship. We have kept contact since he left. In response to my questions, he provided me with over ten pages of answers, in near-impeccable English, I may add.

To begin with, quite apart from the sudden separation from family and home, there was the 'lag' effect of hours, days, of travel – by both air and rail – and of stop-overs and suitcase-living and hostels and reception centres and scrappy conversation with total strangers. As Gábor put it, 'All I knew was that I had arrived and I was lost.'

The new arrival would know nothing about the School apart from what it had said in the prospectus – if indeed he or she had even read that. Gábor did at least have the advantage of age – he was sixteen – and he already spoke good English – slowly but quite surely. His vocabulary was extensive, and his knowledge of English literature was in advance of that of many of his English contemporaries. For example, how many sixteen-year-olds of your acquaintance have read Somerset Maugham? Or have even heard of him?

However, Somerset Maugham and R.L. Stevenson did not save Gábor, or any of his fellow-sufferers, from making the usual mistakes and feeling the same sense of desolation. For example, when asked on his first day whether he wanted to come into the dining hall for tea, he declined, saying he wasn't thirsty, not realising that 'tea' meant something else – namely the last meal before breakfast the next morning. I am sure that any other foreign student, if asked, would come up with a similar memory.

Luckily, the young are the young, and nothing if not resilient, and impressionable. There were so many new sights, sounds, and experiences that it would have been a rare teenager indeed who did not respond at least to some of them. Gábor, for instance, actually liked school lunches – quiche, chips and beans; pizza; braised kidney with scrambled egg and fried bread; pork and apple casserole – and discovered the joys of English desserts; he was completely bowled over by rhubarb crumble. He was too late at sixteen to learn much of rugby, but he developed a remarkable fondness for cricket, if only for watching it. One of the great might-have-beens of his school career, he recalled, was that he never had the chance to try and become a fast bowler.

Others, as I have said, with the advantages of starting younger, responded to the challenges of sport. Not surprisingly, the Asians made their mark in the badminton and squash courts, and at table-tennis. Several found their way into hockey teams. A few made it into school rugby squads.

In other fields, several became adept at, of all things, bell-ringing (see 'Passing Tribute'). Gábor, despite his half-Jewish, half-Catholic background, liked going to church at East Buckland. He responded to the sense of community there, and he enjoyed singing the hymns.

Which brings one, neatly, to villages and rural matters. I have not seen or heard much explicit evidence of this, but I would suspect that the Devon countryside must have made a strong impression on all those young people (and they were in a majority) who came from close city backgrounds – Hong Kong, Canton, Bangkok, and so on. The sheer space must have been breathtaking at first – and all of it on tap, as you might say. Built in. Part of the deal.

The Devon weather certainly made an impression. I once asked a South African boy what he mainly missed so far away from home. He did not mention house, town, family, friends, or anything like that. It came simple, direct, and prompt: 'The sun.' The heat too. Another import from Nigeria, who had left an airport sweltering under a temperature of 90 degrees, claimed that his suitcase, when he arrived, was almost empty, because he had put on nearly all his clothes.

Gábor came from Budapest. He was happy to admit that in Hungary, city folk looked down on their fellow-Magyars in the country. They were, as he put it, 'poor cousins twice removed'. But he 'loved being in the country' in Devon.

In fact he liked almost everything. It was the making of him. His enthusiasm carried him into companionship with contemporary English pupils. His English, which, in the first nervous days and weeks, had threatened almost to desert him, now came back with a vengeance, and of course went on to improve in leaps and bounds. His scholarship soon proved formidable; he simply *knew* so much. Besides his command of English, he understood French and a little Russian, and his Spanish was fluent. (He had attended a school when he was younger where the medium of instruction had been Spanish.) He had actually read foreign literature the titles of which were mere names only to the best-informed of his classmates – and as often as not he had read them in the original language. He was far and away the most articulate and polished speaker in the School Debating Society. He was a film buff able to hold his own in almost any company. He was so far into the language of his hosts that he actually relished the humour of P.G. Wode-house.

I had good reason to remember his command of English. In a History lesson, I had occasion to refer to the Puritan Opposition in the Parliaments of Elizabeth I – known in the books as the 'Puritan Choir'. I remarked that, despite their relatively small numbers, they exerted a strong influence because they were so vociferous. Gábor's hand stole upwards.

'Yes, Gábor?'

The question came, measured and clear, in that dark chocolate voice of his.

'That word "vociferous", sir – that was a very interesting usage. Could you please explain?'

Which I did. I then made one remark too many. I said, pleased to raise a smile among the rest of the class, 'I am glad you find my lessons so interest-ing.'

Gábor gave me no quarter.

'No, sir. I did not say that your lessons were interesting; I remarked that your use of the word "vociferous" was interesting.'

Well, OK, I asked for it, but very, very few foreign students would have been able to give it to me quite so surgically. Indeed, very few *English* students could have done it.

There were times, I suspect, when his very scholarship might have grated on other members of the class, particularly in the matter of foreign lan-guages; he always knew the answer, and was keen enough always to offer it. But one can hardly criticise a boy for keenness, knowledge, and for love of knowledge. Indeed, if one had had a whole class of Gábors, one could have mopped up a dozen syllabuses in the allotted time. But the rest of the class were English; they had reached the Sixth Form by due process of – of evolution, if you like. They took for granted so many things that Gábor had worked so hard for, that he was meeting for the first time. They had the rest of their lives to appreciate everything that was English; Gábor had only two years. Of course he had to devour everything. They did not understand his appetite; all they saw was what they thought was his gluttony. In their worse moments, they would have been tempted to see him as a pedant, a swot, and a creep – and narrow-mindedness would have urged the weak to add the final epithet 'foreign'.

It is a truism that the convert Catholic is far more devout and attentive to the niceties of dogma and ritual than the born Catholic. It was the same with Gábor; he had become smitten with Englishness, and was determined, without of course surrendering his Magyar soul, to squeeze the fruits of English education till the pips squeaked.

He was also particularly sensitive to the fact that he had been offered, by virtue of his scholarship grant, a truly remarkable opportunity. He would not be able to bear the thought of going home in the knowledge that he had not made the very best of it. For this reason, he was particularly grateful to the retiring Headmaster, whose efforts resulted in his stay being extended from one to two years, so that he could complete his full 'A' Level courses. Equally when the new Headmaster made him a prefect.

He did so want to be a good prefect. But here he ran into typical schoolboy cussedness. The more he upheld the rules, the more they made life difficult for him. To them he was a foreign martinet; they did not understand the mainspring of his actions. On his side, perhaps, he had not absorbed enough Englishness to insulate himself against their cheek. The more he tried, the more they played up, and of course the more they attributed his zeal to mere foreignness; the more they became difficult, the more he railed at their lack of humanity and fairness.

Perhaps too it was his very maturity which they resented. He behaved with staff like a young adult. His fearsome learning and fluent delivery made teachers forget at times that they were dealing with a seventeen-year-old. To the younger pupils, he was not 'one of them'; he was getting like one of 'the other side'. (Anyone who has spent any time in a school knows that the real atmosphere in the classroom is not one of peace, partnership, fellowship, and understanding; it is a constant state of friendly hostility, point-scoring, and quick-wittery.)

Friendly – that is perhaps the key. (Even in a real war, the men over the way are 'our friends the enemy'.) This friendship comes only with time, usage, practice, and understanding. Everyone who knows how the machinery works knows too that it does not go round without a lot of oil. The trouble is, for an outsider who is new to it and who has only a limited time to become familiar with it, that he sees the cogs and the wheels but he does not see the oil.

If Gábor had had four years instead of two, he would have cracked the problem. He had cracked innumerable others. He would have acquired the necessary self-confidence, flexibility, sense of humour, and low cunning.

To his credit, though, he did make prodigious strides. For instance, I can remember an occasion when he came to the Common Room, and – I forget the details – I sent him away to get something which he should have brought before. He switched on the charm and apologised, flashed a dazzling smile, turned on his heel, skipped off, and flung a promise over his shoulder that he would fetch it 'in the twinkling of an eye'. I thought that was pretty damned good going.

I think it is fair to say that he won general acceptance among his contemporaries. His fluency in the language, his willingness to try, his obvious enjoyment of nearly everything, provided him with a certain unstoppability, but even quite late in his stay the occasional barb of spite would be let fly. He was watching the football World Cup on TV one day; England were about to play Argentina. When the time came for the singing of the English national anthem, the TV audience sang along, and, so as to join in the spirit of the occasion, Gábor chimed in. After the first line, about 'our gracious Queen', one of the English boys whirled on him: 'She is not *your* Queen!' He also inserted a broad biological expletive with it.

It hurt deeply, the more so as the boy in question had not till then been unfriendly. Gábor left the room, joined other foreign students watching another set in another room, and they all cheered and hugged each other when England lost.

The irony is that that English boy may have been otherwise blameless, both before and after. It may well have been that he was simply taken by surprise by his own sudden resentment at what he saw as a usurpation of Englishness by a foreigner. It was as instinctive as a cat lashing out with a claw – immediately forgotten. Nasty remarks to foreign races and nationalities are not necessarily the result of rabid, deep-seated 'racism'; they can often spill out as a result of any one of a hundred adverse moments brought on by bad news, bad health, bad mood, sudden shock. It is no more a fundamental flaw in character than a spat of bad temper, and anyone who boasts that he has no 'racism' in him is guilty of Pharisaic pride; he would not dream of boasting that he never feels bitter about something, or envious, or selfish. Even if we have not *said* anything derogatory about other races or nationalities, there are very few of us who have not, now and then, *thought* it. We may at once have castigated ourselves for doing so, but there it is; the thought flashed through.

So Gábor had his hurts and his miseries, and, like most other foreign students, he developed strategies for dealing with them. He fell back on reading Hungarian poetry. He went out to the edges of the School grounds and swore in loud Magyar at everything in general. He devoured parcels from home – home-made jam, Hungarian sausages, newspapers. As luck would have it, there was a Hungarian student teacher attached to the staff. Whether or not they enjoyed much in common temperamentally did not matter; inevitably, they gravitated towards each other; they were the only Magyar speakers within a thousand miles.

It is clear from Gábor's reminiscences that he is sensitive, observant, and highly articulate, so he makes his points with force. He is probably mercurial too. He suffers well. He happily concedes that he is a great worrier. Maybe this is all part of the Great Magyar Soul – I wouldn't know.

But he is also fair. He was sharp and shrewd enough to see that part of his homesickness sprang from the very fact that he was, generally speaking, having such a good time. There grew an element of guilt that he was enjoying himself so far away from his parents. There grew another element of guilt as he steadily integrated with his English contemporaries; other foreign students who had not made the same progress he had tended to cast looks which spoke of accusations of betrayal. I have heard this feeling recorded by other successful 'foreigners' as well. It is a sad fact that one can not be everything, one hundred per cent, to everybody. There is only so much space in the psyche.

He was remarkably balanced too in his assessment of the education system he found in England, and at West Buckland. For a start, he said, 'I soon found all the traditional English stereotypes proven false. [Note the verb – not "proved", but "proven". Good, that.] The people I met were not haughty and reserved. They were not cold and unfriendly. The food was not dull or bland. The accent was not like the Queen's.'

On the wider stage, he relished the chances to use his own mind. 'At last I was at a school where not only did they not censure you for individual thought, they encouraged it. I felt this was the stuff to give to the troops.'

I can do little better than continue to quote him, as it shows not only what he thought, but how good he is at expressing it, and in a language not his own. 'The syllabus struck me as strange having grown up in the Hungarian school system. I came from a country where education was all about memorising. . . . Even in Literature, where common sense dictates that students should be shown the way to appreciate different works, given the means to decide for themselves what is good and what is not, Hungarians go about heaping information on the students. We learned when Shakespeare died, but not why his plays were so new or so exciting. We learned that "Don Quixote" was the first modern novel, but not what made it so special.

'On the other hand, in England we were given a set of tools – whatever subject we were studying – to dissect and appreciate whatever we were examining in class. This approach was entirely new to me. Not unappreciated, just new. I therefore had a lot of difficulty at first, adapting to the new requirements and somehow trying to change my focus from the facts to the tools of interpreting those facts.'

However, this handsome bouquet presented to the English educational system did not mean that Gábor had surrendered all his critical faculties. 'Naturally, the comparison of West Buckland School and my Hungarian state-run secondary school is likely to give the English system a falsely clean bill of health. [Naturally!] There are private schools in Hungary, run on the English and American principles, which more closely resemble West Buckland than my old school. And probably there are some English state schools which have more in common with my old school in Hungary, than with West Buckland. However, the statement that the Hungarians teach the students facts and the English teach students what to do with the facts, is still valid.' [So the bouquet still smells sweet.]

Gábor – it should be obvious by now – derived a great deal of benefit from his two years at West Buckland. He had his problems. This account would not be credible if it was claimed that he had not: 'It was not all smiles and roses, and I did have to work very hard at getting myself accepted. There were times when I was lonely and miserable and I really did have trouble with the younger kids.'

But the overall balance in the ledger is, so far as I can see, overwhelmingly on the credit side. He lost his shyness; he 'learned to appreciate the ways of a different people'; he tested himself against a whole cluster of foreign problems and challenges, and was vindicated. He was converted to cricket, and any Magyar who admits to that must be well and truly integrated – even so far as becoming, like the English, a little mad. He also fell in love with an English girl, who became, and remains, the light of his life.

'Besides all these benefits, I simply spent two wonderful years at a school I adored. I met people I am in contact with to this day, students and teachers alike. . . . I forged friendships that will – hopefully – last a lifetime.'

It calls to mind the testimony of another, English, pupil which I quote elsewhere (see 'The View from Below'): 'When I sit down and really think about it I struggle to really criticise WB.' (Although I don't think Gábor would have done anything so outrageous as to split an infinitive.)

Perhaps Gábor was lucky. More likely he was simply good at seizing every chance that came along, so to some extent he made his own luck.

He was certainly articulate to a surprising degree. Small wonder that I have quoted extensively from his reminiscences. I simply do not have the time to shoot similar questions at every foreign student we have on the campus, much less to record and analyse their answers. If I had, I should no doubt come across several who had made fewer strides than Gábor at integration, maybe some who had made little effort at all in that direction, beyond learning enough of the language to be able to pick up the relevant knowledge in the academic syllabus.

Gábor too was European, not Thai or Chinese or Brazilian or Nigerian. That does not mean that these pupils could not, in their way, derive just as many relevant benefits – well, relevant to them – from their stay at West Buckland.

I have certainly come across evidence from an Asian pupil that it is one's very success at overcoming problems and integrating which brings a crop of further problems in its wake. Becoming more 'English' does not always make it easy to return to one's native country. One can not pick up the traces as if nothing had happened beyond the acquisition of some book learning and mobility in another language. Signs of 'Englishness' will show, and they won't always go down well with family and old friends. Things which the pupil had tolerated before he left, for the simple reason that it had never crossed his mind to question them, now became objects of criticism, and dislike – even, possibly, shame. Gábor, for instance, has found perpetual trouble with the Hungarian university system. The reasons are not relevant here, but the fact is illustrative of what I am describing.

What these foreign students discover when they get home is a phenomenon as old as the hills of the country that nurtured them. Success in one sphere leads only to problems in the next. Or, if you like, life is one damned thing after another.

Perhaps, after all my attempts to give a balanced view, the reader may still think I have loaded the argument by using the evidence of someone who became so fond of the place. But, as an exit line, may I leave with the audience this idea: the important thing may be not so much the fact that Gábor liked it as the subtlety and sensitivity with which he explains why he liked it – while at the same time putting in some of the warts – and doing it in such gracious English. Now, he didn't just wake up one morning with all those skills ready grown; perhaps West Buckland had a hand in putting them there.

29. *Vive les Aristos*

A hundred and nine years after the Revd. Brereton had set up his new school for the sons of the 'middle class', the Headmaster made a drastic break with tradition; he accepted one of the sons of the aristocracy – and the French aristocracy at that.

Correspondence exists in the Archive to show that the son of the Comte de Panouse asked to stay at West Buckland, and was accepted. Apparently, there had been some kind of 'exchange' visit made by a pupil of the School to a school in Verneuil – the Ecole des Roches. It was about sixty-odd miles west of Paris, and not far from the Count's chateau at Thoiry en Yvelines. By way of returning the compliment, the School was prepared to accept a French pupil from the Ecole, but there was none willing or available to make the trip at that time. This was the spring of 1967.

The Ecole's Director wrote to the HM of WB to ask whether he would be willing to accept instead, as a paying guest, the son of the Count, for a period of one month. The boy wanted to improve on his schoolboy English. A hint was dropped that his second language was Russian. Another hint was dropped about the possibility of private lessons in English.

The Headmaster replied that the School was indeed willing to accept the boy, and generously offered the services of his wife to give him English lessons. Alas! Russian was not possible, as the subject was not on the timetable.

Father appears to have accepted, as his next letter makes no reference to this disappointment, and is concerned only with arrangements for his son's arrival on 19th June. Father would come with him by car, and would stay a short while in Barnstaple. (One wonders what a French aristocrat would have made of hotel cuisine in North Devon in the mid-sixties.)

The Headmaster had specified a fee of £40 for a third of a term, and, taking into consideration various incidental payments and the boy's pocket money, delicately suggested that a total of about £50 to £60 would perhaps be suitable. It was; M. le Comte duly sent it – £60.

It is a bit of a puzzle to work out what the boy did out of School hours. Father had explained that he – his son – was keen on tennis (well, that was all right), and had spent much time with the local sea scouts. Unfortunately, he was a bit rusty, not having rowed 'since he was about two years old'. As is well known, there is not much scope for sea sports in the middle of Exmoor, and the young Count-to-be was unlikely to be much diverted by cricket. The Count, however, had assured the Headmaster that his son was a willing lad and prepared to have a go at anything. One wonders whether anyone in fact ever tried to convey to him the basic principles of the Leg-Before-

Wicket problem. And how did the History teacher get round the tricky business of the guillotine in lessons on the French Revolution?

Anyway, it seems to have worked out pretty well. Towards the end of the boy's stay, the Count wrote to say that his son, judging by his letters home, was 'interested by his new life' and that 'he very much admired the countryside'. The Count was grateful to the Headmaster's wife for her private lessons, and said he was sure that, overall, his son had benefited considerably from his time at West Buckland. He thanked the School for all its trouble and hospitality, and politely asked the Headmaster to drop in next time he was passing, so that he, the Count, could thank him, the Headmaster, personally.

The Headmaster replied gallantly that he was grateful for the invitation, and assured M. le Comte that he and his wife would indeed try to drop in if they happened to find themselves in that part of France.

And that would have been that – except for a couple of small cuttings that fell out from between the old letters from which I have been quoting. They are a classic example of the fact that, when you trawl through old files and documents, you never know what you are going to come across.

For example, if you were tracing the arrangements for a boy's one-month stay at a country boarding school, would you have expected to stumble across news of a couple of original Chopin manuscripts? No. Well, I did. The first cutting comes from the *Daily Telegraph* of November, 1967. It explained that the original manuscripts of two Chopin waltzes had been discovered in the library of a French chateau not far from Paris. They had been 'provisionally' certified as genuine by the Bibliothèque Nationale. They were of Opus 18, in E flat, and Opus 71, in G flat. These waltzes were in fact well known, but the manuscripts had long since disappeared.

And where had these presumably priceless documents been found? In the chateau of – you've guessed it – the Comte de Panouse at Thoiry. So the Count's forebears were either keen musicologists, or purveyors of hospitality to celebrities. Is it too great a flight of fancy to picture the maestro, replete with the Count's hospitality, sitting at the grand piano in the great chateau drawing room and strumming away while the huge open fire scatters gleams of romance across the silver candlesticks and his fine-chiselled features? An adoring Georges Sand leans across, strokes his cheek, and says, 'Oh, Frédéric, you improvise so beautifully. You should write some of these things down.' And they had a row in the morning, and went off without them.

The second cutting could not be further away from either Chopin or boarding schools. It was about the Count again, and came from a newspaper of May, 1968. The family de Panouse were apparently known in some circles as 'the French Bedfords'. By way of vindicating this appellation, they were planning – in May, 1968 at any rate – to open an African game reserve. The Count and Countess sent out invitations to the opening ceremony which included an etching by Decaris (the cutting quoted his name, with no qualifying clause at all, as if the general reader was *of course* well acquainted with his work). This etching portrayed lions, elephants, crocodiles, giraffes, panthers, rhinoceroses, gazelles, and wild boar, against a backdrop of the main façade of the chateau.

The game reserve was the third commercial venture of this enterprising aristocrat. He had, two years previously, thrown open his grounds to the general public, and in the following year had added a zoo. Now had come the African game.

There cannot have been all that many French aristocrats who flung their estates open to the public with such grand opening ballyhoo. (Come to think of it, after the culling by Madame la Guillotine, there cannot have been all that many French aristocrats – full stop.) One wonders therefore if the Count de Panouse and his great project were the origin of the famous story about the chap who did just that, and, as the *pièce de résistance*, offered a prize of a million francs to anyone who would be willing to swim the moat round the chateau. There was just one small problem: the moat was full of man-eating crocodiles.

The great day came; the crowds gathered – round the moat, naturally. Nobody seemed eager to accept the count's challenge. He tried further persuasion on the public address system. '*Mesdames et Messieurs*, a million francs, to paid at once to the lucky man. And I will offer a further prize as well – the chance to meet the lady of your choice, not matter who she may be – film star, pop star, Olympic champion, whoever you like.'

The crowd fell silent. Nobody moved. Just as the Count was wondering what he could possibly do next, there was a sudden splash, and there was a man swimming for his life, with a clutch of hungry crocodiles in silent, hull-down, pop-eyed pursuit. He made it, but only just; one of his pursuers managed to get a consolation prize of a pound or two of flesh from a trailing leg.

The Count, distraught, went to visit him in hospital, taking, of course, the million francs.

'Now,' he said, 'the second half of the bargain. Who would you like to meet?'

The man turned away in weary disgust.

'I mean it,' said the Count. 'Believe me, I know everybody. Who would you like to meet? Sophia Loren? Gina Lollobrigida? Golda Meir?'

The man turned to look at him.

'Did you say anybody?'

The Count nodded vigorously. He was anxious, for good public relations, to make it up to him.

'Anybody.'

'Well,' said the man, 'in that case, there is someone.'

'Name her.'

'Not a woman. I should like to meet the man who pushed me in.'

I intend no disrespect with the above anecdote; it was just that the train of thought was irresistible.

There remains a sizeable straggle of loose ends which further research could possibly tie up. Most obviously, of course, is one about the story. Did the Count have man-eating crocodiles in his chateau moat? Did he have a moat at all? Is it possible that he arranged for his son to stay a month in England to brush up his colloquial English, specifically to qualify him further for the part of charming host to English visitors? Does he still have in his possession the two Chopin manuscripts? Were they finally authenticated by the scholars of the Bibliothèque Nationale? If he doesn't have them, where are they now? Does his son still run the Thoiry game park and zoo? After all, he would be only about fifty by now. Does he still have fond memories of the 'countryside' which he much 'admired'?

Closer to home, who was the person who remembered the boy's visit and inserted the two cuttings in his file months after he had left – probably never to return? Did the Headmaster and his wife ever find that they just happened to be passing, and so did they ever 'drop in'?

But what a heady mixture to find in a dog-eared buff file in a School archive – French counts, *châteaux*, rowing at the age of two, Russian as a second language, Chopin manuscripts, crocodiles and panthers, and etchings by 'Decaris' – whoever he is.

Light years away from middle-class education for the sons of farmers and local coal merchants. What would the Revd. Brereton have made of that?

Château Reserve 6/5/68

ON Thursday the Count and Countess de La Panouse, whom some call "the French Bedfords," will open a new public attraction at their Château de Thoiry en Yvelines, south-west of Paris. It is

Africa for the French

an African game reserve which, if the etching I reproduce is to be believed, will embrace lions, crocodiles, giraffes, panthers and elephants.

The attractive etching, by Decaris, was sent out by the Count and Countess with invitations to attend this week's opening ceremony. In the background is the château. That, at least, is real.

The venture is a development. The couple opened their grounds to the public in 1966, adding a zoo in the following year.

Part of the brochure for the game park at Thoiry en Yvelines. [School Archive]

30. Holding the Fort II – G.B. Smith

We didn't see enough of G.B. Smith. Nothing like enough. This impression grew upon me as I found out more about him. To begin with, I had nothing but his name, though that was evocative if you consider it by means of the initials – GBS (George Bernard Shaw, for the benefit of those who did not grow up in the shadow of Shaw's reputation as something of a national gadfly and chatterbox, in addition to that of being one of the century's leading playwrights).

Graham Burrell Smith, Headmaster, 1940-41. [Sedbergh Archive]

There it was, in the reference list of the School headmasters – in between Mr. Badger, who left in the summer of 1940 to join the Forces, and Mr. Howells, who, as Second Master, was invited by the Governors to take over the reins when Smith left a year later – for the duration, of course; there was the implicit suggestion that, when more peaceful times arrived, the Governors would appoint someone glittering with degrees and blues, more in keeping with the dignity of the School. (Something must have happened to make the Governors change their minds, because Mr. Howells was later officially confirmed as the 'proper' Headmaster, and continued as such until 1952.)

Badger himself had been in office only since the beginning of 1939, so, what with his early departure, the brief occupation of the chair by Smith, and the 'temporary' arrangement about Howells, all within two years – and the War itself – it must have been a pretty choppy episode for the School. Rather like the notorious Time of Troubles in the late sixteenth and early seventeenth centuries in Russia, when Tsars came and went with alarming rapidity. I am glad, however, to be able to reassure worried readers that none of the headmasters in question met the sort of sticky end which enveloped most of those ephemeral rulers of old Mother Russia.

As I said at the outset, I had little on Smith but his name – and I wasn't even sure of that. Was it G.B. Smith or was it G. Burrell-Smith? I had two theories offered for what the 'G.' stood for. I had one badly-lit photograph of the School Debating Society, taken in what looked like a curtained hall, with G.B.'s spectacles gleaming out of the gloom like a pair of Spitfire pilot's goggles on a moonlit night, and out of nowhere in particular I had received the stray fact that he had once been at Sedbergh School.

So Sedbergh appeared to be the first port of call – indeed the only port of call, except the random chance that I might make contact with surviving Old Boys from 1941 who could possibly, but only possibly, remember something about him. (I was in fact able to do so, but recall of a man who stayed such a short time was necessarily scrappy, especially a headmaster, who does not normally intrude personally in the lives of many small boys.)

And here I unearthed a mesh of coincidence that, at first sight, prompts a near-incredulous shake of the head. In answer to my enquiry, I first received a charming letter from the Headmaster of Sedbergh, Mr. Christopher Hirst, who informed me that he was no stranger to West Buckland, as he had been Chairman of the board of governors of St. Michael's, a nearby preparatory school just outside Barnstaple. Moreover, he had also been the Headmaster at Kelly College in South Devon, so he knew the county well. That was only the start of it.

(Kelly College had a connection with West Buckland too. The Headmaster who had started the turnover in 1938 by leaving, a Lt.-Commander Westall, had gone on to become Head of Kelly College for the next twenty years.)

Yes, indeed, said Mr. Hirst, Mr. Smith had been at Sedbergh, as Headmaster moreover, for nearly ten years. It also turned out that Mr. Badger, who had been Smith's predecessor at West Buckland as Headmaster, had worked at Sedbergh under Smith's headship. I was later to discover that Smith had worked at Osborne and Dartmouth Naval Colleges. Westall, as a naval man, had naturally trained at Osborne and Dartmouth, and, since their dates overlap, it seems more than likely that Smith taught Westall. West Buckland also had an ex-pupil, William Stradling, who later went on to teach at Osborne and Dartmouth during the same period, and so would also have known both Westall and Smith.

Finally, I received a second letter from Sedbergh, from the School's Librarian and Archivist, a Mrs. Elspeth Griffiths, who told me that her brother was an ex-pupil of – guess where – West Buckland School.

Now, I know that there are only so many counties in England, and only so many independent schools, and there must be a certain amount of – shall we say – cross-fertilisation, but by any standards this does seem to be a somewhat unusual series of connections.

It was this obliging lady, Mrs. Griffiths, who, in response to my request, embarked on a steady search for 'Smith' memorabilia, and, over the next few months, it was she who produced the bulk of the material for this piece. The final article, the finished portrait, may be mine, but the bricks and mortar, the nuts and bolts, the paints and pigments, were provided largely by her, and for this I am most grateful.

Graham Burrell Smith (there was no double barrel, it seems) was born in January, 1880 – or April, depending on whether you trust the editors of *Who Was Who* or of the King's College, Cambridge, magazine. His father was a barrister. He – the son – went to City of London School, and won a scholarship to King's College, Cambridge in 1899. It was probably a choral scholarship – which makes sense, bearing in mind the great choral tradition at King's, and his own subsequent success in that sphere. He obtained a First in Part I of the Historical Tripos and a Second in Part II. Then he stayed on for a fourth year, and got a Second in Part II Theology. Had his mind turned towards the ministry during his time there? The influence of all that singing in King's Chapel? He must have spent a lot of time there, and to some purpose. One of the dons remembered years later that 'he was about the best alto we ever had'. At King's, that is high praise.

That, at any rate, took him up to 1903. During the next two or three years, he must have sorted himself out – musician? priest? teacher? – because his first posts were at Epsom College in 1904, and the Royal Naval College at Osborne in 1905. (Again, *Who Was Who* says 1906). In the interval he presumably obtained a Postgraduate Certificate of Education – if such pieces of paper existed as early as 1903. He worked at Dartmouth Naval College too. During that time (1905-1915), as I said, he could well have taught a young cadet called Rupert Westall, later Headmaster of West Buckland from 1934 to 1938. And he was a colleague of William Stradling, the West Buckland prodigy, who won practically every scholarship, race, cup and medal on offer during the late 1890's.

That took him into the War – the Great War – the War to end wars. Smith was seconded to the Intelligence Department of the Admiralty. We don't know whether he volunteered to join up; he was only into his thirties, and a bachelor. Perhaps he did, and failed the medical. He was on the short side, and well covered. 'Rotund' was an adjective that sprang to the mind of more than one writer describing him. In later years he was a great encourager of games, but there is no surviving record of his participating in the usual athletic pursuits. It says in one source that he 'was brought into contact' with Navy Rugger at Osborne, but not that he actually played. The same source was careful to say that he was a 'votary' of cricket – 'votary', not 'performer'.

Or maybe the nature of his teaching and the subject matter of it peculiarly fitted him for intelligence work, which would mean that he would not have been allowed to do military service even had he wanted to. Lots of teachers and dons found their way into such work during both wars. Recent publication of the work of the code boffins at Bletchley Park has made it clear not only that clever young people were recruited, but that they were offered little choice in the matter. There was a lot of heartache among them about the 'cushy' jobs they had while their contemporaries were under fire all over the world.

At first sight this intelligence work would explain the origin of one of his nicknames – 'the Spy' – but not so. More later.

After the War was over, Smith returned to what was clearly now his confirmed *métier*. He went to work at Repton, as Senior History Master and Librarian. He remained there for seven years, till 1926.

It was during this period that he brought to full flower what had become a many-sided personality. He was highly intelligent – Cambridge, a First in History, and so on. He had his singing. To this he had added a notable skill with the clarinet. (He later helped to found a school orchestra at Sedbergh, so he clearly had a good all-round knowledge of and interest in music.) He may not have played games, but he understood rugger, and was a 'votary' of cricket, in the golden days of the inter-War county game, when cricket was the summer sport everybody went to see, when Hobbs, Hendren, Woolley and Tate were household names, and when it was the chosen activity of nearly every schoolboy in a park or up against a cul-de-sac wall.

He had developed an interest in ski-ing. So, though he may have had little ball sense, he was no non-bender. Oh – and he had also turned himself into a very competent photographer.

Scholar, historian, singer, clarinet player, sports-watcher, ski-er, camera craftsman – pretty impressive on a CV. What transmuted this portfolio of skills from being merely impressive to being absolutely invaluable was the final quality that any good teacher needs if he is to succeed – the ability to communicate. To communicate sound knowledge, good standards, and above all enthusiasm. Smith appears to have had this in abundance. Before he had left Repton he had established the School's reputation as 'a nursery of History Scholars', and he had been very willing to put his other skills and experience at the disposal of both pupils and colleagues. He possessed what might be called 'clubbability', and, in the clubby atmosphere of the public school system, a little of this went a very long way.

It secured Smith a headship at the end of 1926. That does not imply that he was a calculating cultivator of 'the right people'. The record indicates that his character and his manner were both genuine and unconscious. It was simply that he had all these gifts, and he was at his best when he was sharing them. If that brought a headship, well and good. If it didn't, too bad. I suspect he would have been content to carry on doing what he had already been doing, and doing very well. He had no wife urging him on to 'better things'. He had therefore no family, the expenses of whom would have necessitated promotion and higher salary. He had a rich, full life, which he obviously enjoyed.

On the face of it, then, he was a splendid candidate for a headship. The Governors at Sedbergh agreed; he was their unanimous choice. At the same time, it was possible that his fellowship on ski-ing holidays with Old Sedberghians in Switzerland, and his friendship with Mr. Weech, the retiring Headmaster, might have helped – just a little bit.

Coincidence reared its head again: one of the final three candidates was from the staff of the Royal Naval College at Dartmouth; and only a month before Smith was appointed, a young graduate from Brasenose College, Oxford, joined the staff to teach Latin – a Mr. H.D. Badger, who was later to precede Smith as Head of West Buckland.

Mr. Weech, by all accounts, was a hard act to follow, despite his apparently harmless nickname – 'Billie'. As the Editor of *The Sedberghian* remarked, 'It is almost impossible for the younger generation to imagine Sedbergh without Mr. Weech. We could hardly believe that a successor to him could be found.' Which, since it was written after the event, at least implies, obliquely but generously, that one had.

The Editor offered the wry comment that one of the results of the intense interest generated by the search for Billie Weech's successor was that nearly every visitor to Sedbergh during the 'search' period was eyed curiously to try and divine what sort of headmaster he might make – including two commercial travellers and an organ blower.

Smith needed to be not only good to follow a man like Weech, but unflappable. For the School was going through a bad time. The post-war boom had played itself out, and prospective pupils were getting thinner on the ground. And if that did not affect all the independent schools, what followed in the early 1930's certainly did – the Depression. So Smith had hardly pulled the School round from one crisis before he was faced by another, even more serious.

But he kept his head up (forgive the pun), and the numbers – just. By his refusal to be rattled by events or circumstances, he maintained morale. By his energy and his acknowledged geniality, he was able to generate the wherewithal for a worthy batch of improvements – a biology laboratory, a new sanatorium, a pavilion or two, squash courts, improved chapel lighting, and a swimming bath.

Well, you may say, isn't that what headmasters are supposed to do – build up the School a bit? It is a poor head who can't manage more than a new bike shed and a set of indoor toilets in ten years. True. So Smith was possibly only doing what scores of independent school headmasters were doing up and down the country. In default of comparative figures for new squash courts and cricket pavilions among HMC schools between the Wars, it is impossible to offer a definitive verdict. But, in the light of the difficulties stated above, it seems nevertheless a creditable record.

But Smith's real contribution lay beyond Governors' Construction Committees and bricks and mortar and local M.P.'s laying foundation stones.

He was, first and foremost, a teacher, and he was interested in the welfare and development of boys. It is pointless to try and argue that, by today's standards, he might appear to be a one-sided, unathletic, quirky bachelor – 'an alto, for God's sake' – who was biased in favour of privileged boys from wealthy families. Pointless, irrelevant, tendentious, and unfair. He was born into a set of circumstances, he discovered within himself a set of gifts, and he generously put to use those gifts in the circumstances in which he found himself. You might as well criticise him for not being interested in state schools or girls' education as you might criticise a missionary in Africa for not being interested in South America. Like the missionary, he gave his life to it – a very long life as it turned out.

He was in the tradition of fine teacher-headmasters, as opposed to the more modern trends of fine administrator-headmasters or smart marketing-headmasters or worldly-wise public-relations headmasters or ego-driven celebrity headmasters. Each set of contemporary needs calls forth a contemporary response.

In Smith's case, History was his subject, music was his second love, photography his hobby, and sport his leisure pursuit, albeit as, probably, a spectator. But running through it all, tying it all together, making sense of it all, was his vocation – boys' education.

He was no dewy-eyed idealist though. In his very first report to the Sedbergh Governors, in early 1927, he pulled no punches. He praised the 'tone and character' of the boys, and the 'initiative and efficiency' of the prefects, but went on to observe that he was 'not equally impressed by the average intellectual calibre of the School'. So he knew perfectly well what he was taking on, and that it would call forth all his many talents. The next nine or ten years were to vindicate him, and his philosophy, right up to the hilt.

Already, from the time he was at Repton, the evidence had been coming through, particularly from *The Repton Letters*, a collection of letters home by the writer, Christopher Isherwood, who studied under him there.

Smith taught him History and Civics. Isherwood is gratified that 'Mr. Smith' appears 'quite pleased' with his essay. So he wants to impress him. He hears papers read by 'Mr. G.B.S.' at the School Literary Society. Like many a precocious young man of letters, he finds plenty to criticise, but the mere fact that he refers to his teacher by his initials – 'G.B.S.' – is usually a sign of fondness and secure intimacy. All right, so GBS was, at that time, an evocative set of initials because of George Bernard Shaw; its use still betokens a boy who is well-disposed rather than the opposite.

Smith gave him valuable advice about university; as this was the 1920's and this was a fashionable public school, that meant, of course, Oxford and Cambridge. Nevertheless, he valued Smith's knowledge and shrewdness. 'He knows all the strings at Cambridge.' And a comment which shows either that Smith was honest or that Isherwood was sharp – 'none at Oxford'. Isherwood was impressed by Smith's knowledge in the Civics class – he 'has been very good on unemployment'.

Smith later invited him, in the summer of 1922, to join himself and a few other boys in a walking tour 'along the Franco-Swiss border'. He offered to 'arrange everything', even to the extent of meeting the costs of unexpected extras. Naturally, he took Isherwood's passport photograph. He took a lot more on the trip (what photographer could resist Alps?). When they returned, Isherwood much admired the enlargements. Isherwood seems to have enjoyed the whole experience, though he thought that three weeks was enough. All this is more evidence, incidentally, that, though Smith may not have been much of a ball-player, he was by no means antipathetic to exercise.

Isherwood later wrote a book called *Lions and Shadows*, and the character of 'Mr. Holmes' is supposed to be a portrait of Smith:

'To look at, Mr. Holmes was a short, stout, middle-aged man [Smith was in his early forties when Isherwood knew him] with reddish hair just beginning to get thin on the crown. He had closely folded, rather prim clergyman's lips and a long, astute pointed nose which was slightly crooked. [Photos bear out the thinning hair at this time, but not quite so conclusively the crooked nose.] His glance was cold, friendly, and shrewd. [Can you be "cold" and "friendly" at the same time?]

'Almost everything Mr. Holmes did or said contributed to a deliberate effect: he had the technique of the first-class clergyman or actor. But unlike most clergymen, he was entirely open and shameless about his methods. Having achieved his object – which was always, in one way or another, to startle, shock, flatter, lure or scare us for a few moments out of our schoolboy conservatism and prejudice – he would explain to us gleefully just how this particular trap, bait or bomb had been prepared. . . . .

'Quiet, astute, disconcertingly witty, he was never widely popular. His brand of humour, and indeed his whole personality, was an acquired taste. A large percentage of his pupils bored him and he showed it. . . . .'

Now, to some extent you can make of this what you like. If the physical descriptions fit – the nose, the hair, the full figure, the middle age – you begin to be persuaded, and tempted to accept the more subtle suggestions about character and behaviour as genuine too. But this was written years after the acquaintance had lapsed, and the original eyes were those of a seventeen-year-old – intelligent and articulate, but immature for all that. He was moreover a pupil, not an equal. From what he says, and from other evidence, it seems that Smith was a practised exponent of the old schoolmaster's technique of keeping one's class on the hop, and of maintaining an inmost keep of mystery which kept them guessing. History teachers too are supposed to make their sixth-formers sit up and question assumptions, to disturb them, to get in underneath them. The fact that he explained his methods afterwards shows that he was not really trying to make them feel uncomfortable; it was all a means to an end.

Then there is the reference to acting. Any teacher who successfully projects himself has to be something of an actor. And a manipulator – it is his job to make things happen, and, if possible, to make it look to his pupils as if they are just occurring by chance. It is interesting too that Isherwood twice uses the comparison of a clergyman – interesting in the light of the fact that Smith read Part II Theology at Cambridge.

What is slightly jarring is the reference to his 'boredom' with 'a large percentage' of his pupils. Of course Isherwood could be plain wrong, but, in view of the fact that we have taken so much of what else he has said seriously enough at least to consider it, we must do the same here. Suppose, therefore, that Isherwood was right, and that Smith was something of an intellectual snob. The trouble then is that it does not square with the bulk of the other evidence, from Sedbergh and, later, from West Buckland.

It could, more harmlessly, be that he responded only to those pupils who showed interest in his subject. Successful teachers are good at creating a lively atmosphere, and can consciously build a 'chemistry' in the classroom, but they cannot do it without a basis of reasonable co-operation and good-will. There has to be a certain amount of two-way traffic. Good teachers may be hypnotists, but they are not wizards; they cannot do it against the will of their subjects.

If an enthusiastic teacher puts on a full show of enthusiasm and energy before a group of indifferent Philistine pupils, he will look silly, and will be dismissed as a buffoon. There can have been few audiences more cruelly critical than a group of 1920's privileged, cocky, public-school, know-all seventeen-year-olds in a room where the only person present showing keenness was the teacher. Smith was far too wily a bird to fall for that. Perhaps all that Isherwood saw was the result – a wary, dry, ironic manner which he interpreted as boredom. I have come across other testimony about so-called sarcastic, unkind teachers (as perceived when the speaker was a boy); when the speaker saw the same man in action years later he was surprised to see how tolerant and understanding that man really was.

What about the remarks that 'he was never widely popular' and that 'his brand of humour' and 'whole personality' were 'an acquired taste'? It could be true. Or it could be that, if Isherwood himself did not quite catch the nuances and the *raison d'être* of Smith's behaviour, then his contemporaries did not catch them either, and if they did not like what Smith had to offer, then it is small wonder that he was not 'widely popular'. There is one enigmatic little postscript to add to this argument, and that is the comment of a man who was a pupil of Smith's years later at West Buckland, and who liked him very much: 'I believe the staff hated him.' But again, pupils often get it wrong.

Finally, all Isherwood's remarks are about a character called 'Mr. Holmes', with the inverted commas, not about Mr. Smith, without the commas. If he had wanted to give a full, accurate pen-picture of his History teacher, he could always have done so, and leave it at that. So, for whatever reasons, Isherwood's portrait is not to be wholly relied upon.

What did Sedbergh have to say about him? I have found nothing to his discredit. History, as one might expect, 'flourished'. So did his new subject, Civics (one of the popular new subjects of the 'tween-war years). Cricket and rugger benefited from his interest and knowledge. So too did other sports like squash, tennis, and athletics (where his 'expert photography' also played a part). He was an inspiration to the musical life of the School, with his re-founding of the orchestra, his enrichment of musical appreciation, his clarinet playing, and his alto singing ('it took the school some time to get used to his pervasive hoot in chapel and chorus').

Much of this is arguably predictable, given his declared personal interests, but Smith's contribution went much further. He set up a Modern Language VIth; he encouraged debating, and participated; he preached in chapel (that Part II Theology again); he built up, stimulated, and developed the teaching of Art – not a favourite gospel in the ruggernaut religion of most public schools then; he looked kindly on the rarefied sport of fell-running (think of Sedbergh's geographical position), and facilitated many a fine performance by granting timely leaves of absence from Chapel.

His reputation as a teacher of History is, if anything, enhanced by the record of his stay at Sedbergh. 'Quite the best teacher of history that I have ever met,' said one of his old pupils. 'His weekly lectures to the sixth form left me spellbound, and for years I kept books of entirely illegible notes taken during them.'

Now comes the evidence that contradicts Isherwood's possibly immature and one-sided verdict. His general manner was said to be less forthright than that of his predecessor, the impressive Mr. Weech – he was 'more likeable'. He was an 'essentially a kind and generous man'. He was not easy to get to know, and could have been shy (he had a slight stammer), but those who did get close enough to know him well 'felt for him not only respect but affection'. One of his staff described him as 'kindly' – not an adjective that teachers usually apply to their headmaster. He was not the dry, academic type who reserved his interest and friendship only for those who exhibited his own interests and inclinations, as Isherwood had suggested. He was indeed praised for his scholarship (he later wrote history books), but he was also praised, and remembered, for his 'sympathetic encouragement of that average type whose interests are not exclusively athletic or bookish'. He was indeed 'interested in everything, accessible to all, the really approachable Headmaster'. You can't have a much finer testimonial than that.

From an educationist's point of view, he does well too. 'His sympathies were liberal and his educational ideas progressive' – the music, the art, the modern languages. He was known, as the above evidence shows, 'for the catholicity of his tastes'.

But the touchstone for judging a teacher is his relations with his pupils, and here Smith comes out with flying colours. The basis for any such relationship is trust, and Smith certainly seems to have had that. He won a great dividend of trust from his pupils because he invested it in them in the first place.

He was a good mixer, according to his obituary in the King's College magazine; he showed 'human understanding' to those in trouble; and he treated the older pupils as 'mature and responsible people'. His obituary in the Sedbergh magazine said substantially the same: 'His relations with boys, at any rate with senior boys, in the classroom and outside, were governed by a complete trust in their being able to behave with good sense and responsibility. Prefects were expected to show initiative in devising measures for the wellbeing of House and School and not to regard their function as merely to carry out orders from above. . . . Finding thus that they were assumed to be mature and responsible beings, boys tended to become such, and there must be many. . . . who profited by this early trust.'

Lest anyone should think that the above material is the distillation of the usual mixture of banana oil, sentiment, and nostalgia which often lubricates such tributes, let a former pupil speak out – one who *wanted* to write something about him. 'He had the knack of making some of our con-sciences prick, and we would even voluntarily confess our sins, clearing up matters which would otherwise have dragged on for ages.' The writer went on to say that, on the one occasion he was sent to the Headmaster for 'correction' for some crime or other, he only 'received a rather languid couple of strokes' on the fundament, admitting that he deserved far worse. And, to his amazement, Smith later made him a prefect.

The present Archivist at Sedbergh, Mrs. Elspeth Griffiths, said the impression that had come through to her from old pupils was of a 'very gentle and civilising influence in the School'.

It was a shock, then, when he left so suddenly, four or five years before his sixtieth birthday. He had never been what one could call robust. He was short, well-covered (or 'rotund', as everybody said), and not especially athletic (although there is a passing reference to the squash court). He wore spectacles. He had a slight stammer, possibly a symptom of a nervous disposition.

He took over the School at a time of falling rolls, and, just when he was getting it back up to scratch, there came the Depression. 410 when he came in 1926. Up to 424 in 1929. Down to 397 in 1931, and down further to 348 by 1934. Enough worries here to consume the energies of a much less committed man. Yet, from the recital of his many activities and interests, it is clear that he threw himself into the life of the School. He lived on site, and there are many similarities between the Headmaster's House in a boarding school and a goldfish bowl. He was a bachelor, and so had no comforts of wife or family to ease the pressure of a life of lonely authority.

There was an outbreak of meningitis, in which several boys died. Imagine the strain of dealing with the worry, the medical measures, the funerals, the welfare of the other boys, anxious parents, and questions in the press. One writer suggested too that he had suffered from the fatigue of trying to take the School too far too fast – which, by its very criticism, indicates a massive investment of thought and energy.

For whatever reason, or combination of reasons, there was some kind of breakdown early in 1936. He resigned suddenly in the Easter holidays. One witness remembers seeing him after the holidays; he had gone completely bald. He had always been a mite thin on top, but now he 'hadn't a hair on his head'. The same writer also claimed that he had been afflicted with diabetes. 'The previous term had done that to him.'

So Smith left Sedbergh.

There is an enigmatic entry in *Who Was Who* which says, after the Sedbergh bit, 'Cornwall Education Committee'. We know he went to live there, because there is an even more tantalising entry in the Sedbergh magazine, which says that they 'heartily wish, to him and to Miss Burgess, long life and happiness in the chosen spot of their retirement' – which was named, appropriately, Mawnan Smith.

So did he take the plunge at last? You might think so, because, in the 1930's, retiring headmasters did not normally announce their intention of cohabiting with maiden ladies in Cornwall, or anywhere else for that matter. Nor did respectable school magazines record such matters – much as many a seditious sixth-former editor might have been tempted by the seismic possibilities to do so. However, it is the disappointing duty of the historian to point out that another source records Miss Burgess as Smith's niece, who had kept house for him at Sedbergh. Of course, it is not beyond the limits of possibility, or the limits of English Common Law, that Mr. Smith did indeed marry his niece. But, in default of further evidence, it would not be seemly to venture into such a tortuous byway of speculation. Suffice it to say that Miss Burgess, having flashed across the screen so to speak, vanishes again. There is no sign of her at West Buckland. No Old Boy remembers anything about a wife. Or a maiden lady. Or a niece.

Whether Smith in fact went to work for the Cornwall Education Committee or not is unrecorded in any source known to the present author. We do know, however, that he wrote – three history books in fairly rapid succession:- *An Introductory History of Europe in the Middle Age* ['Age' – that's what it said, not 'Ages'] (1938), *France, 1815-71* (1939), and *France, 1598-1715* (1940). He was no stranger to the author's craft; while at Sedbergh, he had made a notable contribution to a massive – and very ambitious – History of the World, edited by his predecessor, 'Billie' Weech. The reviewer in the Sedbergh magazine offered it as his opinion that Smith's chapter on 'Islam and Christianity' was 'the most accomplished portion of the whole book, from the viewpoint of brilliant scholarship no less than as a piece of graceful and lucid writing'.

Then he reappears in what one could call public life in September, 1940, as the Headmaster of West Buckland. The previous Head, Mr. Badger, had left to join the Forces at the end of the previous summer term. He was the second headmaster to resign in twenty-one months. It was wartime. Where could the Governors find a suitable, well-qualified, youthful, energetic head in such a circumstance? They clearly decided that they couldn't. Badger had worked under Smith at Sedbergh. It seems inconceivable that he did not mention that his old boss, with a decade of successful headship behind him, was living in scholarly retirement in the next county, and might be tempted to come out of that retirement, at any rate for the duration. (A lot of teachers did in fact do so because of the absence of so many men in the Armed Forces.)

Whether or not Badger set up the deal, an offer was clearly made, and Smith came to West Buckland to take over the reins of office. He must have found a school very different from the one he had left behind in Cumbria five years before.

Sedbergh may have shared with West Buckland a proximity to wild open country – fells in the north and moors in the south – and there was a mutual passion for rugby. But the similarity did not go much further than that. Sedbergh may have been rural, but West Buckland was definitely rustic. It was not so fashionable as Smith's old school; it was not so scholarly; it could not boast the cultural sheen that Smith had given to Sedbergh. It had several long-serving staff who had got used to doing things their own way. Its very remoteness had engendered a strong sense of family unity which embraced (one might be tempted to say 'bound') all its inmates, and made it, possibly, suspicious of newcomers, especially those with new ideas. The new headmaster who had arrived in 1934 had had a lot of new ideas, and, personalities aside, it can be no coincidence that he was, for the most part, not popular. (One or two of his ex-pupils have gone much further than that.)

Badger, who had succeeded the reformer, had not stayed long enough to make much of a mark. The Deputy Head was one of the eternity brigade – Sam Howells, who already, in 1940, had twenty-two years of service behind him, and was to notch up another twelve before he died. He had made the School his life, and he admired the Headmaster who had retired, after twenty-seven years, in 1934 – the Revd. Harries. Every school with any kind of history has at least one great headmaster in its chronicles; well, at West Buckland, Harries was that man. The shadows of his headship and his personality and his philosophy still loomed over everything. Smith was taking on much more than a wartime holding operation.

This situation goes a long way to explain the remark of an old pupil from West Buckland that 'he was not popular with the staff'. This old pupil, however, was definite in his own praise: 'we thought he was marvellous'. Smith's teaching of History clearly made an impact, because he went on to say, 'If I am a historian it is due to him.' He is now the author of several books of military history, and so speaks with authority. He also became a headmaster himself, and so speaks with even more. Finally, he was one of Smith's prefects, and so was in a position to watch him more often and more closely than other pupils in the School.

There was another contemporary who had little to do with him, but who recalled that even 'at a distance, he always appeared to have a jovial air about him'. He also remembered the 'very shiny bald head'. Apparently his nickname was 'Pate'.

The mere fact of a nickname usually indicates a measure of respect and affection, however grudging. Smith enjoyed two. The other one went back to his days at Sedbergh.

There he was known as 'The Spy'. Which might sound appropriate for a headmaster who was forever trying to outsmart the opposition in the corridors and dormitories and byways of a boarding school. But that was not Smith's way. No doubt he was endowed with the successful schoolmaster's usual ration of Machiavellian craft, but there is no evidence that Smith was a snooper.

Nor does the name come from his days in Naval Intelligence during the Great War – which would have been logical, if erroneous.

It came from a board game called *L'Attaque*. Apparently this game was very popular in the 1920's, when Smith arrived at Sedbergh. It bears comparison with another sort of after-dinner craze which struck England about the same length of time after the Second World War – *Diplomacy*. Let an old pupil of Sedbergh tell the story:

'[The game] was played on a board like chess between two opposing armies. The pieces presented a blank face to the enemy. On their hidden side were pictures of soldiers bearing numbers, the greater number taking the lesser when an attack took place. The Commander-in-Chief was naturally the most powerful piece on the board, but there was one insignificant member of the opposing army, a man in civvies, who could be obliterated by everyone else. [His importance lay in the fact that] his sole object was to slaughter the opposing Commander-in-Chief, and he had to be kept hidden safely away until he was sure of his prey, and could pounce on him. He was

"The Spy", and the Headmaster of Sedbergh School bore a striking resemblance to this furtive fellow, as portrayed on the business side of the piece.'

One suspects that Smith would have enjoyed the nickname, because he clearly had a sense of humour. There is the story of a young teacher who, on being told that he was to teach some subsidiary Geography, admitted his concern that he had never studied any Geography since his days at Prep. school. 'Never mind,' said Smith. 'You'll soon learn.' The teacher said that he did (learn), and he 'very much enjoyed it'. The story has no doubt been told about many a headmaster. It does not display dazzling originality or sparkling wit, but it is indicative of an amused sense of perspective. Several stories have come through about misdemeanours which the perpetrators (either trembling pupils or worried young teachers) expected would be followed by condign punishment or severe criticism, but which were met with Cheshire Cat smiles or blind eyes.

This confidence, and sense of proportion, showed constantly in the classroom. Smith had a good enough grip, and enough sense of fellowship with his classes, to be willing to be sidetracked now and then into reminiscence. One anecdote showed not only this (no doubt carefully-rationed) digressive technique, but a penchant for clairvoyance.

He had taught several members of the Royal Family (at Osborne Naval College, presumably), and was happy to retail stories about them. He was asked what the Prince of Wales was 'like', and replied that 'he was rather a slow learner'. Then comes the gem – the throw-away remark that every good teacher (especially of History) learns to toss into the conversation, and which gets remembered long after the exams have been passed and the old notes thrown away.

Smith offered the observation that, in his opinion, the Prince of Wales would never be crowned King of England. Not only that; he was prepared to put a £1 on his forecast with anyone who cared to take him up on it. A boy called Hough apparently did. The writer said he has wondered ever since whether Hough ever paid up.

Stories do not normally stick to nobodies; Smith was a personality. He was a successful teacher and headmaster too. The balance of evidence about him is in his favour – at Repton, at Sedbergh, and at West Buckland. It is possible that Isherwood at Repton had a point about Smith's apparent intolerance and sharpness towards those he thought were uninterested in what he had to offer, and that Smith's Sedbergh pupils were also right about his general *bonhomie*. The change could have come about simply by the passage of time; Smith, as the years advanced, became more experienced, more broad-minded, and more understanding. It could also explain why (if the West Buckland old pupil was right) the staff there did not like him. If he brought a whiff of northern air, and a breeze of greater tolerance, into a Common Room which had done things its own possibly more authoritarian way for a long time, it is small wonder that he ruffled some feelings.

One ex-fifth-former there also remarked that his class did not do well in their History exam. – the old School Certificate, later 'O' Level, now GCSE. This was not so much because they didn't like him as because they didn't understand him. This is more than likely. Smith's approach was academic, casual, relaxed; he treated sixth-formers as if they were undergraduates. It was not going to work with the – shall we say? – slightly rougher-edged members of the fifth form of a less academic school who would probably have benefited more from a regime of 'do-as-I-say-and-learn-your-notes'. This is nobody's fault; it is just as things were at the time.

Interestingly, no evidence remains of Miss Burgess – the niece who was going to share his retirement at Mawnan Smith in Cornwall, and who may or may not have married him. Nobody I have spoken to about his time at West Buckland remembers a Mrs. Smith, or a Miss Burgess, come to that. One ex-pupil does recall that he had a housekeeper, 'a gaunt female', who had a son in the School, who may well have strained Smith's patience and his sense of humour. But that is all.

But it was not his housekeeper that drove him away from West Buckland after only one academic year. It was his health again, or rather the break in it. Apparently the Devon moorland weather beat him. Even Exmoor rain and wind does not normally destroy a man's health, but it is possible that, coming after his previous breakdown and possibly subsequent fragility (and the diabetes), it proved too much. And running a boarding school in war-time, where the staff don't like you much, could have been a strain for a much younger, fitter man.

Whatever the reason, Smith left in July, 1941. The *Register* remarked generously that 'during the year he spent with us we grew to appreciate him, and that appreciation grew from term to term'. Smith did not have enough time to get his message across. If he had, who knows what changes he might have wrought, what goodwill he might have generated? The Editors clearly recognised some of his gifts, because they concluded by saying that 'what is our loss, is Eton's gain'. (That is where he went.)

Such a remark can clearly have more than one dimension, but even equipped with its cutting edge, it gives a sign that it could see many of the sides of Smith's personality.

Another speaker is credited with repeating the remark (or even coining it), and in this case it was clearly intended to have its cutting edge turned towards its subject. The ex-pupil whose evidence has been much used in this essay also recalled that Sam Howells, Smith's Deputy Head at West

Buckland – a man noted for his sharp tongue – said the same thing when the news about Smith's resignation became known: 'Our loss is Eton's gain.' True or not, sarcastic or not, it could throw as much light on Howells' character and tastes as on Smith's.

At any rate, Smith's departure for Eton showed, if nothing else, that his appetite for teaching had not faded. He was to spend seven more years at Eton – happy ones too – teaching History and singing in the choir. So a second public school chapel had to get used to his 'pervasive hoot' of an alto voice.

He retired finally in 1948, aged 68. A good run for a schoolteacher, especially by the standards of present times, when so many practitioners over the age of fifty scheme and scrum to get their names on the list for an offer of early retirement. An even better run for a man whose constitution broke down in his mid-fifties; who suffered, it appears, from diabetes; and who later retired a second time for reasons of health.

But Smith was not finished, by no means. He disappears from the academic record, but went on to live until he was ninety-five, at Falmouth (so he must have liked Cornwall), and finally at Poole. The obituaries say he was 'active and alert' until the end, actually playing bridge on the evening before he died, on 25th May, 1975. The guess is too that he filled much of those twenty-seven years of retirement with a lot of photography, clarinet-playing and musical appreciation – and that his 'pervasive hoot' enhanced the tone of many a local choir.

Like all men who filled a position of authority, and like all good teachers, he did not captivate everybody. He did not have children, and, almost certainly, did not take a wife, so there were sides to his personality which could have been developed further. But take him all round – teacher, sports enthusiast, headmaster, musician, chorister, preacher, historian, author, debater, photographer, encourager of so many subjects beyond his own speciality – he made the very best use of the gifts with which he had been endowed, and he happily put those gifts to the service of the young people around him.

Far and away the strongest impression that comes down in the evidence is encapsulated in the verdict of an old pupil: 'a most tolerant, understanding and reasonable man'.

What a pity that West Buckland had him so late and for so short a time. 'Our loss is Eton's gain.' It was indeed.

31. Getting the Priorities Right

The camel, as someone memorably observed, is a good example of the shortcomings of committee work; it looks, to all intents and purposes, like a horse designed by a committee. Conversely, if you travel the roads of France, you are struck by their pretty universal straightness. This, apparently, was not so much the work of the Romans as of Napoleon. The Emperor, having once conceived his Grand Design for a modern network of communications for France, was not going to let mere village interests (or even villages themselves) get in the way. No planning committees or local enquiries for him. In his view the ideal number for a committee was one.

Education, and its so-called progress, is a classic example of the former of the two approaches. In the chapter about 'The Safe under the Lavatory Basin' in the previous book (*West Buckland School*), I mused on what might have happened if there had been a design committee set up for the new School Chapel. It was, of course, mere speculation, and was intended as little more than entertainment with a tiny moral nestling amongst the fluff of the joke.

However, I recently came across what you may call hard evidence of the truth of this 'moral'.

A departing head of the English Department left for the Archive a fat file relating to the inception, design, and creation of the new English 'suite' which came to replace the old dormitories above the Karslake Hall. There was to be, and there now is, a new Music 'suite' as well, but I have little documentation for this, and in any case I can make my point just as easily with English alone.

The then Head of English circulated the members of his department to canvass their views about the priorities and facilities, both ideal and crucial, that they thought should be involved. Their replies are a good illustration of the general validity of the admittedly light-hearted speculation that I offered with regard to the Chapel. Inevitably, I must condense and simplify, and the authors of the views I shall summarise may think my *précis* work is a mite suspect, so I shall name no names. I am only making a point after all, not agreeing or disagreeing with any of them.

Inevitably, there were complaints about existing facilities. It is a very human trait, when one is asked what one would like, to begin by saying, 'You should see what I've got to put up with right now.' The room was in a 'terrible state', and the restriction on space was being worsened steadily by growing numbers of pupils.

But then the teacher – we shall call him/her Teacher A – got down to brass tacks, with suggestions about a workroom for teachers, space for drama, both in small groups and for performance, store cupboards, make-up rooms, changing rooms, and so on.

Teacher B also wanted rooms divided so as to allow for both big and small groups. He/she wanted the teaching rooms adjacent to the Library, and wondered why a library should be used for teaching at all. Why not use it for the purpose for which it was conceived – as a place for storage, consultation, and reading of books? Why not indeed?

Then there was the ever-practical teacher C, who ended his telegrammatic message, which had briefly nodded towards drama studios, word processors, and centralised resources rooms, with a down-to-earth plea for what he called a 'W.C. area'. I like the addition of the word 'area'. One wonders what extra benefits were to be made available by the supplementary 'area'. His justification came under the heading of 'the-others-have-got-it-so-why-shouldn't-we?' – another very human viewpoint. Or, as he tartly put it, 'It would appear that physicists/sums people are permitted to have bodily functions but English specialists are required to be stoical.'

Teacher D was that rarity in the profession – the one who was pretty generally satisfied with things as they were. 'My present location is in many ways ideal since it is central, has two rooms (essential), and one room is suitably quiet for orals and language work.' He was on to a good thing, knew it, and saw no reason to change it – though he knew that change would probably come. So he prudently put in his requests – books, tapes, cupboards, computer centre, special quiet room, and so on.

Teacher E took the high ground. Teachers of English always have a court card in their hand which is quite un-trumpable: English is absolutely basic, absolutely central, and absolutely vital to progress in absolutely every subject. Try getting round that one in a Head of Department meeting about timetable allocation.

In fact Teacher E took such high ground that he looked with lofty suspicion on the whole prospect and on its provenance. 'I know there is a problem about what use to make of redundant dormitories but I do not believe that should dictate the future of the English Department.' Or, rather more sharply lower down, 'English teaching facilities must not depend on the need to find a use for redundant premises.'

It reminded me of the old farmer who was stopped by a motorist and asked the way to some remote hamlet. 'Well, zurr, if oi wuz 'ee, oi shouldn't staart from 'ere at all.'

To be fair, Teacher E also weighed in with a pretty formidable portfolio of recommendations along the lines of other colleagues' suggestions, and ended by taking a welcome global view of the problem. English was central, true, but it also had the power to influence every other subject and the progress of pupils in every other subject. What should finally influence the decision-makers was the 'benefits to the whole school' rather than to 'those associated with any competing project'. The business was bigger than any mere department. Statesmanlike.

It is to the credit of the Head of Department, and to his *précis* skills, that he melted down all this verbiage to barely two pages. It makes an interesting contrast to the feasibility study produced by the architect, which ran to twenty-four.

That, of course, was only what the teachers thought. I do not have the documents to tell us what the Governors thought, what the parents thought (if anybody asked them), what the staff beyond the English Department thought (if anybody asked *them*), what the builders thought, what the accountants thought, and what the contributors to the Appeal thought.

No wonder it took the best part of a decade from start to finish. What did the English Department think of it when they came to work in it? Was Teacher C satisfied with his 'W.C. area'? Or had he long since left and forgotten all about it?

And, perhaps most interesting, what did the pupils think of it? After all, it was built for them.

What would you, the interested reader, think of it? Why not come to the School and see for yourself?

32. One Jump Ahead

The more you discover about the School's founder, the Revd. J.L. Brereton, the more you marvel at his capacity to surprise you. (See 'Founding Father'.)

In a book commemorating the centenary of Barnard Castle School (which Brereton also founded in 1883 as the North Eastern County School), his grandson, H.L. Brereton, (a former Headmaster of Gordonstoun), recalls a story which was told to him by a local farmer who had known Brereton Senior for a long time. (This could well have been Mr. Miller, who had offered the use of his farmhouse as the first West Buckland school premises in 1858.)

Brereton, naturally, paid many visits to Lord Fortescue at Castle Hill. After all, they were setting up not only a new school, but a new type of school, and there was a lot to discuss – this quite apart from Brereton's multifarious duties and responsibilities as Rector of West Buckland, and Fortescue's equal burden as patron, founder, chairman, and paymaster of practically everything that Brereton organised or set up. They also happened to be personal friends.

Lord Fortescue lived (and his descendants still do) in a wide estate, with parks and lodges and drives and whatnot. Castle Hill was a fair step from Brereton's rectory, so his journey was made on horseback. Brereton, arriving in the evening after a busy day, had to dismount to open the five-bar gate into the grounds, or ask the lodge-keeper to open it.

He then tied his white handkerchief to the top bar of the gate. This was so that he would not have to disturb the lodge-keeper when he rode back to West Buckland, often in the small hours. He just set his mare at the gate, where she could make out the handkerchief in the gloom. And they jumped it.

33. The Comedian's Advice

When I first arrived in Cambridge University, a very green grammar-school boy from the London suburbs, one of the first things that impressed me was the presence of College servants. And not merely that they were there – though that in itself was a sort of culture shock to a lad from a home which did not have a car or a telephone, never mind home helps or nannies. Some of them, too, not only were simply present; they had a 'presence'. I was not the only freshman in mortal dread of our Head Waiter, Bill Kimberley. In my memory, he had only one eyebrow, which went from one temple to the other, straight across above his eyes – twin orbs which shone like jet. Hair was slicked, straight and black. Add in a slightly Mediterranean complexion; a measured, patient voice which gained in menace from its very deliberation; impeccable grooming – a sartorial symphony in black and white; movements like a cat, with the black coat tails twitching behind him like a killer waiting to pounce – and you have an alarming mixture of a capo di Mafia, Count Dracula, and Shere Khan.

What also impressed an eighteen-year-old about these servants was that most of them were old. Well, they were to me. But I soon found out that many of them really were – at any rate old by the standards of normal employment. Like the College buildings, they had been there, it seemed, since the sixteenth century. Even more amazing, they continued to be there long after I had left. Attending a reunion dinner years later, you would still meet one or two of them serving at table or pouring out the sherry at the reception in the Master's Garden – often they had been specially recalled for the occasion. And they remembered you – they really did. You certainly remembered them. (Bill Kimberley turned out to be quite a nice chap, with an engagingly dry sense of humour.)

A freshman soon learned to accept them as part of the College furniture, but, if he had any sense, he also was careful to treat them with appropriate respect, even if familiarity opened the door to some Christian names. Some. By no means all. Jock was 'Jock', over the years, to hundreds and thousands of people; it was years before I learned his surname. But others were addressed much more correctly; for instance, I would never have dreamed of addressing Warren Wright in any other way than 'Mr. Wright'. His manner did not attract familiarity. Nor could I have said anything else but 'Mrs. Hills' to the lady who knocked on my bedroom door every morning – a stooping wisp of a witch in pinafore and tall black hat straight out of the Brothers Grimm. 'Eight o'clock, Mr. Coates.' Voice like a dentist's drill. I cannot recall her saying anything else. She looked about ninety.

My point – I am sorry to have kept you so long – is that colleges, for all that they may have a reputation for tight-fistedness, conservatism, even backwardness, have a trick of keeping their employees. (They also have a pretty fair number of long-serving Fellows as well. Two to my knowledge have recently died in my College after holding their fellowships over fifty years. Old members in their eighties regularly totter back to reunion dinners.)

It is the same with West Buckland School – and for all I know with many other schools as well. Only last year I was engaged in preparing a brass wall plaque to a School servant, Gerald Parker, who retired recently after 51 years of service. A couple of years ago I interviewed Jim Hobbs, who retired in 1980 after 40 years' service. His father, Charles Hobbs, also completed 40 years as Assistant and later Chief Gardener. Incidentally, his wife, sister, and niece all worked in the School.

West Buckland may be unusual in this respect because of two things – the remoteness of the School in the Exmoor countryside, and the proximity of the villages of East and West Buckland. In the days before the railway train and the motor car, where else could the School recruit its domestic staff but in the nearby villages? Remote villages are by nature conservative; habits – including employment habits – once formed, tend to persist. Sons and nephews and granddaughters find themselves going where their forebears went; it's easier. In times of agricultural depression, there may have been nowhere else.

So, to give further examples, Bill Cockram served for over thirty years in the early twentieth century, and became the custodian and nanny of the School's only motor vehicle, which served almost as long as he did. William Skinner served as under-gardener for a mere twenty years, but ran his Sunday School for forty-two. Sylvia Ridd came to the School in the 1960's, to be a maid in the Headmaster's house. She subsequently became Head Cook, and is still here. And the record, so far as I have been able to determine, goes to George Balment, who was in on the ground floor, so to speak. He was hired as general handyman and gardener when the School was founded in 1858, and only the creakings of old age forced his retirement in 1916, 58 years later.

This propensity for long attachment is evident not only among the domestic staff. A history of the School was published in 1983. In the back was printed a list of those who had served over ten years in the Common Room – a whole pageful of them. Over a score in that pageful had served more than twenty. In the Common Room today I could introduce you to six more who have each given over twenty years' service, and at least four more again who have amassed over thirty years each. Even your present author, who, after early retirement, took on some part-time work after twenty-nine full-time years in other classrooms, thinking to himself that he would give it just a term, to see how it would go, is now in his seventeenth year.

It goes on. Tom Hitchins, who, sadly, died only recently, organised an Old Boys' Dinner in Plymouth for over sixty years. His association with the School went back 76 years. Both his son and his grandson have attended the School, and both, uniquely, have been Head Boy. Then there is Sam Heath, who defies categorisation. He has been workman, plasterer, general Mr. Fixit, friend, and teacher of bell-ringing – and a host of other things which momentarily escape me – for well over thirty years. (See 'Passing Tribute'.)

One wonders what it is that holds all these people. Their own skills, professional pride perhaps, loyalty obviously. No doubt too, domestic ties build up, which makes it difficult to move. Possibly a spot of inertia too; if one is fair, one cannot completely rule it out. But is that it? Isn't there anything else?

Does the School have an ingredient in its make-up containing some adhesive quality which makes its inmates stick? Is it the water or the septic tank drainage? Hardly. The hundred-year-old, nicotine-stained cricket pavilion, refuge of rule-breakers (and not only among the pupils)? Oh come now. The narrow, twisting, sheep-shoving lanes and the tractor-jutting gateways that frustrate the approach? Oh – very droll. The draughty old stone buildings and the windswept, pitted passages? The sun-bathed, vine-clad, gentle slopes and the balmy air? Yes, yes, yes – all right – point taken. There is no need to overdo it.

However, talking of the weather, and notwithstanding the above, the School also has a remarkable reputation for health – good health. One health inspector after another has complimented the School on its robust constitution. This has shown itself in a number of predictable ways – the energy of the pupils in activities like Ten Tors, the Duke of Edinburgh Awards, cadet camps, and of course the *Exmoor* (see 'A Shot of the Good Side'), the state of near-dereliction into which the old isolation hut was in danger of falling in the late nineteenth century. It is shown too in an unexpected manner – the longevity of its headmasters.

I do not mean the length of their individual service in the Headmaster's study. With 15 heads in 144 years, it comes out to only about 10 years each. Take out the present incumbent and the three caretaker heads over the years, and the average goes up to about 13. Still not especially long, though reasonably healthy.

No. What I am referring to is their survival capacity *after* they have left. We are told today that secondary school headmasters have to cope with so many pressures both within their schools and without that it is a wonder that

lists of applicants are as long as they are – indeed that there are any applicants at all. Boarding school heads have an extra burden of responsibility,
because they have charge of their pupils twenty-four hours a day, seven days
a week – during term-time anyway. To say nothing of the problems of the
extra staff which such care entails – catering, pastoral, domestic, clerical,
and so on.

They are running a society in miniature, with all the ramifications of a
village or small town, if not the numbers. In the case of West Buckland,
because of its remote setting, this creates a yet bigger responsibility for
making a viable life, and a sociable one, for hundreds of people of widely
differing backgrounds, callings, aims, and characters. After a dozen or so
years of this, on average, one might think that retiring headmasters would
slide quietly into semi-somnolent retirement, and, after a decent interval,
into a merciful grave.

I am delighted to report that the last two incumbents are healthy and very
active, in their sixties and seventies respectively. Three of their predecessors
lived until their mid- or late eighties, and three more made it to their
nineties. Even more mystifying, the first head, Thompson, had at least one
breakdown during his period of service, but returned to complete another
decade before retiring, going on to take up full-time parish duties, and
starting a family. He lived to be 85. Another, Smith, had a breakdown which
necessitated his resigning a headship in Cumbria. He came to West Buckland a few years later, as a caretaker head during the Second World War. He
resigned after a year, giving as his reason the Devon weather (the only
instance of such a cause of departure for any member of staff I have discovered). He promptly went off to teach for another eight years at Eton, and
went on to a retirement of twenty-seven years, surviving until he was 95.
(See 'Holding the Fort – II')

Is there anything in the Devon atmosphere which puts what I can only
call 'survival power' into these men, in some cases men whose health one
would not have described as robust? Is there any agglomeration of School
ambiance which, by some biological alchemy, provides an injection of
longevity? And, while we are about it, is it the same thing which makes
people stay?

What follows is only speculation, and is not provable by any method
known to me. However, here it is, for what it is worth. To begin with, it must
almost certainly be something to do with West Buckland's position and
isolation – and climate. And I don't mean nice climate. People stuck out
here simply have to get on with each other. This was especially so in the
early days, when you could not get anywhere else. A colleague who was a
pupil in the 1960's told me that even as late as that the boys were allowed to

go into town only twice a term. So, I repeat, they had to get on with each other. (They still do; the site hasn't moved.) And you normally get on with your fellow-inmates only if you begin to see some virtues in them.

No doubt there were some festering bad relations here and there, and scope for some pretty underhand human behaviour now and again, as there were in the medieval monasteries. But, as with monasteries, the Rule prevailed, and the monasteries lasted for several centuries. And West Buckland has survived since 1858. Both survived because these bad examples could not have been typical.

Then again, the facilities have, until relatively recently, been a mite spartan, to say the least. We have a photograph of the games washroom before the First World War; it looks far worse than the ablutions block in Colditz. Dormitories were chilly, cavernous rooms like barracks. Diet for a long time seems to have been of the wodge-and-stodge variety – though the School did grow its own vegetables for years. One old boy described the food as uniformly 'grey'. Outdoor pursuits were a constant campaign against the weather for three-quarters of the year, and envelopment by it during the fourth. Overcoming, or at any rate surviving, these difficulties engendered a communal sense of satisfaction and achievement. In a backhanded sort of way, it is possible that the inmates (I use this term frequently because it seems to fit best) came to take a perverse pride in the fact that their school was not like anybody else's. Bit like the Foreign Legion, maybe.

Staff had a lot to do, not only in coping with the boys in their charge, but in dealing with the factors I have listed above. The Acting Headmaster, for instance, in the late 1860's, had to teach a full timetable, run the School, deal with a host of pastoral problems, handle visitors and other outsiders, as well being School Chaplain and curate at East Buckland and studying for an external Science degree. (See 'Holding the Fort – I'.) Hard work. In the early days of the twentieth century, the inspectors noted that the Headmaster – *the Headmaster* – taught in the classroom for *twenty-seven hours a week*. He also appeared in every cricket and football photograph. Hard work. How many heads now spend twenty-seven hours a week in the classroom? How many *teachers*, if it comes to that?

The American comedian George Burns, who was telling jokes – and making you laugh – till he was nearly a hundred, and who therefore had plenty of time in which to ponder the problem, observed that the recipe for a happy life was to fall in love with your work.

I have not found any record of any pupil, employee, teacher or headmaster saying that he had fallen in love with West Buckland; characters of stoical patience (which West Buckland is very good at teaching) are not given to sentimental confession. But staff stay; and a lot of them live a very long time when they retire. As for the pupils, I have recorded elsewhere, more than once, my abiding impression that the place has a most unusual capacity for inspiring affection.

Take Cordy Wheeler. Cordy was born in 1884. He entered the School in 1895. He was good at everything – Captain of football, champion athlete, cricket colours; honours in the Cambridge Local Examinations; Head Prefect. And by all accounts a boy of remarkable dignity and prestige among his contemporaries.

It was while he was still at School that there came the crisis which threatened the School with closure. Cordy went himself to Lord Fortescue to plead with him to change his mind.

Shortly after he left, he returned briefly as assistant teacher, and became a governor when he was only twenty-one. In 1907, he was partially responsible for saving the School a second time, when misfortunes once again rose and overhung like an imminent avalanche. It was he who recommended Harries as the man to save the situation. Harries came in, and became probably the greatest head the School has had. Splendid vindication for Wheeler, and for his faith in the School.

He taught at Blundell's before going up to Keble College, Oxford for a degree in Theology. He served with distinction in the First World War – decorated, mentioned in despatches, and reaching the rank of Lieutenant-Colonel.

Back in civilian life, he resumed his teaching career, and became a headmaster. During all that time, he remained a governor of West Buckland School, and held every office and distinction that the Old Boys' Association had to offer. As Governor, and later Chairman of Governors, he steered the School through the terrible years of shortage and austerity after the Second World War. When the Headmaster, Sam Howells, died in office in 1952, Wheeler agreed – at the age of 68 – to come back as caretaker Headmaster until a replacement could be found. He retired from the Board of Governors in 1962, after 57 years' service on it. Right up to his death in 1972, he maintained his association with the School – which lasted in all for 77 years.

One of the writers of tributes to him in the *Register* was an ex-headmaster, and headmasters do not always see eye to with their governors. This head emphasised the happiness of the relationship they had enjoyed, and said of Wheeler, 'He was devoted to the School.... and believed firmly that an institution was greater than any of those who served it.'

Which of course still begs the question: what did that institution do to instil such faith and affection? So we have come full circle.

It would be easy to get maudlin about this, and one does not wish to be accused of being so. It may be that I have missed the whole point. But the facts are there; these men and women did stay, and do stay, for a long time. And several of the headmasters did live to a very great age. It is simply interesting, and maybe gently provocative, to speculate as to how far the reasons for this went beyond mere coincidence.

34. Fortunes of War

Whitsun Blues

The *Register* of December, 1917 reported somewhat sadly on the Athletic Sports:

'Whit Monday was ushered in with storms of rain, which did not improve either the course or the appearance of the chalk lines on it, and, although we had glimpses of sunshine, it was still raining at one o'clock when we determined to start. At this stage a wind got up, and we were no longer troubled by wet, so that the track appeared none the worse. Once again, we regret to say that the spectators were less than usual, but as the same causes still exist – no trains, no cars, no petrol – we must be thankful that any came at all.'

(Nevertheless, it is an ill wind that blows nobody any good – see 'Shining Examples'.)

The Hideous Truth

An ex-pupil of the War years (Second War this time – 1939-45) told me that, in order to comply with the wartime blackout regulations, huge wooden frames were constructed, and covered with sheets of grey cardboard, which the boys had to put up against the windows of the hall every night, in order to frustrate the hundreds of German bomber pilots who were, of course, cruising regularly and relentlessly all over Exmoor in the search for strategic targets to bomb.

It would have been a huge task to black out the dormitories as well, but some boffin or other in the Air Ministry had discovered that if you painted your window panes blue and your light bulbs orange, it would totally confuse the enemy. So the dormitory window panes were painted blue and the light bulbs were painted orange.

It meant that the dormitories looked oddly sepulchral during the day, and as for the boys' faces during the evenings. . . . as my informant said, 'If you can imagine a dorm of boys all looking orange, it was the most disgusting sight you ever saw.'

The same informant also told me that it was a tradition for newly-elected members of the Phoenix Society (the School's Debating Society) to have to run along an exposed gallery above the Quadrangle (now built over – the gallery, not the Quad) – for about twenty yards – in full view of the Quad's audience, no doubt assembled for the occasion – totally unclothed.

Finally, there was the story of the School dances. Yes, School dances. Between 1939 and 1941. Not many, but clearly memorable. There were no girls of course, except the Bursar's teenage daughter, who was very much in demand. Maybe a couple of female staff would turn up, bravely. So what did the boys do? While the gramophone churned out the latest swing recordings of Glenn Miller and Benny Goodman, they danced – with each other.

(The potential trains of thought that could be set off by this anecdote are truly mind-boggling. However, tall though it may be, I have since had it confirmed by other contemporaries.)

Many Hands

A contributor to the West Buckland Centenary Book recalled that the Second World War, among other things, taught the wartime inmates to make beds. So many school servants – in both dormitories and kitchens – were called up that there was no alternative but to get the boys to take over. Regular chores soon included not only bedmaking, but waiting in hall, water-carrying, washing up, and general dogsbodying in the kitchen and scullery.

When the servants returned after the War, they resumed all their previous duties – except making beds.

According to the Cloth

Children who are taught in primary school projects that food was rationed during the Second World War are not always informed that clothes were rationed as well, at any rate after 1941. The infamous 'clothing coupons'. Pronounced 'koopons', as you might expect, by everybody – except news announcers on the radio. For some reasons these gentlemen, whose accent was so cut-glass that you could stick flowers in it, were made to pronounce it 'koopaungs', in deference, one supposes, to our gallant French allies who had surrendered after a six-week campaign in 1940.

Anyway, these 'koopons', or 'koopaungs', if you prefer, or even 'kewpons' if you lived in London, drove a coach and horses through every school's clothing regulations. You may have been able to get extra butter or a bottle of Johnnie Walker, or even nylon stockings, on the black market, but, to my knowledge at any rate, there were no spivs or wide boys creeping up to worried bursars and saying behind their hand, 'Pssst! Want any extra blue serge blazers? Or 'ow about some kids' flannel trousers – straight orf the loom? Or some Army surplus gym slips – all the regulation pleats – to you, squire, ten bob a go. Fiver a dozen – and I'm robbin' meself.'

In most cases, the rules were quietly allowed to lapse, or parents were discreetly enjoined to 'do their best', and assured that no reprisals would be taken against irregularly-dressed new pupils. West Buckland went a stage further. It actually said in its current regulations that 'for the duration of the War School Uniform is in abeyance'. Boys could wear 'what clothes they possess'. Furthermore, the advice was offered that 'if new clothes have to be obtained, Corduroy Trousers and Leather Jerkins are suitable'.

Corduroy trousers, yes. But do any of our more mature readers recall the outfitters' shelves groaning under the weight of ramparts of leather jerkins? I had always thought that leather clothing was reserved for the likes of bomber crews in Lancasters or ace fighter pilots in the American Army Air Force.

It would be interesting to pick the brains of others who were at a private secondary school during the War and ask them how many times they saw leather jerkins in the Upper Fourth.

35. The View from Below

The School's founder, the Revd. J.L. Brereton, went to school himself at Rugby, during the headship of the celebrated Dr. Arnold (see 'Founding Father'). The young Brereton was so indelibly impressed by the great man that he governed the rest of his life according to how well he thought he would measure up to Arnold's expectations.

So it is a fine irony to discover that, in his early days there, Brereton was so miserable that he begged his father to take him away. It is another irony, perhaps, that he later came to like it, especially when he reached the senior end of the school.

Well, you may say, he would, wouldn't he? When he was bigger, and more used to the place, and could exercise authority over his juniors. This is not fair, either to Brereton or to Rugby. It is based on the facile and slightly cynical view of human behaviour which assumes that we all like to boss somebody about – and very little else.

It is indeed true that most of us enjoy exercising power, and it is also true that power can corrupt. But it is not true that all power corrupts everybody utterly all the time, and it is not true that the desire to exercise power is the only human motivation. It is almost certainly beyond argument that a lot of boys in Arnold's Sixth Form revelled in their seniority and their privileged position, their status as captain of this and monitor of that. But Brereton did not, at any rate not for the usual reasons. He was not a natural games player or a particularly clubbable boy. What he liked was the cloistered seclusion of the Sixth Form, its encouragement of scholarship, the privilege of being given responsibility, the opportunities to get to know, intimately, a charismatic man.

What this lengthy preamble is designed to show – perhaps a trifle ponderously – is that a boy's (or girl's) feelings about his (or her) school may be very mixed. They can vary as they grow up; they can be modified in the light of fresh experience – either at home or at school; they can intensify; they can become more specific, as knowledge and growing perceptive powers give the boy (or girl) greater ability to sort out a bewildering *mélange* of emotions. For certain, they can not be glibly summarised in a couple of natty little clichés.

There can be few people, if any, who have not experienced a butterfly or two on the first day at a new school. Will I make any friends? Where are the toilets? How strict (a favourite word, that, of pupils) will the teachers be? Will I get to the school bus in time?

In a school like West Buckland, there are more. Will I be a good enough sportsman? (The School has a strong local reputation.) Will I be up to the work? (You know – more homework, new subjects like Biology, Chemistry, and so on.) Will I pass all those awful new exams? Will I fit in? One recalled her arrival like this: 'I was very scared and I thought that everyone would be realy snoby [sic] because there[sic] rich and I am not.'

We are back in the land of natty clichés again. Are they really all 'rich' at West Buckland? No – of course not. Nor, by the same token, are they all 'poor'. Are they all 'snoby'? I doubt it. They are not all shiny, squeaky-clean egalitarians either. As with everything else, they are a mixture. (One can argue too about what an eleven-year-old child might mean by 'poor'. Does he mean his family can afford only two foreign holidays a year, or an Audi instead of a Mercedes? Or does he mean that his single Mum can just about manage to put him there and pay for his blazer because he has won a scholarship? Does either of them know what it means to live in a corrugated iron lean-to in a shanty town?) Perceptions, especially the perceptions of children, can often say as much about the perceiver as about the thing perceived.

West Buckland is a secondary school – well, primarily, to perpetrate an awful pun. The 'Prep' School numbers about 200, against about 500 in the main school. The campus now stretches over 100 acres. Many new arrivals come from tiny village schools, with only a handful of teachers. No wonder they are anxious about getting lost, about not finding the Biology Lab., about getting on the right bus in the fleet of them that draws up each day in the drive. This has nothing to do with the School being private, or 'posh', or 'rich', or 'snoby'; it has to do with sheer size, which to a lonely ex-junior, trussed in a stiff new uniform, and bent under the weight of new bags, coats, pens, pencils, calculators, and games kit, can be overwhelming. But West Buckland is only 700 strong. What must it be like for a new pupil arriving in a colossal state comprehensive with over 2,000?

Not fitting in; not making friends; getting lost; not being able to meet the new demands, whether in the classroom or on the games field. These fears are normal, indeed universal; they are predictable; and they are natural. There are always one or two unlikely ones, of course. One new arrival remembered later that he was frightened by the fire alarm in his first week. After all, these children are only eleven years old; they are not so very far removed from the unreasoning phobias of infancy – of feathers, shadows, knobs, close hedges, hoovers, or whatever.

Conversely, there can be the pupil with a very mature approach. One opined that 'it was just the morning, waiting, being excited, anxious all in one'. More than one remembered, despite their own nerves, seeing that everyone else was in the same boat. Many of them concluded by saying that their fears proved quite groundless. Some went further and claimed that the School was 'brilliant'.

There was more individuality in their reminiscences of later times. Rather than sights and sounds, I asked several of them to try and recall smells. Smells can be powerfully evocative. Catch a whiff of something when you are unprepared, and you can be whisked through decades in an instant. Or, to put it another way, smells can be as greedy as sights or sounds in the amount of memory space they take up.

R.F. Delderfield, for instance – one of the School's two distinguished men of letters – effortlessly itemised 'empty trunks, apples, cake crumbs, and cheese rinds' in the 'tuck-house', and 'ink, chalk and new exercise books' in 'Big School'.

I asked my guinea-pigs to imagine that they were looking back on their school life after fifty years, and to try and select the smells that they thought would linger in their memories. I gathered a pretty pungent *potpourri*.

Food predictably came high on the list – mashed potato, sweets in the tuck shop, an old salad prepared for a Food and Nutrition lesson and left for several days in a locker. One recalled, enigmatically, 'spagetti bolinase' which reached you 'from a mile off'.

Freshly-mown grass is no surprise; neither is chlorine in the pool, or stale sweat in a changing room. Two or three referred to the addition to the atmosphere, at any rate in the girls' changing room, of 'different perfumes'. The laundry room opens on to the quadrangle, so that came in for a deal of comment. Toilet cleaner made an impression – which is at least better than remembering the toilets themselves. 'Old pillows' might give some food for thought to the relevant authorities. But not 'pencil sharpenings'. Speaking from my own experience both as pupil and as teacher, it is a rare child who does not have some kind of fixation on sharpening pencils. How much blood has been left on the classroom carpet at the end of negotiations over the appointment of the next pencil-sharpening monitor?

One interesting sign of modern times was the recall by one pupil of 'the smell of the IT sweet [sic]'. So computers also have BO. A sinister sign, perhaps, that they are fulfilling our worst nightmares and becoming human.

One or two imaginative contributors took the enquiry further, into the realms of touching and feeling. The heat on the glass at the hotplate; the pain of soldering iron on the fingers; the wind outside the Karslake dining-hall – these might well cause an old buffer in fifty years' time to nod vigorously in recognition, and sentence his grandchildren to a bout of reminiscence.

The attentive reader – of whom you are a fine example – will have noticed by now that a certain topic is conspicuous by its absence – bullying.

Am I therefore trying to pretend that it never happened at West Buckland? No. I am trying to put it into perspective. I am putting it neither first nor last. I am simply taking it as it comes, and it seems to come naturally here. We have been discussing the worries and fears of new arrivals at West Buckland; they (the new arrivals) are smaller than anybody else, so they are the obvious targets for those creatures (who infest the woodwork anywhere) who want to inflict unpleasantness on people more obviously vulnerable than themselves. Hence we arrive at bullying.

There are those left-wing reformers who discuss bullying in private day- and boarding-schools in hushed tones of shocked loathing, as if such horrors never occurred anywhere else. This betrays ignorance not only of state schools but of human nature. Bullying can, and does, occur everywhere, from the nursery to the retirement home. It is certainly not the preserve – or the fault – of private or boarding schools. And it is not only small children who suffer; in schools of any type, *teachers* also can be bullied, never mind pupils. A minute ago I called you an attentive reader. Let us extend the compliment and call you an honest reader. Now, can you put your hand on your heart and say that you never – never – instigated or joined in the 'playing up' of a weak teacher? Thirty of you; one of him – if that is not bullying, what is?

And what is so special about bullying? Is it 'better' or 'worse' than, say, lying, or theft, or malicious damage? Can any school head, be it in the state or the private sector, day or boarding, single-sex or mixed, tell a journalist or an inspector that there is no lying in his school, no theft, no damage? No – he will simply say that he does his best to keep it to a minimum, to inculcate respect for the truth, for other people's property, and for public property in his charges. By the same token, he will strive to inculcate respect for other people's peace of mind.

Poor leadership, chaotic organisation, shortage of out-of-class facilities to keep pupils occupied, incompetent staff – any or all of these can help to engender the opportunity for bullying. No school – of whatever type – can claim that it has never suffered from one or other of these faults in a history of 150 years.

It is not for this writer to assess the amount or the level of bullying in West Buckland now. It is not his brief, and he does not have the relevant information or statistics on which to base any kind of fair judgment. All he can say is that, from his previous experience of teaching in it (over a decade), from his present vantage point of Archivist (another seven years), and from watching the way pupils and teachers talk to each other, and the way most pupils behave to each other, he would be surprised to be told that it is anything more than a fringe activity.

If bullying *does* take place – or any other malpractice for that matter – the School certainly does its best to ensure that any child, of whatever age, sex, creed, or colour, can have access to an impressive, almost bewildering, array of professional help. A worried pupil can tell his form prefect, his tutor, and his head of house. If that is not adequate, he can go to either of the two deputy heads – one a man and one a woman – or he can ask to see the School Nurse or the School Chaplain. There remains the School Doctor, who can call up specialist reinforcements; and the Board of Governors, who can institute all sorts of high-level inquiries. And thanks to Ms. Rantzen, he can also pick up the phone and dial the Childline.

It almost makes you wonder how he finds time to go to his lessons – which, if he did, might help him to put his problems into perspective by dwelling less upon them. And the multiplying of help agencies does not necessarily multiply in similar ratio the effectiveness of the assistance he might get. Nevertheless, one can certainly not accuse the School authorities of not trying. If they have not completely eradicated bullying, or any other sins, it is not for want of thought or effort.

A few decades ago, or further back, it was probably a worse situation. There were few day pupils. Boys were allowed into town only twice a term. There was not much provision for entertainment or organised leisure activity at weekends. No television; therefore no videos or video games; no computers; no Duke of Edinburgh Award Scheme; no Ten Tors; no motor cars in the Sixth Form – and so on and so on.

Some Old Boys I spoke to after an Old Boys' Dinner emphasised a child's near-total separation from home during term time. There was no access to an inside telephone, except in cases of the utmost emergency. A boy was on his own, unless he had a brother or two higher up the School. He learned to cope.

Wet weekends could be the worst times. There was so little to do. And it wasn't only the moon-faced weeds or spotty wimps who suffered; nearly everyone was on the receiving end at one time or another. 'But surviving stood you in good stead.' One did not complain. One Old Boy told me that he had an older brother, but did not tell him about the regular extortion of his pocket money by a nasty bigger boy. Not because he consciously resolved not to bother his brother, but because '*it never occurred to me* to tell him, or to tell the staff or parents'. [My italics.]

So – one way and another – they survived. And it was not only bullying that one kept quiet about. Again the Old Boys – one of them told me that for years he kept to himself the fact that his parents were divorced. Forty or fifty years ago, the subject was taboo. Nobody spoke of it, and nobody knew; you would die rather than air the problem. Divorce was simply something that happened in the *News of the World* – to other people. It wouldn't have mattered whether or not you had had all those tutors and counsellors and chaplains sitting there with their doors open twenty-fours a day; you would not have gone to see them; it was private. The same Old Boy told me that it was years before he discovered that two other members of his own class had had the same problem, and not one knew about the situation of the other two.

So what is a child supposed to do today? Keep it to himself, or go and tell it to all and sundry? Or find some kind of middle way of common sense and expediency and a friend's arm round the shoulder, and bumble along it as best he can?

It is fair to say that he might find it easier than he would have done, say, fifty years ago, or a hundred, if it comes to that. But then again, a child today is brought up to question things far, far more than he was fifty or a hundred years ago. Headmasters then were figures of fearsome authority. Authority carried with it so much more certainty. And behind authority lurked that 'immortal, invisible, God-only-wise' aura of religious rectitude which enjoined that it was the duty of one and all to 'render unto Caesar'. Just as it is often said that soldiers in the twenty-first century would never tolerate being shuffled forward by the thousand to die in trench warfare, so it can be argued that children today, and parents, simply would not accept the discipline of a previous era. Look at the evidence – where is the dunce's cap now? When did you last see the slipper, the cane? Do children still get tied to chairs?

This does not alter the fact that any child today who suffers from bullying, or from anything else, can dwell in a Stygian depth of hopeless misery than which he can imagine nothing worse – twenty-first century or no twenty-first century. Nevertheless, my point still, I think, remains valid: fifty or a hundred years ago he would have been more likely to weep alone, and suffer, than he is now. Not only are all those agencies there that I referred to, with their doors open; he is constantly being urged to use them.

It was this shortage of hope or help in the past that prompted me to ask those Old Boys at the Dinner whether any pupil of their acquaintance had ever been driven to take his own life. They looked genuinely taken aback by the question.

'Oh, no! Not that I ever heard of.'

Not even to attempt it? No – not that either.

So they managed – somehow? Yes. 'If you had problems, you just go on with them.'

Did any run away? Oh, yes – but not for long. Apparently the Headmaster used to send the School cross-country champion to look for them. (This was Exmoor, remember.)

Before one leaps to condemn the boarding schools of the past, let it be borne in mind that the men I had spoken to were attending a dinner to commemorate their connection with the School, to renew old friendships, to reminisce. They would not have been there at all if their pleasant memories of the School did not significantly outweigh the unpleasant ones.

I had a long and detailed letter from an ex-pupil who had left within the last decade, and he too had plenty of things to recall that had made him miserable. A lot of them sprang simply from being very young and away from home (he began boarding when he was eight, and continued until he was eighteen.) Yes, he had been on the receiving end of bullying. (And yes – he had dished it out as well later on.) He had got into trouble, and felt, in retrospect, that he might have been given more help and understanding lower down the School. However, he was honest enough to admit that he might not have been the easiest of pupils to handle.

Now comes the redress. He also went out of his way to cite examples of help and interest that he did receive – from, for example, a perceptive housemaster (over several years), and from an understanding matron (with whom he is still in regular contact). He was amazed, and gratified, to discover the change of atmosphere when he reached the sixth form. 'I also found that teachers could be friends as well as teachers and that being given responsibility really does shape a young man.' Indeed, he was moved to wonder whether, in giving him so much responsibility in running certain activities, the School had overdone it by neglecting his academic progress. But he felt strongly that it was the opportunities provided by these responsibilities which had had the decisive influence on the moulding of his character. He could see that 'they [the School] struck the balance carefully, gambled and came out trumps in the end.' He also added shrewdly that 'it's not the first and certainly not the last time they'll ever have to'.

I have had occasion before to note the extraordinary capacity of West Buckland to inspire affection among its inmates, often in spite of things rather than because of them, you are tempted to think. This last correspondent, while offering much comment, observed, 'When I sit down and really think about it I struggle to really criticise WB.' He added in a bracket, 'I know I have blindingly rose-tinted specs!' Well, something must have made them that colour.

This correspondent, as it happens, was a good example of how a school like West Buckland can do a lot of positive things for children in a certain situation. Forget the bullying for a moment; forget the distance from parents; forget all the other miseries – imagined, self-inflicted, genuine, and otherwise. Forget that bullying has possibly a greater chance to flourish in boarding schools than in day schools, for the simple reason that young people are in contact with each other for far longer periods at a stretch.

Consider the child who has a wretched, or disturbed, or in some way unsatisfactory home life – for any one of a score of reasons. A spell in a good boarding school can offer a haven, where a child can work without interruption, without noise, without friction, without the burden of severe illness – mental or physical – in the family, without the threat of dispute or violence. In the case of service families, when foreign postings can be unpredictable and uncomfortable, not to say dangerous, a boarding school is the only practical option.

In some cases, this can lead to a child forging a bond of enormous strength with his school. In the case of my correspondent, he became so attached to his school that he positively looked forward to the *end* of the holidays.

Did this mean that he emerged from his ten years' boarding as some kind of warped zombie who had learnt mere survival and little else? A narrow-minded, rah-rah-rah devotee of the Old School Tie? No, I don't think so. He had a successful university career; he did academic research; he now works for a prestigious engineering firm; he looks supremely well; he is good company; and he is happily married to a charming and talented girl.

All right, you may say. So your correspondent liked it. So Delderfield liked it. So did all the others who wrote to you or answered your questions. Delderfield could wax lyrical about the 'web of memory' which is 'either drenched in mistlike rain or sparkling under a bright, warm sun'. Delderfield was a writer; he would say things like that.

Quite likely. He was a poet too, and he wrote a poem about the School.

I have forborne to quote from it because it might strike a non-believer as 'proof' of the School's ability to drown the memory's critical faculties. But the point is not the poem's truth or inaccuracy, or its validity as literature; the point is the mere fact that West Buckland inspired him to write it. He had been to five other schools; he did not write poems about them. Indeed he said that he had 'a profound distaste' for them.

You may pass a devoted middle-aged or elderly couple in the street who are so odd that you are driven to wonder what on earth they see in each other. But again we miss the point: the point is not the oddity; it is the devotion.

Are you coming back for more? I think I may be a little ahead of you.

What about all those Old Boys who have *not* written to me? What about all those past pupils who have *not* joined the Old Boys' Association? (Or, as it is now, the 'Old Members'?) Did they therefore hate it? Some of them – yes, quite possibly. No school, however perfect, can expect all its old pupils to carry rose-tinted spectacles in the pocket all their lives. But it is equally likely that a lot of them simply do not have much to say about their school, either because it was 'well – all right, I suppose', or because they can not remember much – which would also argue that few moments of misery burned themselves into the soul. (It is a commonplace that people who have a happy childhood do not often remember much about it.) Many too are probably lazy, and mean to say something one day, but never get around to it. Many still send their children to West Buckland.

We have talked much of bullying, and we are in danger of slipping into cliché country once again. Just because the world, or the media, or the man on the bacon-slicing machine, think that the thing to talk about in relation to 'posh' schools is bullying, it does not follow that pupils themselves are so taken up with it. Certainly not today anyway. Certainly not when compared with other things.

I asked our School Nurse to come up with a list of topics which, if they do not worry modern pupils into lonely, self-destructive misery, at least exercise their minds from time to time. The minute you look at it, the items make sense. What follows – the batting order, that is – in no way implies any kind of priority.

Just as a new pupil worries whether he will make friends, and whether he will be 'liked', so those higher up the School fret about 'popularity'. What will their 'peers' make of them? A lot of this comes about as a result of the activities of the popular press, teen-age magazines, and television, which have proliferated in the last three decades. Reading and viewing matter cascades all over the young, telling them what they should say, do, wear, and think. A new word has been coined to encapsulate the acme of such correctness – 'cool'. If you are cool, you will be popular and successful with your peers. The very word 'peers' has also been harnessed to served in this context. Thirty years ago, the only reason to mention 'peers' was either to refer to the House of Lords, or to itemise the terms of Magna Carta. Now we do not have classmates, or fellow-pupils, or other kids, or company; we have 'peers'. (Similarly, by the same alchemy of philology, we do not have brothers and sisters any more; we have 'siblings' – which sounds like some species of sardine, or a Norwegian collaborator.)

Anyway, whatever you call them, boys and girls worry about what those around them think of them – they worry about their 'image'. There's another one – 'image'. The chances are that increased co-education has contributed to this; these poor souls have not only to worry about what their mates think of them, but what the other side of the race think as well. And race it is – to get high up the ladder marked 'cool'.

So we arrive – at last, you may say – at sex. No matter how you worry about it – not enough, too much, the wrong kind, the temptation, the guilt, the ignorance, the knowingness of others, 'peer pressure' (there it is again) – it is bound to cross the mind – frequently – of young persons whose bodies suddenly start to hurl at them an onslaught of desires, urges, emotions, crushes, passions, and rages which nothing in their previous life has re-motely prepared them for.

Just as the climate of opinion has become increasingly fixated on sex during the last thirty years, so the attitude to marriage has undergone a similar sea change. The last statistic I saw said that the divorce rate was running at about thirty per cent. That Old Boy I spoke about may have kept his parents' divorce to himself, but there is not much chance of that happen-ing today. Parents divorce, remarry, or take 'partners' – often in a very 'civilised' manner. It is not unknown (though admittedly newspaper anec-dote) for father to turn up to a sports day with his second wife/partner, along with mother with her second husband/partner. They may well be chatting gaily in their civilised style, but the son or daughter may be forgiven, perhaps, for not seeing it quite that way. Such a situation is quite beyond his or her experience or resources. Quite apart from possible ignorance about how one should behave in such a situation, the child can be assailed by a storm of conflicting emotions which do nothing but make it wretched. Anecdote from a national newspaper this may be, but it is still illustrative of a valid point.

Not even usage, it seems – the knowledge that 'it is happening all the time' – can take away from the individual child, or even soften, the shock of the splitting of the home. This, shall we say, 'difficulty' has prompted the Chairman of a recent Headmasters' Conference to draw attention to it in his lead speech. He went so far as to criticise some parents for putting their own gratification before the peace of mind of their children, and of attempt-ing to salve their consciences about a broken home by putting their children in boarding schools. So boarding schools in this instance, far from bringing sadness to their charges, are used by certain parents, for possibly selfish reasons, as a means of *avoiding* sadness, as far as is within their [the schools'] power.

Children talk about things like this. Well, they do now. They are not blind; they know it is common; their intelligence tells them that there is bound to be, in a group, say, of ten of their 'peers', somebody else with a similar problem. Indeed, a senior boy once remarked to me that the members of his class thought it a matter of considerable surprise that not one of them came from a family with a divorce in it.

It will come as no surprise, however, to be told that pupils worry about examinations. A recent government, in its wisdom, has so far 'reformed' the exam system as to increase the number of public tests to be taken by children between the ages of sixteen and eighteen from two to three – one a year. At the time of writing this, most universities have not found a better way of differentiating their candidates than by demanding that they achieve certain grades at 'A' Level. And this still does not take account of Key Stage exams all over the place *before* they are sixteen. Nor does it take account of the internal exams which all schools administer as a means of monitoring a pupil's progress and effort in his day-to-day classwork. Add to that the specialist exams like music, ballet, drama, and so on, and you can easily produce a term's timetable that is bursting with crises and pressure points.

Nor is this necessarily a phenomenon which afflicts senior pupils. The most junior members of a secondary school can reel in the first few weeks from a battery of deadlines. For example, in primary school, they generally stayed put; in a secondary school, they move about – five or six times a day – from one specialist classroom to another. They have to cope with new subjects like Physics, Biology, Chemistry, Computer Studies. They have to become accustomed to a homework timetable which requires work on two, even three subjects a night (this often after a journey of an hour or more each way on the School bus). They have to learn to plan their day with Napoleonic thoroughness, so that they arrive in the morning with all the correct books for the subjects of the day, to say nothing of games kit, towels, trombones, trip money, and doctors' certificates.

It is true that usage pours a little oil into the machinery, and they soon learn that an inventive imagination and a judicious ladling out of soft soap can help one to steer a wary course between the Scylla of one fierce teacher and the Charybdis of another credulous one. But the pressure is there, and I for one often admire the *panache* with which these young people manage to survive, and survive with a smile on their faces and a cheeky lollipop stuck in their mouths. One of the less-trumpeted dividends of life in a busy secondary school is the invaluable apprenticeship it provides for budding business executives; these boys and girls are juggling deadlines all day.

One could go on. Am I going to get the necessary grades to get into university? Is it true that teenage boys can get testicular cancer? Am I going to get too fat? Am I going to get too thin? I know Mum and Dad say they don't want to pressurise me, but they spent a lot of money to put me here; am I going to let them down? Why was I not made a prefect? Why did Peter Wilson not say hallo to me this morning?

If you, the attentive and honest reader, are still with me, you may by now qualify for a third adjective – patient. It has perhaps seemed an overwhelming litany of woes. Makes you wonder why they don't all run away.

But they don't. An adolescent's capacity for worry may be limitless, but so too is his capacity for resilience. And his energy. And drive. Adolescents fortunately are unstoppable. They need to be, with all those monsters waiting in their path to devour them.

However, alongside the monsters – and at the risk of stating the obvious – there must be an awful lot of good things going on as well, or a lot of them *would* run away.

And, since we began by considering what upsets the pupils of a country school like West Buckland – what imposes upon them – it might be apposite at this juncture to point out that the vast majority of the troubles mentioned above would have occurred no matter what sort of school the child attended.

Just as that young man I spoke of said that he found he had to 'struggle to really criticise WB', so one is constrained to suggest that 'WB' does not merit much censure for being what makes it different from other schools – a private, mostly-fee-paying, co-educational, part-boarding school set in the depths of the Devon countryside. Such an identity may attract the criticism, even the contempt, of educational philosophers, doctrinaire reformers, inverted snobs, and those who rent their bonnets to bees, but the subject of this piece is what the *inmates* think of the place. After all, they are the ones who have to live there.

West Buckland may deserve criticism for a lot of features which it shares with other schools, but not much, I put it to the court, for what springs from its specialness, its uniqueness, its 'West-Buckland-ness' if you like.

Brereton dreamed of creating a school that was different. One wonders whether, had he been a boy in his own creation, he would have begged his father to take him away. We can perhaps get close to an answer through the fact that he sent his eldest son to West Buckland. Or – maybe a little closer – through the comment of a pupil in Year 7: 'I can't wait to go in Year 8.'

36. Customer Satisfaction

'West Buckland means a great deal to me, not only because of all of the friends I have made and the opportunities I have been offered, but because it made me feel special and part of a very privileged community. The special thing about West Buckland is that everyone is made to feel the same way, at ease with the person they are and valued because of it. I also feel that another typical West Buckland trait is the amount of support given by staff and pupils.

'What made me luckier than some was the opportunity to show just how much West Buckland meant to me, being made a Senior School prefect gave me a great chance to give something back to a school which had, and still does, give me so much. I feel proud to be a product of, and a part of, such a wonderful place. Hopefully the West Buckland ethos will remain with me for a long time yet, no doubt the memory of it will.

'All I have left to say is thank you very much for everything the school has done for me and how it has enabled me to be the person I have become.'

[An extract from a letter sent by a leaver to the Headmaster, August, 2000.]

37. Gleams in the Kaleidoscope

Claim to Fame

Tom Hitchins, who entered the School in 1928, did the usual things that a sporty boy would have done – played rugger and cricket, smuggled cider into the dormitory in his games holdall, collected colours, and jogged around the campus in his cadet uniform. He passed his School Certificate in 1932, and his Cadet Cert.A, and won prizes in English, Latin , French, and 'Aggregate Merit' (twice).

After he left, he became a local businessman, served in the Armed Forces right through the Second World War, and made a prodigious contribution to the Old Boys' Association, holding every office that was in its gift. By the time he died in 2004, he had been constantly associated with the School for 76 years.

Both his son and his grandson attended the School, and each in his turn became Head Boy – a unique feat, one would imagine.

But his rarest distinction has just emerged from the record: in the *Register* of November, 1932, it notes that 'T.K. Hitchins' served the School Choir in the Summer Term – as 'organ blower'.

Thirst for Conflict

One Old Boy recalled a certain teacher who coached him and his team-mates for rugby. He (the teacher) 'drank healthily', but was nevertheless more than willing to join in the game. 'In the scrum when he was there it smelt like a four-ale bar.'

Devotion Indeed

Ian McLintock, one of the last of the old bachelor-schoolmasters, who served the School for thirty-one years, was a man of many parts – Housemaster of the Courtenay, teacher of Latin and French, officer in the School JTC (the CCF now), organiser of the Home Guard during the War, manager of the Tuck Shop, expert in the Byzantine rules of the Games Committee, impresario of the *Exmoor* runs, dedicated leader of camping trips in France, skilful caricaturist and modeller, and a Common Room 'character'. He was known to be fond of a jar or two, and stories circulated of the noise made late on Saturday nights when his car was backed into the garage of his house in Swimbridge and struck the back wall and surrounding junk.

He was also an inveterate diary-keeper. He died not long after retirement – alone. When he was found, considerably later, it was discovered that he had kept up his diary to the last day of his life.

Thumbnail Sketches

An Old Boy was kind enough to send me a lot of information about individual names in various sports teams whose photographs appeared in the last book (*West Buckland School*). He was thoughtful enough to insert in the margins little nuggets of news, apparently chipped out of the memory by the mere act of writing down these names. . . . .

'Died of TB soon after' . . . . 'Had size 13 shoes' . . . . 'Killed in training in the Royal Marines' . . . . 'MC in Italy' . . . . 'Drank himself to death' . . . . 'Expelled for sleeping with the Matron.'

(If the autobiography of Brian Aldiss, a contemporary, is to be believed, this Matron must have been a most accommodating lady.)

Love's Dignity

The Secretary of the School Association of Old Members received a letter from the wife of an Old Boy, to say that her husband had just died. She wrote a short account of her husband's life and career for the Association's records, and concluded with this touching sentence:

'He was a gentleman who always treated me as a lady and I am proud to be his widow.'

38. The Bard at West Buckland

Two of the stories in the previous book about the School (*West Buckland School* – nothing if not explicit) involved writers. The first ended with the information from a local historian that Shakespeare himself had visited Bideford in 1605; the second was about the racy stories that Brian Aldiss buried in a hedgebank in 1943 in order to escape detection, and which a gang of sixth-formers dug up in 1995 – and which Mr. Aldiss himself authenticated.

Well, I can now reveal a sequel, which will cap both of them: Shakespeare was once a pupil at West Buckland (a much earlier building, you understand), and he too buried some of his early jottings in order to escape the vigilant censorship of his teachers.

The container – a small, lead-lined oak box with its seal unbroken (a small green waxen globe stamped 'W.S.') – was unearthed by the members of a junior lunch-time smoking club in a local spinney, when an ancient badger sett collapsed on them. Since it would have proved impossible to explain how they had all been covered with earth (and escape punishment), the members of the club shrewdly negotiated a deal with the authorities: they traded the box and its contents for a guarantee of immunity from punishment for the smoking offence, and for two hundred and seventy-four similar offences committed over the previous three and a half years.

The contents were something of a disappointment to those Shakespearean scholars who were hoping to uncover a new play, but common sense would dictate that not even the Bard was turning out winners in his teens. The box, however, did reveal a fascinating clutch of jottings, obviously the result of daily experiences, that the young literary lion thought worth recording. As he was a teenager, many of these were critical; this explains why he took such pains to conceal them from his teachers.

He clearly forgot about the box, but many of those remarks must have seeped into his subconscious, because it is surprising how many of them found their way into his later works.

By way of proof, I append below a selection, and, for the benefit of those who would like to prove to themselves their command of the plays, I offer a key further on.

1. *Thoughts during the 'Exmoor':-*

'For this, be sure, tonight thou shalt have cramps,
Side-stitches that shall pen thy breath up.'

2. *The Prep:-*

    'What, are they children? Who maintains 'em?'

3. *Modest inmate of the Art Room:-*

    'An ill-favoured thing, sir, but mine own.'

4. *Orchestral rehearsal:-*

    'Sometimes a thousand twangling instruments
    Will hum about mine ears.'

5. *Remark on a sixth-form essay:-*

    'O most lame and impotent conclusion!'

6. *The First XV:-*

    'Where have they this mettle?
    Is not their climate foggy, raw and dull?'

7. *Long winter evenings:-*

    'Come now; what masques, what dances shall we have,
    To wear away this long age of three hours
    Between our after-supper and bed-time?'

8. *Choir Practice:-*

    'Pray you, no more of this; 'tis like the howling of Irish wolves against the
    moon.'

9. *Cricket weather:-*

    'The skies look grimly and threaten present blusters.'

10. *French oral examiner:-*

    'A stony adversary, an unhuman wretch, uncapable of pity, void and empty
    from any dram of mercy.'

11. *Public exam results by post:-*

    'Read o'er this;
    And after this: and then to breakfast with
    What appetite you have.'

12. *The Locker Room:-*

    'A very ancient and fish-like smell.'

13. *The Duty Prefect:-*

    'I have seen
    Hours dreadful and things strange; but this sore night

Hath tried former knowings.'

14. A Visit to the Changing Rooms:-

'Rammed me in with foul shirts and socks, foul stockings. . . . that there was the rankest compound of villainous smell that ever offended nostril.'

15. The survivors of the 'Exmoor':-

'What are these
So wither'd and so wild in their attire
They look not like th'inhabitants o' th' earth?'

16. Outside the Tuck-Shop:-

'I am not in the giving vein today.'

Key:

1)	*The Tempest* I – ii
2)	*Hamlet* II – ii
3)	*As You Like It* V – iv
4)	*The Tempest* III – ii
5)	*Othello* II – i
6)	*Henry V* III – iv
7)	*A Midsummer Night's Dream* V – i
8)	*As You Like It* V – ii
9)	*A Winter's Tale* III – iii
10)	*The Merchant of Venice* IV – i
11)	*Henry VIII* III – ii
12)	*The Tempest* II – ii
13)	*Macbeth* II – iv
14)	*Merry Wives of Windsor* III – v
15)	*Macbeth* I – iii
16)	*Richard III* IV – ii

39. Thousands of 'em, and All Boys

In the conclusion of the novel *Goodbye, Mr. Chips,* a scene faithfully rendered (for once) by the Hollywood film of it, the dying 'Chips' murmured that he had overheard someone near the bed saying it was a pity that he had no children.

'But I have, you know. I have. . . . thousands of 'em. . . . and all boys.'

In January, 1922, the West Buckland Old Boys' Assocation held its usual annual dinner, and, as usual, they sent an invitation to the Revd. Thompson, the School's first headmaster.

He had always been a keen attender at these functions, a familiar figure in his black clerical dress, with his white moustache and his gleaming monocle. This year, however, was his eighty-sixth, and he was forced to send to the Committee this letter:

> 'I can hardly say how great a pleasure it would have been to me had I been able to be with you to-night; but that pleasure is denied me. Whether I shall ever again be able to attend an Old Boys' Dinner, is, I am afraid, more than doubtful. But to the last day of my life my affection for my own Old Boys will never cease – nor will I fail to regard with great interest those who have since my headmastership become members of the School. To each and all I offer my heartiest good wishes.
>
> 'May the School to which we belong continue to grow and flourish – may there never be wanting a supply of Old Boys to keep up its old traditions and preserve its good name.
>
> 'I am gratified that my son is your guest to-night. I trust and believe that he will take a life-long interest in the School of which for thirty years his father was headmaster.
>
> 'January 12, 1922.'

Five months later Thompson died.

The parallel does not run exact: Chips had no surviving children of his body, and Thompson did. Chips served over fifty years, and Thompson only thirty. But Chips came to a school already steeped in tradition; Thompson had to build his from scratch.

Nevertheless, the parallel runs close enough for it to be worth making the comparison.

J.H. Thompson, HM from 1858 to 1888, with his staff and monitors, 1885. All six staff sport moustaches. Look at the self-conscious poses of the monitors, to say nothing of the bowler hats, waistcoats, and watch chains. [School Archive]

40. Who Wants to be a Benefactor?

If somebody had asked Lady Margaret Fortescue when she was a little girl whether she wanted to be a benefactor when she grew up, she would have looked totally baffled – well, that is my guess anyway.

Let us assume for a moment that she was a particularly knowledgeable little girl, and understood what a benefactor was. She would have been puzzled first because she knew perfectly well that her family had been benefactors of West Buckland School for generations (it would have been like asking the daughter of royalty whether she wanted to be a princess when she grew up); second, because, as a girl, she would not inherit the family earldom, and so the role of benefactor would not fall to her.

The Fortescues, like hundreds of aristocratic families the length and breadth of the country, assumed the role of benefactor as naturally as they took on the mantles of President of the County Show or Justice of the Peace or Sheriff or Lord Lieutenant or any other of the many distinctions which encrusted the hull of county society. It was not something you aspired to, or took exams to qualify for, or put up with, or shouted about; it was just something you did, like shutting the gate. It was not the be-all and end-all of a public life; it was a part, one of many that a busy aristocrat was called upon to play.

And they do not come much more aristocratic than the Fortescues. No newcomers they. None of your career opportunists from the Wars of the Roses, waxing fat on the confiscated lands of defeated enemies; or courtiers oiling up to Henry VIII in his struggle against Rome and keeping an eye to the main chance when it came to snapping up cheap estates snatched from the monasteries; or strutting Whigs and Tories aping nobility to disguise descent on the wrong side of the blanket from Charles II. The first Fortescue was a Companion of the Conqueror – beat that. Saviour of the Conqueror's life too – if the family tradition is to be believed. Three times. With his shield, apparently.

The Latin for 'shield' is 'scutum'. The word for brave, in this context, is 'forte'. (If you want the full monty, the word for 'brave' is 'fortis', but adjectives in Latin had to agree with the gender of the nouns they qualified – masculine, feminine, or neuter – and scutum is a neuter noun, and the neuter of the adjective fortis is forte.) Hence the family name. Since the first forte scutum kept Duke William alive at Hastings long enough to win, he was, you might say, the 'safety' of the Duke. The Latin for 'safety' is 'salus'. 'Of the Duke' comes out in Latin as 'ducum'. In 'full monty' mode again for a minute, ducum is in fact plural – 'of the dukes'. This comes about, presumably, because our first Fortescue saved the Duke's life three times, so by a slow process of linguistic osmosis, the phrase entered the family memory as a good story and seeped out the other side as a proverb: if you are a duke in battle, and you want to make sure you survive to enjoy the fruits of victory, it is a good idea to have a beefy baron on hand with a sizeable shield to slap in front of you whenever danger looms. 'A brave (or strong) shield is the safety of dukes (or leaders).' Hence the family motto: '*Forte scutum salus ducum.*'

At any rate, there they were – in on the ground floor, as you might say. Rewarded with land in Devon, documented as estate-owners as early as the mid-twelfth century. The fact that one can glibly summarise the Fortescue family career for the next seven or eight hundred years as 'pretty routine' or 'what you might expect' – the progression of barons, crusaders, crown servants, judges, ministers, soldiers, sailors, sheriffs, magistrates, and lords lieutenant – is a compliment to – well, to England, if you like. In no other country in the world could such a verdict be remotely valid or relevant. By implication this compliment would extend to the Fortescues. It is certainly not intended to belittle their achievement; in fact, quite the contrary. Along with scores of other ancient families, they did their duty by their family and their sovereign, did their thing, and did their best, according to their lights – for several centuries.

Part of their 'thing' was looking after those under their authority and in their care. At the risk of giving yet another history lesson, this 'benefactor' dimension is not a creation of the industrial revolution or nineteenth-century evangelical do-goodery. It goes right back. Any adult who remembers doing complicated classroom charts of the Feudal System of the Eleventh Century will have engraved upon his memory the impression of authority – the vassal swearing homage. What might have slipped past him, unless his history teacher was a good one, is that this feudal agreement went two ways. True, the vassal swore obedience and loyalty; but the lord also, and by an equally binding oath, swore to provide protection, justice, and security. If he didn't, the agreement was, legally, null and void.

Of course, it would be ridiculous to pretend that every generation of Fortescues, or of any other noble family, maintained an unbroken chain of kind, devoted, generous, head-patting father figures who knew the name of every villein's new-born baby. It would not be necessary to ransack the family cupboard to prove the existence of black sheep, bounders, bullies, and boors; the law of averages can do that. (It can also do that for every other class of society, by the way.)

But what the imprint of the centuries has done is to ensure the presence of an expectation – an expectation of a norm of behaviour. The medieval church laid down rules for civilised Christian conduct. The fact that noblemen (and everybody else) regularly broke them did not invalidate them, or, remarkably, diminish society's respect for them. They still constituted a standard, a bench-mark, which every man, in his heart of hearts, knew was sound and reasonable. (Why else did wealthy bigwigs, as they neared the end of the road, regularly bequeathe land and wealth to the agents of the spiritual world?)

By the same token, then, Fortescues expected, as a matter of course, that, somewhere along the line, one would lend an ear, give a hand, offer a leg up, put a hand (another hand) in the pocket; it went with the territory.

When, therefore, an idea came along about a new school in their area, and a new type of school, it was inconceivable that the Fortescues would not be involved.

Now it so happened that Lord Ebrington, the son of the second Earl, was interested in education. It so happened too that he had been forced by health problems to retire early to Castle Hill (the family seat) after a busy career in Government service. It so happened again that he was a friend of the Revd. J.L. Brereton, whose brain child the school was (See 'Founding Father'.) So the project was off to a good start. But the benefactor element was an ingredient of the mixture too. And it became an ever-growing element as the years went on. Brereton was a great spender – of other people's money – and Ebrington (or the third Earl, as he became in 1861) patiently endured the expenses and the pay-outs and the rescue packages which were the results of Brereton's impulsiveness and poor business sense. There survives a voluminous correspondence between them.

There was also a time when Fortescue had to come to the rescue, not with money, but with tact – or should we say 'economy with the truth'. When an early headmaster, a Mr. Challen, left in 1899 at the end of a clearly profound dispute with the governors, he took with him about two-thirds of the pupils to set up a rival school in Barnstaple. In an attempt to reassure worried investors, Fortescue sent off a batch of telegrams from Filleigh post office, saying 'School prospects now excellent', understanding shrewdly that sharp eyes and busy tongues would speedily insert this intelligence into the local grapevine.

Incidentally, this educational pioneering activity was not confined to West Buckland; Brereton and Fortescue were involved in the new county schools all over England – East Devon, Somerset, Dorset, Bedford, Norfolk (see 'Founding Father'). Fortescue laid the foundation stone for yet another, at Barnard Castle in Durham. The pattern was the same: Brereton was the man with the ideas and the charm and the drive; Fortescue was the man who knew everybody, who could tap the pockets of VIP's – and who had to dig into his own pocket when Brereton overspent yet again. It was to strain their friendship more than once.

The benefactor element was to become even more relevant after the third earl died in 1905. The fourth and fifth earls may not have had his crusading zeal for education, and they were not personal friends of the Revd. Brereton – who had died in 1901. But by that time the School was up and running; it could not be allowed to run dry for lack of funds – although it had twice come close to closing for lack of pupils. The bright idea had become a responsibility. It was on their territory. Literally; the second earl had provided the land for the first permanent buildings.

This does not mean that the fourth and fifth earls were regularly chipping in with dollops of rescue capital or interest-free loans. No. The School was reconstituted in the first decade of the twentieth century as a fee-charging independent school, albeit helped with a grant from the Devon County Council. As such it was expected to balance the books, and, by and large, it did, at any rate until the late 1960's. But the Fortescues were there, taking an interest, doing their VIP bit, being seen, presiding, governing (there has always been a Fortescue on the governing body), and generally just being around, as they had always been. If that meant that certain School functions had to be scheduled to coincide with the Earl's social diary, so be it; it was a small price to pay.

Incidentally, it may come as a surprise to you to be told that I have been able to make no computation as to the extent of the Fortescue financial contribution over the years, for the simple reason that Lady Margaret Fortescue, the present head of the Castle Hill family, has no idea herself. Or put it this way: when I asked her whether there existed a list of the Fortescue benefactions over the years, she said, 'I wouldn't think so.'

Now it could be argued that this was her discreet way of telling me to mind my own business. Possible, but unlikely; she was quite willing to tell me how much she had left to the School in her will. (And she didn't know, for instance, that the third earl had paid many of Brereton's debts.) Much more likely that it fits with the general impression which came through to me that, as I have tried to show, benefaction is important, but it is not *that* important. It is something you do, not something you shout about.

When I asked directly whether she thought that the School was sufficiently aware of the extent of her family's generosity over the years, she thought for some time before saying, in effect, that one doesn't 'blow one's own trumpet' about things like that. She was 'always interested' and 'wanting to know what is going on', and she was 'very proud of the School', and that was that.

She had certainly done her bit towards the running of the School, over and above any monetary contribution. She had been a governor for thirty-eight years – for over a decade commuting from East Anglia, where she then lived. And travelling then, before motorways, was a tedious business. In her young days, 'it took bloody well all day to get to *Exeter*'.

Her daughter, Lady Arran, had succeeded her, and was still a governor. Had Lady Margaret trained her in this calling? No. 'She used to see me go off to Governors' meetings.' It was part of the daily round, the common task. 'I've tried by example to show that it was duty', but it had never been forced down her daughter's throat. There was no teenage rebellion; it had all 'happened quite naturally'. And very successfully, it appears. Lady Margaret offered it as her opinion that 'my daughter does too many things'.

I once asked Lady Arran whether her own daughter would follow in the family tradition of governorship. The answer was similar, if more succinct and positive: 'Oh, yes – she's been told.' As the young woman in question is not only a Fortescue but an ex-pupil of the School, the chances are doubled that the tradition will be continued.

It may cross the mind that this is all very well, and yes, they do some useful work. But there they are, in their enormous house at Castle Hill, groaning under the weight of ancestral portraits, swamped with servants, with nothing else to do but enjoy their wealth. Writing the odd cheque and sitting on the occasional committee is no great strain.

Well, it is a point of view, but not a particularly well-informed one. And it is one held by those in ranks of society usually below the likes of the Fortescues. Yet such families are not necessarily so safe or inviolable as one might think. Nobody wants to abolish the working classes or the middle classes, but there are those who, if they were given the chance, would abolish the aristocracy. The creeping demise of the House of Lords, for example, could easily be seen as a stage in this campaign.

Then again, privilege, possessions, and landed property do not automatically bestow perpetual prosperity. The house Lady Margaret now lives in, though it is referred to on the estate as 'the bungalow', is a bungalow the like of which you and I have rarely seen. But she is no stranger to financial worries. Or to tragedy.

Her only brother was killed in the Second World War, and neither of her parents totally recovered from the shock. They died within four days of each other in 1958. Worse, her mother died first, leaving her estate (she was a wealthy woman in her own right) entirely to her husband. So when *he* died Lady Margaret was left with an appalling burden of death duties. The title – the earldom – had passed to the late Earl's brother, but the Earl had made his daughter Margaret heir to Castle Hill and its land. (Here I am passing over various advantageous marriages since the fifteenth century, which had enhanced the Fortescue holdings, but I am here concerned not with a history of the family, but with its role as benefactor of West Buckland School.)

There was nothing else for it but to sell. The Challacombe estate went, a large slice of Exmoor, most of West Buckland, and a chunk of East Buckland too – mostly to tenant farmers. Why not sell off a painting or two? The popular conception of nobility and stately homes has it that there is usually a batch of Rembrandts and Corots knocking about in the attic or sandwiched between glowering ancestors on the staircase.

Not at Castle Hill.

There had been a fire in 1934, which raged for two days. The damage to the fixtures, fittings, and books was awful, though servants saved a lot of the paintings and furniture. But that was not the end of the trouble. Forty-nine paintings were sent away for restoration. The van which brought them back arrived one evening too late to be unloaded, so it was put for safety in a nearby garage. During the night fire struck again, and everything went up in smoke – garage, van, paintings, and all. The house was rebuilt, but the interiors had been lost for ever. The books and paintings were of course irreplaceable.

Just for good measure there was a divorce in the family, and Lady Margaret returned to Castle Hill in 1968 to run the place, make ends meet, and raise two daughters on her own. She still found time to be a governor of the School, as I said, for thirty-eight years. She has also been the first lady president of the Devon County Show, not to mention countless other local calls upon her time.

There was also the small matter of the day-to-day administration of the estate, which demands all sorts of flair from business sense and imagination to attention to detail and the power of executive decision. Sympathy too. She can, by some accounts, be 'pretty feudal' when the situation calls for it, but estate employees can still leave her surprise birthday presents on doorsteps – and she can still have a little cry about it.

However, she does not spend all her days sitting on the office stool and reeling at the sight of a bulging engagements book. My impression is that Lady Margaret enjoys a full life, even at eighty – maybe more so at eighty. For example, she said, when I rang up to fix an appointment for a visit, 'I can't do Tuesdays, I'm afraid; that's the day I go shooting.' And anyone who greets you in lively blue jeans and white trainers, while fending off the fulsome attentions of Labrador dogs, is not sheltering behind a rampart of fragile seclusion. She gave me two full hours of her time; she was a good listener; she pondered her answers; she enjoyed a good story; and she relished a spot of gossip.

So how had it been? What had it been like to be a governor all that time? How did the others treat her? 'Inevitably, I was a bit different.' Not, as you might think, because she was an aristocrat, but because she was a woman. Governing bodies, especially in places like Devon, tended to be pretty conservative clubs. So they would say to her, 'What would you think – as a mother?' Then, too, she said, she made a change from the sort of professional person who was usually invited to join boards of governors. And let us not forget the obvious – 'the family had founded it'. Of course she was interested, and she became more interested as the years went by. More involved. It helped that she lived so near the School; most governors did not. So headmasters naturally turned to her, because of the sheer convenience of it.

Why do it? As I have tried to show, I think the work of being a benefactor like the Fortescues gets done simply because of the situation. It goes with the territory; it has always been done. It is done because it never occurs to the benefactor *not* to do it. It is so deeply buried in the psyche that it demands thought before it can be explained in words, and then probably not entirely adequately. Lady Margaret had to fish around in her mind before she said words to the effect that 'we've all been very conscious of being large landowners; we're very lucky; it follows then that we should get involved'. 'Fair do's' seems to be what it comes down to (my comment, not hers).

Purely out of personal interest, I asked whether the Fortescues still had a say in the choice of the parish priest in their estates. Lady Margaret, it appears, is still the patron of West Buckland, East Buckland, Swimbridge, Filleigh, and Gunn churches. But the days have gone when 'Father selected them after an interview'. Nowadays she simply listens politely.

The only local post that Lady Margaret has not been willing to take on has been J.P. She offered as an explanation, 'Because I would have been too kind to the persecuted motorist.'

Which little anecdote shows a pretty sharp sense of humour too, and an appreciation of a good story. Some years ago, there had been a chairman of governors called the Revd. Prebendary Andrews, who by all accounts seems to have been quite a character. He lived a bachelor life in 'an arctically cold rectory', where his sister kept house for him, but he had a keen mind and a razor-sharp wit, of truly Saharan aridity. He told rib-straining jokes with a completely straight face. He had many gifts, and was an excellent public speaker. Lady Margaret's summary of him was that, if he had been ambitious, he could have been Archbishop of Canterbury.

When the time came once to select a new headmaster, she and the Revd. Preb. had formed a sub-committee to weed out the pile of applications, and get it down to short-list proportions. One candidate, in Lady M.'s opinion, after a first read, did not merit further consideration, so she set his letter on one side. Andrews noticed this, as he had been reading a copy of the application from the same man.

'I noticed you put aside the letter of Mr. X. May I be so bold, Lady Margaret, as to ask why?'

Lady Margaret had done it, she said, because she felt he was 'not up to scratch academically'. He was moreover a Methodist, and he was a bachelor, and a boarding school needed a married head.

'Very interesting, Lady Margaret,' said the Revd. Preb. 'I rejected him because he split his infinitives.'

It is rare for anyone who is part of a tradition not to be proud of it, and Lady Margaret is no exception. She is proud of Fortescue family history – for instance she volunteered the information that her father and her mother's brother became Knights of the Garter on the same day. (Well, wouldn't you?) She is proud of what she and her family have done to recover from the shock to the family fortunes when her parents died. She is proud of what her daughter has accomplished as her successor.

She is proud of what West Buckland School is and what it has achieved, and so by association proud of her own (considerable) contribution to that happy situation. 'I think it's a very good education' that they offer. 'They do turn out jolly good citizens.' And she laid stress on their 'sense of duty', their capacity for friendship, and their 'right attitude to life'.

The School has moved on, and has recovered from its last bad spell in the late 1960's, which Lady Margaret described as a 'very dicey time'. It is healthy, purposeful, and thriving, and it balances its books. She is not a governor any more, and she does not put money into the School any more. 'I don't think I've got a banker's order.' But, if there is something special needed, 'Yes, I'll stump up.' And she had made provision in her will for bursaries for the children of estate employees.

It was the same with her daughter, Lady Arran. 'She is very good and very generous. She will put her hand in her pocket if necessary.'

By quoting these last remarks, I hope sincerely that I do not induce eager fund-raisers and foundation managers to write ill-timed, ill-judged, and ill-informed importunate letters to Castle Hill. The Fortescues have done their whack, and expect their 'child', after all these years, to stand on its own feet, just as any parents would expect their own children to do. But they are still interested and concerned, and, like parents, will be ready to stand by if –

God forbid – anything really awful happens. It is a deep fund not so much of reserve finance as of interest, willingness, and experience.

By way of illustration, may I quote a small example of the experience. A few years ago I watched Lady Arran give away the prizes at the School Speech Day. As always, the visiting dignitary has to make a speech afterwards. These speeches can be, shall we say, a variable blessing. Lady Arran's was a superb example of what such a speech should be – polished, neat, witty, succinct. No doubt well prepared, but very effective.

As an example of the willingness and interest, may I use Lady Arran again. When I was preparing the illustrations for the previous book to this (called simply *West Buckland School*), I asked if a colleague and I could visit Castle Hill to view and photograph some of the family pictures – those which had survived the fire, or which had come along afterwards. Although she had just returned from a long journey, she greeted us graciously, told us everything we wanted to know, showed us everything we asked to see. My photographer colleague, who has socialistic tendencies – but who had put on a tie for the occasion! – pronounced himself quite charmed with the experience.

Nearly a hundred and fifty years of involvement on the part of a noble family is a huge asset for any school, and any governor or headmaster would be mad to neglect it. Lady Margaret was quick to point out that, by comparison with, say, the Dukes of Devonshire, they were 'not in the same league', but they are still in a league that is miles away from almost everybody else in the county, whichever way you care to look at it. Such prestige, such tradition, such knowledge, such experience – such 'clout' is there, at the School's disposal, as is the Fortescue proximity, interest, concern, pride, and goodwill. When it is put like that, it almost becomes bad taste to mention mere money. But the Fortescues are practical; they know what it is like to have to rustle some up. Perhaps they are not so many miles away after all.

41. Otherwise Known As

In *West Buckland School*, I dug out, from the mine of the past, over eighty nicknames, of pupils and teachers and headmasters and school servants. Clearly I did not exhaust the vein. Here are a few more, gleaned among the disused workings:-

Bam	Ma	Nellie	Duck
Romeo	Dog	Polar	Dreamy
Fleur	J.B.	Johnnie	Yanner (both
Bocker	Barlow	Bungy	father and son)
Moto	Ticktock	Girlie	Flabby
Sam	Babe	Nig	Titch
Rat	Digger	Stinker	Watto
Nipsy	Bung	Taff	Nar
Goon	Baloo	Bullock	Jock
Fruitie	Tusky	Pate	Dac
Nasal	Tina	Bungro	KK
Scoops	Queeran	Bananaby	Co
Mona Lisa	D	Vixen	Gnome
Bristols	Molar	Barch	Gad
Weed	Nipper	Jobber	Piggy
Jasper	Bunny	Joe	Beehive
Clanger	Sabrina	Buttercup	Guzz

42. Ichabod

Hollywood did a lot for me. It did a lot for my generation. Besides being an escape from the drabness of wartime and post-war austerity, and a perfect auditorium for a child's capacity for hero-worship and wishful thinking, it was an enormous fund of knowledge. It would be too much to say that it was a child's university, or even a finishing school, but it was certainly an incomparable starting school.

Thanks to Hollywood, for instance, I knew that all spies spoke with either a German or a mid-European accent, and came from Berlin, Budapest, or Zagreb. I knew that African explorers always wore bush jackets, carried revolvers on lanyards, and slept under mosquito nets in huge tents which had been carried all day by hundreds of half-naked black porters in square packages balanced on their heads. If I saw Europeans in grubby white double-breasted suits, 'natives' with hats like plates on their heads, and inscrutable pigtailed 'orientals' skulking behind piles of cargo in 'junks' on the river, I knew at once that I was in Shanghai or Singapore, or any seaport in between.

Hollywood, in short, was an inexhaustible mine of cliché. Nevertheless, cliché was first-hand knowledge to the young child, before the passage of time turned the exciting into the hackneyed, the original into the derivative, the genuine into the laughable. Even then, something of permanent value could be salvaged from the wreckage of crazes and undiscriminating passions.

This was general knowledge. All spies may not really have spoken with foreign accents, and all explorers may not really have carried revolvers on lanyards, and all villains may not really have worn grubby white suits; but I did at least know that Budapest was the capital of Hungary, that Zanzibar was on the east coast of Africa, that Singapore was the busiest city on the Malay Peninsula. As a result of seeing Hollywood historical films, I knew that Robert Clive was one of the great champions of British rule in India, that Henry Morton Stanley's search for Livingstone began simply as a newspaper assignment, that Prince John got up to no good while his brother King Richard was away on the Crusades.

Hollywood may have got a lot of things wrong, but at the same time it gave us so many points of reference. It is a familiar cry today that the present school generation have no such facility at their disposal. Put another way, they are often accused of being life-threateningly ignorant. (A charge that sixth-formers of my acquaintaince have been only too willing to admit, oddly enough.)

This argument, if you have put up with it this far, is now showing signs of becoming the all-too-familiar bleat of the older generation that 'things are not what they used to be'. Children don't know anything nowadays. They can't punctuate; they can't spell; they can't do mental arithmetic; their geography is pathetic; their history is non-existent; they have memorised no poetry; they have no grasp of basic grammar. Let this hobby-horse ride roughshod over the conversation, and before long the younger generation will have no religion, no morals, no manners, no table etiquette; no capacity for innocent play; no respect for age, tradition, heritage; no regard for anything except iconoclasm and apathy.

So hold on a minute. If you examine the full list of 'things that aren't what they used to be', you may well find that they contain items the passing of which is mourned not by the older generation but by the younger. One can make a case for saying that there is no creature so stuffy and conservative as your average sixth-former, and no hanger and flogger more savage than your average third-former.

Take the Glee. This was instituted at West Buckland by the Revd. Harries shortly after the First World War. It was, and was almost certainly intended to be, an occasion for some plain good fun. It was a competition between the four houses. It involved a singing contest; each house performed its own version of a given song, which was assessed by an outside adjudicator. The rest of the programme consisted of a series of sketches of the sort of topicality that would appeal to a boarding school audience – skits of favourite entertainment vehicles, satirical pieces, and digs at members of staff or other figures of alleged pomposity. The scripts, the acting, and the production standards could vary from the promising to the abysmal, but, as with any amateur performance to a captive audience, everyone involved was so determined to have a good time that quality came very low in the list of desirable criteria.

As is well known, the inmates of an Army barracks in Aldershot or a Stalag in Bavaria or a Japanese prison camp in Thailand had such awful lives that any light relief, however execrable, was more welcome than anything except a lorryload of Red Cross parcels or the end of the War. What is perhaps not so well known is that, for the pupils of a boys' boarding school in the depths of the Devon countryside between the wars, similar circumstances – in principle if not in degree – obtained. Think about it – no permission to visit the local town, except maybe twice a term, in strictly regulated buses; little chance of escaping on a bicycle – town was too far away; no radio till the late twenties; no TV at all; no school film projector; no computers, no mobile phones, no electronic games. Just rugby and cross-country running in the winter, and cricket in the summer. Trips if you were good enough to be in a School team. A reading room and the sixth-form debating society if you weren't. No wonder the Glee was popular.

No wonder it soon passed into the rarefied status of sanctified tradition. No wonder it was mourned when it was abolished – over seventy years later. The pupils, especially the older ones, who wrote and performed most of the Glee, decided at once, with the passion for simplification that is the prerogative of the young (and of the propagandist), that this pernicious decree passed by a new headmaster was proof that he was a heartless, narrow-minded tyrant who had no glimmering of the School's tender soul, no regard for its time-honoured rituals. *Ichabod.*

They had a point; the Glee had provided a great deal of fun, and had kept a very large number of pupils well occupied, over a very long period. But there were only so many square yards of space in a relatively small set of School buildings, and there were only so many facilities available. As numbers grew, there were even more limitations on space, and above all on time. Compare the numbers of activities recorded in the *Register* of the 1920's, and in the *Register* of, say, 1996, just before the new Headmaster arrived, and the problem becomes obvious. Kids in the 1990's had so much more to do, and still only twenty-four hours a day in which to do it. Allow every single activity, and the butter is spread so thinly that everything is in danger of being done badly. The minute that new specialist rooms are built, there is an avalanche of demands for their use. It is a bit like the argument about new motorways; the minute you build a fourth lane to take the surplus traffic, mysteriously a fresh wave of traffic is generated to block it up.

So the Glee went. So did Fives. I can not speak with any authority here, never having played Fives, nor indeed ever having seen it played. But, after a long innings at West Buckland, it went, and no doubt it had its mourners. *Ichabod* again.

What about the great Gilbert and Sullivan tradition so earnestly nurtured by, again, the Revd. Harries? He planned them, inspired them, ran them, and starred in them. Whether it was a great flight of the ego for him is immaterial; they provided huge interest, they involved scores of boys as chorus, principals, make-up artists, scene-shifters, programme-sellers, and general dogsbodies. Look at the photographs of the casts of the various productions, which went on without a break from 1915 till Harries retired in 1934. Look at the standards of costume. Look at the sheer numbers. The School was only about 150 strong, rising admittedly in the 1920's, but dropping again with the Depression of the early thirties. It was a colossal achievement for a moorland boys' boarding school, and must have been a huge event. There were two or three attempts at repeating them just after the War, but they never appeared to attain the stature of the great Harries extravaganzas. Just a glance at the programmes tells you that the later shows were, to say the least, a trifle *ersatz* compared with the earlier efforts.

Not everyone is a lover of Gilbert and Sullivan, admittedly, and not everyone therefore was plunged into inconsolable grief at their passing. But it seems fair to say that something valuable passed out of School life when they went. *Ichabod.*

One could go on. If only a limited number of boys clapped their hands at the prospect of yet another rehearsal of the Chorus of Peers or the Policeman's Song, a very large number of boys, I should guess, would be pleased at the prospect of an afternoon's football. Yet this, too, was abolished in the 1920's. Now, if the Glee and Fives and G. and S. boasted long traditions, they could claim nothing like the venerability of tradition enjoyed by 'foot ball', as it was when the School was founded (or 'foot-ball', as it became in the 1880's and later, till it lost the hyphen). Yet football went. I wonder how many boys thought Harries was a monster for that decision?

Notice how many changes involved Harries. Another execution he was responsible for was that of the School Reading and Debating Society, in 1926. From its Minutes (and we have all of them), it seemed to be bowling along pretty well, but he saw fit to abolish it, though he re-incarnated it in the shape of the Phoenix Society (which is still with us). I would almost put money on the fact that his decision was not met with anything like unanimous approval. Yet, despite all these changes, Harries is generally reckoned to be the School's greatest headmaster. Maybe partly because of them.

He must have had sound motives – not even arbitrary dictators take their decisions lightly, unless they are of the stamp of Caligula. And I think it only fair that we ascribe some worthy motives to a man of the cloth who was viewed as a great head both during his career and after it was over. We do not know why Harries re-vamped the Reading and Debating Society, but there are one or two theories about the demise of football.

The given reason was that the School was running out of opponents (the School used to play local clubs as well as local schools). This is indeed possible. The death rate of young men had been so terrible in the First World War that many clubs would simply not have been able to field teams as they had before the War. Before motor transport became common, simply getting to each other's grounds presented difficulties (though that had, arguably, been just as bad before).

But there were still the schools. Here we run into what was probably a deeper reason. More and more public schools, it seems, were switching to rugby. Now, rugby, as we all know, is a hooligans' game, but it is played by gentlemen. West Buckland School – and, in its former incarnation, the Devon County School – played the gentlemanly game of football. The trouble was that football was played, according to accepted wisdom, by hooligans. Kids in back streets and cul-de-sacs did not punt a rugger ball about or practise their scrum technique round bollards and lamp posts.

Harries was keen to raise the status and public image of his school. He – or the Governors – changed the School's very name, from, as I said, the Devon County School to West Buckland School. He adopted the public school prefect system, and stopped calling his chosen seniors 'monitors', which smacked of teacher's stooges and filling inkwells. He stopped calling them 'dormitories' and renamed them 'houses'. Subjects like Latin began to creep up the ladder of the timetable. So taking up rugby was part of a logical progression; it was a game to be played by gentlemen, and it would bring his rustic novice scrummers into more and more contact, both physical and cultural, with 'real' gentlemen in other (posh?) public schools. (They did rather well too; within a few years of making the switch, they produced three School teams – a First, Second, and Colts' XV – which all went through a season undefeated.)

The Glee, Fives, Gilbert and Sullivan, the Reading and Debating Society, football (or 'foot-ball' if you are a dyed-in-the-wool conservative) – the graves and epitaphs of all of them, and more, are duly marked in the pages of the *Register. Ichabod, ichabod.*

But there have been other disappearances which may not have been accorded their individual obituaries. Did anybody see fit to pass comment on the removal of toast and dripping from the breakfast menu? Or daily porridge? Has any memorialist called attention to the final melting of the ice in the washbasins? (No reminiscence of any Old Boy over the age of fifty is complete without a reference to 'ice in the washbasins'.) Is there any entry in the *Register* recording the removal of wintry draughts in the dormitories?

This could be because nobody saw fit to mourn the departure of these time-honoured features of School life.

By the same token, I don't suppose anyone complained about the ending of fagging. Certainly not juniors anyway, who had to do it. No doubt there was a clutch of sixth-form fogies who had had to do fagging when *they* were juniors, and who had been looking forward to perpetuating that fine school tradition. So they would have had something else to blame the Headmaster for.

There are changes, of course, which do not result necessarily, or exclusively, from the initiative and creativity – or spleen – of a restless headmaster. The demise of fagging is a case in point. That peculiar, but very powerful agency, the climate of opinion, had a big hand in it. So it did, too, in the abolition of corporal punishment. Prefects were banned from inflicting it in the early 1970's, surprisingly at the instigation of the new Head

Prefect. According to the story I was told by a teacher with a long memory, he (the prefect) disapproved of it, and issued an ultimatum to the Headmaster, to the effect that if the Head made him Head Prefect, he (the Head Prefect) would not continue it. The ultimatum was accepted.

The abolition of caning by staff came as late as the mid-1980's. The institution was already withering before the European Court pronounced on it. The ultimate demise came with the arrival of a lot of girls from a nearby convent school which had just closed. This precipitated a situation in which any continuation of caning was made ludicrous by the implications of this female influx: if you couldn't cane girls, you obviously couldn't cane boys either.

Then there are the changes which come about because the Headmaster sees them as unavoidable – if the School is to continue. The classic example of this at West Buckland came in the late 1960's. The new Headmaster was dismayed to discover, when he had a good look at the accounts, that the financial viability of the School was a good deal less promising than he had been led to believe before he was appointed. Numbers were limited too. A lot of maintenance and repair needed doing around the campus. Bank managers were rubbing chins and shaking heads and pulling long faces. Something Would Have to be Done.

The 'Something' turned out to be an alarming menu of change (alarming, that is, to the conservatives): the extension of day-pupil facilities; the broadening of the admissions policy in order to get more boys' buttocks on benches; dark hints about the possible entry of that peculiar species – girls; and so on. (I am simplifying – perhaps over-simplifying – a very complicated and painful period in the School's history in order to make a point in my own argument, and I have no wish to hurt anybody's feelings. For this reason I have named no names.) This was seen by many senior staff and governors, and Old Boys, as going against a century of School tradition. Which it was. But, according to the Headmaster, it was either that or closure. Which did they want?

There was quite a lot of drama before he made his point. The School survived. Whether it was because or in spite of him is immaterial; it survived. Did something valuable disappear in the process? Quite probably. Not even the demise of the aristocracy in the French Revolution was one hundred per cent progress. But in such situations the vital factor is that change becomes even more valuable than preservation, no matter how cherished the tradition. Not just invaluable – indispensable. So – Ichabod no doubt to the Old Guard, but not to everybody else.

So it will always be. Why 'Ichabod'? I was wondering when you were going to ask that. It is Biblical, as you may have guessed. It comes from the first Book of Samuel (iv, 21). The Judge Eli's daughter-in-law, in an advanced stage of pregnancy, had been told that Israel had been defeated by the Philistines (those Philistines had a lot to answer for, one way and another), that they had stolen the Ark of the Covenant, and that her husband and father-in-law were both dead. The shock brought on the birth pangs of her son, whom she named 'Ichabod', which meant something to the effect that 'the glory is departed'. (Well, after all that, it would be, wouldn't it? She too died shortly afterwards, of grief – having refused to 'regard' the child. No grandfather, no father, no mother, rejected, and with a name like Ichabod – the poor lad didn't much of a start in life, did he? One wonders what became of him.)

Now how on earth did I know that? Well, I'll tell you. Because I spent one lesson every week throughout my first year at a grammar school wading through a relentless little tome entitled *A Short Old Testament History*. Our teacher was equally relentless, and imposed on us yet more relentless revision tests every week. The penalties for poor performance were dire.

The result is that I can tell you to this day about Judges called Othniel and Ehud and Shamgar, and Deborah and Barak, and the plains of Jezreel, and Hophni and Phinehas (the sons of Eli), and I don't know what else. And *Ichabod*.

Believe it or not, but that last piece of information actually came in useful later on. One of our set books for the 16+ English Literature exam was a collection of *Essays by Modern Writers*. One of these 'modern writers' was Max Beerbohm, who was born in 1872 – which shows you just how modern he was – and the title of his 'essay' was *Ichabod*. I knew at once what the general theme of the essay was. So you see? No knowledge or experience is ever totally wasted.

This could be my cue to jump on the *Ichabod* bandwagon with all the other fogies I have been talking about, and bemoan the passing of so much knowledge and information that used to be current in the lives of well-educated boys and girls. But what is the point? The earth, as Tom Paine is supposed to have said, or at least implied, belongs to those on it, not to those underneath it.

Knowledge goes in fashion like anything else. If something goes out of fashion, it goes out of fashion. What is the point of saying 'Ichabod' – that the glory is departed? What if it is? What is the point even of knowing what the very word 'Ichabod' *means*, if your average school child rarely goes near a church, and wouldn't know a prophet from a judge, or an epistle from an apostle, or the Sacred Host from the Holy Ghost? There are indeed answers to this question, but they are not germane to the present issue. The point I am making is that at certain times certain types of knowledge are deemed to be no longer relevant, for better or worse.

Whole subjects disappear from the curriculum, with many or few mourners according to their own educational backgrounds or personal preferences or experiences of the subject in question. How many schools teach Latin nowadays? West Buckland has recently abolished it. How many schools teach Greek? How many teach actual religious faith in the Religious Knowledge lessons? How far has 'General Science' superseded the tripartite Chemistry, Physics, and Biology? How many schools do 'Integrated Humanities' instead of History and Geography? (Probably not so many, because History and Geography have made a comeback.) How many girls learn typing and shorthand today? Not all that long ago, it was the key to a good living for millions. No more.

I don't suppose that anybody today deplores the passing of Estate Management or Euclid from the curriculum at West Buckland, but there were plenty to deplore the more recent removal of Politics from it, and Business Studies, and General Studies, and Communication Studies – to name only four recent casualties.

All this is in the nature of things. At least it is in the nature of organic bodies. We are told by the biologists that the body's cells undergo a near-complete renewal every seven years or so. Not all at once of course – the changeover is gradual, cell by cell. So it is with schools with any kind of a history. Subjects, habits, institutions, even traditions come and go, just as do pupils and teachers. It is a sign of growth, not of decay. The School's heart is beating.

Maybe too all is not completely lost. We like to think that something of our forebears lives on in ourselves. The experiences and joys and sufferings of a person's life may have slipped into history, may even have slipped from the memory, but they are present in the lines and the wrinkles and the faraway eye. Just so with a school: traces of all those changes and abolitions and crises and dramas are still present, deep in the woodwork and the well-scored walls. The lines and the wrinkles are there just as much there as they are there on a pensioner's cheeks. Curiously, young people, who tend to find the ageing process frightening, find age itself comforting. They don't often listen to the voices of time and experience, but, given the choice, they would, on the whole, prefer them to be there – just in case. Given the choice, they would prefer having their stone steps worn down in the middle to having them sharp-edged and gleaming.

We in our turn must take comfort from youth, from our children. All is not lost here either. They may indeed be unblushingly ignorant, and ignorant of the extent of their ignorance, but they are probably much more *aware* than we were. How many of us, in our teen years, knew about world famine, the ozone layer, global warming, fossil fuels, rain forests, genetic engineering, lung cancer, calories, human rights, the whales, the seals, the bears, the badgers, and a menagerie of endangered species? Young people of today probably get them all wrong (as Hollywood once did), but they have at least heard of them. Set against these priorities (as they see them), it is no surprise that they do not stop to wonder what is the capital of Hungary, or why Stanley was looking for Livingstone, or what Prince John was getting up to in his brother's absence.

A witness of change, of whatever age and taste, may indeed shake his or her head and mutter 'Ichabod, *ichabod*' – things are not what they used to be. But then they never were.

And a good job too.

43. Entertainment and Insurance

Into Injun Country

On 7th June, 1869, 'the whole School made an excursion to Lynton, and spent a very pleasant day. Sixteen waggons and carts were required as conveyances.'

[It must have looked like the Oregon Trail – the only difference being that the whooping savages were the ones *inside* the waggons, not around them.]

The First Silver Screen

The *Register* of June, 1914 contained this entry:

'During the term, by a special arrangement, the kinematograph film, "Quo Vadis", was shown for the benefit of the School in the Dining Hall. It proved of very great interest to everyone, and much light was thrown upon the customs and habits of the Romans; for days after boys might be seen greeting each other from a distance with outstretched hand after the Roman fashion.'

[The more you think about this, the more dimensions it grows.]

Bonny Brown Hair

Frances White came to work as a dormitory maid at West Buckland School when she was only thirteen. In the first decades of the twentieth century, particularly in the country, this early employment was nothing unusual, though perhaps young Frances did attract attention by virtue of the fact that she was still wearing pigtails.

It certainly attracted the attention of Edward Timms (not his real name), a pupil at the School; he used to creep up behind her, slip the knot on one of her pigtail ribbons, and run off with it. It was a typical piece of schoolboy teasing.

What was not typical was what he did on the day he left. He came up to Frances – to her face this time – and presented her with a beautifully wrapped and decorated cardboard box. When she undid the parcel and opened the box, she found every single one of the ribbons he had taken from her.

Providing for the Future

A first-former (or 'member of Year 7', as we should say now), writing a piece for John Clark, a Geography teacher, had occasion to make these remarks about him and about other members of staff:

'During IT, time passes as quickly as a slug runs across the QWERTY keyboard if we are typing.'

'The French teacher is a lenient man whose strongest concern is the "masculine" or the "feminine".'

'Our physics teacher is cool! And we do lots of cool experiments. It all stays cool until he sets fire to something, then things warm up.'

'Geography is taught us by Mr. J. Clark, a tall strict man who is the head of the best house in the school, "the Grenville". He is a wondrous teacher and I would like a House tie.'

44. The Buck at West Buckland

John Vick became the Headmaster of West Buckland School in 1997. After the usual preliminary visits and briefings and study sessions, and boning up on names and accounts and staff CV's and so on, he arrived at the end of August to begin for real – only to be completely upstaged by Princess Diana's sudden death.

Still, there is something about education which is blessedly unstoppable; school, like the show, must go on. Perhaps the fact that the eyes of the world were all on London during those first few days may, in an indirect sort of way, have been a help. You must ask John Vick that.

He liked being here, that was for sure. West Buckland had put out its equivalent of the red carpet – glorious summer sunshine. He told me that the day he and his family moved house, he sat on the front steps of the main building (which was, then, the Headmaster's official residence; a new, more homely one was built shortly afterwards) and thought, 'This is the most wonderful place to live.'

Alas! It rained on and off for the next seven or eight years, but that did not dampen his original conviction that it was 'a remarkable place to live your working life and bring up your family'. He still stands by that conviction.

How had he come to be a headmaster? By the normal route. At least normal once he had secured his degree. There was something of a break-through before that; he was the first member of his family to attend university. (His sister had been to a teacher training college.) But, once he had a History degree from St. John's College, Cambridge under his belt, the progress was, as I said, normal enough – post-graduate certificate of education; housemaster for five years; Head of History at Stamford for five years; and then Deputy Head at Woodbridge in Suffolk.

Had he always had a headship in his sights? No – not at the outset. But, like Topsy, the idea must have 'growed'. As he said, 'You don't move to a deputy headship unless you're thinking of a headship.' After two or three years at Woodbridge, he started looking. West Buckland was not his first shot at the target.

Before he saw the advertisement, he had never heard of West Buckland – along with ninety-nine per cent of the population. His wife had once lived in Devon, and, coincidentally, had just been reading *To Serve Them All My Days*. So that was a start. (If there is anybody not *au fait* with that work, it was written by R.F. Delderfield, an Old Boy – one of the two literary 'figures' the School has produced – and is a fictional account of the career of a young teacher between the Wars at a school called Bamfylde, which is a thinly-disguised West Buckland. It was turned into a major television, thirteen-episode drama round about 1980, and the School duly basked in some vicarious publicity for a while.)

He was intrigued, did some homework, and sent in his application. As a result of his homework, he did not arrive for interview too burdened with arrant misconceptions about the School or the problems facing it. 'I had seen enough schools to know what the challenges would be. I knew the School had few financial resources beyond fees. I knew that the Assisted Places Scheme was about to be run down.' And there were about a quarter of the children on Assisted Places support; so, as and when they went, how were you going to attract another 120 fee-paying pupils?

It might be appropriate here to make a point which often may slip past critics of independent schools, particularly critics from the state sector. In the Old Days when local government funded everything in state educational establishments, nobody – least of all teachers – ever worried about costs. You ordered your new picture-books and your fancy new building kits which you had been told about on your latest course (you were always encouraged to 'go on courses' as a vital step in your 'career development'). You cheerfully tore up and threw away sheet after sheet of paper which the old Banda duplicating machine had spoilt. You ordered coach after coach to take the children on yet more excursions to yet further distant parts. You dismissed a school secretary's misgivings about expenditure with the airy assertion that 'education is free' and 'a child's right'. Indeed, if you were of a left-wing disposition and the local council was Tory, you positively revelled in spending money, if only to give 'them' another headache. You joked proudly about going over budget year after year, as if it were a national pastime like fiddling the income tax. Teachers – not to put too fine a point on it – were (and, dare I suggest it, some still are) shocking business managers.

The handing over of budgets to schools themselves gave many of them a rude awakening. But while all this has been going on, the independent schools have always lived under the shadow of the First Commandment of their race – namely, that if you don't balance the books, you don't survive. 'In the red' means 'dead'. If the money doesn't work out, there is no US cavalry from the Local Education Office to gallop to your rescue. You are on your own, and you deal with the creditor Indians as best you can.

John Vick was well aware of their type, strength, and number, and duly set about dealing with them. He may not have had the US cavalry, but he did have other support, less tangible but no less real. The School had recovered well from a bad spell in the late 1960's, thanks to the stern discipline, corner-cutting, and gifted improvisation of the Revd. George Ridding; and his successor, (and John Vick's predecessor), Michael Downward, had, in his long tenure of office, patiently and quietly built up the numerical strength and the scholastic reputation.

The contribution made by both these men – totally different but complementary and equally vital – is a good illustration of the truism about the extent to which a school depends upon the leadership of its headmaster. In an article published in the *Times Educational Supplement*, the national inspectorate went so far as to say, in its discussion of successful secondary schools, 'Without exception, the most important single factor in the success of these schools is the quality of leadership of the head.'

Now it was time to build on the work of these two precursors, to face challenges that were simply not there thirty, twenty, even ten years before, and to find the wherewithal to keep going. So the pressure was on.

There is something to be said for having a lot to do; you do not have time to worry about what sort of figure you cut while you are doing it. 'You would be ill-advised to present yourself as anything other than what you are.' Cards were put on the table. For example, John Vick let it be known at once that he was happy to be addressed by his Christian name. (By his colleagues, I hasten to stress – not by his pupils.) This was not the result of any doctrinaire philosophy about egalitarianism. 'I wasn't aware of what levels of formality existed beforehand.' But he had seen the uncertainty created by a lack of explicitness on the part of headmasters with whom he had worked previously. 'I simply wanted to get it clear.'

So 'John' it is. But not universally; there are still those who prefer 'Sir' or 'Mr. Vick', even 'Headmaster'. Well, so be it. As long as the respect is there. 'I hope I am more than a title.' And he hopes the human dimension is apparent too.

At an Old Boys' Dinner, he cheerfully recounted the incident when one of his sons was engaged in some agitation against School uniform. (Both his sons have been pupils.) The boy was getting up a petition against it. 'How many signatures do you need to get the rules changed?' he asked his father. 'Only one,' was the reply. 'Mine.'

At School assemblies, he has shamelessly introduced everybody to his teddy bear. Not to any old teddy bear. Not to a pretend teddy bear. To his real, live, genuine, actual, kept-all-these-years, still-with-him teddy bear.

Support came from other directions too. If he felt the glow of the sun on his arrival at the School, he felt the glow too of human kindness. So did Lynne, his wife. 'She is much more of an urban person', and had not been quite so taken at first with the idea of a rural existence, but she agreed with him that 'the warmth of the welcome was extraordinary'.

It was clear too that the people who provided this welcome liked working there. 'I responded to the clear attachment people had to the place.' There are countless instances of loyalty and long service (see 'The Comedian's Advice'), in all types of staff, and John Vick was soon very grateful for it. He quickly came to appreciate too 'having a good governing body'. To say nothing of a vigorous and very partisan Old Boys' and Girls' organisation. He has seen several such bodies in other schools where he has worked, but affirmed that the OWBA ('the Old West Buckland Association' – the newer format set up to accommodate Old Girls as well as Old Boys) was more intense in its commitment to the School than any others he had seen.

So he was not alone. Nevertheless, only one person could sit in his chair. It followed therefore that the awkward decisions were going to be his; that is, among other things, what he was appointed for. New brooms have to sweep clean. If they don't, there is not much point in having them. Innovation often means abolition first. Neither is ever going to be universally popular. 'There are those who find it difficult to accept that I have made a decision, and that it must be accepted and abided by.'

That did not mean that every decision, awkward or otherwise, was going to be right. Headmasters are human; in the course of their well-intentioned reforms, there are going to be some mistakes. Had he made some? Of course. I asked, inevitably, what the worst one was, not expecting a reply, for obvious reasons of discretion, security, and care for individual sensitivities. 'I know what it was. I regretted it, but I've also lived to be quite pleased about it.' Work that one out.

Another of the early things a headmaster must do is to secure an inner circle of colleagues and assistants he can trust. Cabinet government is not limited to Downing Street. John Vick was lucky when he arrived; he had, either side of him, a husband-and-wife team on whose integrity he could rely completely. David Clark was Deputy Head and his wife was Secretary. Purists would observe that this was not an ideal situation, but it is to the credit of all three of them that they made it work. Indeed, my impression as a mere observer was that their mutual respect during the time they worked together – six years – went up rather than down. (See 'Other People's Letters'.)

No man is a hero to his valet, so the saying goes. By the same token, no headmaster is Mr. Wonderful to his secretary. But, without sinking into the sugar, it is fair to put in here the comment that Helen Clark spoke well of her boss. The best you can usually hope for is no comment at all.

It is not for me to pass judgment on the nature of the relationship between John Vick and his senior teaching staff, the Bursar, the Catering Manager, the Caretaker, the Chief Groundsman, the Head Prefect, the Maintenance Manager, and all the other departmental heads whose work contributes to the oiling of the wheels at West Buckland. I don't see much of it, and even if I did, I am not qualified to offer a verdict on their efforts.

But the place seems to bowl along pretty well. You have only to observe people talking to each other, witness teachers pulling pupils' legs (and see the pupils enjoying it), listen to the badinage in the Common Room, watch children simply going about the place (and children from the ages of three to eighteen). You have only to note the huge amount of work that is put in, by all manner of people, over and above their contracted duties and for no monetary reward. You have only to skip through the accounts of the legion of activities that staff and pupils get through in a year, as recorded in the School magazine, to see how many quarts are regularly, and constantly, being squeezed into pint pots. You have only to notice how good colleagues are at rallying round when one of their number is up against it.

If, as those inspectors claimed, the first prerequisite for a successful school is a headmaster with powers of leadership, then some credit is due to the present incumbent of the West Buckland equivalent of the Oval Office, where, as Harry Truman famously said, the buck stops. Dammit – the world is only too quick to criticise when something goes wrong, and any headmaster worth his salt must be prepared to answer for everything that goes on under his roof and under his rule. So it would be churlish indeed to withhold all praise when things go right.

Once again – staying clear of the sugar – this in no way implies that everything is, as Bertie Wooster would have put it, 'Oo-ja-cum-spiff' all the time. Take a look at the variety of topics that a headmaster of West Buckland must be responsible for, or take a hand in, or have a policy about, or make a comment on, or deal with, or react to, in the course of an average term.

Before we do that, let us make an attempt to chip away just a little at the obdurate idols of facile cliché and music-hall joke and tabloid jibe and cinema melodrama. Headmasters of independent schools do *not* spend their working day swanning around quadrangles between gothic doorways and mullioned windows, with billowing gown and lopsided mortar-board, carrying a Book of Common Prayer in one hand and a cane in the other. This denial could be repeated a dozen times in a dozen places, and there would still be plenty of people prepared – nay, eager – to believe it when such a picture is presented to them by cartoonists or chat-show hosts or tabloid journalists – or films featuring Will Hay and the Belles of St. Trinians. So the best one can hope for is that a few small chips have come off the idols, not that they have tumbled completely.

To try and show how inept this concept is, let us take the example of politicians. If every comment or cartoon about politicians portrayed them as looking like William Gladstone, complete with high collar, frock coat, and righteous glare, people would just laugh. They know that this is simply not so, because they have the evidence of their own eyes, from newspapers and the television screen. We all know what politicians look like, behave like, and sound like; God knows, we see and hear enough of them every time we turn on the box and are foolish enough to switch to the Perpetual News Channel – the twenty-first century's answer to the Inquisition.

But people generally – well, the vast majority of them – do not know what goes on in an independent school. Neither – I dare to imply – do a lot of chat-show hosts, tabloid journalists, and cartoonists. So they fall back on cliché; that's all there is. It is much easier, and more entertaining, to be rude about something you know next to nothing about, and your audience knows next to nothing about. Here endeth the lesson.

All right, so they don't behave like that. Well then, what do they do? What are their concerns, their worries, their duties?

What you would expect, really, if you stop to think about it. In no particular order – staff appointments, naughty pupils, the curriculum, staff salaries, relations between staff and governors, the Parents' Association, the accounts (remember? – 'in the red' means 'dead'), School public events, examination results, fund-raising, marketing – that sort of thing. Then there is the correspondence; you should see the size of the post bags that come in every morning. The delivery is so substantial that the School even gives the postmen breakfast! A lot of that post, after suitable filtering by secretaries, finds its way to the Headmaster's desk.

Letters have to be read, pondered, and reacted to. Answers must be framed, often discussed with relevant staff, and checked and signed. Government official documents have to be studied. The fact that the School is independent does not mean that it is free from control by the powers that be. Besides being a school, the School is a charity (in the eyes of the Inland Revenue, anyway), a work-place, a provider of accommodation, a catering establishment, a repository of machinery, an open-air recreation centre, a haven for medical and pastoral care, and an examination headquarters. Every one of these functions attracts to it volumes of rules and regulations. Of course a headmaster does not have to deal with the detail of each one himself, but he has to be aware of what those responsible are doing; remember, he carries the can if they get it wrong.

This still does not take account of the legislation, local and national (and, with the growing interest – I nearly said interference – of the European Union, international), concerning child care, safety at work, toxic chemicals, gymnastic apparatus, swimming pools, electrical devices, military equipment (the cadet force), athletics meetings, speed limits, parking spaces, kitchen hygiene, washing facilities (for pupils with ages ranging from three to eighteen – of both sexes), computer security, fire prevention, and I don't know what else. If something goes wrong with any of these, not only does the Headmaster carry the can; he can be hauled into the witness box – or the dock – for a damages case – which, even if it is dismissed, will generate the usual crop of rumours that 'there's no smoke without fire'. (The Bursar would not get off lightly either.)

In between all this desk work – and attempts to foresee trouble – there is the small matter of overseeing the educational progress of nearly seven hundred pupils, and the professional performance of over half a hundred academic staff – writing reports, interviewing candidates for entry and for scholarships (those that remain after the demise of the Assisted Places Scheme), visiting lessons, monitoring the work of individual teachers, assessing possible candidates for promotion, encouraging career development in younger, and older, staff, selecting new prefects, making good deficiencies caused by retirement, promotion, illness, departure, pregnancy – even, if necessary, suspension. Once again, the Head of course doesn't do it all (though he does write on every child's report), but he has to know what is going on – if he doesn't want a nasty surprise just after breakfast on, say, a harmless summer's morning.

The School, as we should all know by now, if we have been paying proper attention, is independent. That means that people send their children to it because they have chosen to. They choose to because they have looked around; they have done some homework; they have compared notes; they have tested the water in several places; they have done some sums. And they have been to see for themselves. There are five hundred children in the main school; that means – apart from the usual crop of brothers and sisters – the Headmaster has spoken to five hundred sets of parents. All right – not all in a single year. But divide 500 by 7 (that's the number of years a child stays if he enters the Sixth Form) and you get about seventy-odd coming in every year. That's about 150 parents who must be seen, put at ease, made to feel special, told the same thing as the other 148, and generally persuaded that West Buckland is just what they are looking for. Plus of course those who end up deciding that it isn't.

So much for the routine. Then there are the more, what we might call, irregular topics. It could be a full inspection, when anything up to a dozen or more ladies and gentlemen descend upon the School and look at absolutely everything. A School's reputation can rise or fall on their report.

It could be a recruiting trip to foreign parts to make contact with prospective parents in, say, Thailand or Hong Kong. Again, it is not just a case of a free air tour for the Head; there is a lot of preparation, correspondence, and assembling of promotional material to be tackled – the submerged nine-tenths.

It could be arranging assistance for traffic-calming in the nearby village, where near-medieval narrow streets were obviously not built to take the volume, or size, of traffic generated by seven hundred children (and a lot of parents) making the journey between school and the main road twice a day.

It could be deciding whether to give the nod of approval to the latest educational wheeze cooked up by a professor at some prestigious department of education, and which may have been, for deep reasons never fully understood by the humble teacher, espoused by the inspectorate. 'The Engineered Classroom' is one which comes to mind. 'Child-Orientated Resources' might be another. There have been countless such ideas, some elevated to the status of near-philosophies. Some last for a decade or two; many slip quietly between the floorboards in only a few years. Within another decade, some sink to the ignominy of heresy. A few get resurrected, re-named, garnished with suitably pretentious jargon, and presented to an admiring world as something Totally New. Good for a chair in education any day.

It could be a hundred things. Talk to any group of headmasters, and I am sure they could, between them, come up with another hundred.

Regular things and irregular things. Does that take care of it all? By no means. Life, as we all know, does not consist only of things which get done frequently and things which get done only once. Spliced in between the laws governing the School's existence, survival, and development, there lurks yet one more, totally unpredictable and totally arbitrary. I refer to Murphy's Law, which can be variously summarised. Some say it lays down that no matter how foolproof a thing is, it will go wrong, and at the very worst possible time. Others claim that it arranges that, as soon as one has taken elaborate precautions to avoid a punch in the face, one will be kicked in the small of the back. No doubt there are other variations, but everyone knows the general idea.

How, for instance, can you prepare in advance for an outbreak of foot-and-mouth? This happened in 2001. The vast majority of schools, in both public and private sectors, are, naturally, in built-up areas; in the normal run of things, nobody would even see a cow. Indeed, we are told that there are city primary children who do not know where milk comes from.

West Buckland did not enjoy such insulation; it was right in the middle of it. The precautions against spread of the disease reached right into the daily routine. Indeed, there were pupils from stricken farms, or adjacent to stricken farms, who could not come into school. The epidemic forced the Head to cancel, for that year, the oldest and most cherished tradition in the

School's history – the annual cross-country run across Exmoor. (See 'A Shot of the Good Side'.)

A headmaster can walk in one morning, rubbing hands, ready to roll, and raring to go, to discover that two of his pupils have absconded; that some particularly nasty disciplinary incident has occurred; that some foreign students will have to be quarantined because of a SARS outbreak on the other side of the world.

In the middle of any one of these crises, the phone will ring, and there will be a journalist on the line, asking leading questions, putting suppositions, suggesting comments, seeking opinions, and tempting the careless speaker to ghastly indiscretions. The only thing one can say about their published pieces at best is that they will almost certainly get it wrong, misunderstand, or cloud the issue. At worst, they will often, by omission – deliberate or otherwise – by stealthy choice of adverb or adjective, or by shift of emphasis, and despite their claim to be serving the cause of public interest, fail to serve the greater cause of truth.

How does a headmaster weave his way through all that? (And I have probably not told you the half of it.) If he is a worrier, the answer is 'with great difficulty'. If he has a sense of perspective and a sense of humour, the answer is 'as best he can, and he looks forward to a cup of tea at the end of it'.

A cup of tea at home with his family too. Family life is 'the bedrock'. Apart from that, John Vick cheerfully admits that, during term time at least, he does not get much relief in the way of activities much removed from school activities. Though he does allow himself one luxury – partisan contemplation of the fortunes of Sunderland Football Club.

However, life on the campus is not such a goldfish-bowl experience as one might think. He would not have liked existence in the old main-building Headmaster's house. He looked at the offices, the endless buses pulling up outside, the lack of a garden, the stone staircase, and decided that family life there was simply not on. So a new house at the rear of the campus was built into the deal of his appointment. Its windows look out on to fields as far as one can see, and there is a spacious garden, much to his wife's delight.

But are there not still too many interruptions to private life – new house and all? No. 'Most of the interruptions come from our sons' friends. Colleagues are very good at respecting my family's privacy.' Indeed, during holiday time, it becomes so quiet – three miles from a main road, five miles from a shop, eight miles from a supermarket, nearly ten miles from a railway station, forty miles from a sizeable city – that it is their sons who tend to find it oppressive.

This remoteness is, of course, the thread which runs right through the whole history and atmosphere of West Buckland, and governs its thinking and behaviour, as much as the fact that Britain is an island governs the nation's history.

John Vick is well aware of this, and is well aware of the special qualities it engenders. I have had occasion to refer to them elsewhere in this book. Time and again, those who have been involved with the School for any length of time talk about the atmosphere of an extended family. People simply have to get on with each other.

Despite the advent of emails, faxes, and mobile phones, the basic fact of geography has not changed. West Buckland is still 'a school apart'. In both senses. The fact that this has stayed constant for nearly a hundred and fifty years only lends strength to the pull the School has over its inmates. 'Former pupils feel a greater bond than in other schools I've worked in.'

For this reason too John Vick is adamant that the money invested a few years ago in new boarding blocks was money well spent. Foreign students have to be accommodated, obviously. So do the children of parents in the Armed Forces, diplomatic work, and several other callings. More to the point, boarding would have died if that money had not been spent; the old accommodation was simply not up to scratch, and parents would have taken their business elsewhere. Expectations are constantly rising. And not only in school accommodation; look at what we expect now as a matter of course in hotels and holiday lets, and compare it with what we put up with thirty years ago.

Good boarding makes good boarders. 'Boarding here is good value in the way of fees.' Another permanent concern – I nearly said headache – for a headmaster: how do you pitch your costs? How do you calculate them? High enough to pay for the sort of service which people have come to expect, and low enough not to frighten them off? How can you close the gap between the percentage rise in inflation and wages on the one hand, and the percentage rise in fees on the other?

It probably helps that the School has a long tradition of boarding. John Vick's history training has given him an appreciation of the significance of that. Indeed, he is pretty chuffed about the whole history of the School. 'To be part of that history is quite wonderful.' It was his enthusiasm for this facet of the School's personality which led him to set up the Archive in 1998, and which allowed the present author to continue in gainful employment. So I suppose I must declare a slightly special interest.

That did not prevent me, I hope, from asking one or two questions which, while not especially searching, may have induced a little consideration before answering. My impression was that the answers came without awkwardness or undue hesitation, and were pretty balanced and human. At the same time, John Vick was clearly answering from his corner, as you might say. And why shouldn't he?

For instance, I asked about bullying. 'It is as common as any other sins, and it appears everywhere. It is not the preserve of schoolchildren.' (It came uncannily close to what I wrote about it in 'The View from Below', which I composed without any reference to the Head.) 'We are alert to the fact that it exists, and it can be destructive.'

The same kind of commonsense comment came about abuse of drugs. Of course it was pernicious. But tobacco and alcohol were much worse. Nor could any school claim that it had no sex problems. 'Our children are all blessed with their fair share of original sin.' He did allow himself a small swipe, however, at parents who had double standards, who were down on drugs, for example, but who showed an irresponsibly complaisant attitude towards sex or alcohol or smoking.

'You have to try and adopt a fairly philosophical approach. . . . I've had problems, but I hope I've been able to deal with them in the context of a good school which is going well. . . . There are policies which all staff are expected to subscribe to and support, despite their private views. . . . We try to establish guidelines which make sense to pupils and parents.'

All pretty bland and reasonable, perhaps, but occasionally the spark of self-awareness and humour broke through.

Did he know all the children personally? No – but 'I know *something* about all of them. . . . I can identify the overwhelming majority. Maybe not the younger ones, whose hand I have not shaken or whom I have not suspended.'

He freely conceded too that 'you can never spend enough time sharing the activities of the children. . . . I don't think I'm an abject failure at it, but you can never be visible enough.'

It's true: however hard you try, there will always be some game or team or competition which you have to miss because the Chairman of the Governors has dropped in, or there is a fire in the kitchens; however many thank-you letters you write or however many congratulatory notices you pin on the notice board, on a campus of a hundred acres and with a pupil body of seven hundred and a staff of a hundred – academic, clerical, technical, domestic, catering, and so on – there is going to be somebody, somewhere, who feels that his or her efforts were not sufficiently appreciated.

There is, however, one little perk which goes with the job, and which allows a headmaster to do a little to redress the balance noted in the previous paragraph. He has, I hope I have been able to show, a thousand responsibilities, and he may get through scores of separate jobs in the course of a working day (and evening – don't forget the numerous public and recreational activities at which he must at least appear). But, unlike the classroom teacher, he is bound by no timetable. His day may be crowded, but it is all his to do as he likes with.

As with the President of the United States, the buck stops with him. But, like the President, he can afford 'gestures'. And he uses them well. He will go outside to talk with a blind person who is starting a sponsored walk at the School. He will devote a lot of time to an elderly lady visitor (whose father – whose *father* – had left the School in 1896!) while he is waiting for the Archivist to be found and to turn up.

He will conduct a conversation like this with a small boy who came into the Secretary's office with a problem.

'Can I have permission to miss History, sir?'

'Why?'

'I've got a guitar lesson, sir.'

'Got your red form?'

'Here, sir.'

'Now, where do I fill it in?' (He probably knew perfectly well.)

Now, he needn't have spoken to that boy at all.

He will pass remarks to pupils as they file past him outside the Hall on their way in to morning assembly. He may be merely suggesting that their shirt tail would be better off inside their trousers than outside, but words are exchanged.

He will sit down anywhere in the Dining Hall with his lunch tray and talk to any child. True, the conversation may not exactly sparkle and may not flow thick and fast, but any adult who has any conversation with any child knows that you have to work at it harder than the child does. The important thing is that he works at it; he makes the contact.

This freedom and distance also enable him to take a more dispassionate view of a problem which may have arisen between a teacher and a pupil. The teacher involved, who has been having his patience tried over a long period, may be hammering on the desk for drastic action to be taken in the interests of discipline, security, common sense, classroom atmosphere, his own peace of mind, and a dozen other priorities. John Vick may have to assume the role of sweet reasonableness, champion of the underdog, Devil's Advocate, bland pacificator, and a dozen other guises – none of which is going to endear him to the aggrieved member of staff. Particularly if it turns out that his suggested policy, or – worse – his imposed remedy, goes wrong.

The sugar vat is looming again, so we must beware. Napoleon may have been unique among great men in that his valet thought he was wonderful, but there were plenty of people all over Europe who heartily detested him.

Helen Clark may have spoken well of John Vick, but I daresay, if you looked hard enough and asked the right questions, you would unearth a fair number of people who could wax eloquent on his shortcomings. But the man himself appears able to live with this. Indeed, anybody in his position has to.

He takes a certain amount of what he thinks is legitimate pride in what he has achieved so far. Remember those 120 Assisted Places which had been abolished? Well, he has replaced those 120 pupils on assistance with 120 pupils whose parents are prepared to pay fees. So the ship is still afloat.

That does not mean that he would prefer to have only fee-payers. In common with other independent heads, he would like to see the sort of opportunities enjoyed by the present pupils to be made available to whatever child wants to take advantage of them, regardless of status or bank balance. But he has to react to the world as it is.

He is pleased with the progress made towards a genuinely co-educational atmosphere. When a boys' school takes on girls, there must inevitably be a period of adjustment, during which the female newcomers may feel that their sex and its needs and interests are not being fully catered for. The machine, if you like, is being tinkered with, simply in order to generate more capacity, when what is really needed is a custom-built, completely new one. Well, twenty-five years on, John Vick feels that the new machine is in place and fully operational; both sexes are getting a fair crack of the whip.

He thinks too that the staff, overall, are better than they were. Both individually, and as a group; there is, for instance, a better balance *vis-à-vis* age and sex.

There is a new Preparatory building. The Prep. in particular will generate more revenue, naturally, and will introduce to West Buckland a range of parents who may well consider making the investment for their child's secondary education. Put crudely, it is a foot in their door. But John Vick believes that it is a healthy development on its own terms – not just as a means to an end.

There is a new centre for the performing arts. West Buckland's sporting tradition has not been neglected either; there is the new all-weather hockey pitch. The recent crops of exam results are pleasing. Better care is being offered to children with learning difficulties. Boarding has become more civilised, comfortable, and homely. The School has a new IT block. And so on.

He is optimistic about the future. The Sixth Form looks good. The Prep. looks good. Devon population is low by density standards, so the challenge is there to maintain numbers. But he takes hope from the fact that parents are prepared to stand a rise in fees (and not just in West Buckland) which exceeds the inflation rise, and from the fact that the percentage of children in independent schools is rising.

He does not think that independents are under the sort of threat to their very *raison d'etre* that they were twenty or thirty years ago. There is still a body of opinion which does not favour them, but the war-cry now is not to abolish them outright. Strategies are now more 'sideways' – like removing their charity status, raising employers' contributions to teachers' pensions – things like that. (I suppose governments could always try making state schools better; that would be the most 'sideways' one of all.)

At West Buckland, there is still a tremendous lot waiting to be done, and there is still, naturally, nothing like enough money with which to do it. How long should a headmaster stay around to see that such plans were carried out? He replied judiciously that 'neither change nor longevity is good in itself'. So pick the bones out of that.

There are grey hairs evident that were not there when he arrived. But the zest and the cheerfulness and the relish appear undimmed. He is understandably proud of the laurels he has won, but knows that they are only for occasional display, not for leaning on. 'I meet a lot of fascinating people. I have had some desperately sad things to do, but I also have a lot of happy things to do.' At the very least, that sounds pretty positive.

If, as those inspectors said, a head is the prime factor in creating a school atmosphere of purpose and a climate of self-esteem, how much more is this applicable in a school like West Buckland, which is so distant and self-contained? John Vick is aware of this, and does his best to show that he is aware of it. He values the intangibles of school life. He appreciates what staff do – and is appreciative too of the many talents they possess which do not immediately relate to their classroom activities. He values the fact that children feel cared for and known.

It all comes down to the human dimension. 'It is much more important to get soaking wet on the *Exmoor* than it is to get a new sports hall. . . . What West Buckland has is difficult to build, and terribly easy to damage.'

45. I Say, I Say, I Say

George Henry Douglas White joined the School in 1910, from Weston-super-Mare. He became what seems, from the record, a typical run-of-the-mill schoolboy. He did not win races in sports; he did not distinguish himself in the many School cross-country runs; he did not gain promotion in the cadet force; he did not sing in the choir; he did not win his football colours. He did play cricket a bit, though; he won his Second XI colours in 1913 and played for the First XI in 1914. About par for the course, you would say.

The only remarkable thing about him seems to have been his Christian names. We know three of them, but apparently he was blessed with four; he is referred to when joining and leaving as 'G.H.J.D.' So what the 'J' stood for we can only guess. Four initials were clearly too much for most authorities, for, in the succeeding four years, he is referred to variously as 'J.D.', 'J.G.', 'J.H.', and 'G.D.' I can find no other White on the roll during this period. He left in July, 1913, but, mysteriously, returned in February, 1914, where he is welcomed back as 'G.H.'

Most curious of all, he refers to himself, in the only document we have in his own hand, as 'J.H.G.D.' There is in the School Archive a sixteen-page pamphlet entitled *The Educator*. It is dated June, 1914, and its editor was Master White, who had obviously squeezed this enterprise in between hours at the nets and out on the square.

It consists of four sheets of foolscap, which, when folded, make sixteen pages in all, each about the size of a school exercise book. In case you should think that J.H.G.D. had probably *pinched* them from a school exercise book, I must leap to his defence. Since he clearly ran off several copies, it is asking a lot of his ingenuity, not to say his cheek, to suppose that he successfully purloined so many sheets of paper in one go. Secondly, the pages are plain; nine exercise books out of ten have lines, in order to provide minimum containment of a schoolboy's wayward handwriting. And finally – the clinching piece of evidence, my lord – there are no holes left by the removal of the retaining staples. As Holmes would have said, 'May I draw to your attention the curious incident of the staple holes.' I rest my case.

Whatever the provenance, the whole is painstakingly bound with a single strand of white cotton. It is hand-written, naturally. It would have been a resourceful boy indeed who had gained access to a typewriter at West Buckland in 1914. I doubt if there was more than one in the entire School. (I am put in mind of a stray fact which I gleaned from a history book about Europe in the eighteenth century. It regaled its readers with the knowledge that, although the printing press had been developed in Germany in the middle of the fifteenth century, no press was set up in Constantinople until 1726.) I do not suggest that West Buckland School was as sunk in medieval darkness as was the Ottoman Empire, but it was, in its moorland fastness, just a little behind the times.

Anyway, *The Educator* is the oldest example in the Archive of a totally pupil-driven publication. A few pupils had had items printed in the *Register* before 1914, and plenty more have since, but this is the first piece known to me which has been written, edited, and produced entirely by pupil-power. Just what method of reproduction was employed I am not qualified to say. We are back in the deep past – not only Before Scanner and Before Xerox, but Before Roneo and Before Banda. Almost Palaeolithic then. And there can't be many readers with longer memories than that. (It might even – come to think of it – have been simple carbon paper. Think of the work!)

It was no mere flash in the pan either. The edition which comes down to us is 'Number 2', and the Editor refers proudly to the 'many improvements that have been suggested to us by our readers' since the appearance of Number 1. He hoped therefore 'to give more satisfaction'.

He went on, in his editorial, to declare his gratitude for any further communications from his readers, but warned his potential correspondents to avoid 'political and religious subjects'. 'Any letters containing such questions will be returned unopened.'

There followed light-hearted commentaries on recent School cricket matches: 'our fellows came in and out too rapidly to be counted'; 'the 1st XI were looking confidently forward to a crown of glory when Time, "the enemy", cut them short and the match was drawn'; 'Perry's 57. . . . was one of the features of the game. The Editor's bowling was another but nobody seemed to notice it'; 'our First XI make a wonderful show in the nets but are very modest in matches. Politeness prevented them from winning against Wellington and Taunton.' And so on and so on.

There was an ode about *The Sports*, examples from which show that certain things have not changed much in ninety years.

'The day of days, and bore of bores
For those who cannot run. . . .
And regularly about this time
We fly our nice new banners
And hear from someone's earnest lips[3]
Our yearly rules of manners.
We learn it is not nice to sit
And listen to the band.
We are reminded, if we slack,

---

[3] The Headmaster's Christian name was Ernest, and he was known far and wide as 'Ernie'

Our elders have to stand. . . .
All this we knew before but still
The yearly tale is told.
After about the 30th time
It grows a little old.
And then while they give out the cups
Amid the roaring cheers,
Our boredom culminates at last;
We think of tea with tears.
Then after tea our hope revives,
And brisker grows our step,
For when we've cleared the flags away
We know we'll get off prep.
Then having seen the sports as well
As parents too have seen them,
We settle down and thank our stars
There are twelve months between them.'

That could have been written by any schoolboy at any time in the last hundred years, and still been relevant.

There was an extended piece about the Officers' Training Corps Field Day (OTC then; CCF now), followed by an even longer Ode about the same thing. Pretty nifty scansion and rhyming too.

Scattered around in between these weightier pieces were little squibs and crackers like:

'Question: What is a canard?

Answer: It is a story one canardly believe.'

Or

'Question: Why is the Garden of Eden like a box of bad cigars?

Answer: Because when you've Adam you 'Eve.'

Yes, I know. But this was the heyday of the old Music Hall. Double acts – 'I say, I say, I say – ' were doing things like this all over the country in a thousand variety theatres. It sounds now like the corny jokes you get in Christmas crackers, but it was probably pretty jolly up to date in 1914. Even now you have to crack a reluctant smile; they are so bad they're good, like the *Carry On* films.

There were cheeky little digs at Euclid, like: 'A polygon is a figure that has more sides than it knows what to do with.'

There was a neat parody of History lessons, which shows that the authors of *1066 and all That* were by no means the first in their field; Editor White had beaten them to it by nearly twenty years:

'Sir Walter Raleigh was the first man to see the Invisible Armada. He invented potatoes and tobacco and died from giving water to a soldier in the

Battle of Zutphen. Prince William was drowned while crossing the Channel in a butt of marmalade and he never smiled again.'

Finally, Editor White printed answers to some of his correspondents. To a 'IInd Form-ite' he said, 'No, St. Andrew was not the "patient" saint of Scotland. He was the "patron" saint of Scotland. The "patient saint" of England is the Editor of *The Educator*.'

Naturally, I have picked out what I think are the best bits, and I have no way of knowing what percentage of the copy was the work of White himself. But his was clearly the initiative and the drive – and the work. By any standards, and considering the conditions that prevailed at West Buckland School in the second decade of the twentieth century, *The Educator* was a pretty good effort. Editor White was no great scholar or intellectual; he chalked up routine passes in the Junior and Senior Cambridge Local Examinations, which were the current public tests throughout England. I have been able to find only one instance in the record of his being awarded a prize, though it was, perhaps significantly, an English prize. (*History of the Church of England* – which served him right.) So – all credit to him.

He left – for the second time – in July, 1914. War broke out on 4th August. When the next *Register* was published in October, it listed sixty old members of the School who were already in uniform, and the editors knew that 'many more are preparing to do so'. This from a school roll lower than 130.

'G.H.' joined the Coldstream Guards. He was killed three days before Christmas – the second of fifty-six.

G. H. J. D. WHITE, 1910-1914. 1st Btn. Coldstream Guards.
Killed in action, December 22, 1914.

G.H.J.D. White, and the announcement of his death
in the *Register*. [School Archive]

46. A Legionary's Underwear

It is a commonplace in the world of archaeology that much of the valuable material which assists our understanding of bygone civilisations comes not from what people keep but from what people throw away – or what simply gets lost.

I had confirmation of this truism when one of the School carpenters left on my desk a slender file containing pieces of paper which he and his colleagues had dug out from underneath the floorboards when they had been doing some holiday alterations near an old boarding block.

It was confirmation of another kind too – confirmation of a cliché. A cliché about what archivists do. What do they do? They delve into neglected corners and come up with dusty documents, which they carefully store in their 'cubby-hole' in some other neglected corner of the School.

I hasten to point out that I do not work in a cubby-hole, but it is an undeniable fact that on this occasion I was indeed presented with a tiny collection of dusty documents. Indeed, they showed a remarkable capacity not only to scatter dust, but to generate it. No matter how many times I examined them, turned them over, shook them, and blew across them, they continued to scatter dust over the desk every time I picked one of them up.

I have no doubt that Sherlock Holmes could have pored over this dust with his famous lens, and come up with fascinating details about it – that the oldest dust dated at least from the 1870's because it contained wood particles which could only have come from a particular kind of timber which had been eradicated from the local forests by the deadly Siberian larch-weevil in that decade; that thirty-seven per cent of it was impregnated with a cheap, substitute creosote which placed it firmly in the Second World War, when so many commodities were makeshift, substitute, artificial, 'utility', or generally *ersatz*; that a small proportion of it was in fact dried tobacco, which testified to the long-lived juvenile preoccupation with the furtive consumption of nicotine. And since Holmes had written a trifling monograph on three hundred and seven-nine types of cigarette ash only three years before, no doubt he could have identified the brands.

We do not have Holmes' passion for micro-analysis, his deep knowledge of chemistry, or, frankly, his spare time in between investigations. All we have is our eyes, and maybe a little imagination – although we can perhaps employ a little of Holmes' doctrine of observation and inference.

There were two envelopes, one postmarked 'Romford and Dagenham' – which is hardly surprising; we took boys from most counties in 1960 – and the other postmarked 'Bideford', 1973 – which is. Not because the boy's home was North Devon, but because only thirty years ago, parents or friends were still communicating with the inmates by letter. Boys could not get at a phone in School unless there was a dire emergency, and as late as the 1960's they were allowed out into Barnstaple only twice a term. For a present generation whose pockets bulge with mobile phones (and, one suspects, a good deal of money), it is almost unimaginable.

And – something to give a few greybeards a chance to wag their heads – the stamp on one cost 3d. (barely more than 1p.) .

There were two luggage labels, both with the names of pupils. One was in capitals, in a mature hand, so Mum or Dad had seen to the details. The other was in lower case, 'joined-up' writing – very joined-up. So clearly in the hand of a well-taught, diligent boy who had not yet fallen into the anti-calligraphy habits of his elders. To clinch the matter, the address contained the name of the village – 'Filliegh' [sic].

So these dated from the days of the Taunton to Barnstaple Railway, the demise of which must have been an inconvenience, not to say a shock, to hundreds of pupils. Sad too, since the railway, or rather the station, had originally been built to cater for their needs. Way back in the 1860's, the tireless Revd. Brereton, School founder, rector of West Buckland, governor, educational reformer, prophet, do-gooder, and local ball of fire, had been the driving force in securing this facility. (See 'Founding Father'.) For generations, boys had unloaded their trunks from the train, and put them on the cart which had been sent from the School specially for the purpose. There was no room for themselves; they had to lug their overnight bags and hoof it over Leary Hill, all the way to the School – two or three miles.

(Much later, in the nineteen-twenties, there apparently existed – according to an Old Boy – a handcart, which was used to bring up goods from Filleigh Station to the School. Whether it had also been used to bring up boys' luggage the Old Boy did not specify. But he did say that a squad of boys enjoyed manhandling it from the School down to the station, because one boy went in the shafts and the rest counter-balanced themselves carefully behind, so that on the long run down the hill the feet of the boy in the shafts seldom touched the ground. 'The fact that these boys were never involved in an accident,' he said, 'reflects on the little use made of the local roads in those days.')

No train now. But no hoofing it either. Not only do parents have motor cars; a lot of the pupils do too. We even have parking spaces dedicated exclusively to their needs. How many members of the School would care to carry a case three miles now, in their shiny new uniform, bought specially for the new term, up hill and down dale – as likely as not in wind and rain? There was indeed a School automobile between the Wars – a venerable

Austin. But it is hard to see how it could have accommodated every single arrival at Filleigh Station, even on a shuttle service.

Mind you, the fact that times may have been hard during the term does not necessarily mean that times were poor during the holidays. A letter dated February, 1969, from 'New Barnet, Herts.', informs the recipient that his flight has been booked from London to Zurich for the winter sports, and that the writer has recently attended a champagne party to celebrate the launch of the new Ford Capri. 'Uncle Alan', moreover, had 'one on order for delivery in a couple of months'.

The recipient was, one guesses, pretty young, because enclosed in the letter were 'two cut-outs of the new Ford Capri for you to play with'. And it was signed 'Daddy and Mummy'. It is further illustration of the point I made above about the need for writing letters instead of phoning.

It raises too the deeper matter of just how much contact parents had with their offspring once the term had started. It is worth noting – the text makes this clear – that the letter was enclosed with the two cut-outs, not the other way round. It is also clear from the text that the boy is to fly by himself – 'they expect you at Zurich airport on the 29th March'. And later 'all we have to do now is get you a separate passport – or I shall have to come along as well!'.

The last paragraph of the letter makes one wonder how much thought some parents gave to words of encouragement, morale-lifting, and sheer companionship. It said, 'Lets [sic] have a few more capitals, full-stops and better spelling in your future letters, please.' This kid was young, he was separated from his family for months at a time, and he was two hundred miles away.

It ended like this: 'Yours aye, with much love [typed]

Daddy and Mummy'.

Times do indeed change: how many fathers today would finish a letter like that – 'Yours aye'? How many fathers at any time in the last fifty years – or more? It has a curious ring of half-business, half-club-member formality about it, like something out of the nineteenth century. Almost as if he did not really know how to talk to his son. Had he been to boarding school himself? If he had not, it might help to explain it. If he had, it might also help to explain it.

One of the scruffiest, most-handled documents was a timetable – the sort of thing a boy would carry around with him, at any rate for the first two or three weeks of the academic year, until he had memorised it from sheer usage. Again, it is surprising to note the extent of yet another revolution which has taken place in the last thirty years. This timetable is dated 1974, and it belonged to a boy in what was then called the Second Form, and is known today as Year 8 – twelve-to-thirteen-year-olds. It is full, as you might expect, of squares filled in about Maths, and French, and English, and Geography, and History, and Biology, and so on. The Latin lessons are entered in conjunction with 'E.E.' – which means Extra English. The boy's name is foreign, so presumably he was let off the dead language in order that he could become fluent in the live one.

It is interesting to compare this with what appears on a Year 8 timetable today. I obtained a print-out of one and had a look. Frankly I was looking for more changes that I actually found. Maths, English, French, History, Geography, the three Sciences, are all there, and in similar quantities. Latin has gone, and been replaced by Spanish, which is hardly surprising. Drama collects two periods a week, as does Art, and Music clicks for one – so the old regime has lost its Philistine rough edge. What appeared as 'R.E.' (Religious Education) in 1974 now emerges as plain 'Religion'. I have no idea what is the significance, if any, of the removal of the word 'Education'. It is quite remarkable to note the number of guises under which this subject has appeared over the years – Scripture, Bible Knowledge, Religious Instruction, Religious Education, and Divinity. And now 'Religion'. One thing – it can't get much shorter – unless you call it simply 'God'.

The two biggest differences, which reflect some at least of the changes over the last generation, involve pastoral care and computers. Whereas in 1974 the form master would have done the register, read one or two absence notes, and collected some money for something or other – all in about ten minutes before lessons, now there is a whole lesson set aside – just after lunch on a Wednesday afternoon – for what the modern timetable calls 'Tutor'. This is the new pastoral care spot. This is no place to comment on the variety of things that go on, or are supposed to go on, in a weekly session of a tutor group. I just mention it here as a sign of the times.

Lastly, there is 'Clait' – which is a mnemonic to do with Information Technology. In short, computers. The number of computers on the campus now runs into three figures. Enough said.

As a pupil moves up the School, new subjects do tend to creep in rather more – Food and Nutrition, Design and Technology, Health and Sex Education. We have also seen Social Studies, Community Studies, Classical Studies, and Business Studies. Some of these have not only come; they have gone as well. The latest newcomer is Psychology. It will be interesting to note the extent of its staying power. Quite apart from the relative merits or otherwise of all these new subjects, it is surprising to see how *recent* they all are. The fact that some of these new items have not only come but gone is testimony not only to the amount of change, but to the rate of change.

Would a philosopher see in this a further symptom of the Disposable Society?

At any rate, one choirboy, it seems, had seen fit to dispose of a 'Choristers' Leaflet', published by the Royal School of Church Music, Addington Palace, Croydon, Surrey in June, 1960. Perhaps he found a little indigestible the paragraph in the Editor's Letter about the temptation presented by the summer weather 'to forsake church in favour of a day out'. ' The Church badly needs people like *you* who are going to take a firm line and say politely but firmly "My place today is in my church choir".' And more of the same. Can you imagine any red-blooded boy not being tempted to stuff it down the wainscot?

Incidentally, one might easily imagine a history teacher stuffing it down the wainscot too. In a paragraph about the history of Church Buildings, the writer blithely informs his readers that 'between 1530 and 1660 the Church went through troubled times, with first the Reformation and then the influence of Puritanism, leading to the Civil War and the Commonwealth'. It is worse than a party political broadcast. He goes on: 'Many abbeys fell into ruin after the Dissolution of the Monastries [sic], and many other churches were seriously damaged by Roundhead soldiers in the Civil War. Also in 1666 the Fire of London destroyed many fine churches.' It is a wonder he didn't accuse the Puritans of that too.

Public announcements are often a good barometer of the fortunes and the style of the School. There is in the collection a programme for Sports Day, 1968. It is one single foolscap sheet, printed by the old Roneo method, and folded once to make four small sheets. The School crest is hand-drawn in the top left-hand corner. It is a far cry from the more handsome little printed booklets from between the wars, and light years away from the computer-generated efforts of today. And it is no coincidence that the School in 1968 was entering upon the worst period of its fortunes probably since the beginning of the twentieth century. It shows; it shows.

Nevertheless, appearances must be maintained. There is also a letter on headed notepaper, from a housemaster, from about the same time as the Sports Day programme. It draws the attention of members of the House to the fact that 'the Headmaster has complained about boys walking about in dressing gowns before breakfast'. Gad! *Before breakfast!* Worse was to come. One boy 'was seen in VI Science in a dressing gown'. The end of all civilisation as we know it. 'He wishes it to be known that when you get up you dress.' So there!

Finally, a pupil had seen fit to obtain a copy of his father's work permit for Zambia for the late 1970's and early 1980's. Judging by the elaborateness of it, it seemed an awful lot of trouble to go to only in order to let the thing slip down between the floorboards. Was he himself applying for a permit, and intending to show his father's as a sort of testimonial? Did he, when the thing disappeared through the crack, swear gently to himself and set about obtaining another? Or did he say, 'Oh, what the hell; I'll go and work for Marks and Spencer's instead'?

Now – did these gritty pieces of much-folded paper tell us mighty truths about the School's career? No – of course not. Not put like that. Not when put beside the massive records in the three hundred-odd past numbers of the School magazine, or the countless photographs, or the Minutes of Governors' meetings, or whatever. But they do tell us something for all that.

It is as if the great collections of documents inform us about the massive edifice of the School's history; but what these humble little scraps of paper do is show us a glimpse of what the doorknobs felt like, or how long the splinters were in the benches, or what colour the rust was. And it is these details which are more likely to stick in the memories of past pupils than all the turgid detail about nineteenth-century educational philosophy or Labour Government policy or the inquisitions of past teams of inspectors. Show an Old Boy one of those luggage labels, and I venture to say that scores of vivid images would float at once past his memory's eye.

Years ago, on a conference, I met a teacher who told me that he had once gone to endless trouble to prepare a series of lessons on the Roman Army and the Roman Occupation of Britain. This was for a secondary school first form – or 'Year 7', as we must now call it. (Year 7, by the way, does not mean that the pupils in it are seven years old; they are eleven, rising twelve – so much clearer that way, isn't it?)

Anyway, this colleague had read all about legions and cohorts and centurions; he was expert on tortoises and catapults and throwing-spears and short swords; he had mastered, blow by blow, the ups and downs of the Roman invasion; he was fluent in the careers of Aulus Plautius, Agricola, Boudicca, and Hadrian (he of the Wall). In short, he was ready for any question which the most bespectacled little swot could throw at him.

He was bowled out first ball. A hand went up, and its owner said, 'Sir – what sort of underclothes did the Roman legionaries wear?'

Well, that's what these scraps do: they shed just a little light on what Roman legionaries wore under their – under their uniform.

47. The Real Natural History

My Archive Office is on the first floor of the original stone building of West Buckland School, facing to the front. From my window I look out over a forecourt, some tennis courts, assorted trees, cosseted grass running down to a country lane, and, beyond, miles and miles of rolling fields (the School is on rising ground midway between the villages of East and West Buckland). On a clear day I can see Dartmoor. It is difficult to imagine a more pleasant prospect.

On a dry morning (it doesn't rain all the time), as I drive between the high banks of primrose or fern or flame-leaved beech hedge, or swerve to avoid a directionless pheasant, or look around from the top of Leary Hill, or weave through the village of West Buckland, with its twenty-mile-an-hour speed limit and its hugger-mugger of jutting cottages, and gaze across at the cluster of School buildings a quarter of a mile away – ensconced in its green cushions of surrounding fields – I sometimes feel it should be necessary to pinch myself and say, 'Berwick, you're going to *work*.'

Does a pupil catching up on an overdue essay on the back seat of a school bus, or a full-time member of the teaching staff belatedly running eight sets of lesson notes past his mind's eye, as he changes gear for yet another bend – does either of them ever say something like this to himself? Possibly not. They must speak for themselves. But I would hazard the assertion that they will *remember* all these sights. These images will still register on the inward eye, and therefore the memory. And they would miss them if they were not there. And they – both pupils and staff – will be grateful for them in later years. It may be one reason why so many staff stay so long.

Mind you, we must not let the sun-drenched nature-ramble dimension completely skew the picture. It does rain in West Buckland – just a bit. And when it is not raining, it spends a lot of time looking as if it might make up its mind to rain. You can rarely trust 'it'. Put the rain together with the tractors, muck wagons, and farm animals that regularly pass up and down the steep-sided lanes (always at the wrong times), and you have a recipe for exasperation and despair; Murphy's Law dictates that, as soon as you have cleaned your car, you can rest assured that the rain and the mud (with helpful additives from passing cows) will conspire to ruin the effects of your hard work in a matter of seconds. If it doesn't, two sharp brakings, followed by a necessary surge through a four-inch-deep, fifty-foot-long puddle, should do the trick, and your vehicle could easily have come straight from the Monte Carlo Rally.

Stoicism is the only way to avoid tears of mortification and shredded patience. Drivers soon absorb the spirit of compromise too. Aggression which might win the day in a busy city street or an open highway counts for very little when you come face to face with a double-decker bus as you climb a slope. School bus drivers – noble souls – are noted for their determination to get their charges to their destination, regardless of obstacles. They are also determined, with equal nobility, to get their empty buses back to the depot when they have delivered their load. They are a bit like the tide coming in. There is nothing for it but to back up – or rather down – to the nearest passing bay, while the bus waits motionless, like a hypnotised bear. As you crane and twist, you cast the odd glance to the front to make sure that it hasn't woken up and decided to pounce.

If by that time – and it is of course always the rush hour, by definition – you have been caught up by half a dozen cars behind you on the same mission, you can see where the stoicism comes in.

So – yes – there are the bad moments too. And not only for parent and teacher drivers. Generations of new pupils must have quailed at the sight of Leary Hill. Until the advent of the motor vehicle, they had to negotiate it on foot. When they were decanted from the train at Filleigh Station, their trunks may have been loaded on to the School cart, but they had to walk. Teachers and visitors may have had the luxury of a pony and trap. One young appointee, back in 1864 (See 'Holding the Fort – I'), arrived late into Barnstaple on the train (there was no Filleigh line in those days), and had to hire a cart to bring him all the way out from Barnstaple Station, to arrive at nearly midnight. In January. What must he have thought! Even the present Headmaster, as he turned off the main road on his first exploratory trip to West Buckland, wondered what he was letting himself in for. And he had ABS and air-conditioning!

The sheer topography therefore has a lot to answer for. And it had not escaped the notice of that indefatigable contributor to the *Register*, Mr. R. P. Chope (see 'Lorna Doone at West Buckland'). The long-suffering editors of that magazine, no doubt under severe pressure, allowed Mr. Chope to put in no fewer than nine pages of detailed, and very scholarly, information about the geology of the Bucklands. If he cares to take the risk, the attentive reader of Mr. Chope's article can wallow in references to plutonic rocks, brown micaceous sandstone, and silicious ooze chert, with a strong Latin seasoning of verbal spices like *foraminifera, posidonomya,* and *goniatites*. To be fair to Mr. Chope, he does offer an English explanation of what these latter exotic fossil organisms are – or rather were. For example, we are told that trilobites are 'three-lobed animals with a head-shield and compound eyes – now extinct' (thank God for that); and that *Radiolaria* 'have their skeletons composed of silica or flinty matter, instead of carbonate of lime . . . . not soluble in carbonic acid' (so now you know). As an illustration of the fact that 'solid rocks [could] be bent in the way we see them in cliffs, railway cuttings, and quarries', he offered the useless but fascinating information that 'even such a brittle substance as sealing-wax can be bent into a circle by applying pressure gradually'. Knowing Mr. Chope, I should not be in the least surprised to discover that he had actually proved it in his study at Hartland – must have taken him weeks.

But, as I have said elsewhere, Mr. Chope was not a mere dryasdust antiquarian; he could sit back and observe perspectives, and he did have a sense of humour, of a kind. He noted the irony of the fact that he was writing in a magazine which was celebrating the golden jubilee of the School (in 1908), while the School was built on land which had been laid down originally ('sedimentary', if you want the correct word) 'some twenty or thirty millions of years' before.

Modern scholarship has now pushed back the earlier estimate to nearly four hundred million years ago, but that is not Mr. Chope's fault; I am sure he was up with the latest research of his time (he knew everything else). He was right about the rock being called Devonian – Upper Devonian to be precise. Devonian – very apt, considering.

Then, apparently, 'deposits of the Carboniferous age' were possibly laid on top, but most of these would 'have since been worn away by the combined action of rain, frost, and wind'. He was right there too. So nothing much has changed at West Buckland for the last three hundred-odd million years. Comforting. No wonder Devonians are what they are.

It is inescapable therefore that a little of this has rubbed off on the pupils of West Buckland School. They can not have been rained upon, chilled, and blown about for three hundred million years without developing an above-average resilience. There are countless instances of this. Early cadet forces, when they went to army camps in the holidays, were observed by their opposite numbers to be able to take more pressure and punishment than any others, with barely a blink. One health report after another complimented the School authorities on the glowing vigour of their charges. The School's oldest and proudest tradition is a compulsory annual cross-country run of nine miles (to say nothing of a six-mile walk to the start). Talk to any old boy of more than fifty, and he is practically guaranteed to tell you, within twenty minutes, about breaking the ice in the wash-basins of the dormitories. Older old boys who were cooped up as prisoners of war found conditions in the bleakest *stalag* quite bearable; after WB, it was a doddle.

One might expect literary Old Boys to wax lyrical about the countryside of North Devon – which is indeed well worth lyricising. So R.F. Delderfield, one of the two famous authors who attended the School, would recall 'the invigorating moorland air', 'gold in the beeches', 'white clouds a-sailing', 'Buckland, timeless and ageless', and so on.

But it got through to other inmates who made little claim to descriptive flair or literary distinction. One of them remembered – over a span of sixty years – 'the luxurious vegetation of the lanes, with fly-blown and dusty blackberries'. More than one foreign pupil has recorded his liking for the surroundings of West Buckland (see 'Foreign Legion'). I myself was not a pupil of the School, but I was evacuated to Swimbridge, only a few miles away. As a child of the London suburbs, I found 'the country', as we knew it, a totally different planet. I can remember being captivated by primroses and violets in the tall banks – and I was only seven. But it stuck. When the teacher read to us from *The Wind in the Willows*, I naturally placed the adventures of Toad, Rat, Mole, Badger, and Otter around Swimbridge. It was quite a shock to discover, decades later, that Kenneth Grahame was writing about the Thames round Pangbourne.

Memories, moreover, are not merely mentally decorative; they can have their uses too. One correspondent of Delderfield's, who was forced by circumstances to spend time in a desert where the temperature soared to 110 degrees Fahrenheit, claimed that 'the only thing that keeps me going is day-dreaming of the blessed Buckland rain'.

He added that another thing that kept him going was 'the scum on the surface of the school swimming baths' – which, some might argue, is perhaps taking the value of reminiscence a little far. Especially when one remembers how many kinds of primitive life might be present – and not much of it very beneficial.

But it highlights the fact that 'life', in every sense of the word, is always *there*. It is hard to get away from the weather at West Buckland. It is equally hard to get away from living things. Again, there are countless examples.

With the proximity of fields all around, there must be, for instance, a higher incidence of occupation, or at least visitation, by legions of creepy-crawlies. I have done no census on this, admittedly. Perhaps there is scope here for a biology project.

I am on firmer ground when I record the well-attested fact that, three or four decades ago, boys used to help with lambing on nearby farms. They were nearly all boarders, and all too often left to their own devices, especially at weekends. It was something to do. There was a member of staff who tried to give the boys some absorbing activity by introducing them to bird-watching. A reminiscence by one of the three original pupils of the School recorded that he and his friends dammed up a nearby stream, for the usual reasons that boys dam up a stream – to try and bathe, to chase water life, and just for the hell of it.

For years the School kept pigs. Indeed, there still stands the building where the carcases were hung. There are still members of staff who remember 'the piggeries'.

Until quite recently, very few School photographs were complete without the Headmaster's dog. One of them, Bob, was credited with giving the alarm on the night of the famous School fire in 1930. There exists a vague tradition, which I have never been able to nail down, that the Head Boy is allowed to keep a dog as well. No Head Boy to my knowledge has ever tested the validity of this against the current School rules or the Ministries of Health and Education regulations.

However, a senior boy did once bring a cockatiel to School. Name of Bruce. Bruce had had a mate who had escaped, so he was lonely. His owner, a sixth-former, knew that he could not keep him in his room, so asked if he could be kept somewhere else on the campus, promising that he would do everything necessary for Bruce's care.

The Headmaster was not wild with enthusiasm about the project, but it so happened that one of the lady secretaries, Mrs. Yvonne Reed, had been thinking of having some goldfish in her reception office, partly for local colour, partly to give visitors something to look at and talk about while they were waiting. The close similarity between goldfish and a cockatiel can readily be seen, and it will be equally readily understood that a lady who can keep huddles of visitors at bay in her office with one hand tied behind her back can muster formidable powers of persuasion when the situation demands it. The Headmaster was not only swayed by Mrs. Reed's advocacy; he was quite won over by Bruce's personal charm. So Bruce took up residence in the outer office. His owner was as good as his word, and came regularly to feed and water him, and to change his tray. I am told that his Friday visits to give Bruce his weekly shower engendered quite an audience.

He (Bruce, that is) still pined, however, for a partner, so one was found – Fiona. By that time, Bruce had taken up residence in the inner office, where another lady, Mrs. Millar, enjoyed his, and Fiona's, company. Then, one day, Fiona was found with her head down in a bowl of water. Bruce, as fickle as Henry VIII, was asking for another mate almost within minutes (I don't know how you detect these things). By that time, his owner had left school to go on his gap year, and there was nobody to do the business with the bowl and the tray – or the shower. So Bruce now lives with Mrs. Millar at her house in Braunton, where, I am told, he has now developed a taste for roast potatoes. And he is still looking for a mate.

They couldn't even keep animals out of the School Museum. This shadowy institution ran for about twenty years during the headship of the Revd. Harries. I have not yet been able to establish where it operated, how it started, or why it closed down. But the *Register* periodically recorded with editorial gratitude the contribution of a wide variety of disparate objects. In November, 1919, it thanked W.H.L. Woodman for the donation of a mongoose and a snake. (Totally irrelevant, but worth recording for sheer incongruity, in the same issue it thanked W.C. Chapman for 'some fragments of a Zeppelin'.)

Then there was the terrapin saga – also quite recent. It happened at the height of the foot and mouth epidemic in 2001. Such an event may be no more than another news item in urban Britain, but it was of enormous significance in farming areas, where West Buckland is placed. Even the School felt its weight; they had to cancel their oldest observance of tradition that year – their annual cross-country race, the *Exmoor*. Some pupils were unable to attend school, because their farm had been quarantined. Local herds, which had taken decades to build up, were slaughtered, and went up in obscene smoke. The countryside was, in effect, out of bounds to everyone.

In the middle of all this, two girl pupils smuggled a couple of terrapins into the School from Hong Kong. Very foolish of them. For one thing it was against the School rules. For another it was against the law of the land. Confiscating them was the easy part; arranging for their removal and care turned out to be rather difficult. The tutor of one of the erring pupils spent one free period after another – when she really needed to be preparing French lessons – trying to find an agency which would take an interest, never mind take responsibility.

She tried the RSPCA, HM Customs and Excise, Paignton Zoo, Heathrow Airport, the Department of the Environment, and the Police. In the end, I believe the situation was resolved by a gentleman called a Wildlife Liaison Officer, and only just in time. While this patient French teacher was trying to find a home for them, they had been boarded temporarily in the Biology Department, and they were in a bad way *then*. The Biology teacher charged with their care said that the two girls had had no idea how to look after them, and 'they were nearly dead by the time we got them'. He added, 'They were quite a rare breed actually.'

With foot and mouth in mind, I said, 'Can they transmit diseases?'

'Oh, yes,' he said. 'Quite nasty ones too.'

Mercifully, he didn't specify, but I was taken by the matter-of-fact way in which he offered this intelligence. Scientists and medics have an alarmingly detached attitude to what we humble mortals regard as quite important matters of life and death.

Most animals, it seems, end up in the Biology Department, though by a variety of routes. Smuggling was one. Request was another. One boy was particularly attached to a gecko, but was told, as with Bruce, that pets were not allowed in sleeping accommodation. He asked the Biology Lab. to look after it, and produced a handsome dark wood box for the purpose, to be lit by a single pearl bulb. It was comfortably furnished with a log full of boles and holes, and embellished with a sort of creeper like a periwinkle. There was a bowl of water, a sliding door, and a thermostat. What more could a discerning gecko ask?

He received permission, plugged in the thermostat, and blew all the circuits in the whole laboratory. While another home was being found for him (the gecko), he had to be placed in a room which had a guaranteed warm atmosphere, regardless of the vagaries of the weather. So he spent several days in the Common Room.

After that came Mactavish. Mactavish was a snake. But he too fell victim to the uncertain temperature of the Biology Lab. They found him one morning – on his back. Did you know that snakes turned over when they were ill? 'So', said Neal Gwynne, the teacher in charge, 'he had to be put down.'

I murmured my sympathy, and innocently asked how you put down a snake.

'Decapitation,' said Neal.

I decided to move on.

'Any other animals in the Lab. at the moment?'

'Yes – we had a couple of tarantulas.'

'Isn't feeding them a problem?'

'No – they eat anything. One in fact ate the other.'

Here I thought I could show off my scientific knowledge.

'Ah – the female ate the male.'

I should have known better.

'No,' said Neal. 'The other way round. The female eats the male only after mating.'

It was the best recipe for abstinence I had ever heard of.

'Are they poisonous?'

'Oh, yes.'

You see? That detachment again. All very chatty. But my curiosity brought me back for more.

'Surely, if you are afraid that such a – such an accident – might happen, why don't you keep them in separate cages?'

'We did. But he crawled out of his cage, over into hers, and back again after – after the – er – the meal.'

'I see.'

'But he fell ill. And the heating went off again, and he got cold. So he died.'

'Ah.'

Neal was still so detached about it that you almost felt you wanted to take your hat off in an attempt to sort of restore the balance.

'How did you look after them during the holidays?'

'Oh, the Headmaster took them. He put them in the spare bedroom. When his mother came to stay, he put her in there as well. But only for one night.'

Perhaps we had better change the subject.

Let us get outside again, into the fresh air. Plenty of life there too – even I can identify a dozen or so wild flowers, and I can barely remember the difference between pistils and stamens from my primary school Nature Study. All round the classroom of our school at Swimbridge we had little meat-paste pots filled with speedwell and campion and herb robert. I learned to recognise king-cups and dead nettle and wild garlic. Round the cottage where I lived we had dog rose and wild honeysuckle. When I came to live in North Devon thirty years later, I made the acquaintaince of hogweed, cow parsley, and rosebay willowherb. And there they all are, in the lanes and fields of East and West Buckland, if a child only has eyes to see. Even if he does not know what they are called, he will recognise them for the rest of his life, and, when he comes to find out the names, welcome them as old friends. Vetch, foxglove, early purple orchid, bluebell, celandine, periwinkle – they are all there on the doorstep.

Trees too – though trees are more difficult. But West Buckland is equally generous there – and I mean West Buckland the School as opposed to West Buckland the village. The School developed very early the engaging tradition of planting trees and shrubs to commemorate an event, a visit, an achievement, a life – as I am sure many other schools have done. In 1863, Lord Fortescue persuaded the Archbishop of Canterbury, no less, to come down and present the prizes. Such an event demanded something permanent by way of memento. Archbishop Longley duly planted an evergreen oak in the quadrangle. It soon became one of the School 'sights' – 'the Archbishop's Tree'. A later benefactor put an octagonal seat all round it, and it became the 'general place to meet and gossip', as a later pupil and headmaster recalled. When the Old Boys came back for the 'gathering' every Whitsun, after the cricket match against the School and the celebratory dinner and the speeches and the cheerings, everybody gathered round the Archbishop's Tree, which had been hung with Chinese lanterns. Songs were sung, and the evening closed with 'Auld Lang Syne'. Even for an outsider, it is not difficult to imagine how emotionally charged such an occasion would have been.

The Archbishop of Canterbury was not the only celebrity who came to WB. They got the Chancellor of the Exchequer down in 1874. He planted an ilex. Lord Fortescue promised an araucaria (no, I don't know either) in honour of the exam achievement of T. Stone, a Somerset farmer's son who had just become the top junior in the whole of England in the Cambridge Local Examinations. When the first Oxford examiner, the Revd. Curgenven, came down in 1864, they asked him to plant a tree right in front of the School. He must have enjoyed the experience; he came back eight more times to conduct the exams. But they didn't ask him to plant any more. (See *Toujours la Politesse.*}

Over the years, there must have accumulated quite a lot. When the first headmaster, the Revd. Thompson, retired, he said in his farewell speech that he could remember the occasion of each and every planting of a tree or shrub. And he was Headmaster for thirty years. Indeed, in 1908, it became necessary to clear away some of them, because they were beginning to clutter up the place, and there had to be some clearance to make way for further development. One of the casualties was the very first – the Archbishop's Tree. That was in 1908. The weather has accounted for several more since, but there are still plenty left. And there are still more being planted. The most recent marks the passing of a teacher less than six years ago.

If you knew your trees, and all the plaques on them had survived, you could have written a passable historical sketch of the School. And though Exmoor itself is not a great favourer of trees (for all that it is called the 'Exmoor Forest'), the farmland surrounding it still supports a fair number in copse and hedgerow.

One could go on. The Biology Department (again) runs a Pond Project. I checked up on this with my regular informant, Neal Gwynne. The pond had been created by laying a tarpaulin in a hollow, but there had been a problem with maintaining the water supply. Then it was discovered that there was a spring underneath, so another Biology teacher had the bright idea of making a hole in the tarpaulin to let the spring water in. Instead all the remaining water ran out. On the last count, Neal said he had seen some pupils very busy with wheelbarrows and spades, but he was not sure what they had yet achieved.

The second Biology teacher stoutly maintains that there is more to it than that, but he readily accepts the old maxim that the truth should not be allowed to get in the way of a good story. However, fairness dictates that he should be allowed the credit for the department being awarded a prize for an ecological project – the Cashmere Cup. For that and much other work, he himself was short-listed for Teacher of the Year. And a third biology teacher is currently running yet another scheme known as the Foxglove Project. White foxgloves too – quite rare apparently.

Not to be outdone, the Geography Department has recently opened its own internet weather station. There had been some 'meteorological observations' begun in the School way back in June, 1904, and for several years the *Register* printed a summary of the weather for the term. But nothing compared with this. How those early fifth-form weather-men would have drooled over the technology available to the present boffins hunched at their screens. You can log on through the School website, and find out about any weather system or region you like in the British Isles. You can type in 'Barnstaple' and get the local picture. You can ask whether it is going to be a good day to go and chase the usual game creatures.

Many pupils come from farming families, so ferrets and rabbits have been the staple of much sport – and, in the old days, of necessity. The fox and the stag, over the years, have figured large in the leisure life of West Buckland and neighbouring villages. A while ago, I was stopped by a colleague as we were walking across the campus. He told me to cock an ear. 'Hear that?' he said. 'The hunt.' (What you might call the West Bucchanalia.) The Revd. Harries was a keen horseman, and photographs survive of him, mounted, chivvying laggards on the cross-country runs. It wasn't all that long ago that some boys' means of getting to school was still a horse.

According to a local naturalist, you can come across evidence of, or, if you are persistent and lucky, actually *see* long-eared owls, hares, pine martens, minks, otters. Even red squirrels not so long ago. Though he offered the gloomy epitaph: 'The martens probably ate the squirrels.'

As Exmoor is a 'wilderness', it boasts, like every self-respecting wilderness, its own horror. Dartmoor has the Hound of the Baskervilles; Exmoor has its 'Beast'. As my naturalist correspondent observed cryptically, 'Mostly of the black variety.' He offered instances both 'genuine' and 'inconclusive'. He claims that 'the cats are out there' (in the countryside at large), and that 'the police and DEFRA are aware of it'. I daresay, if you wanted more 'evidence', you could get it in a score of well-oiled pubs in the area.

It is not just what is on or under the ground; the School has taken note of what is up there, above. Devon skies are refreshingly free from pollution. The School Astronomical Society is a thriving concern. The Devon Astronomical Society helped them to put up a thirteen-foot fibreglass dome at the back end of the School golf course. It has also provided, on permanent loan, a seventeen-inch telescope. Parents as well as pupils, I am told, are regular attenders.

This natural history dimension was particularly evident during the last six months or so of 2003, which saw some of the hottest weather for years. The fine weather carried over into the autumn, when the colours in the trees and hedgerows were absolutely ravishing. I understand it is something to do with the long period of sunshine, and sugar, but don't ask me to explain further. If I ask the Biology Department, Neal will weigh in with more lurid details about little-known features of chlorophyll or osmosis or plant digestion that I would rather not know about.

All I know is that I greatly regret not pointing a camera at the dozens of sights I saw around the School grounds during the months of September and October – even November. In these heady new days of digital photography and computer-generated manipulation of images, what magical scenes might we have engineered?

Speech Day – prize-giving – at West Buckland used to be in July. Then, in more recent times, it has become switched to September. Round about the end of the third week, before the July leavers have to go up to university for their first term. The West Buckland weather, as I have tried to show, is no respecter of carefully-creased trousers and high-heeled shoes and best bibs and tuckers, but, once in a while, you get a perfect autumn day. The wind has taken a holiday; the sun is out; the sky is blue; the air is balmy; wherever you walk your eyes, they are seduced by siren scenes of colour.

As a Chairman of Governors, an Old Boy, once observed in welcoming the guests, 'On such a day as this, West Buckland is a jewel.'

48. Likely Lads

The Power of Prayer

About a couple of generations ago, a parent sent the following letter to the Headmaster (the underlinings are his, not mine):

'. . . . This is to inform you that my son . . . . will be leaving . . . .
'I hope and <u>pray</u> [sic] he will pass his 4 "O" Levels to enable him to enter . . . . Without these "O" Levels I'm afraid he stands <u>no chance</u>. My wife and I have tried to impress upon him – how important "hard work" – right now – is, and I <u>know</u> you have.
'All we can do now is hope and pray.'

[He got three. So God had just a little to answer for.]

A Mystery Wrapped in an Enigma

'Health excellent, home surroundings limited culturally, intellectually possible, but good all the same.'
(From a teacher's testimonial for one of his pupils.)

A Worthy Educational Aspiration

'The general Physical Education is producing a virile set of boys.'
(From the Board of Education Inspection Report, October, 1938.)

[One wonders what the Inspectors would have said about a similarly vigorous girls' school.]

The Tyranny of the Machine

The writer of this testimonial for a pupil – taken from personal records of the fifties and sixties – was clearly no touch typist. Or perhaps he had a very cold study and preferred to type with his gloves on. Perhaps the keys simply had a will of their own.

'C—— is a good porospectfor the university. he dies not yet have his elder brother's meticullus thoroughness; but he shows consideranle ina insight into gographiclsl problems. Although Economics is for him a sidelime, he is expected to obtain a high frade in "A" level. In Mathematics he has the potential to go futrther.
'He takes part in a wide range of extra curriclular activities. He is a sjool prefect, sith charge of the Library. He is also secretacy of the school Debating Scociety. In all these posts he has shoewn a fine sense of judgement. I think he will be a considerarle personality atl th university.'

[If the writer had this sort of trouble with a mere typewriter, the mind boggles at the struggles he would have had with a computer – or rather the computer with him. What, for instance, would his spellcheck program have made of 'frade', 'futrther', and 'porospectfor'? It would surely have crashed in despair.]

49. A Shot of the Good Side

A View of the 'Exmoor'

If a psychiatrist laid you down on his couch, fed into your ears words and phrases like 'mud', 'rain', 'wind', 'cow pats', 'swollen streams', 'biting cold', 'bursting lungs', 'leaden legs', 'up hill and down dale', 'blisters', 'cramp', and 'straining muscles', and then invited you to say the first thing that crossed your mind, it is most unlikely that you would come out with the word 'magic'.

Yet that is the word which has been applied more than once to the extraordinary events that take place annually on a day in late March at West Buckland School. Applied moreover not by sentimental purveyors of apocryphal stories or hack journalists steeped in cliché and hyperbole, but by eye-witnesses, organisers, and above all by actual participants. I nearly said sufferers. For suffer they most certainly do – well, most of them anyway.

A walk along roads to the start of the race, a pause for a quick munch-lunch out of anything which has been providentially stuffed into track-suit pockets, a further half-mile up a hill to the start, and then the run itself, by way of moor, woodland, field, and river-crossing back to the School. There are three other runs which take place on the same day – for senior girls, junior boys and junior girls, with the course appropriately curtailed according to sex and age. But the mud, wind, rain, cold, and river are all there in just as full a measure. Exmoor is not noted for providing much in the way of sunshine, especially at that time of the year, and it is not generous in its efforts to push the mercury very far up the tube.

There was a time when the races were spread over more than one day, but so many other demands upon a pupil's time have been coming in from eager protagonists of other sports, and from harassed directors of studies who are at their wits' end to find enough timetable space for more and more subjects and more and more examinations, that the papal consistory which decides these things took one of their infallible decisions and decreed it as an article of faith that all four *Exmoors* would in future be run concurrently.

Mind you, as the greybeards will tell you, if you go back far enough, when there were fewer junior boys and no girls at all, there were even more races. They were spaced out over three or four months of the winter, and had become so entrenched in the folklore of the School that they had all been given names – the *Westacott*, the *Stoodleigh*, the *Filleigh*, the *Crossbury* – mostly for juniors. Seniors had their own *Crossbury*, the *Beeches*, the *Bray*, and the *Long*. Scan the *Registers* for yet earlier years, and you will also find the *Railway* Run, the *Short* Run, the *North-West*, the *Leary*, and the

Tuck. They were all designed as preparation, as a (forgive the pun) run-up to the big one.

These races became victims of a variety of circumstances – PE staff who wanted more time to spend on shorter training runs which could be more closely supervised; the demands of school team training in other sports; the advent of hockey; increased volume of road traffic which could pose a danger to straggling lines of muddy schoolboys weaving a choppy course down a country lane; and the construction of new roads which cut across old cross-country courses.

So only the *Exmoor* survived. Not because it was the longest, but because it was the oldest. Its origins go back to 1859, when the School was less than a year old. One of the founders and directors, Sir Thomas Dyke Acland, who was himself a great lover of Exmoor, was also well aware of the convenience of the Moor to a new school; it was close, it was large, it was wild, and it would be a wonderful mopper-up of boys' surplus energy. He therefore suggested a course which began out on the Moor and finished at the School, and was conducted as a hare-and-hounds handicap exercise. The course could be, and was, variable, at the whim of the 'hares' laying the track. It became a 'proper' race in 1908, quite probably as part of the re-vamping of the School begun by the new Headmaster, Harries. It is also possibly no coincidence that 1908 was the year of the School's golden jubilee. Harries and one of his assistant teachers, Adelbert Taylor, mapped out the course which is still, with some modifications, followed today. The original map showing their work is still in the Archive. The *Exmoor* has been cancelled only twice in nearly 150 years – once in the Arctic winter of 1947, and once in 2001, because of the foot-and-mouth epidemic.

In actual fact, the longest of the races, was, unsurprisingly, the *Long*. It certainly lived up to its name; it was – to quote a teacher reminiscing about its passing – 'a bugger'. The same teacher claimed that there were usually more casualties and drop-outs in the *Long* than in the *Exmoor* itself. 'If you survive the *Long*, you'll do the *Exmoor*.' He should know; he organised it for twenty years.

All of which brings us to the matter of the actual length of the course. Estimates vary between seven and twelve miles (according to the rosy depth of the spectacles, the bitterness of the memory, or the amount of alcohol consumed beforehand by the storyteller) – that's the running part. We must not forget the six miles or so of road walking that have to be done in order to get from the School to the start at Kinsford Gate – by way of the *Poltimore Arms* (pause for refreshment and for attention to the needs of nature). By dint of twisting and turning a ruler across an Ordnance Survey map, and then by complicated computations involving centimetres, inches, and map scales, I make the run about nine miles. The *Register* of May, 1908, recording the laying down of the new course, confirms this, I am pleased to say. Bob Clarke, however, who organises it, says that it is nearer eleven. Practically a half-marathon. We still lack a precise computation. To my knowledge, no member of the Geography Department has ever come up with a scientific, properly-surveyed measurement. The Maths Department computer had a go, but did not allow for contours and gradients.

Perhaps the lack of precision is a good thing. It enables the School the more easily to claim that the *Exmoor* is the oldest, longest, toughest, regular, scheduled, compulsory school cross-country run in the length and breadth of the land. Should any other educational establishment ever see fit to challenge this claim, it could lead to voluminous correspondence, both in the columns of the local press and between each other, followed possibly by mutual campaigns of one-upmanship. It would be only a matter of time before somebody suggested a solution – two competitive races, one over each course, and a comparison of times and relative performances, and two respective geography department boffins hovering all the time with sextants and theodolites and tape measures. Though even that might not be the end of it; more academics would then weigh in with statistics about anti-cyclones on the day, depth of river crossings, level of rainfall, gradients, contours, prevalence and consistency of cow-pats, and a host of other allegedly relevant material. On second thoughts, it might be better to let the School (and whatever other school thinks the same thing about itself) continue in its vague pretensions – which after all do no harm to anybody. And which do the school in question a great deal of good.

For the plain fact is that West Buckland School likes the *Exmoor* – actually likes it. Or rather likes the *idea* of it. No sane boy faced with the prospect of a nine-mile run (or eight- or ten- or whatever) across one of England's last wildernesses, purely as a task *in vacuo*, would clap his hands and say 'Hooray!' No – it is what the *Exmoor* has come to mean. It is a tradition – in logic as meaningless as the ceremony of the Keys at the Tower of London. But in sentiment – ah, that is another matter.

One would be tempted to think that your average legal minor is inclined to be dismissive of tradition; to perceive it as yet another piece of Machiavellian machinery devised by the world of adults in order to contain and frustrate the energy, creativity, and pure sanity of the young; hence tradition is to be questioned, challenged, derided, and generally knocked at every possible opportunity. Not a bit of it. The truth is that the young are absolute suckers for tradition. They love doing things they have done before. They have since infancy; it is an avenue of security in an unknown, unpredictable, unsafe world. If anyone should doubt this truism, let him or her try telling the favourite goodnight story to their offspring on Thursday night slightly differently from the way they did it on Monday, Tuesday, and Wednesday – and stand by for mutiny. Let him, or her, try putting up a familiar Christmas decoration in a different place one year – and let them have their defence brief ready. Let a new headmaster abolish a practice that has been part of school life for a while – no matter how valid his reason, he will be 'trampling on tradition'.

So the *Exmoor* has been, like Everest, 'there' for 146 years. Value accrues almost by a law of ethical physics. Then there are the sub-traditions, which have grown up over the years, and which have been absorbed into the overall image – the *Exmoor* assemblies, and the songs; the stories about previous *Exmoor* exploits – apocryphal or otherwise; the jokes, the prodigies, the geography. All these features of the image become burnished more and more highly over the years with each re-telling of the story, until the *Exmoor* becomes almost a School heirloom – meaningless and incomprehensible to an outsider, but beyond evaluation or criticism – as an idea – to the inmates (they are only too happy to criticise the factual detail within their four walls, and to take advantage of loopholes in the organisation outside them).

It is possible to argue that these inmates do not actually think about it much, any more than they would think about their parents or the trees in the road where they live. It is simply part of being at the School. They like it because it is just that – a part of their lives. It is special; they all have a share in it; it belongs to *them* – and to nobody else. (Not that anybody else would want it.) Take the course. Names like Long Wood, Heasley Mill, Barton Pits, and the 'Planty' take on a significance rather like that of First World War battlegrounds – Vimy Ridge, Loos, Hill 60, and so on. The crossing of the Bray sounds a bit like the Charge of the Light Brigade. And what could one make of the immortal 'Charles Bottom'?

The *Exmoor* has thrown up its heroes, its star performers. For instance, Arthur Pearce, the son of a governor, came first in every run in the School's calendar for two full seasons, 1906-08. (His grandchildren attended the School over seventy years later.) There was Cecil Farmer, who arrived at the School from India just before the First World War. In the space of two or three years, he took part in twenty runs – the *Exmoor* and the others – and won nineteen of them. He would probably have won the twentieth but for an accident. He also mopped up almost every cup and medal going on the athletics field, in his spare time as it were. (See 'Shining Examples'.) A generation gap was spanned with the two Tullys, father and son, who each won the *Exmoor*. Tully senior won it twice, in 1935 and 1936, after coming second in 1934. In addition to that, he won the Colts race twice in 1930 and 1931, and the Junior *Exmoor* twice in 1932 and 1933. Some runner. But his record was eclipsed, as records always are, by that of J.R. Jones, who, in the mid-1950's, won four *Exmoors* on the trot, as you might say.

Incidentally, with a tradition like this, the School, you would have thought, would be able to boast a string of international cross-country champions. Well, here is another irony – it can't. At least, it couldn't until 2002, when Isabelle Stoate became the first WB pupil to be selected to run for England. This international meeting was due to take place just after the *Exmoor*. When the selectors heard about the coming event at West Buckland, they requested that she should not take part, because of the risk of injury. So she was not able to compete in the School race – which, on form, she should have won by miles.

There have been those who have won, so to speak, by mistake. It is not unknown for markers to wander, or to be misplaced, or to get *themselves* lost. Or for mist to obscure the course to such an extent that in certain areas the markers – misplaced, absent, lost, or present and correct – become invisible. In 2000, the first two senior boys home found out that, because of this problem, they had not taken the same course as everybody else. Regardless of whether it was shorter or longer, they promptly refused to accept their cups and medals.

This is no criticism of the organisation, which has developed dimensions and intricacies over the years which would delight the head of any civil service red tape department. Some time ago I came across the arrangements for an *Exmoor* race in 1959 – the hundredth *Exmoor*. This information, handwritten, was to be pinned on to a quadrangle notice board. It consisted of a single sheet of quarto, with about twenty words on it. In the millennium year, somewhat fuller, and individual, computer-printed requirements were transmitted to all those concerned – it took 85 sheets of A4.

Verbal instructions to the assembled school on the morning of the race can sound like a briefing for the Normandy landings. Everybody has to listen, because, even if they are not actually running, most of them will be involved in one way or another – as markers, messengers, or general dogsbodies. (All lessons shut down for this event.) By this means the authorities can still sweep up in the day's proceedings those who have wheedled their way out of the race by means of heartrending accounts of sudden incapacitating indispositions – hence the annual joke about 'wooden legs'.

There is also the opportunity to work into the proceedings a topical joke or two. For instance, in 2000, the teacher in charge, Robert Clarke, gave out detailed instructions about the precautions to be taken at the crossing of the Bray below Newtown Bridge. There were to be security ropes and volunteers in wet suits to give any necessary assistance, because, as he said, the water can, in bad years, get up to five or six feet deep if you stray into the wrong places. He paused, as if to savour his next announcement – which was to the effect that the teacher to be the marshal at the crossing 'will be Miss Barson', who was by a long way the shortest member of staff.

There is another traditional joke about the presence of cows in many of the fields. But one must never talk, as I have hitherto done, of 'cow pats' (or worse); it is always 'bovine residue'. This is the legacy of the famous *Exmoor* assembly songs, which were begun about thirty-odd years ago by a Classics teacher, Ian McLintock. When McLintock left, Paul Thornhill, an art teacher and housemaster, took up the torch of authorship, and produced further refinements and embellishments to the tradition. A natural versifier, with a mischievous streak of sedition in him, and a wicked penchant for sailing close to the wind, he continued the tradition of composing an ode about the *Exmoor* set to a well-known tune – like the Policeman's Song from *The Pirates of Penzance*, or the Gendarmes' Duet, or something by Noel Coward. There would be scurrilous references to individuals and nefarious practices, in addition to dire warnings about the horrors awaiting the audience when they got out on to the Moor. Chock-full of in-jokes quite unintelligible to an outsider. Indeed not always intelligible to an acquaintance who reads them only a decade or two later.

Mr. Thornhill has recently presented a full set of them to the School Archive. There is, one feels, a case for a 'limited edition' of a 'slim volume' for 'private circulation'. (In fact, as I came to check these lines, I heard that this is precisely what has just happened. Send your cheque to the School Secretary.) The general tone of the collection, and of the author's attitude to them, is summed up in his email message to me when I acknowledged receipt of them: 'I am glad to hear that the Scrolls have arrived safely.'

Then there are the jokes and stories that have shaded imperceptibly into legend, and which defy analysis or proof. The first one, admittedly, does seem fairly well rooted in truth, and concerns the markers. In the old days, apparently, they were simply parked out on the Moor, in twos and threes, about mid-morning, and left there until nearly tea-time. Old hands took care to be well muffled and shielded against wind and rain. The next priority, before the drinks and the smokes, was, naturally, food. Old boys have talked to me misty-eyed about packets of sausages and tins of baked beans and camp fires and solid fuel stoves.

One over-zealous, or over-successful, bunch of pioneers engineered such a blaze in the shelter of nearby barn that, so myth would have it, they frightened away the sheepdog, and cooked not only the sausages but the barn as well. What you might call 'hot dog with corn on the hob'.

And then we have the saga of the missing chicken. This exploit apparently involved not only cooking a bird but stealing, slaughtering and plucking it as well. Looking for a culprit for this is like trying to find a Nazi in Germany just after the war. Plenty of suspicions but no clinching clue – which in no way diminishes the story's potency. It makes you tremble to think what such anarchists might have got up to if left alone for ten minutes in a chemistry lab. Anyway, there they are, in the School's folklore – the Phantom Chicken-Stranglers of West Buckland – as outrageous, as immovable, and as unfathomable as Jack the Ripper or Sweeney Todd in the folklore of London.

From time to time, well-meaning reformers have taken it upon themselves to 'improve' the *Exmoor*. The *Exmoor* is, as I said – if you noticed – compulsory. In theory, every boy (and now every girl too) who is able-bodied on the day is supposed to run. One new headmaster apparently thought this was going a bit far, and could be a danger to the health of the over-willing participant (if such a rare creature has ever existed). He insisted upon the runners having a medical examination before the race. In the memory of the old boy who told me this, he caused 'a near-mutiny'.

It makes an outsider feel that the *Exmoor* has become rather like a running family row. The family members – the inmates – can argue, criticise, complain, wriggle, and hurl abuse to their hearts' content. But let an interloper – however well-intentioned – begin to tinker with it, and the unified wrath of the School descends upon his head. In the same way, there was a move some years ago to abolish the *Exmoor*, because it was said to be too tough, inhuman, and out of date – a relic of a male-orientated, upper-lip, empire-building past. There was a referendum taken, and the voters decided overwhelmingly to keep it – and to keep it compulsory.

Well, what was it that they wanted to keep? What actually happens on an *Exmoor* day? The events of Wednesday, 20th March, 2002 will serve as an illustration as good as any. (I have cheated so far as to insert one or two incidents and remarks taken from 2000 as well, but the spirit is the same.)

It begins well before the day, with, as I said, Bob Clarke circularising every member of staff with his or her own personal set of instructions. Then he has to visit the farmers over whose land the runners must pass. In 2002, he found, to his gratification, that they were more compliant than usual. Devon farmers are not noted for open-handedness, *bonhomie*, or eagerness to co-operate, and can usually be relied upon to locate the unpromising side of any proposition. However, this year they were, said Bob, quite pleased to see him. This was because of the previous year's terrible outbreak of foot and mouth. One of its by-products had been the cancellation of the *Exmoor* for only the second time in nearly 150 years.

By early 2002, the pestilence, the loss, the misery, and the general awfulness were over. Suddenly the prospect of hundreds of teenage boys and girls scrambling over their moorland and through their fields represented not an automatic threat to livestock but a welcome return to normality. So the *Exmoor* got off to a good start.

Then there is the vital precaution of negotiating with the licensee of the *Poltimore Arms* to make sure he is going to have his doors open on the morning of E-Day. Licensees of remote moorland hostelries are not exactly besieged with thirsty patrons during weekday mornings in the off season, and they tend therefore to be rather arbitrary about their hours of closing. So special arrangements have to be made. Catering for the dry throats of dozens of staff – never mind pupils – is a serious matter that has to be attended to, and ensured well in advance.

Bob Clarke's assembly went down well. You can tell when an audience enjoys something, and it is not always to do with clapping afterwards. Schoolchildren are experts on assemblies – past-masters, veterans, connoisseurs. God knows, they've had to sit through enough of them. But they like this one. They liked the latest *Exmoor* song too – performed by Paul Berry – modern languages teacher, compulsive raconteur, and experienced entertainer – dressed up as Bud Flanagan (though the significance of the long fur coat would have been lost on ninety-eight per cent of the audience, young staff and all). 'Running on the Exmoor', set to the music of *Underneath the Arches*, and accompanied by Mrs. Priscott ('Rosalie' to everybody on the staff – the financial guru of the Bursar's Office, and spare-time music teacher and J.P.), struck just the right note. They picked up all the jokes and references. The song gained immeasurably from Paul's delivery.

This general good humour continued outside in the quadrangle, where everybody waited around for the word to start on the long walk to the *Poltimore Arms*. A local TV company had got word of the event, and had sent a cameraman and interviewer. Watching the competitors talking to them, you would hardly guess that a long, a very long, ordeal lay immediately in front of them. One girl in particular I recall – Anna Makarova. (The School takes in a sizeable number of foreign students, particularly at the senior end.) As the name suggests, she was Russian, and so far had spent her time in the sixth form in a semi-permanent state of Slavonic gloom. But here she was, looking more animated than anyone could remember. Her refusal to speak to the TV crew was quite clearly the result of very human, and engaging, shyness, not of East European aloofness and frigidity. The *Exmoor* had brought out the *glasnost* in her.

That TV team worked hard. They clambered all over Exmoor, taking every kind of atmospheric shot, and promised us a full report in the early evening local news. Then, at about three o'clock in the afternoon, a current celebrity's famous sailing boat broke in half in mid-Atlantic sea trials, and our item never appeared. I think we got about fifty seconds behind the credits the next day. Show business, you see.

We had another visit from a camera crew in 1959, the year of the hundredth *Exmoor* run. Two in fact – one from the BBC and one from ITV. The School did its best to co-operate with both crews; it was the only *Exmoor* in which the competitors left by the East Drive past the Headmaster's house instead of from the back fields, and the only *Exmoor* with two beginnings and two finishes. The BBC team had to get further up the drive to film the competitors leaving the premises, so had the start repeated. The ITV team missed the finish because of a misunderstanding in a muddy lane with some local sheep, and persuaded the first seven or eight runners to 'finish' again. Eager viewers of BBC were rewarded with all of sixty seconds that evening, and another two minutes on Children's TV later. The ITV film did not come out at all. More show business.

Markers leave early, of course – over a hundred of them. These are mainly the first formers – or, as we must say nowadays, 'Year 7'. The organisation aims to have a marker (or pair of markers; you can't leave twelve-year-olds on their own out there for all that time) at every gate, fork, bend, or stile – anywhere where an alternative route could present itself. Dozens of marshals among the staff must transport them, position them carefully, and make sure they know exactly where they are and what they have to do. And of course take care to pick them up afterwards. It would be a juicy titbit for the local press if we were to get all our runners in and lose a brace of markers.

There are also officials known as Sweepers – which can be left to the imagination. Others again – drivers of minibuses full of competitors to the starting points for the 'lesser' races, recorders, timekeepers, kit-luggers (bearers of huge bags of track suits doffed by the runners at the start), housemasters, cheerers-on, camp followers, and general trouble-shooters. Spectators are not, as a rule, very thick on the ground, partly because vantage points are not always accessible to motor vehicles, and partly of course because the weather can be bad. And on this day, the weather surpassed itself; it was diabolical.

It was difficult to recognise members of staff, never mind pupils, behind layers of anoraks, leggings, gaiters, and adjustable storm visors. The only creatures bearing any visible resemblance to the human race – who were left behind – consisted of three types. First were the kitchen staff, whose job it was to produce the *Exmoor* 'tea' – soup and home-baked bread roll. I did some research to find out if the traditional pea soup was still provided; it wasn't. Instead there were two enormous – I don't know what you would call them; the nearest is perhaps – buckets of 'spring vegetable' soup. Home made, like the bread? Alas, no – packet soup. Heaven knows how many packets. I found it difficult to believe that they intended to get four hundred or more mugs of soup out of these two receptacles. Urns! Urns – that's better. Urns of soup. *Le mot juste* at last.

In the main offices the ladies of the clerical staff were knee-deep as usual in memos and invoices. I offered the trite speculation that, with the whole School out on the Moor, they would perhaps have a quiet day. Wrong again. The morning had already been 'absolutely manic'. The 'phone had never stopped ringing, with calls from two types of parent – the ones who wanted to know how they could find a means of contacting or watching their competitor offspring; and the others who were calling up to inform the School of sudden, disabling – nay, nearly life-threatening – indispositions which, with the best will in the world, made their son's or their daughter's participation in the forthcoming event an impossibility. They much regretted it, and their children were absolutely heartbroken, but. . . .

If there was usually a steady trickle of staff into the office on a normal day, on this day of days, there was a relentless stream of them – each with errands of vital urgency – drawing pins, laminations, photo-copying – vital because of the immediacy of the event. Only the Headmaster's Secretary was optimistic. She was looking forward to the moment when the Headmaster put on his storm jacket and his Goretex mitts and left to start the race, because then she could 'get on'.

The third, very small, group sat in the hall, up by the silver cabinet. They were up to their elbows in overturned cups, dusters and Duraglit. Undaunted by my previous wrong diagnoses, I ventured to ask knowingly of one of them, 'Are you a volunteer or have you been a naughty boy?'

There is nothing that has the put-down power of the total truth.

'Neither, actually, sir. I've had the 'flu', so I can't run. My Dad asked if I could be relieved from marking cos we're going ski-ing on Friday.'

I was not the only one to get a surprise or two that morning. A lot of the girls very nearly did not get to the start of their race. I overheard a teacher remark afterwards that 'we had to dig Charles out of his ditch'. Rigorous questioning revealed that Charles Dawson, a Science teacher and something of an expert in outdoor activities, had suffered a skid on the muddy road, and had tipped a cargo of senior girls, and the minibus, into the roadside ditch – two wheels of it anyway. The big girls bounced in the back, the rest shoved, Charles thoughtfully engaged the clutch..... They arrived only ten minutes late at the start, where Bob Clarke was having one of his many nervous breakdowns of the day.

Hardly surprising – nobody in his right mind expects the *Exmoor* to go without a hitch. Further proof would have been offered if you had sat in the

Common Room after it was all over; you would pick up stray, half-finished conversations like this:

'Then we ran into this flock of sheep. . . .'

'I got to Heasley Mill and there wasn't a single marker there. . . .'

'The mud out there was so bad that they couldn't stand; we had to pass them down the hill from hand to hand. . . .'

It is scarcely necessary to repeat, but I shall nevertheless: the weather was absolutely terrible – cold, windy, and wet, with a savage drizzle that enveloped one and all like a cloud.

However, the senior boys were still in fine form when they reached the *Poltimore Arms*. Old hands many of them, with several *Exmoors* already behind them, they made their way familiarly into the bars and soaked up the last available heat before the log fires. A lot of staff arrived – in cars of course. Nobody seemed to mind the crush, but something had to give; the proprietor had to make a living. When Bob Clarke announced that the competitors would have to leave in favour of the paying customers, they went with a good grace.

Another half a mile up the hill to the start, where the runners have at last to take off their track suits and other outer clothing and shove them into the enormous plastic bags held by house officials. It was a maelstrom of bending and hopping and wrenching, stooping and tying, jumping and slapping, and blaspheming in disbelief at the Icelandic winds and Finisterre drizzle that lashed bare legs. A last slug of Coke, a final furtive watering of the primroses in the hedge. A few moments of marshalling and hectoring, last-minute adjurations about what to do in case of drop-out, a drop of a handkerchief by the Headmaster, and they were gone.

Those remaining scrambled into the parked cars, and raced off along the road to the start of the other three races. Suddenly the place was empty, deserted, void – just the wind and the cloud and the wet and the cold. Sixteen hundred feet up, and nothing to be seen beyond fifty or sixty yards. It was like the top of the world just after the Creation. It made you wonder whether you had actually seen what you had just seen.

If, to reassure yourself, you wanted to see it again, you would have to drive pretty smartly to North Radworthy to see the start of the Senior Girls' race, then to Barton Pits for the Junior Boys, and finally to Stowford Cross for the Junior Girls.

There have been others who have wanted a closer identification. Over the years, Old Boys have come back to compete again as guest runners. Well, not compete, because it was clear from what little I have seen that they were by now accomplished athletes, but they were happy to join in. There was a headmaster twenty or thirty years ago who was an Oxford blue at cross-country. He used to take part regularly. According to the story, he would finish so quickly that he had time to go to his house, have a shower, get dressed, and get back in good time to see nearly everyone else come in.

The *Exmoor* has also been a regular challenge to new young staff. Fresh-faced twenty-somethings who have come to coach rugby or teach PE often feel the need to demonstrate to their new pupils (and to themselves) that their talents, and their physique, can take in more than drop goals and back somersaults. We have even had, and still have, a young lady English teacher who has a London Marathon to her credit, and who now has a couple of *Exmoors* under her belt as well. One of the young lions, Richard Mace, rashly announced his intention (or at least his hope) not only of finishing, but of keeping up with her. You'll have to wait a page to find out.

So off they went – across Fyldon Common and down into Buttery Wood. Down again, past North Radworthy and into Long Wood. Down, down to Heasley Mill, on past Barton Pits, Hunniwins Farm, and Stowford Cross. Up a bit out of the tiny valley, through Walscott Farm, and then down again – down, down to Newtown Bridge and the wading of the Bray. But just because the School is at 650 feet above sea level and the race starts at 1,600, it would be ill-advised to suppose that it was downhill all the way. The *Exmoor* hoards its best surprise for the end – or nearly the end. For just after the River Bray comes the Cleave (that's how they spell it round here), and in the Cleave the rising contour lines cluster, close and cruel, like bandits in ambush. As one survivor put it, 'It's the last part that crucifies you.'

Finally – after the crucifixion – past Charles Bottom (there is a village called Charles nearby), past a disused mineshaft or two, through Pitt Wood, across the Carriage Hill road, and on to the School campus. Into the funnel of red tape, give your name to the recorders licking their sharp pencils, and it is over. For another year.

The end is remarkably low-key. Hardly more than about twenty people. Understandable. The competitors are still out there, and those who have finished soon stump, stagger, or limp off to the showers. Vital to get out of the wind and rain. No point in surviving cramp and pulled muscles if one is going to succumb to pneumonia instead. Nearly all the staff are out some-where on duty. Apart from a scattering of parents and a harassed-looking journalist, who spent his time keeping the rain off his camera and chasing after early arrivals to ask them their names and how to spell them, that was about it. Barely a quorum of an audience; barely a stutter of applause. It could easily have been a routine games afternoon.

It brings back to the memory the lady who won the Wimbledon Tennis Championships just before 1900. She lived to a great age, and scores of years later she told of how she went to the courts at Nursery Road (long before they built the modern complex up Wimbledon Hill), duly won her final, received her cup, put it in the basket on the front of her bicycle, and pedalled home. This lack of fuss brings home once again the intimacy, the domesticity of the affair. It is not a major championship (though the School's four houses compete, naturally, and there are cups and medals for the winners). It is not trumpeted in the local press, any more than you would broadcast a family reunion from the housetops. It is not even a race for athletes, though of course some athletic ability is a help. It is just something which everybody does.

Look at them when they arrive back. Pink-legged, stiff-legged, tight-legged (and there is a difference), bow-legged, loose-legged, wobbly-legged – everything except cross-legged (unless they had had no chance to seek relief in the hedges *en route*). Hardly the traditional image of the public-school, clean-limbed, swift-striding paragon of British youth.

Indeed the only finisher who looked remotely like a 'proper' athlete was our London Marathon young lady from the staff, Louise Pugsley. She arrived looking as if she had been for a two-mile training jog on Instow beach. Richard Mace, at her side, rather more frayed but glowing with smug satisfaction, thought he knew better:

'I stayed with her. And she's tired!'

Talking of 'clean-limbed', it would have been impossible for anybody to come home in such a state – unless you were Louise Pugsley. They had mud on their shoes, their socks, their ankles, their calves, their thighs, their shins, up their backs, on their necks, in their hair, in some cases all over their faces. One or two girls looked like Apache braves.

Now it is quite likely that when a boy or girl in such a situation gets to a certain stage of muddiness, they cease to care, and may even seek to incorporate upon their persons further levels of moist covering, just for the hell of it. But that in itself indicates a certain sense of occasion, even in such awful conditions. If they had been completely wretched, they would have simply stumbled on – or given up. Instead they arrived in surprisingly good humour. They congratulated each other, stopped for a short while to see later arrivals come in, posed for photographs, and put up with aches and pains – which in some cases must have been very unpleasant. One girl reached the finishing line, put her hands on her hips, looked round, and said to no-one in particular, with the air of someone just making a discovery, 'That was fun.'

It probably wasn't fun for everybody; that goes without saying. Indeed Angus Calder, a PE teacher acting as marshal out on the Moor, became worried as he watched so many stumbling past in what looked like bad shape. 'I don't think I've ever seen so many so unfit.' Hunching himself against the weather, and looking at the lines of dripping, squelching young humanity, he began to doubt the wisdom and validity of the whole idea of the *Exmoor*.

His doubts were dissolved when he suggested to one or two of the most wretched-looking staggerers that they might like to drop out, and no pack drill afterwards. He was met with immediate, stoical, and flat refusal.

Godliness, we used to be told, is pretty adjacent to cleanliness. Well – an hour and a shower later – it may not have been a very godly company that assembled in the dining hall, but it was, as they said in the old stories, a goodly company. Once again, one was struck by the sheer good humour of everybody. There were no hectoring prefects and senior staff to usher them into straight lines; people just drifted in as and when they were dried and dressed – and very smartly too. Full School uniform. The shirts positively sparkled. Perhaps it was because it was the first time they had worn them that day. It made an ironic contrast with the staff, who were coming in with half of Exmoor still clinging to their clothes.

Everyone secured their mugs of soup and rolls, sat down – where there was room – and just talked. Proceedings did not begin at the advertised time, and they continued to talk. More and more came in, squeezed on the ends of tables, or stood in crowded aisles, and still just talked. When some of them were asked to make room for medal-winners, they shuffled up into yet more crowded aisles, and just talked again. Four or five hundred of them in the end. As Sherlock Holmes said of the dog in the night-time, it was the absence of incident that was remarkable.

When at last the recorders had done all their sums and produced their results, Bob Clarke opened the proceedings. He began by saying that the day had produced possibly the worst conditions he had seen in twenty years (cold, wind, and persistent rain after weeks of previous rain), and he was bound to say that he had never seen the School show up so well – both in their level of tolerance and in their initiative. It had really brought out the best in them.

It might be easy to suggest that Bob was getting a little mellow because this was his last *Exmoor*, but the example he gave of what he meant seems to back up his claim. One boy, in ordinary clothes, had seen a competitor in trouble in the river, had jumped in, and had gone to his assistance. His only regret, as he discovered afterwards, was that he had ruined a perfectly good packet of cigarettes in his trousers pocket.

The cups and medals were presented by Richard Cooper, the President of the Old West Buckland Association. By a neat coincidence, the occasion was the anniversary of his last previous participation in the *Exmoor*, in 1952 – exactly fifty years before. That is, all the cups except one – the *Exmoor*

Average Cup (too long to explain). This had been donated by a Mr. and Mrs. Hellewell, who had lost a son – an old pupil – in tragic circumstances, and who wished to preserve his memory and their bond with the School. They visited as often as they could – on *Exmoor* day – all the way from Derbyshire. Bob's invitation to Mrs. Hellewell to present it was succinct, kind, gracious, and quite charming.

Throughout the proceedings, everyone listened, clapped and cheered in all the right places, and fell silent for the next announcement. If you can imagine a family of over four hundred people looking at the family snaps, this was it.

Bob Clarke said his matter-of-fact farewells at the end of his last *Exmoor*, and stepped down with no fuss. At the end, the Headmaster – still in his multicoloured jumper – was just as brief and to the point. He thanked everyone – he repeated 'everyone' (some of the markers, for instance, had been out there for over four hours) – and said they had all been splendid. And he meant it. And they had.

He left. The staff left. And everyone else left. Just like that.

It would be foolish to claim that everyone at West Buckland is bewitched by the *Exmoor*. Of course they are not. But anyone who witnessed the events of Wednesday, 20th March, 2002 would have been forced to admit that the balance of feeling in 'the House' was unquestionably and overwhelmingly in its favour. As a body – as a clearly-indentifiable body – they had tackled a task of truly daunting proportions, and they had beaten it, and they were extremely pleased with themselves. It had brought them all together in the best traditions of companionship.

Young people are not adults; they do not have mature, rounded characters. But they have many facets and subtleties for all that – maybe not fully formed, realised, or controlled, but definitely there. And any teacher or parent will tell you that they are capable of depths as well as heights, of sins as well as virtues. Just as they can be, at times, merciless monsters – say, with a weak teacher – so, at other times, they can surprise us with their resource, resilience, and self-respect. *Exmoor* day was just such an occasion.

Point a camera at them at a time like this, and you see their good side. The Moor had thrown us its worst, and the School had responded with its best. For so many young people to show so much of their best – all at the same time – must indeed have required a touch of magic.

50. Endpiece

I said in the Introduction that I hoped to show you that the School was, on the whole, not a bad place for a child to be. If I haven't, then I'm afraid you have had your near-three-hundred-page read for nothing. Sorry.

If I have, fine. But there may well lurk the thought that, yes, this is all very well, but it costs money. Yes, it does – true. And a lot of people can't afford it. True again. So it's unfair. Well, yes, but only in a way. So let's scrub all the independents and start again.

Now hold on a minute. It is not the *School* that is unfair. It is the system, the social set-up, the 'economic situation', the whole damned thing – Life, if you like – that is unfair. We can't all afford a Mercedes, or a holiday in the Seychelles. But you wouldn't join a campaign to abolish the Mercedes factory, would you, or to obliterate the Seychelles?

That is silly. Nobody would claim that it is a child's right to own a Mercedes, or to disport itself on a beach in the Seychelles, but it should have a right to a free education. Yes, I agree. But a child in this country *does* have a right to a free education – and gets it. So what's the beef?

The 'beef' can only be that a child is somehow missing out because it cannot go to a private school. Now this can only be a legitimate beef if what the private school offers is better than what the state school offers. If it is worse, then there is no case; no reasonable person can complain if its child is deprived of access to an inferior article.

One is forced then to the conclusion that perhaps the education offered by a fee-charging school might in some way be 'better'. (Why else would anyone be complaining?) At the very least, the parents who send their children to such a school do so because they *think* it is 'better'.

Incidentally, what these parents are doing is in line with a long tradition in English history. If the Government can't or won't do something or other, groups of people get together and do it themselves. This goes right back to Saxon village elders and crime-prevention, Elizabethan poor relief, eighteenth-century turnpike trusts, and nineteenth-century railway companies. Men were prepared to put their money where their desires were.

In the same way, parents have decided, and have been deciding for a long time, that the Government is not providing the education that, in their opinion, it should be providing, so they are prepared to pay for it elsewhere. Rightly or wrongly, they perceive the private schools to be superior.

And here we run into a bit of a mystery. What is it that makes them superior – or, if you wish, *seem* superior? It should have become obvious from what has gone before in this book firstly that West Buckland School can fairly claim to be an example of a pretty straightforward, middle-of-the-road, get-on-with-it school (indeed a recent inspectors' report made the general comment that 'West Buckland is not a school that puts on airs'); and secondly that what it has to offer is nothing out of the way or marvellous or mind-boggling. It teaches the national syllabus; it enters candidates for all the normal subjects in all the normal public examinations run by all the normal boards; it prepares its senior pupils for all the usual universities; it encourages children to play games and to enjoy and appreciate the countryside around them. It tries to inculcate good manners, kindness to those at a disadvantage, and a sense of service to the community. It is staffed by teachers who are trained in the same colleges of education and universities as those in state schools.

Now what reasonable parent could object to those arrangements, activities and aspirations? No matter where he lived, no matter what his bank balance was.

It seems to follow then that parents who send their children to West Buckland School do so because they feel that the state schools are in some way falling short of that standard. If they were not – if the children who poured out of state comprehensives looked and behaved like those who pour out of West Buckland and their like, and registered the same level of success, in and out of the examination room, and enjoyed the same easy relationship with their teachers – those same parents would not need a cheque book. No parent in his right mind would shell out six thousand or eight thousand or twelve thousand or sixteen thousand pounds a year for something he could get up the road for nothing.

Oh, no, you've got it wrong, say the egalitarians. They do it because they went to these schools themselves; they do it because it gets their kids on to the Old Boy Net; they do it because they're snobs.

No – I disagree. Of course there are snobs, and there always will be. Human nature sees to that, and no amount of social engineering will get rid of them. But snobs are no danger to a market-driven society; they are no more nuisance than warts on a face – at worst an ugly blemish; at best a wry joke.

No – parents choose the independent schools because the independent schools deliver the goods. They have to, to stay alive. When the Labour Government did for the grammar schools, the independents made huge efforts to smarten up their act, for fear that the ex-grammar-school parents would shrug their shoulders and send their offspring to the shiny new comprehensives, or for fear that the Labour reformers would point the accusatory finger, shout 'Dinosaur!' and maybe have some justification. The result was that, in a new age where prospective parents became far more discerning and well-informed (they needed to be because they were faced with the prospect of parting with a lot more money), more and more of them decided that the independents, on balance, offered a better deal – a deal that was worth a few sacrifices.

Now, if the state comprehensives – in other words, the Government – were to smarten up *their* act, if they were to look at themselves full in the mirror – as the independents did a generation ago – it seems not beyond the bounds of possibility that they could come up with a deal which would make the 'independent' parents think again – Old Boy Net or no Old Boy Net, snobs or no snobs.

If the products of the state comprehensives were so successful that it was *they* who were mopping up the top jobs in academia and commerce and industry and the Foreign Service, those 'Old School Tie' parents would soon change their minds. What would be the point of teaching their sons and daughters how to open doors for old ladies and talk with a plum in their mouths, if they were going to be out-manoeuvred in the great game of Life afterwards? If the Old Boy Net had been bypassed by a New Boy Net? Nobody keeps a Rolls in his garage if it doesn't go.

At the moment, however, it would seem that the Government's conception of 'doing what is best for the nation's schoolchildren' does not satisfy everyone. Over a million parents think there is a better deal available elsewhere, and are prepared to pay for it – and sensible, concerned, informed, articulate, citizenly parents at that.

Now – who is right?

At the very least, there is a discrepancy between state and private education. There are those who would affirm, as I described earlier, that it all comes down to money. If you have enough of it, you can send your kids to a 'posh' school. But there are plenty of parents, who would not be seen dead in a posh school, but who might spend huge sums financing trips to foreign capitals – all over the world – to see their favourite soccer and rugby teams play. Why is it 'snobby' to pay out four figures for your child's education for a year in a school of your choice, but not 'snobby' to pay out what might come to four figures on a single weekend in Budapest or Ankara or Perth to take your child (or children) to watch a football match? But we are not going to get far in this comparison of spending habits; it could so easily degenerate into a tit-for-tat row.

In any case it blurs the issue. The issue is not – or shouldn't be – how much the 'posh' schools cost, but what sort of education they offer to their pupils. Not why they're expensive, but why they're good. The fact remains that over a million parents think that what they offer is *worth* the cost. Those who disapprove of the independents – for whatever reason they *say* – really ought to make up their minds: either private education is better, or it isn't.

If it isn't, then any critic of it can send his kids to the local comprehensive, and all the private schools in the world will not interfere with his kids' education. Private schools do not syphon off public money or use up government buildings. Indeed the presence of over half a million children in independent schools eases the pressure on the comps. If our critic is proved right, every other parent will slowly see the light, and the private schools will wither away. So there will be nothing for our critic to get hot under the collar about.

If, on the other hand, it can be shown that private education, taken all round, is better, then it should be the concern, the responsibility, almost the duty, of every parent and politician of whatever political shade to ensure that this level of education is made available to every child in the land. As every politician and educational reformer is fond of emphasising – especially those who have a season ticket to the moral high ground – 'the children come first'. Well, let them live up to it.

Certainly headmasters of independents would agree; at any rate that is my impression. I have heard one head put forward his view that any principal of a private school would, if asked, deem it a great shame that the education offered to his pupils is not available to everybody.

West Buckland, in short, and scores of schools like it, is offering an education which should, in an ideal world, be accessible to any child whose parents want it. It is not the fault of West Buckland that such an ideal world does not exist. And it is surely a worthwhile aspiration to keep such an education going, even if at the moment only a minority can benefit from it. Whether or not the world is ideal – and it usually isn't – is irrelevant; if a thing is worth doing, it is worth doing. In case that ideal world should ever come into being, we shall need to have some models to learn from. Is it altogether too fanciful to talk of torch-bearers?

In 1858, the Revd. Brereton opened a school at West Buckland which was a pioneer in its field – the cause of middle-class education. In the same year, there was set up the first system of university-sponsored public examinations which would provide some kind of national yardstick with which to measure the educational progress of the nation's young people. The four men most tightly involved in that were Brereton, Fortescue, Acland, and Archbishop Temple – all of whom were closely associated with West Buckland School.

Now the School – this time not alone – is at the heart of another, nationwide, debate which continues about the validity and *raison d'être* of private schools, and the worth of what they offer. Will the problem be resolved by the proof of the pudding, or will it be skewed by prejudices, misconceptions, social hang-ups, and party slogans? And parsimonious chancellors of the Exchequer?

Should those charged with building an educational system for the future concern themselves not with new, fashionable subjects like Feminist Studies; nor with the debate about school uniform; nor whether to have contraceptives on sale in the boys' toilets; nor whether the competitive principle should be banned from all forms of exercise; nor whether the concept of 'passing' and 'failing' should be abolished; nor whether certain percentages of pupils from politically correct backgrounds should be assured of university preferment regardless of relative ability. Not with toning down, slowing down, talking down, running down, playing down, and dumbing down.

Rather with cheering up, backing up, and paying up. Above all, with setting up – setting up a national system of schools where all children are expected to work, and to mind; to be courteous and considerate; to respect the ethics of consistent effort and attention to detail; to be made aware and respectful of a national heritage; to accept that people sometimes succeed and sometimes fail; that excellence is something to be aspired to and admired. Where teachers agree that they are there not only to encourage and enlighten, but to lead, to control, to guide, and to set an example. Where the social unit is still small enough for there to exist some kind of family atmosphere – however 'extended' that 'family' may be. Where – as that leaver said – 'everyone is made to feel the same way, at ease with the person they are and valued because of it'. And where, at the back of it all, there sits a government whose ministers are not terrified of putting a penny or two on the income tax to help pay for it.

Is this the real 'sharp end' of education at the beginning of the twenty-first century? If it is, then West Buckland can feel with some justification that, after nearly 150 years, it is still doing its share of pioneering. The Revd. Brereton, one feels, would have approved.

~ THE END ~

John Cornwell stands by his gun at Jutland. [School Archive]

The portrait of the Revd. J.L. Brereton, by George Richmond,
R.A., which hangs in the Memorial Hall. [Mrs. Lorraine Millar]

Brereton's friend and fellow-pioneer, Hugh, 3rd Earl Fortescue, whose picture hangs beside him. [Mrs. Lorraine Millar]

George Richmond's portrait of Frances Martin, who married Brereton, and bore him sixteen children. Also in the Memorial Hall. [Mrs. Lorraine Millar]

The Brereton family plaque in Little Massingham church, Norfolk. [Author]

The muzzled bear, from the choir stalls in Little Massingham church. [Author]

Two views of the old County School Station, North Elmham, Norfolk. [Author]

The view from the Archivist's office. [Mrs. Lorraine Millar]

The Exmoor – Two examples to show how conditions can
vary enormously from year to year. [the late Derek Holt]

A competitor from the other side of the world. [Robert Moor]

Note the boy in the wet suit on hand for those in difficulty. [the late Derek Holt]

The first three girls home in a senior race. [David Clark]

The first three boys home in a junior race; the little one
in the middle was the winner! [David Clark]